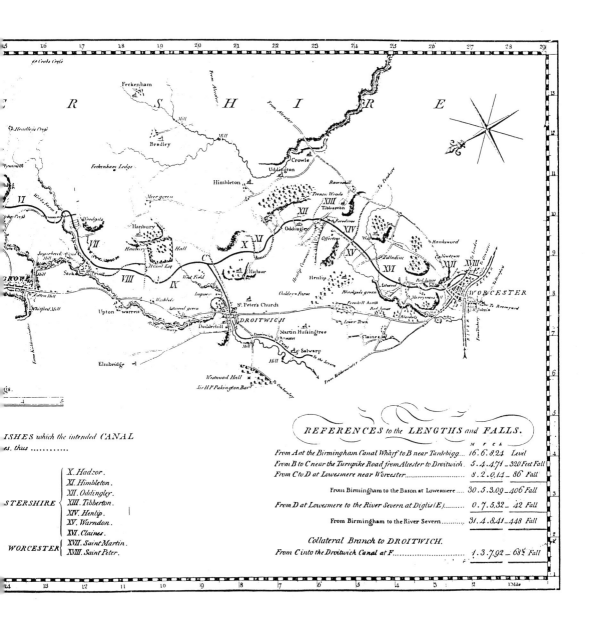

ISHES which the intended CANAL
es. thus ....

STERSHIRE {
X. Hadzor.
XI. Himbleton.
XII. Oddingley.
XIII. Tibberton.
XIV. Henlip.
XV. Warndon.
XVI. Claines.
}

WORCESTER {
XVII. Saint Martin.
XVIII. Saint Peter.
}

REFERENCES to the LENGTHS and FALLS.

	M. F. C. L.	
From A at the Birmingham Canal Wharf to B near Tardebigg....	16.6.8.24	Level
From B to C near the Turnpike Road from Alcester to Droitwich.	5.4.4.71	320 Feet Fall
From C to D at Lowesmere near Worcester.......................	8.2.0.14	86 Fall
From Birmingham to the Bason at Lowesmere	30.5.3.09	406 Fall
From D at Lowesmere to the River Severn at Diglis (E).........	0.7.5.32	42 Fall
From Birmingham to the River Severn...........	31.4.8.41	448 Fall

Collateral Branch to DROITWICH.

From C into the Droitwich Canal at F................................ 1.3.7.92 — 68½ Fall

THE WORCESTER AND BIRMINGHAM CANAL

BIRMINGHAM CANAL

—— *Chronicles of the Cut* ——

By the same author:

Worcestershire Salt
A history of Stoke Prior Salt Works

A Worcestershire Dynasty
The history of a North Worcestershire family
farming and business empire

Tardebigge School 1815-2000
A short history

THE WORCESTER AND BIRMINGHAM CANAL

—— *Chronicles of the Cut* ——

The Revd. Alan White, M.Sc., M.A., M.Ed.

BREWIN BOOKS

First published by
Brewin Books Ltd, 56 Alcester Road,
Studley, Warwickshire B80 7LG in 2005
www.brewinbooks.com

Reprinted October 2006

ISBN 1 85858 261 X

A Cataloguing in Publication Record
for this title is available from the British Library.

Typeset in Times
Printed in Great Britain by
Cromwell Press

CONTENTS

LIST OF ILLUSTRATIONS

Front Endpaper: John Snape's 1789 plan of the the proposed W/B Canal
Frontispiece: Tardebigge Church and countryside from the tunnel mouth

Rear Endpaper: Table of distances from place to place along the canal

WEIGHTS, MEASURES AND MONEY

1 lb (pound weight) = 454 grams (approx.)
1 cwt (hundredweight) = 112 lb
1 ton = 20 cwt = 1 tonne (approx.)

1 inch = 2·5 cm (approx.)
1 foot = 12 inches = 30 cm (approx.)
1 yard = 3 feet = 90 cm (approx.)
1 mile = 8 furlongs = 1760 yards = 1·6 km (approx.)

1d (old penny) = 0·4p (approx.)
6d = 2·5p
1s (shilling) = 12d = 5p
£1 = 20s = 240d

INTRODUCTION

The Worcester and Birmingham Canal (generally abbreviated throughout this book as the W/B Canal) is some thirty miles long. It runs from Gas Street Basin near Broad Street in Birmingham to Diglis, Worcester, and links the Birmingham Canal Navigations (B.C.N.) with the River Severn. It took 24 years to complete from the passing of its 1791 Act, delays being mainly due to monetary inflation during that period. It is level for about 15 miles from Gas Street Basin to Tardebigge at 453ft above mean sea level. It descends by fifty-six narrow locks from there to Diglis, Worcester, and by two barge locks down from the basin to the River Severn. It has five tunnels, including the long tunnel at Kings Norton, sometimes called Wasthills Tunnel, though it is consistently referred to as the West Hill Tunnel in the original company records and I have held to this. It boasts one of the deepest narrow locks on the canal system of Great Britain, giving a 12 feet change of level, this being the top lock at Tardebigge which replaced a working boat lift. The canal also includes the famous Tardebigge Flight of thirty locks of which the deep top lock is one, the other twenty-nine being separated by short lengths of canal (now called 'pounds', but formerly known as 'ponds'), the largest number of locks in so short a distance in this country.

The canal passes through suburbs of Birmingham which, when the canal was constructed, were mainly countryside. Contemporary maps show fields and orchards then to the south of Broad Street. Places like Selly Oak and Kings Norton were rural hamlets and villages. Likewise at the Worcester end, where the canal was constructed round the east and south sides of the city, outside the old city walls, there were fields where, soon, industries and dwellings would be located.

The canal, besides adding a new feature to the landscape, attracted a variety of amenities and industries. It also affected the lives of a great many people, some of whom were employed by the canal company; others, men, women and children, worked on the boats; yet others made a living running public houses, shops and canalside industries such as brickworks, gasworks, factories, mills and boatyards.

Some people were adversely affected by the canal. There are for instance, unfortunately, many recorded cases of drowning especially of boatmen, lock-keepers and children. For others the canal brought great benefits, including employment and also romance as many families of those who worked by and on the canal became interlinked by marriage. There were those, known as 'The Proprietors', who, in the early years, invested their money in shares in the canal and whose hopes of a good return were so soon to be disappointed. There were individuals, engineers and surveyors, administrators and committee-men, contractors and workmen, involved in the construction and maintenance of the canal. About some of these we are well-informed; many are mentioned by name; but the names and deeds of countless humble workmen are unrecorded in the surviving records and minutes of the canal company, in many cases because they were employed by contractors.

Concerning the W/B Canal we are lucky to have many volumes of detailed minutes of the biannual Assemblies of shareholders and of the proceedings and decisions of the elected Committee of Works which managed the construction, maintenance and use of the canal. We are fortunate too that there are many surviving maps and plans, and other sources of information, from which to gain a comprehensive picture of the canal's history, its creation and its effect upon the environment and the lives of many people associated with it.

In using the available records a certain amount of caution is needed. By no means all of the things ordered by the Company or its Committee of Works to be done, according to the minutes, were actually carried out; some were abandoned or postponed due to lack of money, or a change of plan, or because of difficulties or objections.

Not all factual statements in books are to be trusted. For instance, in a number of county directories giving information about Kings Norton, including Littlebury's Directory of Worcestershire 1873, it is stated that Thomas Dobbs of Lifford, "took an early interest in the introduction of canals, and superintended the cutting and construction of the Birmingham and Worcester and Birmingham and Stratford canals." In fact, as will be seen, Thomas Dobbs remained throughout the time of the construction of the canal a "thorn in the flesh" to the Canal Company, as he profiteered out of the land needed both for the canal and for Lifford Reservoir, and he made use of the canal himself, often illegally, erecting buildings without permission on the canal banks and avoiding tolls. He played no constructive part in the actual construction of the W/B canal nor of the Stratford-upon-Avon Canal.

Another instance occurs in A.Rees' Cyclopedia, 1819, in an article on canals which contains a number of misleading statements about the W/B Canal, including one that it was engineered by John Smeaton and that "the great anxiety and fatigue which Mr.Smeaton underwent in this arduous undertaking, are thought to have injured his health and to have shortened the days of that very able and excellent man." In fact Smeaton was approached in January 1792 and asked if he would agree to examine the line of the canal as surveyed by John Snape, but he refused. He was 67 years old at the time and he died that same year.

A more curious myth about the canal was included in "Dictionary of Birmingham" by Walter Showell, 1885, where it is stated that "The tunnel on the

Worcester and Birmingham Canal, near King's Norton, is 2,695 yards long, perfectly straight, 17½ feet wide and 18 feet high. In the centre a basin is excavated sufficiently wide for barges to pass without inconvenience; and in this underground chamber in August 1795 the Royal Arch Masons held a regular chapter of their Order, rather an arch way of celebrating the completion of the undertaking." Apart from the fact that the West Hill Tunnel is, in fact, 2726 yards long and was not completed until 1797, there is, of course, no such mid-tunnel basin.

In tracing the early history of the canal, we are greatly helped by the fact that both Birmingham and Worcester had, from the outset, their weekly newspapers, Aris's Birmingham Gazette, founded in 1741, and Berrow's Worcester Journal which originated in 1709. These newspapers, together with others started during the period of the construction of the canal, such as the Worcester Herald, are invaluable sources of information about events not, or only briefly, referred to in the Canal Company's records. Relevant documents, such as copies of Acts of Parliament, the Commons Journal, Company reports, notices, calls upon the proprietors and receipts, are available in libraries and record offices, and some are in private hands. For the more recent history of the canal, canalside industries and amenities, and of families and individuals associated with the canal, I am indebted to those people, many elderly and with remarkable memories, who have supplied information and, in some cases, photographs.

Over the past 200 years or so of the canal's history there have been changes in spelling, especially of place names. Thus, Tardebigge until fairly recently was usually spelt 'Tardebig' or 'Tardebigg'; likewise Wychall, spelt earlier as 'Witchall'; and Bittell, often spelt 'Bittal'. The original spellings are retained in quotations from documents. Punctuation in many earlier documents, both handwritten and printed, is often very erratic, and I have taken the liberty of correcting it where necessary. Sums of money, weights and measures, are usually quoted as they were in the original non-metric units. A table of conversion to metric equivalents is provided for those who may find it useful.

It will be apparent that the coverage of the history of canalside industries and amenities such as public houses in the relevant chapters varies a great deal in its extent, some being mentioned only briefly, others covered at length and in detail. Where little information is given it is usually because little has been available.

I am aware that boats of around 7ft beam using the narrow canals used to be generally known as longboats before World War 2. Today they are usually called narrowboats, the result, it appears, of being so-called by L T C Rolt in his book "Narrow Boat". I have used the term "narrowboat" as it better describes a vessel able to navigate the narrow canals.

ACKNOWLEDGMENTS

I am indebted to many organisations and people for help and information, documents and photographs. In particular I acknowledge the assistance of the following organisations: the Public Record Office, Kew; the Worcestershire County Record Office; the Worcester Local History Centre; the Birmingham Central Reference Library Local Studies and Archives Departments; the National Waterways Museum and Archives Department at Gloucester including the curator David McDougall and archivist Roy Jamieson; and local public libraries in places close to the canal, especially at Bromsgrove and Kings Norton.

Individuals who have helped include the late Tim Brotherton of Bromsgrove for copies of many old maps and documents; John Brown of Romsley for extracts from Berrow's Worcester Journal 1804-11 and 1822-30; the late George Bate, B.E.M., foreman-carpenter at Tardebigge Canal Depot, who kept a canal diary and wrote articles for Tardebigge Parish Magazine in 1969-70 and for "Fifty-Eight", the magazine of the W/B Canal Society, over many years. Other individuals who supplied particular information are mentioned in the text or named in the lists of sources for each chapter. I apologise to any whose names may, inadvertently, have been omitted.

At various times I have learnt much about the structures and the working of the canal from present and former officials and employees of British Waterways and wish to thank especially David James, Roger Hatchard, Neil Bedford, Brian Parker, Mick Hansford and Allan Troth. Of those with experience on working boats before, during and/or immediately after World War 2, who have shared with me their reminiscences and to whom I remain grateful are Daphne St. Joseph (nee March), Tom Mayo, Eric Rice, and Jack Merrell (all now sadly deceased). Others who have helped with specialist or personal knowledge of aspects of the history of the canal include Ian and Rachel Hayes, Colin Scrivener, Stanley Holland, Tom Preen, Alan and June Picken, Phillip Coventry, Doris Colledge and her sister Phyllis Scriven.

One vital source of information about facts and dates concerning the history of the canal over the past thirty years or more has been articles and reports in "Fifty-Eight", the monthly magazine of the W/B Canal Society. For the use of this material and quotations from articles I am grateful to the Canal Society and contributors to its journal.

I have been taking and collecting photographs and slides of the W/B Canal over the past thirty years. Most recent photographs of the canal are my own; the names of people and institutions who supplied the others, if known, are acknowledged, permission to include them having been obtained wherever possible. Abbreviations used in the acknowledgments are:

BRL   Birmingham Central Reference Library
BW   British Waterways
NWMT   National Waterways Museum Trust
WBCS   Worcester and Birmingham Canal Society
WCCHS   Worcestershire County Council History Centre
WRO   Worcestershire Record Office

Researching the history of the W/B Canal, as time has allowed, has been a long and enjoyable task. I am very grateful to all the very many people whose help and information have contributed to the creation of this book.

Alan White

View of Tardebigge Church and countryside from within the south portal of the Tardebigge Tunnel. (Rosemary Troth)

Chapter 1

THE CANAL THAT
MIGHT HAVE BEEN

THE PUBLICATION OF PROPOSALS

The first public notice of plans for a canal from Birmingham and the Black Country to Worcester appeared in Berrow's Worcester Journal dated 13 January 1785. It was repeated with a minor amendment in the next four issues of that weekly newspaper. It read as follows:

"Intended Navigation from the Collieries to Worcester.

"It being apprehended, that a navigable Canal from the Collieries at Tipton, Bilston, Dudley, and Stourbridge, to communicate with the Severn at Diglis, below Worcester, would greatly reduce the Price of Coals, as well as be the Means of supplying many distant Markets, where the present high Price of that necessary Article of Life deprives the Poor of the Comfort of a good Fire, and the Public of the Benefit arising from so great a Traffic for the Produce of our Mines, and the Employment of such an additional Number of industrious and hardy Men. - And that very considerable Advantages would also arise to the Public, by conveying Merchandize from Birmingham, (either by a Communication with the Birmingham Canal at or near Tipton, or by a Line directly from Birmingham to Worcester) whereby the Merchant would be certain of at least one Day more in every Fortnight, to prepare his Goods for the Spring Tides to Bristol. - And that the Price of Tonnage would not only be reduced, but Coals and Merchandize would be more expeditiously conveyed into the deep Water below Worcester, whereby the Delays and Expences arising from numerous Shallows in the Severn, between Stourport and Worcester, would not only be avoided, but the talk'd of Experiments of erecting Locks and Wears upon the Severn would be rendered totally unnecessary, which, instead of improving, may eventually destroy an old and free Navigation, by raising the Price of Tonnage on all Trade thereon, to the Oppression of the Public, and the great Injury of much private Property.

"And whereas Surveys have been made of the Country through which such Canal is intended to pass, whereby it appears that Coals may be brought from the Tipton and Bilston Collieries, above 11 Miles nearer, and sold at Worcester for 1s.8d. a Ton cheaper than they are at present, and from the Dudley and Stourbridge Mines proportionally nearer, and sold in Worcester for 1s. a Ton cheaper than the Bilston, with equal Advantages to every Market down Severn, and up the Avon from Tewkesbury, and from the Severn, Coals and Merchandize may be conveyed on very easy Terms through Stroud, by the new Canal now making at Letchlade and Cirencester, and by the Thames, Charwell, and Isis, into Hertfordshire, Berkshire, and even Middlesex.

"And in order that a Work of such magnitude and uncommon Utility may receive every additional Support that intelligent and public spirited Men can bestow upon it, the Surveys may be seen at the Bell in Broad-Street, Worcester, between the Hours of Eleven and One o'Clock, every Wednesday and Saturday Mornings, and any Information that may throw Light and Improvement on the present Plan, previous to a public Meeting for the Purpose of applying to Parliament for Powers to carry the same into Effect, will be thankfully received by Mr. Collet, in Foregate-Street; or Mr. Brampton, Attorney, at Hawford, near Worcester."

From this announcement it is clear that during 1784, and possibly earlier, certain persons had been considering the possibility of a canal to connect the collieries west of Birmingham with the River Severn at Diglis below Worcester. Who these persons were we cannot be sure, for they evidently deemed it prudent to remain anonymous and to plan in secret so as neither to alarm prematurely those who might be adversely affected nor to forewarn and forearm the likely opposition. It is, however, clear that the main initiative for the canal came from the Worcester end, for it was there that the need for cheaper coal and industrial products was deeply felt; it was there in the local weekly newspaper that the proposals were first published; and, as we shall see, several Worcester citizens were the most zealous promoters of what was soon known as "The Worcester Canal".

The purpose of the planned waterway was, as stated, to bypass the River Severn between Stourport and Diglis for two reasons; first, because this stretch of the River Severn with its shallows was notoriously difficult to navigate at the best of times, and during a dry summer it could be unnavigable for laden trows and barges for many weeks, even months, on end; secondly, because even when the river was navigable, the route to Worcester from Birmingham via Aldersley, or from Dudley or Stourbridge via Stourton, and along the Staffordshire and Worcestershire Canal, was circuitous, time consuming and costly.

So the canal was desirable; but was it feasible? The first practical step was to engage a reliable surveyor with canal experience to investigate one or more possible routes. The obvious choice was John Snape, already well established as a land and canal surveyor. Living then at Wishaw, Warwickshire, where he was born in 1737, Snape had by 1784 already surveyed and mapped many parishes and estates, including, in 1776, 1777 and 1779 the parishes of Tibberton, Himbleton and Birmingham, through which the proposed canal was to pass. He is believed to have assisted Brindley with the surveying of the Birmingham Canal from 1765 to 1771, for he produced little else in that period. He resurveyed the Birmingham Canal in 1777, was surveyor for the Birmingham Canal Extension and Farmers Bridge locks in 1782, and in 1783 he surveyed the Birmingham and Fazeley Canal and also collateral branches of the Birmingham Canal. In 1784 he was engaged with John Bull in surveying the Dudley Canal Extension which was intended to link Parkhead on the Dudley Canal with Tipton on the Birmingham Canal via the Dudley Tunnel. Snape undoubtedly undertook the preliminary surveys for the Worcester Canal which were displayed at the Bell Inn in Worcester in January 1785, and he was to remain the principal surveyor of the canal both before and during its eventual construction from Birmingham to Worcester.

Parliamentary approval for the Dudley Canal Extension to link the Dudley Canal with the Birmingham Canal was obtained on 4 July 1785. Because of the impending construction of this link it was soon decided that the Worcester Canal, instead of joining the Birmingham Canal directly, would join the Stourbridge Canal at the terminus in Stourbridge, which was the nearest point to Worcester on the then existing canal network. Accordingly Snape produced a survey and plan for a canal from Stourbridge to Worcester via Bromsgrove, together with an estimate of its cost.

CONTROVERSY

Convinced from Snape's initial surveys and estimates that the canal was possible, the promoters carefully drafted their press announcement of January 1875 in which they invited the constructive support of "intelligent and public spirited men". Alas, their anticipation of a hostile reaction from those whose interests could be threatened by the new waterway was soon justified. The first news of organised opposition came with the advertisement, in Berrow's Journal of 24 February, of "A Meeting of the Owners and Occupiers of Estates through which such Canal is intended to be made or which may be affected thereby", to be held on 3 March at the Lion Inn in Kidderminster. At this meeting the landowners were joined by other parties, "Gentlemen, Merchants and Manufacturers". A committee representing landowners, millowners whose water supplies might be affected, carriers on the River Severn above Worcester, and proprietors of the Staffordshire and Worcestershire Canal, was set up, and subscriptions received to finance the opposition to a Parliamentary Bill for the new canal.

The original announcement of January 1785 spoke of a public meeting to be held for the purpose of applying to Parliament for powers to construct the canal. Such a meeting was usually necessary to indicate the degree of support for a proposed canal, and also to enlist subscribers who would become the proprietors (or shareholders) of the canal company if an Act was obtained. However, in this case, no such public meeting was advertised. Instead, the promoters and known supporters were notified privately of the latest plans and invited to subscribe. Belatedly, a report in Berrow's Journal of 20 October 1785 spoke of the likely benefits of "the New Canal intended to be cut from Birmingham to this City to pass near Bromsgrove", and concluded "The expences, we are informed, will amount to 120,000 l., and so well convinced are the people of Birmingham and this City of its great publick utility and advantage that, on opening the Subscription in September, 60,000 l. was subscribed in three days." The lack of any public meeting and the secrecy with which the promoters acted was to be one of the complaints of the opponents of the canal in newspaper propaganda and during the 1786 Parliamentary proceedings. In December 1785 and in January and February 1786 there appeared a spate of advertisements in Berrow's Journal, some arguing for, some against, the canal, and amongst the latter was one addressed "To the few Proprietors of the new Intended Canal who are in the Secret."

During 1785 and early 1786 each of the local canal companies at their meetings (some held specially) considered the likely impact of the Worcester Canal on their own undertakings. Opposition on the part of the Staffordshire and Worcestershire Company was to be expected, as its monopoly as part of the waterway link between the Black Country and the River Severn was directly threatened. In newspaper notices they argued that the tonnage on coals from Tipton by way of the new canal would be little different from that by way of Stourport, especially as they were willing to reduce their own tonnage by a half-penny a ton per mile. They also included the heart-rending plea that, if because of the new canal their dividends should fall, it would cause much suffering to widows, orphans and others dependent on the income from their canal shares.

The Staffs. and Worcs. Company tried to persuade the Birmingham Canal Company to support their opposition, and complained that John Meredith, Clerk to the B.C.N. since 1768, was an active supporter of the Worcester Canal. The reply of the Birmingham Canal Committee, agreed at their meeting of 3 March 1786, was "This Committee wish well to the Staffs. & Worcester Canal Co. but desire to be excused taking any active part in the matter in dispute between the contending parties", and "Mr. Meredith is engaged in the service of the Worcester Committee but merely as a Professional Man, and not on the behalf of or by direction or desire of this Committee." So the Birmingham Canal Company decided to maintain a neutral position.

The Droitwich Canal Company hoped that the new canal might be joined to their own at or near Droitwich, and offered £20 towards the Worcester Canal survey on this condition. When they realised that the new canal would by-pass Droitwich a mile or so to the east, they decided in January 1786 to organise a petition to Parliament to include in the Worcester Canal Bill provision for a branch canal from it to their own. In

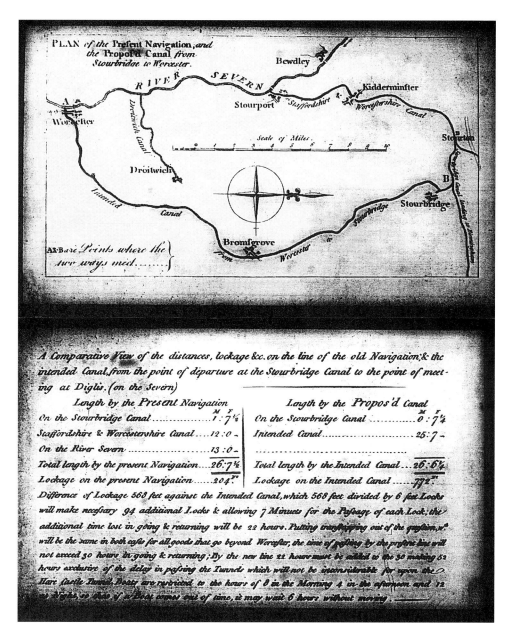

A plan c. 1785 of the existing and proposed waterway routes between Worcester and Stourbridge, together with a critical comparison of distances, lockage and estimated passage times by the two routes, evidently circulated by opponents of the intended canal (WRO).

February they further proposed at a meeting with representatives of the Worcester Canal Committee a merger with the new canal and support for it on condition that 5% interest should be paid in perpetuity on Droitwich shares at their current value of £140 from the date of the passing of the Act. This condition was agreed to; a similar one later in the W/B Canal Act was to be a financial burden on the W/B Canal for many years.

The Dudley and Stourbridge Companies saw a real advantage to themselves in a shorter and more reliable route from, and through, their canals to Diglis and so were strong supporters of the new canal. In fact many of the promoters of the Worcester Canal were, at this stage, also shareholders of the Dudley and Stourbridge Canals.

Meanwhile the Staffs. & Worcs, Canal Company, acutely aware of the delays and inconvenience caused by the unsatisfactory state of the Severn above Diglis, had, in 1784, commissioned William Jessop to produce a plan for improvements to the River from Worcester as far as Coalbrookdale, involving the construction of locks and weirs. This was "the talk'd of Experiments of erecting locks and wears upon the Severn" referred to in the initial announcement of the Worcester Canal proposals. Jessop presented his Plan and Report to a meeting held at Stourport on 21 September 1785. He proposed the construction of four locks and weirs between Worcester and Stourport and twelve between Stourport and Coalbrookdale, designed to maintain a 4ft depth of water in this stretch of the River even in the driest season. At a meeting held in Bridgnorth on 20 January 1786, a committee was formed to promote a Bill in Parliament for these improvements, and a subscription was started towards the estimated total cost of £50,000. Support came chiefly from the Staffs. & Worcs. Canal Company which stood to benefit from trade up and down river from Stourport, from the ironmasters of Coalbrookdale, and from some owners of barges and trows on the river. Opposition came from riparian landowners, fearful of resultant flooding, whom Jessop tried in vain to reassure in a long letter in Berrow's Journal of 9 February 1786, also from carriers in favour of maintaining the natural toll-free status of the river, and from the Worcester Canal promoters who argued that their Navigation would render the intended Severn improvements unnecessary.

So, round about the same time, supporters and opponents of both the Severn Improvements scheme and the Worcester Canal were getting their acts together in readiness for their Parliamentary Bills to be presented early in 1786.

THE ORGANISATION OF THE CANAL PROMOTERS
Steps taken by the Worcester Canal promoters included the appointment of Hooper and Pratt, The Cross, Worcester, as their bankers, and Wilson Aylesbury Roberts Esq., solicitor, of the High Street, Bewdley, as their canal agent. One of the partners in the Worcester Bank, Dr. Thomas Hooper, was to play a dramatic part in the early fortunes of the W/B Canal. He and other members of his family, William Hooper, William Hooper Junior, Mary and Lucy Hooper, had substantial business interests

in Worcester and were subscribers to the canal. The other partner in the bank, Isaac Pratt, of Henwick, Worcester, was on the Committees of the Stourbridge and Dudley Canals, an entrepreneur with coal interests, who gave his name to Pratt's Wharf on the Staffs. & Worcs. Canal, and who later in 1787 took charge, for a brief period, of the construction of the southern end of the Dudley Canal Tunnel.

The canal agent, Wilson Aylesbury Roberts, appointed to attend to the legal side of bringing in the Parliamentary Bill, was an interesting character who, besides having a professional interest in the promotion of the Worcester Canal, also became extensively involved as a shareholder and as a long-serving committee member of the W/B Canal during its construction. He was born in Droitwich in 1736, the son of Richard and Dorothy Roberts and a grandson of Henry Roberts who had settled in Droitwich about the year 1705 and was proprietor of a salt works there. He was christened Wilson Aylesbury after his mother's brother, Wilson Aylesbury Esq. of Packwood, and he was heir to this childless uncle's estate. His fortune increased when, after legal training, he went to live and work in Bewdley and married an heiress, Betty Caroline Crane. He became Bailiff (Chief Magistrate) of Bewdley in 1768 and 1772 and Deputy Recorder (equivalent to Town Clerk) in 1775. His interest in canals may have been kindled by the construction of the Droitwich Canal in 1768-71. Certainly members of his family were shareholders in this canal and served on its Committee, and he himself acted for the Droitwich Canal Company in protecting its interests in negotiations with the Worcester Canal Company, for which he also acted. This looks like professional double-dealing (and as such was remarked on by Charles Hadfield in his book "Canals of the West Midlands"), but it was in the interests of both the Droitwich and the Worcester Companies that an agreement satisfactory to both should be reached.

When he agreed to act for the Worcester Canal promoters, little did W A Roberts realise the hazards involved. On 2 January 1786 Aris's Birmingham Gazette reported: "We are sorry to lay before our readers the following extraordinary instance of the depravity of human nature; the solicitor employed by the subscribers to an intended canal was unfortunately called by business to Stourport; he with great confidence trusted himself to the barber of the place to be shaved, when, shocking to relate, the operator, as soon as he had got him in the suds, cut his throat. - The motive that induced this man to commit such an atrocious act, is supposed to arise from his apprehension, that if the proposed canal should take place, he would not have a man to shave at Stourport." Fortunately, W A Roberts survived this frightful ordeal.

PARLIAMENTARY PROCEEDINGS; THE WORCESTER CANAL BILL
Proceedings in the House of Commons began on 22 February 1786 when "A Petition of the several Noblemen, and the humble Petition of the several Gentlemen, Clergy, Freeholders, and Manufacturers of the County and City of Worcester, and

of several other Persons whose Names are thereunto subscribed, was presented to the House, and read; Setting forth, That it appears, by Levels and Surveys already taken, that a Navigable Cut or Canal for Boats, Barges, and other Vessels, may be made from the Stourbridge Canal Navigation, at or near to the Town of Stourbridge, by or near to the Town of Bromsgrove, to join and communicate with the River Severn, at a Place called Diglis, near to the City of Worcester." One of the Noblemen amongst the petitioners was Lord Dudley and Ward, owner of limeworks and collieries in the Dudley area and a prominent promoter and proprietor of the Stourbridge and Dudley Canals. Another was the Earl of Plymouth, landowner of the Hewell Estates in the Parish of Tardebigge, near Bromsgrove. The interest of Lord Dudley and Ward is easily understandable on commercial grounds; that of Lord Plymouth, who took an active part in promoting the canal, is less easy to understand, since its only likely benefit to him was the prospect of cheaper domestic coal and the transport of timber and agricultural produce from his estates. He just seems to have been a canal enthusiast, as were some of the other promoters, though all, no doubt, hoped for some return on their financial investment.

Following the initial Worcester petition, the Commons agreed to the Bill being prepared and presented, and it received its First Reading on 10 March 1786.

The Bill, a copy of which exists in the Worcestershire Record Office, begins by listing the names of the 193 subscribers who would become "The Company of Proprietors of the Worcester Canal Navigation". The route of the canal was from the Stourbridge Canal at Holloway End across the River Stour, up to the Gig Mill Forge, then through the parishes of Old Swinford, Pedmore, Hagley, and Clent (passing near the mansion house of John Amphlett Esq.), through a tunnel about a mile and a quarter long at Madeley Heath in the Parish of Belbroughton at a summit level of 500 feet, then passing near Barnsley Hall and north and east of Bromsgrove via the Crab Mill, then on through Stoke Prior, following from there the route of the W/B Canal as eventually constructed down to Diglis, Worcester, with the tunnel at Dunhampstead. The canal, 26 miles in length, needed 128 locks of about 6 feet rise or fall, some 48 from Stourbridge up to the summit level and 80 from there down to the River Severn. The canal's principal water supply was to be a large reservoir, about 50 acres in extent, on the slopes of the Lickey Hills at Lickey Common. No water was to be taken from a long list of streams and brooks crossing the line of the canal. There was to be a canal basin at Lowesmoor in Worcester. To finance the canal, £120,000 was to be raised in £100 shares, the maximum holding by any proprietor being 20 shares. The Company could raise another £50,000 more, if necessary, by Calls on the proprietors. General Assemblies of the proprietors were to be held on the second Monday of January and July each year, commencing on 10 July 1786 at the Bell Inn, Worcester. A Committee of Works, with fifteen members each holding at least five shares, was to be elected at each General Assembly. Rules and regulations for the use of the canal were prescribed, also the maximum tonnage to be charged on the various goods carried. In making the canal, agents and workmen had right of access to private property, with safeguards and compensation for land used and damage caused. Some landowners, including John Amphlett of Clent, Henry Cecil of Hanbury, and Marmaduke Langdale of Stoke Prior, were granted special protection against intrusion and the making of public wharves on their land. Other interesting details include permission for canalside landowners to use pleasure boats without payment, provided no locks were used and no goods carried; penalties laid down for throwing rubbish into the canal or damaging lock-gates; and the provision of a side cut to the road to Burcot from the canal between Barnsley Hall and the Crab Mill, near Bromsgrove, probably for the convenience of the Earl of Plymouth. The format and details of this Worcester Canal Bill are of interest since they set the pattern for the Worcester and Birmingham Bills of 1790 and 1791.

Accompanying the Bill was John Snape's Plan and Survey which included "a Navigable Cut from the said intended Canal, at or near Ashford Coppice, to join and communicate with the Droitwich Canal (which is only about the distance of one Mile)". This link to the Droitwich Barge Canal was included in response to pressure and the petition from the Droitwich Company.

FAILURE AND AFTERMATH
Debate in both Houses of Parliament was accompanied by a plethora of petitions for and against the Bill from places, organisations and groups of people. In favour were petitions mainly from Worcester and places to the south and west, as far away as Ledbury, Cirencester, Bridgwater, Taunton, Exeter, Bodmin, Barnstaple and Camelford; also from the Stourbridge and Dudley Navigations, and from Lord Plymouth and inhabitants of Bromsgrove. Against the Bill were petitions from places such as Stourport, Kidderminster, Bewdley, Wolverhampton and Shrewsbury, from the Staffs. & Worcs. Canal Company, and from landowners and mill-owners. These petitions, containing many signatures and requiring considerable effort to compile, were important evidence to Parliament of the degree of support for, and opposition to, the canal.

Eventually the Bill, with various amendments, including provisions for the removal of shoals in the River Severn below Worcester, received its Second Reading in the Commons and, at the end of April, it passed to the Lords where, following the receipt of further petitions, representatives of the promoters and the opposition were heard and questioned, amongst them John Snape and John Nichols, Engineer, for, and William Jessop against. On Tuesday 16 May 1786 the Worcester Canal Bill was defeated in the Lords by 42 votes to 17. Amongst those Lords against the Bill were the Bishops of Llandaff, Chester and Salisbury, who maintained that canals were a threat to the mariners of coastal vessels, and other Peers who voiced their apprehensions about the inevitable damage caused by canals to private property.

On receiving the news of the defeat of the Canal Bill, its opponents were jubilant. Berrow's Journal reported: "We hear from Wolverhampton that in consequence of the House of Lords having rejected the Worcester Canal Bill, and thereby given permanence to the property of the original adventurers, a very respectable meeting of the gentlemen in the town and neighbourhood was held at the Lion Tavern on Thursday last, where an elegant dinner was prepared on the occasion, after which many loyal and constitutional toasts were drunk. The reported thunder from six pieces of cannon planted on an eminence called Bunker's Hill re-echoing to the peals of St. Peter's bells; the hilarity of the company and the acclamation of the populace (who were plentifully regaled with the best October) composed the happy scene of mirth and festivity." Aris's Birmingham Gazette also reported "great rejoicings at Kidderminster, Stourport, Chaddesley &c. .... the bells were immediately set a ringing, and great quantities of liquor given to the populace. In the evening there were illuminations, bonfires, firing of cannon &c., &c."

As for the unhappy promoters of the canal, the only persons to benefit were the paid professionals, including Wilson Aylesbury Roberts who, at a meeting of the proprietors of the Droitwich Canal Company on 19 October 1787, was voted "the Sum of One Hundred Guineas in full Satisfaction for his Trouble and Expences on the Behalf of this Company."

Meanwhile the Severn Navigation Bill also had a stormy passage in Parliament, being opposed, not only by supporters of the ill-fated Worcester Canal scheme, but also by petitions from "Bowhallers or Watermen working on the River Severn" on the grounds that there would be delays at locks and an end of night working, from riverside landowners alarmed about possible flooding and other disturbance, from anxious fishermen, and from barge-owners not wanting to pay tolls. Due to the strength of the opposition, the Bill was withdrawn and abandoned after its Second Reading. Apart from some dredging between Stourport and Diglis and the gradual introduction of horse towing paths, the river was to remain virtually as it was until the 1840s.

It may be of interest to speculate about what might have been the future of the Worcester to Stourbridge Canal had it been constructed. Whether a broad canal "for Boats, Barges, and other Vessels", as intended, or a narrow canal, it would have meant a tiresome haul with 128 locks to negotiate and a long tunnel. From Birmingham there would have been, in addition, 35 locks and the long Dudley Tunnel to Stourbridge. When the Severn was navigable, carriers might well have preferred to use the river route via Stourport to and from Worcester, especially downstream. So the canal could well have been a financial disaster, and have been long abandoned. In the light of events it was providential that its Bill was rejected and that the W/B Canal was constructed instead.

Chapter 2

GETTING THE GO-AHEAD

RENEWED ACTIVITY; ABANDONMENT OF THE STOURBRIDGE ROUTE

We have little or no news of the activities of the frustrated promoters of the Worcester Canal, following the defeat of their Bill, for the next two years. The need for a canal from the Birmingham area to Worcester remained as urgent as before, as interruptions to navigation on the River Severn continued, the severe drought of 1786, in particular, causing a long disruption to river traffic. Eventually, during 1788, the promoters decided upon another attempt to get Parliamentary sanction for their proposed canal from Stourbridge to Worcester. This time, to win over the millowners, they proposed the construction of reservoirs for the sole use of the mills to safeguard their water supplies. On 25 December 1788 and 2 January 1789 Berrow's Worcester Journal carried the following advertisement:

"INTENDED WORCESTER CANAL
"The Owners and Occupiers of Mills upon the River Stour are requested to meet the Committee appointed by the Subscribers to the intended Worcester Canal at the Talbot in Stourbridge on Tuesday the 6th. of January next, at eleven o'Clock in the Forenoon, in order, not only to point out such Clause or Clauses to be introduced in the intended Bill as will effectively secure the said River or any of its Branches from loss of Water by the said Undertaking, but also to settle in which Place or Places Reservoirs may be made, wherein all Flood Water may be impounded and preserved for their express Use and Benefit."

However, in spite of this generous goodwill gesture, the millowners of Stourport and district remained distrustful and uncooperative, so the Worcester Canal promoters began to consider seriously the alternative "line directly from Birmingham to Worcester" mentioned in their original press announcement of January 1785. Unfortunately this meant alienating many of their supporters from the Dudley and Stourbridge Canal Companies, but there was no alternative in view of the continuing hostility of landowners and millowners in the Stourbridge area. A canal direct from Birmingham would have its disadvantages, including major civil engineering works, there being several valleys and hills to traverse, requiring substantial embankments, cuttings and tunnels, and water supplies were also problematical. On the other hand there was the advantage that, with a long summit level from Birmingham to Tardebigge and only a descent of 428ft from there to the River Severn at Diglis, the number of locks required was less than half the total needed for the canal from Stourbridge. There would be objections from other landowners and millowners, but the hope was that these would be more cooperative if offered generous safeguards and compensation.

PLANS AND PREPARATIONS FOR A W/B CANAL BILL

The aim of the promoters was now to present a new Bill to Parliament early in 1790 for a canal which would run from the Old Wharf of the Birmingham Canal near Broad Street, Birmingham, to the River Severn at Diglis, Worcester. The first step was for John Snape to produce a new plan and this he did early in 1789. It was a remarkable achievement on his part that he was able to work out a level

Other Hickman, Fifth Earl of Plymouth. He took a great interest in the creation of the W/B Canal and helped to promote it in the House of Lords. He was the Chairman of the first meeting of the proprietors in July 1791 and of their fourth meeting in January 1793. He held twenty of the £100 shares in the Company. Unfortunately he died in 1799, long before the canal reached the Old Wharf at Tardebigge within his Hewell Estate. (Portrait by Pompeo Batoni, courtesy of Viscount Plymouth).

route for some fifteen miles from the Birmingham end of the canal through undulating countryside as far as Tardebigge. The fact that substantial cuttings and embankments and several tunnels, including the long West Hill Tunnel, would be needed was no deterrent to the canal promoters.

One of the first tasks of the promoters was to begin to negotiate with landowners, millowners, and the neighbouring canal companies who would be affected by the new canal in an attempt to allay their fears and gain their support.

The three major landowners on the line of the W/B Canal were Sir Henry Gough Calthorpe of Edgbaston, Henry Cecil of Hanbury, and Richard Amphlett of Hadzor. Their properties were to be specially protected by clauses in the Bill prohibiting the construction of wharves, warehouses and other buildings without their consent; towpaths were not to be sited on the same side of the canal as their stately homes; and they were to be granted concessions including fishing rights and tollfree transport for their goods. In addition, Lord Calthorpe, on whose land an embankment was to be made, was to be protected from possible flooding by adequate drainage provision, and there was to be no brick-making on his property.

At this time there were many water mills on the Rivers Rea and Arrow, both of which rose in the Lickey Hills and crossed the line of the proposed canal. Many of these mills had been, and still were, grinding corn for flour and animal feeds; others had been converted or newly built for metal working, since Birmingham industries, before the advent of steam power, made use of water power on all available rivers and streams. On the River Rea there were rolling mills at Wychall, Lifford and nearer Birmingham, and grinding and boring mills producing scythes, swords, gun barrels etc. at Hazelwell, Moor Green and Speedwell Mills. The Bourn Brook. a tributary of the River Rea, supplied power for Harborne and Bournbrook Mills. Mills on the River Arrow, from Cofton downstream, included many in the Redditch area for needle making. The millowners and their employees were naturally fearful of the possible disruption to, or diversion of, their water supply by the proposed canal, and the canal promoters saw the need for gaining their confidence and support by making generous and costly provision, as they had offered to do for the River Stour millowners, of reservoirs to store floodwater and improve the flow of water to the various mills. Hence the agreement to include in the W/B Canal Bill the mandatory construction of two reservoirs on the River Rea at Wychall (20 acres) and Kings Norton (9 acres), one at Harborne on the Bourn Brook (19 acres), and two on the River Arrow at Cofton (14 acres) and Bittell (22 acres); these to be made for the sole use of the mills as soon as the canal was completed over each river. Also, no water was to be taken for the canal from any rivers or brooks crossed, and each watercourse was to be piped or culverted under the canal.

Of the neighbouring canal companies, the Droitwich received most consideration. It was assured that a branch canal (included in Snape's plan) would be made to link it with the W/B Canal, but this would be the subject of a another separate Bill. The W/B Bill was, however, to contain a directive that every year, from the date of the passing of the Act, the Droitwich Company should be paid whatever amount was needed to bring its dividend up to 5% of the value of its shares, now valued at £160 each; i.e. £8 per share. This guarantee was negotiated by W A Roberts on 8 February 1790, as recorded in the Droitwich Company's Minute Book:

"I W.A.Roberts Agent to the Intended Worcester Canal and One of their Committee Do Consent and Agree to the Aforesaid Terms, And that the same shall be inserted in the said intended Act of Parliament It being on this Condition that the Droitwich Canal Company Navigation have given their Consent to the said Intended Act - As witness my Hand this Day and Year above written.

(signed) W.A.Roberts."

The W/B Canal promoters were soon to regret this commitment which was to force them to subsidise heavily the Droitwich Canal for many years, long before their canal was sufficiently advanced to affect its traffic.

The Stourbridge and Dudley Canal Companies were now threatened by a waterway direct from Birmingham to Worcester which would take traffic from the Birmingham area away from the route via the Dudley Tunnel, being constructed, and their canals to the Severn. Hopefully to retain their support, the W/B Canal promoters arranged to include in their Bill eventual dividend guarantees. The interest of the Stourbridge Canal was to be made up to £9 per share, if necessary, once the new canal was completed. The Dudley Company would be compensated up to the level of its average annual dividend following the completion of the Dudley Tunnel until the completion of the W/B Canal. In the event, the guarantee to the Dudley Company lapsed, well before it could be implemented, with the construction of the Dudley No.2 Canal from Netherton to Selly Oak in 1793-98.

The Birmingham Canal Company, though not opposed to the W/B Canal, nevertheless insisted that their own water supply should be safeguarded by a 7ft wide land barrier between the new canal and their own, to be kept water-tight under their direction but at the expense of the W/B Company. A clause to this effect was to be included in the W/B Canal Bill, but with the proviso that the Birmingham Company would have the right, if they later so decided, to make a navigable communication across the barrier in such a manner as would protect also the water supply of the W/B Canal.

The Staffs. and Worcs. Canal Company remained implacably hostile to the W/B Canal proposals and was not to be granted any concession.

PROMOTING THE W/B CANAL

This time the W/B Canal promoters avoided the charge of secrecy by organising a public meeting which took place on 22 January 1790, as reported in Aris's Birmingham Gazette: "On Friday last was held in Bromsgrove a respectable meeting of the subscribers to the intended Worcester Canal from this place; the Earl of Plymouth took the chair, and it was unanimously agreed that a Bill should this Session be presented to Parliament for making the said Canal." One of the people who attended this meeting was William Brookes, a glazier of Bromsgrove, who subscribed for 2 shares in the canal. Amongst his surviving papers are notes he evidently made at the meeting, as follows:

> "The Intended Canal from Derington through the parishes of Birmingham Edgbaston Norfield, Kingnorton Alvechurch, Tardebidg - Stoke prior Dodderhill Hanbury Hadzor Himbleton Oddingley, Tibberton Hinlip Warndon Claines Saint Martin Saint Peter a Tunnill near Lea end a Tunnill near Tardebidg, the Summitt at London Barnes 16m 6f 8c 24x nearest to Bromsgrove at and fall from the Levell to Droitwich 5m 4f 4c 71x fall 68 feet.
>
> "To Lowesmore 8.2.0.14 fall 86 feet after 42 feet fall.
>
> "From Birmingham to the River Severn 31m 4f 8c 41x Fall 448 feet.
>
> "From Near West field to Dhich 1m 3f 7c 92x fall 68 feet ½.
>
> "The Vessels to carey 60 Tons."

These incomplete and slightly muddled details of the planned canal were, it seems, culled from information supplied to the meeting by John Snape, for they mostly tally with the list of parishes and the statistics included in his plan of the canal, including distances given in miles (m), furlongs (f), chains (c) and yards (x). The two tunnels mentioned are West Hill and Shortwood (there was no Tardebigge Tunnel shown on Snape's plan - a deep cutting may have been intended instead). "Derington" is Deritend, marked on Snape's plan, but actually some way from the Birmingham end of the canal. Snape's plan gives 320 feet (not "fall 68 feet") as the drop from the summit level to the Turnpike Road from Alcester to Droitwich. The canal was clearly intended to be, like the existing Droitwich Canal and the previously intended canal from Stourbridge to Worcester, a barge canal. A canal link from the W/B near West Field Farm to the Droitwich Canal was included in Snape's plan as an integral part of the project.

Another step taken by the W/B Canal promoters early in 1790 was the publication of a pamphlet entitled "Additional Reasons in favour of the Worcester and Birmingham Canal." Accompanied by a map of local canals, existing, under construction and planned, and showing coal mines both opened and unopened, it compared the distances and tolls from Birmingham to Diglis by way of Autherley, Dudley and the Intended Canal, as follows:

> AUTHERLEY. By Stourport which is the only way from Birmingham to Worcester, by water 60m 7f. Price per ton 12s. 6d.
>
> DUDLEY. Which the Opposers of the Bill call the present Way, although very far from being completed, and perhaps never may be, so as to render it a tolerable Passage 46m 5f. Price per ton 11s. 8d.

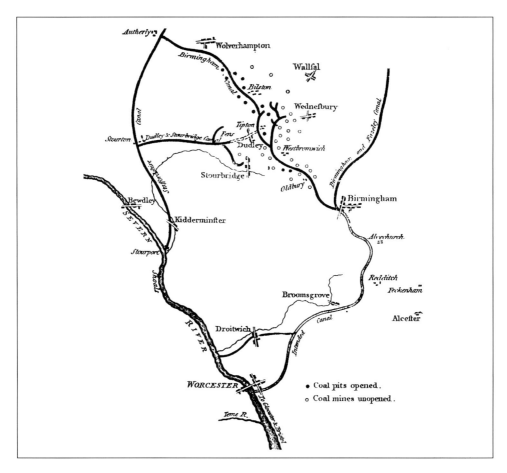

The Midlands canal system with the proposed course of the W/B Canal, 1790.

INTENDED CANAL. From Birmingham, through a Country supplied with Coal by Land-carriage only, to which no Canal has at present any Access, and with the Approbation of Three-fourths of the Land-Owners, and almost all the Mill Owners to Diglis, by a Barge Navigation for Vessels of 60 Tons Burthen 31m 4f. Price per ton 5s. 0d.

The pamphlet went on to list the benefits of cheaper coal to places along and near to the line of the new canal, advantages to mill-owners and occupiers by the reservoirs to be constructed for their sole use, new markets for coal from pits in the Birmingham area, and much cheaper and shorter carriage for goods between Birmingham and Bristol and the South West.

PARLIAMENTARY PROCEEDINGS AND FAILURE

It was after much preparation and with high hopes that, early in 1790, proceedings in Parliament were initiated a second time, as before, with "A Petition of the several Gentlemen, Clergy, Freeholders and Manufacturers of the County and City of Worcester and of several other Persons whose Names are thereunto subscribed." This petition was presented to the Commons on 2 March 1790, and a committee was appointed which on the following day closely questioned John Snape about his experience of constructing canals, about the necessity for the canal, about its proposed dimensions, levels and locks, and, at some length, about arrangements for its water supply. The many questions put to John Snape and his replies, which were reported in detail to the Commons on 4 March, and recorded in the Commons Journal, make interesting reading. Here are a few extracts:

"Mr. John Snape, an Engineer and Surveyor, being examined, said, That he hath taken Levels and Surveys whereby it appears, That a Navigable Cut or Canal for Boats, Barges and other Vessels may be made .....

"And being asked, whether he was ever concerned in the Execution of any Canals? he replied, Not in the executive Parts; but that Canals have been executed from his Plans and he alluded to the Birmingham and Birmingham and Fazeley Canals, as having been executed on the Plan of the intended Canal.

"And being asked, What Part of this Canal he calls the Summit, and what the Extent of the Summit? he replied, The Part between Tardebigg, being in length about Sixteen Miles and an Half - That this Canal does not communicate with the Birmingham Canal - That there will be Four Pounds, or Summits, on this Canal; the Locks are to be about Sixty-six Feet by Sixteen in the Chamber, and the Falls Six Feet - That the Canal is to be supplied with Water from the various Springs which are found in the Bed of the Canal in digging; and Steam Engines are to be erected to raise more Water, so as to form a general Supply.

"And being asked, Whether it is meant to raise Water by Engines to supply the Summit of the intended Canal from the River Severn? he answered, What is not found in digging is to be supplied by Engines from that River; the Distance of this Summit from the River Severn is Fifteen Miles, and the Fall from the Summit is 448 Feet - That the Birmingham Canal is amply supplied with Water by Engines; the Locks of the said Canal are about 74 Feet long, and Eight Feet wide.

"And being asked, Whether the Water raised by the Steam Engines upon the Birmingham Canal would not supply this Canal, if wanted? he said, he apprehended it would."

Satisfied with this report, the Commons on the following day gave the First Reading to "A Bill for making and maintaining a Navigable Canal from, or from near to, the Town of Birmingham, in the County of Warwick, to communicate with the River Severn, near to the City of Worcester". From this time until 15 April, the date fixed for the Second Reading, there was the usual flood of petitions. Many in favour were from towns and villages by and near the route of the canal; from places to the South and West of Worcester as far away as Cardiff, Haverfordwest, Exeter, Barnstaple and St.Ives, Cornwall; from merchants and manufacturers and the owners of coal mines in the Birmingham area; and from "Owners of very considerable Estates and Water Mills, and other works, upon the several Rivers, Brooks and Streams lying between the Town of Birmingham and the City of Worcester, upon the line of the intended Canal." Against the Bill were petitions predictably from places such as Wolverhampton, Bewdley, Stafford, Dudley, Kidderminster and Stourbridge; from the Staffs. and Worcs. Canal Co.; from Sir Thomas Gooch who owned land needed for the canal as well as water mills in the Birmingham area; from the "Owners of Vessels, Barge masters, Carriers and others, Traders upon the River Severn"; and from William, Lord Viscount Dudley and Ward and others, owners and proprietors of coal mines near the Stourbridge and Dudley Canals.

On 14 April, the day before the scheduled Second Reading of the Bill, Sir Edward Littleton in the Commons proposed an Amendment that this Reading should be postponed for three months, which, since the last sitting of the Session was in June, would mean the rejection of the Bill. In the debate one argument against the canal was that "the Scheme would be injurious to the Navigation of the Severn, as the Water for the new Canal was to be taken from thence." Another was that, by increasing the export of coal from Birmingham, it would cause a scarcity and an increase in its price. Both arguments were easily countered, since all water pumped from the River Severn for the canal would be returned, and there was an abundant supply of coal and unopened pits along the Birmingham Canal. However the strength of the opposition was still considerable; the Amendment was passed by 53 votes to 29 and the Bill rejected.

Again there was rejoicing in enemy territory. Aris's Birmingham Gazette reported: "At Wolverhampton the bells were rung, as soon as the account of the rejection of the Worcester Canal Bill by the House of Commons was received, and on Monday last a grand entertainment was given there by the Proprietors of the Staffordshire Canal, upon the same account."

VICTORY AT THE THIRD ATTEMPT

This second defeat must have been a great blow to the W/B Canal promoters, but having worked so hard and spent so much, they were determined to fight on. They prepared to re-present their Bill, substantially unaltered, early in 1791, meanwhile making further attempts to gain support and petitions in their favour.

On 18 February 1791 proceedings again began in Parliament with a petition from Worcester, and the setting up of a Commons Committee. The Bill received its First Reading on 28 February, and it was ordered "That the said Bill be read a Second Time upon Tomorrow Sevennight, the 8th. Day of March next." There followed a deluge of petitions from the same sources and with much the same arguments as before. One of them, from Birmingham, in favour of the canal, contained as many as 6058 signatures and was 14 yds long. Following a petition from the Executors of the late Lord Dudley and Ward, complaining that their names had been included in the list of subscribers to the canal without their consent, a committee was appointed to look into their allegations. This caused the Second Reading of the Bill to be postponed, but it was successfully achieved on 28 March.

After its Third Reading a week later, it was the turn of the Lords to read and examine the Bill and to hear representatives of the promoters and petitioners. Finally on 9 June, after several amendments were defeated, the Lords gave the Bill its Third Reading by 19 votes to 17, a narrow majority of 2. On the next day, 10 June 1791, it received the Royal Assent. So at long last, the third time lucky, the promoters had gained the go-ahead, the Act for the construction of their canal.

It was now the turn of the supporters of the canal to rejoice at their hard-won success, achieved after over six years effort and at great expense. Berrow's Journal reported:

> "On Thursday last our Canal Bill was passed in the House of Lords, and the news thereof immediately dispatched by one of our coaches, the arrival of which on Friday morning with the display of a flag announced the gladsome tidings. .... No sooner were our fellow Citizens apprized of the obtainment of this grand object, than a general joy seemed to have diffused itself thro' all ranks, which was testified by the ringing of bells, bonfires etc., etc. .... The above Bill has been one of the most expensive bills of the sort ever presented to Parliament.
>
> The subscribers alone, it is said, have expended ten thousand pounds upon it; and the expence of the Opposition amounts to near twenty thousand pounds."

There seems to have been little jubilation in Birmingham where canals were no novelty, and news in Aris's Birmingham Gazette was confined to one brief sentence: "On Friday the Royal Assent was given to the Birmingham and Worcester Canal Bill." But several weeks later there appeared the following lyrical appraisal of the benefits of the new canal to Birmingham and elsewhere. In verse 2 there is an allusion to the Thames and Severn Canal completed in 1789, and in verse 6 to ideas circulating for a possible canal to bypass the Severn ("Sabrina") from Bristol to Worcester.

SONG, on obtaining the BIRMINGHAM and WORCESTER CANAL BILL.

COME, now begin delving, the Bill is obtain'd,
The contest was hard, but a conquest is gain'd;
Let no time be lost, and to get business done,
Set thousands to work, that will work down the sun.

With speed the desirable work to compleat,
The hope how alluring - the spirit how great.
By Severn we soon, I've no doubt on my mind,
With old father Thames shall an intercourse find.

Redditch, where the sons of the Needle reside,
Who commerce revere, and make friendship their pride,
The prospect enraptures - and Bromsgrove no less,
Has cause at the victory joy to express.

In Europe's grand Toy-Shop how pleasing 'twill be,
Well freighted the trows, and the barges to see;
The country 'twill charm, and new life give to trade,
When the seat of the Arts shall a sea-port be made.
With pearmains and pippins 'twill gladden the throng,
Full loaded the boats to see floating along;
And fruit that is fine, and good hops for our ale,
Like Wednesbury pit-coal will always find sale.

So much does the rage for Canals seem to grow?
That vessels accustom'd to Bristol to go;
Will soon be deserting Sabrina's fair tide,
For shallows and shoals sailors wish to avoid.

As freedom I prize, and my Country respect,
I trust not a soul to my toast will object;
"Success to the PLOUGH, not forgetting the SPADE,
Health, plenty, and peace, Navigation and Trade."

The Seat of the Arts, July 5th, 1791.   J.F.

Chapter 3

INITIAL ORGANISATION AND PREPARATION

THE TERMS OF THE 1791 CANAL ACT

The Act of Parliament for the canal began by listing the 253 subscribers who now constituted "The Company of Proprietors of the Worcester and Birmingham Canal Navigation" with the power and authority to acquire compulsorily the land necessary for "a Canal navigable and passable for Boats, Barges and other vessels", and to enter and use adjacent land, during the construction of the canal, for access, brick-making etc. Measures were included for the protection of the property of landowners and tenants and to provide fair compensation for any damage done. As already agreed, the estates of Henry Cecil of Hanbury, Richard Amphlett of Hadzor and Lord Calthorpe of Edgbaston were to be specially safeguarded.

No water was to be taken from any river, brook, or watercourse crossed by the canal, and they were to be bridged, piped or culverted, as the case may be. The water supply of the canal was to be only from "any Springs which may

(1651)

ANNO TRICESIMO PRIMO

Georgii III. Regis.

CAP. LIX.

An Act for making and maintaining a Navigable Canal from, or from near to, the Town of *Birmingham*, in the County of *Warwick*, to communicate with the River *Severn*, near to the City of *Worcester*.

WHEREAS the making and maintaining a Canal for the Navigation of Boats, Barges, and other Vessels, from, or from near to, the Town of Birmingham in the County of Warwick, to join and communicate with the River Severn, at a Place called Diglis, near to the City of Worcester, will be the Means of opening a certain Communication for the Conveyance of Goods and Merchandize between the Ports of Bristol and Hull, and also between the Town of Birmingham, the large Manufactories in the Neighbourhood thereof,

The first page of the Act of Parliament of 1791 for the making and maintenance of the Worcester and Birmingham Canal (WBCS archives).

happen to arise in the Bed of the said Canal, and also all such Rain Water as shall fall on the Surface of the Canal", together with water raised from the River Severn by steam engines and stored in reservoirs situated "between the Entrance of the Parish of Tardebig and Diglis Meadows". The five reservoirs agreed on for the use of the mill-owners on the Rivers Rea and Arrow were to be made immediately after the making of the canal over each. The owners of the lands on which these reservoirs were to be made were allowed the right to have the water let out of them in November every seventh year "for the Purpose of taking the Fish therein".

The width of the ground to be taken for what was intended to be a barge canal, together with its towing paths, ditches, drains and fences, was not to exceed 30 yards, "except when the said Canal shall be raised higher, or cut above Five Feet deeper than the present Surface of the Land and in such places where it shall be judged necessary for Boats and other Vessels to turn, lie or pass each other". Any coal, limestone or minerals unearthed in cutting the canal could be claimed by the landowners. At its terminus in Birmingham, the canal was not to be extended into the neighbouring land of Sir Thomas Gooch; any buildings or wharves constructed were not to interfere with "the Lime Works on the said land of the said Sir Thomas Gooch, now in the occupation of John Wall or his Undertenants", and there was to be the 7ft wide water-tight land barrier, soon to be known as the 'Worcester Bar', between the W/B Canal and the Birmingham Canal, as had been agreed.

Disputes between the Canal Company and landowners or other aggrieved parties over land values, damage and compensation etc., were to be resolved by Commissioners, drawn from a long list of people named in the Act, who might refer judgment to the Sheriff of the County and a jury; but such litigation could prove costly for the losers and was best avoided by negotiation and compromise.

The Company was authorised to raise £180,000 (the estimated cost of the canal) in 1,800 shares of £100, each proprietor to hold no more than 50 shares, and the work was not to begin until the full amount was subscribed (i.e. promised in writing) and 10% of each share received. The balance on each share was to be paid, as required, by Calls on the subscribers at intervals of not less than one month. A further £70,000 could be raised, if necessary, either by further Calls upon the shareholders or by mortgages on the security of the canal's assets, interest on the latter to take priority over dividends. Those defaulting on payment of their Calls would, after due notice, forfeit their shares. Any proprietor paying the full £100 in one sum for a share was entitled to receive £5 interest on it after one year only.

The Act required the Company of Proprietors to hold two General Assemblies each year, one in Worcester on the first Tuesday in July, the other in Birmingham on the first Tuesday in January, "at or before Eleven of the Clock in the Forenoon". Each proprietor present, or represented by proxy, was allowed one vote per share held, and if those actually present held between them less than 500 shares the meeting had to be cancelled and re-advertised for three weeks later. Any ten or more proprietors could call a Special Assembly at any time to deal with any urgent matter. Included in the powers and duties of each Assembly were (i) the appointment, re-appointment or dismissal of treasurer(s) and clerk(s), (ii) the election or appointment of a Committee of 15 proprietors, each holding at least 5 shares and not being a salaried official of the Company, to manage the affairs of the Company, including the construction and maintenance of the canal, (iii) the overseeing of the Company's accounts and declaration of dividends, (iv) the authorisation of Calls upon shareholders, (v) approval of new shareholders and the disposal of forfeited shares, (vi) overall responsibility for the satisfactory state of the canal, its structures, towpaths, fences etc., (vii) the framing of by-laws for the use and protection of the canal, and (viii) the determination of tonnages on freight within the maximum limits laid down by the Act.

The canal was to be a public waterway which any boat-owner had the right to use upon payment of the required tolls, "but no Boat, Barge or other Vessel, of less Burthen than Thirty five Tons, shall pass through any of the locks to be made on the said Canal, without the Consent of the said Company of Proprietors, or their lock-keeper or Agent" (a barge canal being clearly intended). All vessels using the canal were required to carry identification plates on each side, and to be gauged at the expense of the Canal Company so that the total weight of the cargo carried could be checked. Penalties were laid down for the infringement of by-laws, giving false information about goods carried, causing damage to the canal and its structures, obstructing the navigation, wasting water, and leaving goods for over 24 hours on a public wharf.

The dividend guarantees to the Droitwich, Stourbridge and Dudley Canals were included, as agreed. Another liability upon the Company was the required payment to the City of Worcester of £40 per annum in perpetuity, after the completion of the canal, in lieu of "The Water Bailiff's Tolls", i.e. the duties payable on cargoes carried by water into, through, or out of the City. This annual payment is still paid by British Waterways to the City of Worcester.

THE FIRST GENERAL ASSEMBLY

The implementation of many of the provisions of the Act, as outlined above, in regard to the use of the canal, could await the opening of the waterway to traffic. The first task of the proprietors was to set up the organisation for the construction of the canal at their first General Assembly, which, as the Act stipulated, was held at the Hop Pole Inn in Worcester on 5 July 1791. A report in Berrow's Journal of the proceedings of this Assembly gives the impression that the day was mostly spent in celebration:

"Tuesday last, the first Meeting of the Gentlemen Proprietors of the intended Canal from Birmingham to Worcester (the Right Hon. the Earl of Plymouth in the Chair) was held at the Hop-Pole-Inn in this City. When the preliminaries of the business upon which the meeting was convened were settled, and dinner over, the noble President, charging his glass, gave 'Success to the undertaking of the intended Navigation!' which was drank by the company with three times three. After passing a most convivial day the evening was concluded with drinking several loyal and patriotic toasts, and the company began to break up about nine o'clock. During the whole time of the Meeting the bells of St. Nicholas continued to ring their merriest peals, with very little intermission."

We know from the Minutes of this first Assembly that, in fact, important business was transacted and decisions made. Of the 253 subscribers listed in the Act 74 were present (no ladies, though many were subscribers!) and 52 others were represented by proxies. It was reported that all 1,800 shares had been subscribed and deposits paid, so that work on the canal could begin. New subscribers admitted since the passing of the Act included John Snape, now living in Birmingham. Messrs. Thomas Hooper and Isaac Pratt were confirmed as Treasurers (they had 48 and 50 shares respectively) and Benjamin Parker, Attorney, of Snow Hill, Birmingham, with 32 shares, was elected Clerk to the Company; he had been active in promoting the canal at the Birmingham end. The Committee of Management with, as stipulated, fifteen members, was chosen and comprised Sir Henry Gough Calthorpe, Bart., W A Roberts of Bewdley, Messrs. John Bingham, James Bingham, Wm. Smith, Wm. Astbury, and Mr James Godrington, of Birmingham; Joseph Berwick Esq. and Messrs. Thomas Carden, Benjamin Pearkes, Thomas Williams, and Hugh Paine, of Worcester; Messrs. John Wall and Richard Jesson of West Bromwich, and Mr Jenkins of Saltley. This Committee was selected to comprise a balance of representatives from the Birmingham and Worcester areas, so that subcommittees could be formed to meet at each end of the canal, as required.

Those persons who had shown "unremitted assiduity and very great perseverance in the prosecution of measures until the Act was obtained" were then thanked, and it was agreed that Messrs. Hooper and Pratt should each be presented with a piece of plate valued at 100 guineas, and Messrs. W A Roberts and Joseph Berwick each with one valued at 50 guineas. Such presentations had become customary on the passing of a canal Bill.

Finally, to finance the initial planning and preparation for the canal's construction, the Assembly agreed "That a Call of Two Pounds on each Share be made from the Proprietors, and which is to be paid on or before the 20th. Day of August next, at the Worcester and Birmingham Navigation Office, at the Cross Inn, Worcester, or at Messrs. Goodall, Dickinson and Goodall, Bankers, in

Birmingham." This decision was to be notified through the Worcester and Birmingham newspapers and also by letter to each proprietor with a copy of the clause in the Canal Bill relating to Calls.

THE ELECTED COMMITTEE BEGINS ITS WORK

On the following day, 6 July, members of the Committee of Management met at the same venue, no doubt with a sense of urgency and responsibility. Their chairman was Thomas Carden, proprietor of a successful retail clothing business in Worcester, a man prominent in public affairs and in service to the community, a magistrate and city councillor, mayor in 1790 and thereafter an alderman until 1828. He had been one of the subscribers, in 1785, to the originally proposed canal to Stourbridge, and now he was keenly involved in the construction of the W/B Canal which he believed would be a great asset to his city. His wise counsel, his business acumen, his energy and dedication were to be an inspiration to all involved in the making of the canal, on whose Committee he served for the whole of the 24 years it took to complete, and later; and for most of that time he remained its chairman. Yet he seems neither to have expected nor to have received acclaim for his efforts. He made a great contribution, especially at the Worcester end, in negotiations with landowners and contractors, and in dealing with the financial claims of the Droitwich Canal Company.

During their first two-day session, the Committee must have spent much time discussing the basic strategy for creating the canal and the things to be done in preparation before a start could be made on the construction work. One urgent necessity was the production, as soon as possible, of an accurate detailed survey of the line of the canal with all the levels carefully verified. The route needed to be finalised before negotiations could begin with the landowners over their land needed for the canal and for access. It was vital that the long summit stretch from Birmingham to Tardebigge via the West Hill Tunnel should be absolutely level; likewise the other long pounds between Tardebigge and Diglis. Snape was retained as the Company's local surveyor, on whom most of this responsibility would fall, but it was imperative to obtain

Portrait of Thomas Carden (1738-1836) at the age of ninety, by Robert Evans R.A. (Worcester Guildhall).

the services of an experienced canal engineer to collaborate with Snape over the surveys and to advise on the construction work. It was decided that Mr Clowes of Cirencester, Engineer, be written to "to know if it will be agreeable to him to survey the Line of the Canal with Mr. Snape".

The choice of Josiah Clowes as consulting engineer was a wise one for he was already well experienced in canal and tunnel construction. He had lived at Middlewich, Cheshire, on the line of the Trent and Mersey Canal, and was involved in its construction. Through his older brother William's marriage to Jane Henshall, Clowes was related to her brother Hugh Henshall and also to James Brindley, married to Ann Henshall. When Brindley died in 1772 and Henshall took over from him the supervision of work on the canal, Clowes became the contractor for finishing the 2880 yards long Harecastle Tunnel which opened to traffic in 1775. Then following his minor involvement in the construction of other waterways including the Stroudwater and Chester Canals, he was engaged in 1783 as resident engineer by the Thames and Severn Canal Company, his duties being to assist Robert Whitworth, the engineer in charge, as "Surveyor, Engineer and Head Carpenter". This experience, which included the making of the 3817 yards long and 15 feet wide Sapperton Tunnel, was invaluable to Clowes and established his reputation. Soon after the completion of the Thames and Severn Canal in 1789, he was called upon to supervise the final stages of construction of the Dudley Tunnel. In 1791 he was busy directing the building of three locks on the River Thames near Lechlade and also in making a survey for the proposed Hereford and Gloucester Canal. Being so busy, it is not surprising that he was unwilling, at that time, to take on the supervision of the W/B Canal survey and its construction. Following his refusal, the Canal Committee decided on 10 August to approach Mr Bull, Engineer of the Birmingham and Fazeley Canal, instead.

A sealing-wax impression of the seal of the W/B Canal Navigation, used to validate official documents. The design includes the coats of arms of the City of Worcester (left) and the Town of Birmingham (right). Of the two females one may represent Sabrina, goddess of the River Severn, the other the Spirit of Birmingham. The motto on the seal reads "Tandem Triumphans" (Victory at Last). Other details are problematical. (NWMT)

At their initial meeting, besides deciding which consulting engineer to approach, the Committee also turned their thoughts to the question of materials and the tools that would be needed. One member of the Committee, John Wall, who managed a lime wharf near the Birmingham Canal Company's Old Wharf and the site of the Birmingham end of the W/B Canal, had contacts with suppliers of building materials. So it was resolved "That Mr. Wall do at his discretion search and prepare Bricks and Stone for the use of the Canal."

A minor, but nevertheless essential, requirement of the Company at its outset was its own unique seal. A cylindrical die, cast in steel, with an artistic engraving in the centre surrounded by the title of the Company would be kept under lock and key at the Company's office, and be used to apply the Company's embossed seal (using red sealing wax) to documents, agreements and Assembly Minutes to indicate their official authorisation. Accordingly the decision was made to order "A Common Seal to be sunk in Steel".

OTHER EARLY DECISIONS AND PREPARATIONS

Following the initial meetings in Worcester, the Committee was kept busy. A subcommittee of Birmingham based members, known as the Birmingham Committee, met as needed to deal with matters at that end, and at the other end there was similarly a Worcester Committee. Full Committee meetings were held at a half-way venue, usually the Golden Cross Hotel in Bromsgrove, every four to six weeks whilst work was in progress.

As the Committee considered its strategy, it soon became clear that because of all the preparation needed before the cutting of the canal could commence, it would be best to aim to start this in the early spring. By this time, hopefully, the worst of the winter would be over when, during spells of icy weather, digging and brick-making would be difficult, if not impossible, and men would have to be laid off. Whilst it was intended to put in hand construction work along the whole line of the canal with a view to its early completion in a very few years' time, it was soon seen to be wise and expedient to concentrate on the Birmingham end and to open the canal in stages from there. Because of the long summit level the canal could be opened as far as Tardebigge without loss of water, and useful revenue would be increasingly earned as each new section was open to traffic.

In order that negotiations for the purchase of land could begin, John Snape soon received urgent instructions to make a more detailed survey of the line of the canal, including "the plot and contents of every piece of land, roads, lanes etc. in the line of the Canal, starting with the first 2 miles from the Birmingham end". At the Committee Meeting in Bromsgrove on 12 September it was resolved "That a letter be written to Mr. Snape informing him that if he does not enter upon the Survey on or before the 19th. day of September instant and proceed thereon from Day to Day 'til it is finished, the Committee will be under the necessity of employing another in his stead". Stung by this ultimatum, Snape went into action forthwith and produced the survey. In November he was ordered to "make a correct Profile on Vellum of the Line", assisted by John Bull. In December a suggestion was made that the engineer John Smeaton should be invited to come and look over the line of the canal, and on 4 January 1792 it was resolved "That Mr. Snape do wait upon Mr. Smeaton and present the Compliments of the Gentlemen of the Committee & to represent to Mr. Smeaton that they are very desirous from the very high Opinion entertained by them of the Ability and Experience of Mr. Smeaton that he will be so obliging to favor them with his Attendance to examine the Line marked out by Mr. Snape." Two weeks later, on hearing that Mr Smeaton had been unmoved by their flattery and had declined to attend, it was decided to make a new approach to Mr Clowes. This time Clowes agreed to serve. Early in February he was paid 20 guineas for going over the summit line and it was agreed that thereafter he should be paid 2 guineas per day and 5 guineas each journey for travelling expenses, such times as he may be wanted, and that he should devote not less than one third of his time to this canal.

The Act for the canal left some scope for variation from Snape's original 1789 plan so that alterations could be made, if possible, to shorten the route and reduce costs. In January 1792 Snape reported to the Committee "that by the last Survey he has shortened the line upwards of two Miles and that the New line will be executed at less Expense than the old one." This reduction in length was to be achieved by forsaking the contours, by tunnelling, as at Tardebigge, and by traversing the valleys of some rivers and brooks more directly with embankments further downstream, as for instance near Selly Oak where it was decided "That the straight line across the Valley below Harbourn Mill be adopted rather than the more curved line nearer the Mill." The greater difficulty and cost of the civil engineering work involved would presumably be offset by the saving in length and in the cost of the land needed.

Besides the appointment of a part-time consulting engineer to oversee the surveying and construction work, there was also the need to find a hard-working and competent resident engineer to direct and supervise the day-to-day construction work. At a Committee Meeting on 4 January 1792 "Mr. Thomas Cartwright, having applied to be engaged as a Superintendent of Locks and Bridge Building, and Mr. Bough attending also and giving him a very good Character, but he having demanded one pound eleven shillings and sixpence per week," was engaged at this salary. Cartwright's home was in Northfield, through which parish (at Selly Oak) the canal would run; he was evidently a reliable builder; he was soon to be an expert in other aspects of canal construction, and he was destined to serve the Canal Company well for some twenty years until ill-health forced him to retire.

The cutting of the canal, it was decided, would be carried out by contractors who would find the labourers, whose wages would be paid by the Company, and who would be supplied with tools and equipment by the Company. Early in March the Company issued the following advertisement:

> "Persons willing to contract for cutting different parts of the Line between BIRMINGHAM and TARDEBIGGE CHURCH are desired immediately to give in their Proposals for performing the same to Mr. Benjamin Parker, Attorney, Snow Hill, Birmingham, Clerk of the Company of Proprietors, where a plan and section of the line may be seen, and any further information obtained."

LAYING IN A STOCK OF MATERIALS AND TOOLS

Of the materials required for the construction work, good quality bricks in large quantities were an urgent necessity for the building of bridges and aqueducts, for lining the tunnels, and for making wharves and warehouses. At the Birmingham end, it would be economical to have bricks delivered from the Black Country by canal. But elsewhere, bricks being heavy and therefore difficult and costly to transport, especially by road, it would be best, if possible, to make them from local clay near to the line of the canal. So the Committee asked John Wall to search for clay for brick-making and to make contracts with brick-makers. Fortunately the route of the canal was found to pass through extensive areas of clay soil (Keuper Marl) along much of its length, and brick-making would be possible at many locations. For the making of bricks large quantities of coal would be required for firing the kilns, so an advertisement was inserted in Aris's Birmingham Gazette in February 1792:

> "WORCESTER AND BIRMINGHAM CANAL.
> Any Person willing to serve the Company with about Two Thousand Tons of Coal, for burning of Bricks, in the Course of the ensuing Season, delivered into Waggons or Carts on the Birmingham Canal Coal Wharf, free from Expence of Loading and Weighing, are requested to deliver their Terms in Writing to Mr. Benjamin Parker, Attorney-at-Law, Snowhill, Birmingham, Clerk of the said Company, on or before the First Day of March next - The Coal must be sound and good, such that will bear Carriage."

The footnote to this advertisement was necessary, for in being transported over rough roads, poor quality coal tended to crumble to dust, and as early as the following June the Committee had occasion to complain that "the coal from Oldbury crumbles very much in carriage from Birmingham to the brick-kiln".

Large blocks of stone were required for the under-water foundation of bridges, for coping and wharf edging, and eventually for locks and other structures. So supplies of stone were sought near the line of the canal, together with permission from the respective landowners for the quarrying and carriage of this commodity. Supplies of timber for strengthening embankments, for lock-gates and stop-gates, and planks for barrow runs, scaffolding etc. were also needed. Amongst the tools required in large quantities were spades, shovels and wheelbarrows. In February 1792 the following notice appeared in Berrow's Journal and Aris's Birmingham Gazette:

"WORCESTER AND BIRMINGHAM CANAL NAVIGATION
Persons willing to contract with the Committee of this Undertaking, to supply them with Deal Baulks and three Inch Deal Planks, from 16 to 20 Feet long; Coppice Oak and Elm and Ash Timber, in the Round; and good building Stone, for Locks and coping Bridges, by the cubic Foot; Bricks for Locks and Bridge Building, and Canal Wheelbarrows, and Lime fit for building Locks and Bridges. All the above Materials, except the Oak, Elm, and Ash, to be delivered on the Land adjoining Mr. Wall's Lime Wharf, at Birmingham. Those Articles to be delivered where directed, on the line of the intended Canal, are requested to send Proposals (sealed up) to Mr. B.Parker. Attorney, on Snow Hill, Birmingham, the Clerk of the Company of Proprietors, on or before the 1st. Day of March next.

The Timber must be all good, clear, and sound, and the Wheelbarrows firm, and of good seasoned Stuff.

N.B. Some very large Oak Trees will be wanted for Engine Beams; also a large quantity of Oak Posts and Rails will be wanting."

OBTAINING THE REQUIRED LAND

Negotiations with landowners actually began as early as the end of July 1791, when the Governors of the Birmingham Free School (King Edward's Foundation, then situated in New Street) were approached for the land they owned which was needed for the Company's basin and wharf. Also at this early stage, Lord Calthorpe informed the Committee that he wanted his land needed for the canal in Edgbaston to be rented, but he later agreed to sell it at an inflated price. During February 1792, when the route of the canal had been finalised, land valuers were engaged by the Committee to assist in the negotiations with landowners, which, in some cases, went on for many months as agreement was sought.

One particularly awkward landowner was Thomas Dobbs of Lifford, Kings Norton. He was to remain a thorn in the flesh to the Canal Committee during the whole period of the canal's construction, not only over the value of his land taken for the canal and later for one of the reservoirs for the water mills, but also because of his encroachment and trespass on the Company's canalside land at Lifford where he set up a vitriol works, and over his avoidance of tolls as well as money owed to the Company. Thomas Dobbs had bought part of the Lifford Estate, including Lifford Hall and Lifford Mill, from the family of the late James Hewitt, First Viscount Lifford and Lord High Chancellor of Ireland. When he discovered what was to be the route of the canal he quickly, in February 1792, purchased more of the land through which it would run for a low price and then proceeded to demand four times that price from the Canal Company, as reported to the Committee:

"The Revd. John Taylor and Mr. Thomas Green reported that Mr. Dobbs, having demanded One hundred and twenty pounds per Acre for his Land, they had viewed the same and found it to be Tillage land of a cold, low, nature and no Advantage of Situation, that the highest Estimate which they conceived could be put upon the Land was 24s. per Acre per Annum, and that upon that high Estimation they had thought fit for Expediency sake to tender him £60 per Acre being 50 years purchase upon that Estimate; that Mr. Dobbs had since called upon a Mr. Wyatt an eminent Surveyor who had before (it appeared) been called on by Sir H.G.Calthorpe and had rather enhanced the Price of that Land and for which reason it may be presumed he was called on by Mr. Dobbs whose first Cousin he is, who has valued it at £90 per Acre Altho' the fact is that only eleven Months ago Mr. Dobbs had purchased the Land at only £25 per Acre. It appeared also that Mr. Dobbs had refused the Tender of £60 and had obtained a precept for the purpose of calling out the Commissioners. The Committee are unanimously of Opinion that the Tender made to Mr. Dobbs is so liberal a tender that it ought to be persisted in and Mr. Dobbs be left to pursue the threatened remedy if he shall so think fit."

ADMINISTRATION

A very early step had to be the setting up of the necessary administration, including the use of an office, book-keeping and accounts, payment of bills and wages, and the keeping of minutes and records and an inventory of tools and equipment. The Clerk to the Company, Benjamin Parker, was responsible for maintaining an up-to-date list of the names and addresses of shareholders, for sending out notices to them, and for placing advertisements and notices in newspapers; he worked from his own offices in Snow Hill. To keep the day to day records of employees, wages, materials, tools and progress made, the Committee, in December 1791, appointed James Jones as principal clerk with a salary of 52 guineas a year plus house, and Stephen Hodge as assistant clerk at £45 per year. Because considerable amounts of money needed to be kept in the canal office for the payment of wages, it was soon decided, for safety reasons, "That Mr. Jones purchase a Blunderbuss for the Office with a Spring Bayonet and a Brace of Pistols for his Pocket." We have cause to be grateful to those clerks who from the beginning wrote up the minutes of the Assemblies and Committee Meetings of the W/B Canal so meticulously and often in copper-plate handwriting. Their records now constitute an invaluable source of information for the history of the canal.

Chapter 4

CONSTRUCTION FROM BIRMINGHAM TO HOPWOOD, 1792-97

MAJOR WORKS TO BE UNDERTAKEN ON THE SUMMIT LEVEL

Unlike the earlier Brindley canals, which mostly followed the valleys of rivers and streams and so required few major civil engineering works, the W/B Canal followed no significant watercourses. Along its summit level from Birmingham to Tardebigge, it had to traverse a number of hills and valleys, requiring tunnels, cuttings and substantial embankments with aqueducts over roads, rivers and streams.

The first aqueduct needed was about 200 yards from the Birmingham end of the canal over a country lane (now Holliday Street). The second was in a lofty embankment at Edgbaston over the Chad Brook which flowed into Edgbaston Pool on Lord Calthorpe's Estate. The third crossed the Bourn Brook whose broad valley extended beyond Harborne Mill and between Selly Oak and Metchley Park and required a large embankment. The fourth aqueduct, in an embankment spanning Gallows Brook Valley, was over the watercourse, later known as Griffins Brook, which now flows through the site of Cadbury's Bournville Factory. In the same embankment nearby it was decided to construct an aqueduct over Stirchley Street (now Bournville Lane), this being a cheaper alternative to a bridge over the embankment which would have needed steep embanked approaches and extra land. The sixth and only other aqueduct needed as far as Hopwood was over the River Rea in an embankment at Kings Norton, and was really just a large culvert, the river there being little more than a stream. None of these aqueducts was very spectacular. Nevertheless, the long and lofty embankments in which they were situated must have been very impressive when they were first made and before extensive tipping over the years, and the making of the railway alongside the canal between Birmingham and Kings Norton, raised the level of much of the adjoining land to the height of the embankments.

Of the two tunnels on the summit level between Birmingham and Hopwood, the one at Edgbaston was needed to avoid having to make an unwelcome cutting through the small hill on Lord Calthorpe's Estate together with a bridge across it to take the existing road (Church Road) which passes over the brow of the hill. There was no alternative to the long tunnel to be made under the West Hill at Kings Norton. Its construction was a daunting prospect, but already on the canal system there were other tunnels even longer, two of which had already been successfully completed, namely the Harecastle Tunnel, 2880 yards long, on the Trent and Mersey Canal in 1777, and the Sapperton Tunnel, 3817 yards long, on the Thames and Severn Canal in 1789. A third, the Dudley Tunnel, 3154 yards long, was due to be completed in 1792. Of these the Harecastle and the Dudley were only 9 feet and 9¼ feet wide respectively. The Sapperton Tunnel, however, was 15 feet wide, and the West Hill Tunnel was intended to be as wide, if not wider, to take barges. It was reassuring that Josiah Clowes had been involved in the construction of at least two of the other long tunnels, and would be on hand to supervise the one through the West Hill.

There was a need for several cuttings, one through higher ground between the Edgbaston and Bourn Brook Embankments, one through Fielding's Hill south of Selly Oak which needed a bridge across it for Fieldings Lane (now Raddlebarn Road), and, of course, the cuttings required for the approaches each side of the two tunnels.

EARLY CONSTRUCTION WORK IN 1792

Work on the construction of the canal began in the Spring of 1792. Clowes and Snape had been ordered by the Committee at the end of February "to make and mark the Line of the Canal without loss of time." This staking out was done along the summit level during March and April, and some Committee members were out and about inspecting its progress, as on 9 April, when they met at Tardebigge Church at 11.00 am with Clowes and Snape and a local man, John Moore, to consider the route in that locality.

One of the first major operations was the excavation of the deep approach cutting at the north end of the West Hill Tunnel. As early as the end of February 1792 advertisements were placed in the Birmingham and Worcester newspapers for a contractor to take on this work, as follows:

"WORCESTER AND BIRMINGHAM CANAL.
"DEEP Cutting at the End of the Tunnel in the parish of King's Norton. - From 40 feet deep at the Tunnel End to level Cutting, about half a mile in length, at the Top Water level. The Canal to be 40 feet wide at Top Water, and 5½ feet deep. Towing Path 9 feet wide - Benching on the opposite side 4½ feet, within 1 foot of Top Water. Slopes to be as 4 feet horizontal, to 3 feet vertical. The

Canal will be contracted in breadth near the End of the Tunnel, as will be shown in the Plan and Profile in the hands of B. PARKER, Attorney, Snow Hill, Birmingham, the Clerk of the Company of Proprietors, to whom Proposals in writing for cutting the above are requested to be sent under seal.
SNOW HILL, Feb. 25, 1792."

At the same time, another advertisement, dated 27 February 1792, asked for "Persons willing to contract for CUTTING different parts of the Line between BIRMINGHAM and TARDEBIGGE CHURCH" to deliver their proposals for performing the same to Mr Parker's Offices, "where a plan and section of the line may be seen, and any further information obtained."

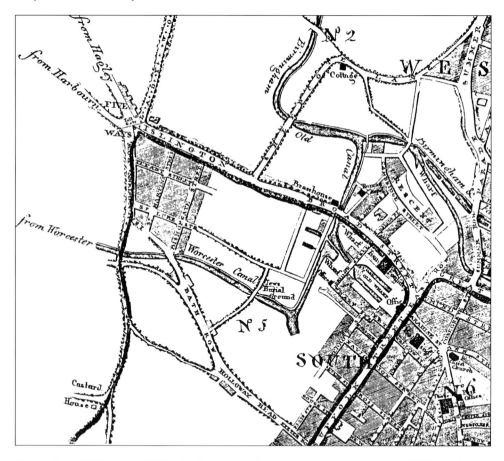

Part of an 1810 map of Birmingham showing the Bar separating the W/B and the Birmingham Canals and the arms from each canal under the street later known as Gas Street (BRL).

The contract for the West Hill approach cutting was, it seems, given to Messrs. Morecroft, for in March they were asked to deliver their estimates for the first 3 miles from the north end of the West Hill Tunnel towards Birmingham, which included the half mile of tunnel cutting. They were also appointed contractors for making the Birmingham end of the canal through Edgbaston, including the Chad Valley embankment.

The canal from the site of the Worcester Wharf to that of the Edgbaston Tunnel was cut in the early summer of 1792. By August, the Committee, impatient at Lord Calthorpe's delay in giving permission for work to begin on his land, informed his lordship that, "having a great number of people ready to begin on his land and sustaining great loss by being so long kept from beginning, and having begun on the land adjoining his land", the contractors had been ordered to move in and start work regardless.

Another section of the canal on which work started in June 1792 was the Gallows Brook Embankment, the contractors being Messrs. Ellis & Allen. Unfortunately this work meant the destruction of growing wheat on the land of Mr Guest of Barnbrook, and he was promised compensation for his crops, as were other farmers similarly affected on the line of the canal as the work proceeded.

By the autumn of 1792 the number of canal workmen, or "navigators" as they were called in advertisements for their labour, had increased considerably, and it was necessary that many of them who had come from far afield, and had been camping and sleeping rough, should be accommodated "on site", before the onset of wintry weather. In December the Committee resolved "That Barracks be erected on the Land by the side of the Lane at the deep Cutting opposite to Edgbaston Hall sufficient for 100 Men to lodge in, with a Building for them to eat in - Messrs. Morecroft having agreed to furnish Beds and other necessaries." A similar barracks was to be erected on land near Bourn Brook Valley for 120 of Messrs. Morecroft's men, and another at Gallows Brook Valley for 100 men. These barracks would probably have been large wooden huts which could be moved, as the need arose, to other sites, and each would most likely have been in the charge of one or two tough elderly women who would have undertaken some cooking and cleaning.

Another move made to promote the welfare of the navvies was the decision in November 1792 "That the Company advance twelve Guineas towards establishing a Club for sick and maimed Workmen under Regulations to be approved by the Committee." In February 1793 James Jones reported to the Committee "that Articles for providing for sick and lame Labourers on the Canal were agreed on by them, and that they had fixed on Mr. Steen of Birmingham and Mr. Turville of Alvechurch as their Surgeons and Apothecaries." Mr Tomlinson of Birmingham was also appointed to assist these two gentlemen, and was to be paid by the Company. The workmen were expected to subscribe a penny or two-pence a week from their wages towards the running of this sick benefit club, a practice which was common in the days before the start of the National Health Service.

In readiness for the construction of bridges, tunnels and the arches of the aqueducts, steps were taken early in 1792 to lay in stocks of bricks at strategic places. By April, three brick kilns had been set up along the line of the canal to make use of local clay, and by the end of the year there were altogether six in operation from Selly Oak to Ley End, south of the West Hill. In August James Wall was engaged to look after the brick kilns, to keep a check on stocks and the quality of the bricks. Some brick-makers had to be discharged for turning out poor bricks unsuitable for the work intended. In November, John Wall was "desired to provide about 40,000 Bricks for the Aqueduct and get them on the best Terms he can." These bricks for the aqueduct, as well as others for the wharf, in Birmingham, came by boat from brickworks along the Birmingham Canal.

The dimensions of the Holliday Street Aqueduct were settled by Clowes and Snape and the Birmingham Committee in October 1792. The brick archway over the lane had to be long enough to take the width of the canal and also the width of the Worcester Wharf at that point. The shape and size of this extensive wharf were also considered in October by Clowes with the help of Isaiah Danks and Thomas Sherratt, both local canal carriers and shareholders, the latter newly appointed to the Committee. On their recommendation the Committee decided "That the Canal be cut 70 feet wide from the Bason to the Jews' Burying Ground and 42 feet wide through the Gardens as recommended by Mr. Cartwright" and "That a Bason one hundred feet wide be made by the side of the Birmingham Canal at the proposed Junction therewith with a space of seven feet between the two Canals and thirty feet between the Bason and Mr. Wall's Lime Wharf." All these details having been settled, Clowes and Snape were directed to "nick out" the wharf and basins, following which, work on their cutting and on the construction of the aqueduct soon started.

THE TRANSPORT OF MATERIALS

Much of the local transport of earth and materials was by wheelbarrows. These were company owned, as were also the large quantities of deal planks used for barrow runs over rough and muddy ground and up and down cuttings and embankments. For transport over a distance, carts and horses were mainly used initially, and this required the provision of "waggon roads" and stabling. In August 1792 Messrs. Wall and Jenkins were instructed "to purchase a team of horses and carriages and provide such accommodation for them as they shall think fit". In the following December and January further waggons and horses were obtained by Thomas Sherratt.

In October 1792 Messrs. Morecroft were instructed "to do all the cutting to make the Canal navigable for Flats from the North side of Bourn Brook Valley to the Turnpike Road between the Five Ways and Holloway Head." At the same time

Thomas Cartwright was directed to get 40 flats made, these being large open rectangular wooden boxes, made watertight by caulking, and able to float, like punts, in shallow water. As soon as a length of the canal was puddled and partially watered, flats could be used to convey earth and materials with far less effort than by carting. They were useful for moving soil from cuttings to embankments, and bricks from the kilns to locations where they were needed. Eventually about 70 were in use up and down the canal during its construction.

The process of "puddling" to make a canal watertight involved mixing clay and sand with just sufficient water to make a thick paste or "puddle", spreading this upon the bottom and sides of the channel and then firming it down by treading and tramping on it, several layers being applied as necessary, to a thickness of about 2 feet. Water for this, also for watering the canal a foot or so deep to take the flats, and finally for filling the canal to take boats, could not be obtained under the strict terms of the W/B Canal Act which stipulated that, apart from water to be pumped from the River Severn, the only supply permitted was from "any Springs which may happen to arise in the Bed of the said Canal, and all such Rain Water as shall fall on the Surface of the Canal." In the event, water for puddling was obtained, by agreement, from local landowners and, at the Birmingham end, Allcock's pool was dammed to put water into the canal for flats. In March 1793 the Committee sent a deputation to the Birmingham Canal Company requesting water to fill the same stretch of canal to a depth of 4 feet so that soil could be boated to make the embankment of the aqueduct at the Worcester Wharf. Boats were ordered for this purpose, but it was towards the end of the year before the Birmingham Company agreed to supply the water (presumably by syphoning it over the Bar) and Messrs. Morecroft were able to use four "dirt-boats" on the canal, now usable on the Birmingham side of the Edgbaston Valley.

TUNNEL DIMENSIONS SETTLED; EDGBASTON TUNNEL COMPLETED
Plans for the Edgbaston and West Hill Tunnels were considered in the Autumn and Winter of 1792-3 by the Committee in consultation with Clowes and Snape. Careful surveys were made to check the line and levels over the West Hill, and on 4 February 1793 Messrs. Jones and Cartwright were directed "to prepare an Estimate of the Tunnel Road without a Towing Path and another Estimate of the Expence of a Tunnel with a Towing Path." On 20 February it was decided "That the Tunnel at Edgbaston be made with a Towing Path on a plan prepared for a Towing Path thro' the King's Norton Tunnel." The width of the Tunnel was to be 21 feet, and its height above water level 13½ feet.

Work on the Edgbaston Tunnel began in March 1793, a shaft being sunk midway to allow tunnelling from the centre as well as from each end. A horse gin was installed at the top of the shaft "to raise Soil and a ten yards length got out with the Gin ready for the Bricks to Arch." At the end of July it was reported in Aris's Gazette that "one of the Workmen making the Tunnel of the Worcester Canal near Edgbaston was killed by the sudden falling of a Quantity of earth.", a reminder of the hazards involved in tunnelling. Experience gained in the making of this short 105 yards long tunnel in 1793 was a useful trial run for the ensuing construction of the 2726 yards long West Hill one.

WORK DONE IN 1793 AND 1794, INCLUDING ROAD BRIDGES

In the spring of 1793 work began on the Bourn Brook Valley embankment and aqueduct, the contractor being John Pixton. In May it was decided that the "Culver", or arch, of the aqueduct should be 13 feet wide and 11 feet in height. By November some 70 men were employed on the embankment, and Mr Pixton was allotted an extra £10 per week to expedite the work, which took well over a year. Included in Pixton's contract was the excavation and moving of earth from the cutting at Fielding's Hill to raise the embankment. It was vital that this embankment, like the others, should be stable and capable of withstanding the pressure of water in the canal. To this end, on the advice of Clowes, timber baulk piling was used with wooden ties across; this would last whilst the embankment settled and consolidated. Similar strengthening was used in other embankments.

During 1793 it became necessary to build some of the bridges to take roads over the canal. On 12 August it was decided "That the Bridges be built 22 feet wide in the clear including the Towing Path, and l0ft. 6in. from top water to the underside of the Arch as advised by Mr. Clowes this day." In fact nearly all the road bridges on the line of the canal were built to this specification, with a span of 22 feet, and with the roadway 14 feet wide between the parapets. The bridges for the Turnpike Roads at Selly Oak and Breedon Cross were started before the end of the year, others in 1794 and later, as needed. At each bridge location the road or lane would be temporarily diverted alongside whilst the canal was cut and the bridge constructed, usually with stone foundations up to water level and brick arches, and sometimes, as at Selly Oak, with stone Ashlar (dressed stone) facing. In August 1794 the Committee ordered the Clerk, James Jones, to "number the Bridges on the Line of the Plan, No.1 nearest Birmingham, and that the Bridges when finished be numbered accordingly." Jones had already been assisting Thomas Cartwright in his oversight of work on the canal, especially with plans and drawings, and in the previous February he had produced a section of an accommodation bridge (to connect the two parts of a farm or estate separated by the canal) which the Committee approved and requested him to cost. These early accommodation bridges were wooden drawbridges which had to be raised to allow the passage of boats. In use they were subject to rough treatment by boatmen with whom they were not popular. One such bridge located at "Lot's Hole" in Edgbaston Parish had to be repaired in 1809 and it was replaced in 1818 by a brick bridge. Another at Leay House Farm, located where Mary Vale Road now crosses the canal by Bournville Railway Station, was replaced by a brick bridge in 1810. Of the original road bridges on the summit level between Birmingham and the West Hill Tunnel, all have been replaced over the years due to urbanisation and the advent of, first, steam and then motor vehicles.

In January 1794, as the prospect of the completion of the canal as far as Selly Oak drew nearer, the Committee ordered "The Towing Path and Benching to be staked out by Mr. Cartwright." Benching was the level strip of land, about 4 feet wide on the non-towpath or "off-side", needed for access and to allow the tying up of boats on that side of the canal. The surface of the towpath would have been consolidated with brickends, rubble or stones and a top dressing of gravel. Finally fences or hedges of "Quick" (i.e. Hawthorn) were put in to mark the boundary of canal property and to protect it and adjacent land from straying animals.

At the Birmingham end preparations of the wharves and basins ready for the commencement of trade continued with surfacing of the wharves and approach roads, the installation of a weighing machine (weighbridge), sheds, and the building of perimeter walls with gates. The wharves were on the eastern side of the canal. The Worcester Wharf at the south end was for coal and goods arriving and departing by road for places in Birmingham. The wharf at the north end, known later as the "Albion Wharf", was used mainly at first for coal and goods transferred across the Bar. In October 1793 one of two sluices cut from the Birmingham Canal into the W/B Canal Company's land, and shown on early maps of the wharf, was authorised. It was for the Birmingham Timber Company who set up a timberyard there, which supplied timber and generated rent for the W/B Canal Company. Both sluices were filled in when the wharf land was later developed. Their site was eventually occupied by the Severn and Canal Company's warehouse and latterly by the James Brindley Public House.

At Selly Oak there was much activity. Besides the brick kiln, a timberyard, a carpenters' shop and a smithy were set up there. At this works depot the stop-gates, ordered to be installed at each end of the embankments to prevent excessive loss of water and damage in the case of a breach, were probably made, and repairs to tools and other equipment carried out. A wharf for Company work-boats was prepared towards the end of 1793, and then in the summer of 1795 as the opening of the canal to Selly Oak drew near, the landowner, Mr Gaunt, was requested to build a wharf as soon as possible. It is likely that one or both of the two canal arms or sluices at the Selly Oak Wharf were made at or soon after this time.

PROBLEMS OF THEFT AND VANDALISM

Security at Birmingham and elsewhere on the canal was an ongoing problem. In February 1793 it was reported that "mischievous persons on Sundays do considerable damage to the Company's Stores at the Bason, Birmingham", so six watchmen were engaged to "attend next Sunday and take into custody such as commit any damage to the said Stores". A few months later a notice was inserted in the press:

"A FELONY
"Whereas in the Night of Sunday the 12th. of May Inst. some evil minded Person or Persons broke down a part of the Towing Path and Bank of the Worcester and Birmingham Canal and let off a large Quantity of Water out of the said Canal, A Reward of Twenty Pounds is hereby offered to any Person or Persons who will discover the Offender or Offenders, to be paid on his or their Conviction of the Offence by me.

Benjamin Parker, Clerk etc."

There were reports later of "persons maliciously and wantonly pulling up the Land Marks of the Canal and damaging Bridges and other Works." With construction work extending through many miles of what was then countryside, it was not easy to combat vandalism and the theft of tools and materials.

THE ADJOINING NETHERTON AND STRATFORD CANALS
During 1793 there was extra activity at Selly Oak as surveying and construction work began for a new canal to link the W/B Canal at that location with the Dudley Canal at Netherton. This canal had been conceived by the Dudley Canal Company in the Summer of 1792. It had been supported by the W/B Company on condition that a stop-lock was incorporated within 500 yards of its proposed junction with the W/B, with its sill one inch above the level of the sill of the top lock of the W/B to be constructed at Tardebigge. The Act for this Dudley Extension, or Dudley No.2 Canal, received the Royal Assent on 17 June 1793. It had been surveyed by John Snape, and Josiah Clowes was appointed its consulting Engineer. It was to be on one level throughout, but needed two tunnels, the Gosty Hill Tunnel (577 yards long) and the Lapal Tunnel (3795 yards long). Work started on this canal at Selly Oak, and the W/B Company supplied 100,000 bricks for it from their Selly Oak kiln in June 1794.

Early in 1792 a meeting in Stratford-upon-Avon was held to plan a canal from there to Birmingham, and it was soon decided that it should run from a junction with the W/B Canal at Kings Norton on the level via Hockley Heath to Lapworth, then lock down to Stratford via Wootton Wawen. This canal was also surveyed by John Snape, its Act received the Royal Assent on 28 March 1793, and Josiah Clowes was likewise appointed to be its consulting engineer. As with the Dudley Extension, a stop-lock was, at the insistence of the W/B Company, to be constructed within 500 yards of the junction at Kings Norton, and the water level of the new canal kept 1 inch above that of the W/B. Because of this only slight difference in levels it was possible to decide on the installation of the famous guillotine stop-lock, which fortunately still survives in situ, though unused, below Lifford Lane Bridge, on the Northern Stratford Canal at Kings Norton. A financial liability imposed on the W/B Company for its support of the Stratford Canal was the obligation to pay George Perrott, proprietor of the Lower Avon Navigation, and his successors, £400 per annum compensation for possible loss of revenue, since the new canal made possible an alternative route between Stratford-upon-Avon and the River Severn via the W/B Canal from Kings Norton. This annual payment is now paid by British Waterways to the Lower Avon Navigation Trust.

Cutting of the Stratford Canal began at Kings Norton in November 1793, and in February 1795 the W/B Committee gave permission for Thomas Cartwright and James Jones to assist Clowes with the construction of the Brandwood, or Kings Norton, Tunnel (352 yards long and 16 feet wide) on the Stratford Canal three-quarters of a mile beyond the Guillotine Lock.

So the W/B Company was interested in, and involved with, the two new canals which were to join it, and which would soon generate increased traffic on its own waterway.

The lofty embankment constructed for the canal across the Chad Valley at Edgbaston, which also later carried the Birmingham West Suburban Railway, viewed from the roof of High Hall, Birmingham University.

THE OPENING OF THE W/B CANAL TO SELLY OAK

It was on Friday 30 October 1795 that the first section of the W/B Canal was officially opened from Birmingham to Selly Oak with due ceremony and celebration, as reported in Berrow's Journal:

"Friday last a tier of boats, laden with coals, passed, for the first time, on the Worcester and Birmingham Canal to Selly Oak, attended by two bands of music, and accompanied by the Committee and others of the Proprietors.

"Previous to the company's going on board, the music struck up 'God save the King,' and after a short and pertinent address from T.Carden Esq. the Chairman of the Committee, to Dr. Hooper, the Father of the Canal, whose reply was replete with modesty and politeness, immediately on the boats being in motion, three cheers were given by the numerous spectators, and the tune of 'Rule Britannia' was performed with a thunder of applause.

"In the course of the trip, with allusion to the perseverance of the Proprietors in this arduous undertaking, and to the motto of their Common Seal, Tandem Triumphans, was played 'See the Conquering Hero comes.'

"In passing along those stupendous embankments over Edgbaston and Bourn Brook Vallies, the success of the undertaking was hailed by repeated cheers from the workmen who had been employed in it, and those heartfelt applauses were followed with the exhilarating tune of 'Come cheer up my Lads, 'tis to Glory we steer.'

"On their arrival at Selly Oak, the Father of the Canal landed the first coal, and the workmen were regaled with a roasted ox and ale, which, to their praise be it mentioned, the men partook of with such prudence and discretion, as to keep aloof from intoxication and the smallest instance of quarrel or disturbance.

"A wharf is preparing at Selly Oak, where a due supply of coals will be stacked to be in readiness at all times for the public; and it is also understood that another wharf will be established at Kings Norton, and the navigation compleated to that place about Christmas next at farthest, where it will communicate with the Stratford Canal, which will be compleated as far as Hockley Heath by May-Day next, for the commencement of the trade upon that line.

"We congratulate the public on the benefit which will necessarily be derived along this line of country and its vicinity by the reduction of the price of coal; and it cannot be doubted but the Proprietors will receive very considerable profits from the tonnage which even this short line of their navigation will produce."

It had been eleven years since the idea of a canal to Worcester had first been mooted, it seems, by Dr Thomas Hooper, supported by Thomas Carden and others. It was now confidently expected that the W/B Canal would be finished to Worcester in two and a half years' time. Little did the proprietors realise that, for a number of reasons, their perseverance, which had been so commended, would be needed for another twenty years.

The vessels used for the transport of coal along this isolated four-mile section of the canal opened between Birmingham and Selly Port (as the location of the Selly Oak Wharf and Depot was immediately called), at the ceremonial opening and for some time later, were Company owned. They were probably some of the work-boats which had been renovated. Efforts had been made as early as the winter of 1792/3 to induce the Birmingham and Birmingham & Fazeley Canal Committees to open a communication across the Bar "by the side of Mr. Wall's Lime Wharf with such lock as shall be approved", but to no avail. Without this communication and until a further length of the waterway was completed, with access to other canals, there was little incentive to carriers, at this stage, to invest in boats or barges on this restricted length of the W/B Canal.

OPENING OF THE EXTENSION TO KINGS NORTON

During the winter of 1795/6 the Gallows Brook Embankment was completed and the canal opened, without fuss, as far as Kings Norton. On 25 May 1796, only a little later than forecast, the Brandwood Tunnel was finished and the Stratford Canal was opened from Kings Norton Junction as far as Hockley Heath, where the basin and wharf were known as Hockley Port. With some 9 miles of the W/B and 10 miles of the Stratford Canal now navigable, carrying became a more attractive proposition. Within a week or two of the opening of Hockley Port, the Hockley Boat Company was established there by Messrs. Chambers, and in August 1796 the W/B Committee agreed to lend them 10 of its flats for navigating coal from their wharf along a shallow channel to Hockley House, a few hundred yards away, the hire charge being 2 shillings per flat per week.

Also in August 1796 the W/B Committee ordered that adequate supplies of coal should be stocked at Kings Norton, as well as at Hockley Port, for the supply of the trade. They also ordered "4 vessels to be built, two feet high on the outside and 14 feet wide on the Beam, the sides to be of 2 inch Oak Plank", to be used, presumably, for supplying coal to these wharves and to the brick kilns.

With the canal open to navigation, arrangements had to be made for the calculation and collection of tolls, and the regulation of traffic. The tolls permitted by the Act were 3d. per ton per mile on coal and other commodities, except lime and limestone on which 1d. per ton per mile was chargeable; roadstone and manure to canalside landowners went free of toll. Accounts were kept at the canal office on the Worcester Wharf. At Selly Port, James Wall was appointed wharfinger. At Kings Norton Junction the Stratford Canal Company avoided the obligation imposed upon them, in their Canal Act, of building a lock house there by contributing £100

The Junction House erected in 1796 at the junction of the W/B and Stratford Canals.

towards a joint one. This large house was built at the Junction in 1796, and is still there. The first lock keeper, Joseph Williams, was paid £200 a year.

In June 1796 the W/B Committee heard that "Joseph Payton breaks open the Stop Gates with his Coal Boats", so they ordered that Richard Barnett be engaged as lengthsman to look after the canal between Birmingham and Stratford Junction, and that "he be directed to lock the Gates at 8 o'clock in the Evening and unlock them at 5 o'clock in the morning", and "to take note of miscreants and prosecute them."

CONSTRUCTION OF THE WEST HILL TUNNEL

Preliminary work on the West Hill Tunnel had started back in 1792 with careful surveys and checking of the levels over the Hill in May, and trial borings in July which revealed that its soil content was chiefly red marl. The northern approach cutting was being excavated during the latter part of 1792. Work began on the south side early in 1793 to expose the tunnel end and enable work to begin there, but the rest of the approach cutting was left until 1795 when it was completed under contract by John Pixton at a cost of £2740.

Decisions had to be made as to the dimensions of the cross section of the tunnel, its width, its height above water level, the depth of water, and whether or not to include a towpath.

Estimates were made of the costs of the alternatives, and by the summer of 1793 it had been decided that the tunnel should be 16 feet wide and without a towpath. In

March the Committee had received "a letter from Matthew Boulton offering to furnish an Engine to convey Barges thro' the Tunnel without a Towing Path." This possibility may have influenced the decision to do without a towpath, but the offer was never taken up. It was decided to install metal hand-rails on each side of the tunnel as a safety measure and also to enable boats to be pulled through, but this was hard on the arms, and legging was the usual method of propulsion in tunnels with no through towpath.

Worcester and Birmingham Canal.

DEEP Cutting at the End of the Tunnel in the parish of King's Norton.—From 40 feet deep at the Tunnel End to level Cutting, about half a mile in length, at the Top Water level. The Canal to be 40 feet wide at Top Water, and 5½ feet deep. Towing Path 9 feet wide—Benching on the opposite side 4½ feet, within 1 foot of Top Water. Slopes to be as 4 feet horizontal, to 3 feet vertical. The Canal will be contracted in breadth near the End of the Tunnel, as will be shewn in the Plan and Profile in the hands of B. P A R K E R, Attorney Snow Hill, Birmingham, the Clerk of the Company of Proprietors, to whom Proposals in writing for cutting the above are requested to be sent under seal. SNOW HILL, Feb. 25, 1792.

The newspaper advertisement for a contractor to undertake the excavation of the approach cutting north of the West Hill Tunnel.

The method of constructing the tunnel was to be the established one of sinking a series of shafts, spaced out along the line of the tunnel, from the surface to the depth of the tunnel bed. Tunnelling would be in both directions at the bottom of each shaft, and also from each end of the tunnel, to make a headway, or passage, along the length of the tunnel. Once this was done, work could begin on excavating the tunnel to the required width and height and lining it, where necessary, with bricks. Because the West Hill Tunnel was to be entirely through clay soil, it needed a brick lining throughout.

In March 1793 work began on sinking the shafts, which were to be circular, 8 feet in diameter, and brick lined. The Committee had received an offer from Joseph Malin, experienced in mining techniques, to supervise the tunnel work under the direction of Clowes, and he was engaged at a salary of £80 per annum. He and Thomas Cartwright were responsible for the day to day operations above and below ground, and were provided with "Mining Dresses". The first two shafts were near each end of the tunnel and were 40 feet deep. Others were made, as tunnelling progressed from each end, over the ensuing months. We do not know how many shafts were made since no plan of the tunnel has survived and there is no mention of their number or their distance apart in the Committee minutes, but they were probably about 140 yards apart, as in the making of the Sapperton Tunnel with which Clowes had been involved. At the bottom of each shaft a wood frame was laid level with the inverted arch, or base of the tunnel, and a pit 4 feet deep sunk below this and bricked to act as a sess-pool for water to drain into. Workmen would climb up and down the shafts by ladder, but the water and spoil were raised, and bricks, mortar, candles, and other materials lowered, in wooden tubs using horse gins, the horses being bought for this purpose by Thomas Sherratt of the Committee.

In November 1793 an advertisement was inserted in newspapers as far afield as London, Oxford, Gloucester, Hereford and Manchester, as follows:

"WORCESTER & BIRMINGHAM CANAL NAVIGATION
"Persons willing to contract for making the Tunnel through the West Hill on the Line of this Canal are desired to apply at the Company's Office in Birmingham for a View of the Plans of the Tunnel and other Particulars and deliver in Estimates sealed and addressed to the Committee of this Undertaking on or before the 31st. Day of December next. The Contractor will be provided with all Materials. The Tunnel will be about 2600 Yards long."

The Committee, in January 1794, reported that they had received only one proposition for this contract, from Richard Jones. However, it was not until a year later that he was taken on as one of several contractors "for excavating the West Hill Tunnel and winding up and clearing off the Soil and for letting down the Bricks and Mortar there at £4.10.0 the yard forward, Jones finding his own Sharpening, Horses and Candles."

At its January meeting in 1794 the Assembly of Proprietors directed the Committee "To proceed in carrying the Head Way through the whole length of the great Tunnel with all possible Exertion". Work on this soon began and proceeded from both ends as more shafts were sunk, but the final breakthrough of the whole headway was not to be until the end of October 1796.

In July 1794 the Committee ordered, and attended, a trial at the south end of the tunnel, using four bricklayers, to assess the cost of lining the tunnel, and it was found that 3500 bricks were needed for every yard. This meant that close on 10 million bricks would be required altogether. Many of these were made at brick-kiln no.4 near the site of Kings Norton Wharf, at brick-kiln no.5 at the north end of the tunnel and at brick-kiln no.6 at the south end. Others were made at Selly Oak, and some 3 million were imported from Tipton in 1796 by canal. As well as the lime needed, about 2000 tons of sand was obtained for making mortar.

The north end of the tunnel was only about 400 yards from the Alcester Turnpike Road running parallel to the canal, and on the fields between the road and tunnel mouth a works depot was set up, with timberyard, carpenters' shop, smithy and store. In February 1795, Thomas Cartwright was authorised by the Committee to build huts or barracks for the increasing number of workmen needed, and this was done "upon the Waste in convenient situations for 50 men" using inferior bricks unfit for tunnel use.

Work began on opening up the headway and lining the tunnel from each end early in 1795 and took two years to complete. The brick lining included a shallow concave base and arched walls and roof consisting of three layers of brick. The brickwork of the archway was constructed on wooden formers which were moved along the tunnel as successive sections of brick arching were completed. To provide firm anchorages for the handrail supports each side of the tunnel, stone blocks were embedded in the brickwork at regular intervals, and these can still be seen, though the handrails have long been removed. The rate of progress during 1796 was reported to be about 130 yards of brick lining per month.

One of the problems faced was an accumulation of water seeping into the workings. At the north end a second-hand steam engine, costing £100, was set up by Joseph Dudley in May 1795 to raise water out of the tunnel. It was evidently located above one of the tunnel shafts, for when the tunnel had been completed and in use for about ten years the Committee ordered that "the Engine Pit in West Hill Tunnel be arched over and filled up."

At the south end where the cutting at the tunnel mouth had been made across Hopwood Dingle which was a little valley with a brook flowing south-eastwards from the Wast Hill, a channel was made to run off the water from the severed brook and from the tunnel workings into the Dingle at a lower level. The brook now drains into the canal by a cascade to the left of the tunnel portal.

To the credit of those in charge, there is no record of any fatalities amongst the tunnel workers, but the navvies and bricklayers, working in the cold, dark and damp of the tunnel by the light of flickering candles for long hours, were prone to illness and injury. As we have seen, the Company employed its own doctors, but in October 1796 "The Committee, taking into consideration the great number of accidents that happen to the workmen on the line of the Canal and which have received relief at the General Hospital", resolved "that this Company should subscribe 5 Guineas per Annum to commence from Michaelmas last, and that the accountant Clerk pay the same with a Benefaction of 10 Guineas."

On 4 January 1797, as the tunnel was nearing completion, the

The original quite imposing north portal of the West Hill Tunnel as it was c.1900, in need of repair. Unfortunately the plaque is unreadable. The circular stone embellishment below the sloping roof effect may have represented the W/B Canal Company's seal (Birmingham Museums and Art Gallery).

Committee ordered that "A temporary wharf be made at Hopwood Lane and a weighing machine put down there." It was also decided "That dressed Tipton Bricks be used in doing the ends of the Tunnel."

THE OPENING OF THE TUNNEL AND CANAL TO HOPWOOD

During March 1797 the tunnel, structurally complete, was watered, and it was opened with due ceremony on 27 March. Unlike other long canal tunnels of its time which had, or developed, faults, and were eventually closed to traffic, the West Hill Tunnel is dead straight and has stood the test of time, a tribute to the men who surveyed it, engineered it and made it. Unfortunately, Josiah Clowes, its architect, did not live to see its completion, for he died early in 1795. It must have been a source of great satisfaction to the others to see the result of their endeavours, to witness its opening and use by loaded barges, which were legged through by three men each side, according to the memory of James Jones, a grandson of the contractor Richard Jones. Aris's Birmingham Gazette reported the opening as follows:

"WORCESTER AND BIRMINGHAM CANAL TUNNEL.

"This great tunnel is at length completed. The first brick of this stupendous work was laid on the 28th of July 1794, and it was wholly arched over on the 25th of February 1797. It is also worthy of remark, that seventeen hundred and eighty-two yards, two feet, and eight inches, were finished from the 1st. of January, 1786, to the 1st. of January, 1797. At the commencement of this undertaking, the practicability of it was treated with the greatest ridicule and reprobation; it was said that the embankments, the deep cutting, and the tunnel, could not be executed; we can, however, at this moment say, that by the great skill and attention of the Engineers, Messrs. Jones and Cartwright, the whole of this business is most substantially finished. The extent of the tunnel is upwards of a mile and a half, and yet so straight, that it may be seen from one end to the other; and the accuracy of the brickwork is well worthy the attention of any architect or bricklayer.

"On Monday last (for the first time) the Committee's barge, attended by other vessels of 80 and 60 tons burthen, laden with coals, passed through it, and landed their cargoes at Hopwood wharf. The country manifested their cordial satisfaction on this occasion, by the ringing of bells, &c. and the vessels were received in their passage through the tunnel (which occupied one hour and four minutes) by the discharge of guns; and the music of horns, clarionets, &c. added to the pleasure of the day. Alvechurch, Redditch, Beoley, Studley, Feckenham, &c. will now be plentifully furnished with coal by this canal, and the farmers in the neighbourhood of its line will find a very ready and cheap conveyance for their grain, &c. to this populous town."

Chapter 5

FINANCIAL PROBLEMS AND
DELAYED PROGRESS
TO TARDEBIGGE

With the opening of the canal to Hopwood in March 1797 work on its further construction came to a halt and was not resumed until the beginning of 1805. There was, of course, tidying to be done of the spoil heaps and the clearance of bricks and other materials from beside the shafts on the West Hill and from the construction site near the north end of the tunnel. Also, although some of the shafts were left to provide ventilation and only needed safety protection at the top, the majority had to be arched across at the bottom and filled in. The urgency of this became apparent when a near disaster was narrowly averted only three months after the tunnel opened. As reported to the Committee later, Mr Cartwright was "sent for from Birmingham on 29th June last at about 1 o'clock in the Afternoon on account of a Cloud having burst over West Hill and inundated it, by means of which the Shafts into the West Hill Tunnel near where the Cloud burst were in imminent danger of being washed in and that part of the Tunnel being filled up, and Mr. Cartwright being almost up to his Waist in Water from 2 o'clock that Afternoon 'til almost 4 o'clock next Morning by which he took a severe Cold and was seized with inflammation on his Lungs and in that Condition went to Worcester on the 2nd day of July last to attend the General Assembly where on his Arrival he was so ill that his life was despaired of." Happily, Cartwright recovered and the Committee ordered that, towards the cost of the expenses of his treatment by a physician and stay in Worcester, he should be paid £20 "when the Money can be conveniently spared."

THE COMPANY'S FINANCIAL DIFFICULTIES

The seeming reluctance of the Committee to compensate Thomas Cartwright for the unfortunate consequences of his devotion to duty in time of crisis was due not to their lack of sympathy but rather to the parlous financial state of the Canal Company at that time, which was the cause of the temporary cessation of further construction work. As early as 1793 the Committee had begun to realise that the canal would cost far more than was originally estimated. In April 1793 expenditure was reduced to £800 per week and the number of cutters limited to 420. Six months later total payments to the three contractors, Morecrofts, Pixton and Ellis, were cut down to £400 per week, and in July 1794 the overall average expenditure reduced to £600 per week. Expenditure was limited to keep within the rate of income from Calls upon the proprietors, many of whom were in arrears or began to default as progress on the construction work dragged on. By the end of 1795 the £180,000 originally estimated and authorised had been almost spent, and at the General Assembly on 3 January 1796 it was resolved that the further £70,000 permitted by the Act should be raised by Calls upon the proprietors. By the time the canal was open to Hopwood, as much of this extra sum as could be raised by a series of £5 Calls was exhausted.

When their Bill was before Parliament, the W/B Canal promoters could not have foreseen the monetary inflation which was about to start. One cause of this was the canal mania of the 1790s and the demand by competing canal companies for experienced engineers, surveyors, clerks and labourers, which meant that, in order to keep their best employees, the W/B Company had to increase their wages. For example, Cartwright's salary which was initially £82 per annum in 1792 was raised to £140 in July 1793, to £180 in February 1794 and to £200 in July 1794; and over the same period the salary of the clerk, James Jones, increased from £52 per annum to £180 plus a house. The price of materials also rose; bricks for which the brickmakers were paid 6s.9d. per thousand in 1792 had increased in price to 26 shillings per thousand by 1809, partly due to the imposition of a duty on them. The value of land also rose as soon as it was known that a canal was to be built across it. The compensation paid to landowners for damage was also an unpredictable drain on finances. Then there was the war with France into which Britain entered in January 1793 and which helped to fuel the inflationary trend.

Besides having to contend with rising costs, the Canal Company was handicapped by the dividend guarantee to the Droitwich Canal Company which came into effect from the passing of the W/B Act in 1791. The first claim made by the Droitwich Company was for the year from midsummer 1792 to midsummer 1793 and amounted to £300. Thereafter a demand was received each July which varied from £86.5s. for 1796-7 to £786.15s. for 1804-5. Each year the W/B Assembly instructed Thomas Carden and other Committee members to examine the Droitwich accounts, and the payments were delayed as long as possible, causing, on several occasions, the threat of legal proceedings. There was no incentive on the part of the Droitwich Company to be efficient, and eventually in November 1810

Messrs. Carden and Wall of the W/B Committee recommended that the Company should take over the management of the Droitwich Canal under the inspection of the Droitwich Canal Committee, and this was done. This arrangement was to last until 1821; it probably minimised the compensation payments, but they continued to be a drain on the resources of the W/B Company.

Besides the economy measures already mentioned, in February 1794 the Committee reported that "The expences of the Dinners at General Meetings is become enormous; suggested a ticket be sent to each Proprietor entitling him to receive 5 shillings at the Bar for his Expences, or the Company's Clerk to present it." At the same meeting another economy move was the decision that, in future, work on cutting the canal should be done as much as possible by contract at an agreed cost and with agreed conditions as to the supply of materials, and so John Ellis's contract for the Gallows Brook Embankment, made a few weeks later, was for an agreed £869, and similarly with other later contracts.

Another far more drastic step was a proposal by the Committee to the General Assembly of 9 July 1793 that a boat canal be considered instead of a barge canal, from Bittell Hill down to Worcester which, it was estimated, would save £100,000 and take 10 months less to complete. This proposal was favoured by the proprietors present at the Assembly, but the Committee soon received a strong letter of protest, dated 1 August 1793, from Samuel Worrall and James George, Carriers, of Bristol, pointing out that the Act was for a canal for barges, the object of the waterway being "to reduce water carriage between Birmingham and Bristol for barges of 60 Tons burthen", and that the proprietors "have no power in the Act to alter the dimensions of the Canal". In spite of this protest the Committee immediately ordered Thomas Cartwright and James Jones to produce comparative estimates of the cost of the West Hill Tunnel 16 feet wide and 9 feet wide at water level. In January 1794 Richard Jones delivered a proposal for making a boat tunnel at £6.10s. per yard and was told he would hear from the Committee when they had decided what sort of tunnel it should be. It was not until the July Assembly that year, when a considerable length of the headway had been dug, that it was finally settled that all the tunnels should be broad to take barges.

In 1797, following the completion of the canal to Hopwood, the Company, faced with outstanding bills and payments due to suppliers, contractors and employees, decided to sell off surplus land, buildings and equipment to raise money to pay its debts. To this end James Jones was ordered to prepare plans of land in the Company's possession which was not needed. In November 1797 the steam engine on the West Hill Tunnel was sold for £110. In February 1798 the Committee ordered "That the Brick kilns and Stable in the Brickyard No.5 on West Hill Tunnel be advertised to be sold by Auction .... also 5 Gins at the Shafts next the North End of the said Tunnel, also the Huts and Blacksmith's Shop in the Lane near the said

Brickyard." Cartwright was asked to furnish the Committee with an inventory of all the materials belonging to the Company along the line of the canal; this he did and valued them at £3257.17s.2d. Those he advised as being of use to the Company were retained, the rest sold.

In July 1797 the Committee, looking for further ways to save money, decided to cut down on salaried staff. Williams, clerk and lock-keeper at Kings Norton, and Barnett, lengthsman, were given notice of dismissal. In July 1798 James Jones' offer to quit his Birmingham house and move to live and work at the Kings Norton Junction House was accepted, and it was ordered "That the stock of Wines and Spirits in Mr. Jones' House be taken an Account of and the Wine distributed amongst such of the Committee as will take it, at 36/- per doz. Lisbon and Red Port, at 42/- per doz. the Sherry, the price paid for it by the Company." In 1799 the Committee reluctantly decided on further staff redundancies and a reduction in the pay of others. The clerks' salaries were reduced in May, and in July the salary of the Company's Clerk, Mr Parker, dropped to £50 per annum, Mr Cartwright's to £100, and that of Mr Hodgkinson, the Accountant Clerk, to £52.10s. In September Cartwright offered to forego his salary, and it was agreed that he should be paid up to Christmas, and that thereafter he should be paid on a contract basis for whatever work he agreed to do. In December James Jones was told he could retain his job only until the following June, and that he was at liberty to go at any time. Although taken on initially as a humble clerk, he had proved his worth as Jack-of-all-trades, including draughtsman, designer of bridges, assistant to Cartwright, and keeper of the Company's Cellar. It seems probable that, through their close association, Cartwright met and married Jones' sister Sarah, for, of their seven children, the Christian names of the first two sons were Thomas James and Mark Jones, christened at Kings Norton Parish Church in 1795 and 1798.

THE THOMAS HOOPER SAGA

As if the W/B Canal Company had not enough financial worries already, a further unforeseen blow fell early in 1798 when it came to light that its Treasurer, Dr Thomas Hooper, hailed as "The Father of the Canal" when it opened to Selly Oak in 1795, owed the Company a large sum of money, nearly £9,000. Dr Hooper had become sole Treasurer when, in January 1794, his fellow Treasurer, Isaac Pratt, resigned, having financial difficulties and being unable to pay the Calls on his shares. It must have been a shock to the proprietors to learn of the Company's deficit due to Hooper's appropriation of its funds. Nevertheless, when at the July 1798 Assembly Mr Daubeny, the Company's Auditor, proposed and Mr Hellicar seconded "That Dr. Hooper be removed from the Office of Treasurer of this Company", the motion was lost by 653 votes to 568 (at one vote per share), perhaps because of all that Dr Hooper had done to promote the canal, and in the belief that the money would soon be forthcoming. The Company had taken the usual precaution, when Hooper was appointed, of insisting upon two sureties, each depositing bonds in the sum of £5,000. One of these was William Hooper, a relative, the other the Company's Agent, Wilson Aylesbury Roberts. The latter offered to pay the Company his £5,000, and this was accepted. A few months later, in October, the Committee received a letter of resignation from Dr Hooper and, at the Special Assembly held on 26 November to elect Isaac Spooner as his successor, he was given until 31 January 1799 to make up his accounts and until 25 December, just one month's time, in which to repay the balance of the Company's money he owed. Of this money some £8,878 was still outstanding in April 1801 when the Committee was surprised to receive from Dr Hooper, in his own handwriting, a counter-claim for £15,592.10s., the total of a long list of expenses claimed by him for journeys to London and elsewhere on behalf of the Company, for land bought for the use of the canal at Kings Norton and Worcester, and for bailing out Isaac Pratt, buying his shares and paying the Calls on them. The Committee ordered a printed copy of Hooper's claim to be sent to each proprietor, together with their view that Hooper had already been amply recompensed for all his expenses, and their unanimous resolution "That Mr. PARKER, Clerk of the Company, do, as soon as conveniently may be, commence an Action or Actions against the said THOMAS HOOPER and his SURETY, in order to recover the Balance which appears to this Committee to be due and owing from the said THOMAS HOOPER, to the said Company, on Account of his late Treasurership." Legal action against Dr Hooper was, in fact, delayed and, at the July 1802 Assembly, called off; but two years later the executors of the late William Hooper, his surety, were served a writ for payment of the £5,000 bond still owing. Legal action continued after the death of Thomas Hooper against his executors until, in 1815, the saga came to an end when Lord Beauchamp of Madresfield, near Worcester, a relative, paid £3,947.7s.8d., the outstanding amount claimed against the Estate of the late Dr Hooper.

INCREASING TRAFFIC ON THE CANAL

One ray of hope amidst the financial gloom was the opening of the Netherton or Dudley No.2 Canal to Selly Oak on 28 May 1798, when two boats from Dudley arrived at the W/B Canal Company's wharf in Birmingham with coal. The Dudley Canal Company itself began to carry coal and lime to Birmingham and to promote the sales of these commodities there, but after five years this ended as other carriers, including Danks & Co., took over. From Netherton a packet boat to Birmingham, carrying passengers, began operating in October 1798, being charged by the W/B Company 2 shillings for the return journey along their canal from Selly Oak. The Dudley Coal Company soon had the use of a canal arm or sluice cut on the west side of the W/B Canal Basin near the Bar.

Further traffic on the W/B Canal between Selly Oak and Kings Norton Junction was generated when the Stratford Canal, after a four years' lull in building due to shortage of money, obtained a new Act to raise capital to extend their canal along a new line to Kingswood, and opened a short cut to communicate with the newly-constructed Warwick and Birmingham Canal in 1802. A through route was now open between Dudley and London via the Netherton, W/B, Stratford, Warwick and Birmingham, Warwick and Napton, and Oxford Canals, and the River Thames.

To prevent loss of water to the W/B canal at their stop locks, the Dudley and Stratford Companies, in 1801, each offered to lend the W/B Company £400 to raise its canal banks to enable its water level to be raised to that of theirs. This offer was accepted on condition that the loan was to be repaid after 2 years out of the anticipated increased tonnage along the W/B Canal between Selly Oak and Kings Norton Junction. To encourage traffic along this section the W/B Company reduced its tonnage on coal passing into the Stratford Canal from 3d. to 1½d., a concession abused by Thomas Dobbs, who, it was reported, "makes a practice of navigating his Coal from the Dudley Canal along the Worcester and Birmingham Canal into the Stratford Canal and back to his Aquafortis Works (at Lifford) to avoid paying 3d. per ton per mile and to pay only 1½d. per ton per mile."

One of the first businesses to make use of the limited accommodation at Hopwood Wharf when it opened was the Alvechurch Coal Company. To be competitive with coal by road from Selly Oak and Kings Norton they asked for, and were granted, reductions in tonnage on coal from 3d. to 2½d. for a time, and then in 1799 to 1½d. per ton per mile between Birmingham and Hopwood, on condition that they sold it for not more than 10 shillings per ton at Hopwood. Besides carrying coal, the Alvechurch Co. also began to run a packet boat for parcels and passengers, concerning which the Committee agreed to implement the following proposition from Thomas Cartwright and John Hodgkinson, dated 7 July 1802:

> "The Packet Boat belonging to the Alvechurch Coal Co. which they run from Hopwood to Birmingham and back once a Week is found by experience to do very considerable damage to the Canal by washing the Banks thereof, which damage will be more when the Embankments are completed and the Water in the Canal raised to its intended Level. We therefore think it would be right to advance the Trip from 2/- (which is now paid) to 7/6 and to restrict the owners not to permit it to run at the rate of more than 2½ Miles an Hour under such penalty as you judge proper."

To meet the requirements of increasing traffic on the canal, various developments were put in hand at the Worcester Wharf in Birmingham, including the making of a public street, later to be called Gas Street, in 1798 on the west side of the basin between the Aqueduct and Broad Street, giving access to the two sluices and wharves alongside. In 1799 two warehouses were built and let to the Hockley Boat Co. and the Alvechurch Coal Co. Negotiations with the Birmingham Canal Company in 1805 and 1806 for the removal of the Bar failed due to the excessive guarantees, conditions and tolls demanded, and in 1807 a crane was erected on the Bar to facilitate the transfer of goods across it.

THE W/B CANAL ACT OF 1798

In October 1797 the W/B Company, having run out of money, held a Special Assembly which decided to try and raise extra money through a Bill to be presented at the next Session of Parliament, giving them powers to raise tonnages and to borrow and take up interest on mortgages of the canal, or by any other means Parliament might think fit. In May 1798 an Act was passed which empowered the W/B Company to raise the additional sum of £149,929.1s.1½d. either amongst themselves by the creation of 1259 new "half shares" each of value £69.8s.10½d., by granting annuities, or by mortgage of the tolls and rates. It also raised maximum tonnages to 1 shilling for coal and other goods, except lime and limestone which could be charged up to 4d. per ton per mile. At a Special Meeting in November 1798 the Assembly, under these powers, decided to ask the proprietors to subscribe £12.10s. per share by 8 equal instalments, upon which 5% interest was to be paid. This money-raising effort failed to raise a significant sum, and a further attempt in 1802, on similar lines, also failed.

CONSIDERATION OF A RAILROAD
FROM TARDEBIGGE TO WORCESTER

With little prospect of the canal being continued to Worcester in the near future, the Committee on 27 November 1798 was attended by Joseph Wilkes Esq. of Overseal, near Burton-on-Trent, who suggested "the consideration of a Railway, either as a permanent Matter or as a temporary Expedient, from the Summit of the Canal to Worcester, and recommended Mr. Benjamin Outram, Butterley Park, near Alfreton, Derbyshire, as a proper Person to examine the line of the Canal from the end of the Summit at Tardebigg to Worcester." It was decided to write and invite Mr Outram to come and report on the feasibility and the expense of such a railway. Outram came over, and a copy of his report, dated 8 January 1799, was sent to each member of the Committee, then printed for the General Assembly of 2 July. In his report, Outram recommended a railroad from the south end of Tardebigge Tunnel to Worcester, 15½ miles long. "The conveyance would probably be best done by dividing the railway into three stages; and, suppose twenty tons of coals to be loaded in twelve or fourteen waggons, two horses would take them down the first stage from Tardebigg to below Astwood; four other horses would take the same loading along the middle stage, which would be on a level to Offerton; and three other horses would convey the same to Worcester; each set of horses would return with a gang of waggons and their share of back loading and make two of these journeys every day; proper stables would be erected at the divisions of the stages to hold a sufficient number of horses for the trade. The return or upgate loading, being estimated at one fifth of the downgate loading, each nine horses and three drivers which would convey forty tons down from Tardebigg to Worcester, would bring back eight tons to Tardebigg each day." Outram offered to construct a double cast-iron railway, "set on blocks of stone, bedded and backed with small stone or gravel, and fenced on both sides, the rails of one road being of strength sufficient for waggons of two tons burthen; and those of the other road, being one fourth lighter for returning carriages", at a cost of £35,200. A single railway with passing places might cost £25,000. Outram argued, in conclusion, that "By means of a railway as now proposed, full trade may be established in two years, and, in case the Canal should be finished and the rails taken up and sold, the savings in building the locks and bridges would fully compensate for the expences, and loss of making and re-selling such railway, and the Company would be gainers by the amount of 2 years tonnages, which would probably exceed £40,000."

We are informed by the minutes of the July 1799 Assembly that "Mr. Outram attended and stated to this Company his opinion on railways in general and the proposed railway to Worcester in particular. Resolved that further consideration of the Railway be postponed 'til the Canal is nearly finished to Tardebigg." Outram was paid £57.15s. for his report, and the matter rested until a year later, when the Assembly of 1 July 1800 "resolved with one dissenting voice of six shares that a single Rail-way from the Summit of the Canal to Worcester as recommended by Mr. Outram be adopted." This was to be a temporary rail-road to be completed in two years' time. It was then hoped to complete the canal to Worcester in 4 years' time at an estimated cost of £19,127. Almost two years later, at a Special Assembly on 5 May 1802, it was unanimously agreed that "with all profitable dispatch the Canal should be compleated to the end of the Summit at Tardebig whence a considerable Increase of Tonnage would indubitably arise, and that from thence a single Rail Way should as soon as practicable be made so as to open a Communication with the City of Worcester, agreeably to the plan recommended by Mr. Outram in his report." However, by the time the canal was opened to Tardebigge, five years later, the railway scheme had been dropped in favour of continuing the construction of the canal. By this time it had probably been realised that the transfer of cargo from boats to waggons and vice-versa at each end of a connecting railroad, the limitations on uphill loads because of the steep gradient below Tardebigge, and the use of so many horses would have meant much extra cost and inconvenience to traders; also, a temporary railroad would have been a time-wasting project and a burdensome expense to create and dismantle.

THE 1804 W/B CANAL ACT

In 1803 the Canal Company, faced with the threat of legal action on the part of River Rea mill-owners for the delay in constructing their reservoirs, and wanting to resume construction work on the canal between Hopwood and Tardebigge, urgently needed more money. At the July 1803 Assembly it was resolved that "the Company should apply to Parliament for Power to raise a further sum of £49,680 to enable them to discharge their present Debts, to make the Reservoirs at this time necessary to be made, and to complete the Canal to the Lane at the North end of Tardebigg Tunnel, which £49,680 will be £27.12.0 each Share, - That the same be called for in 6 Payments of £4.12.0 each, the Calls not less than 4 Calendar Months distant from each other."

The W/B Canal Company's Bill, as proposed, was passed by Parliament and received the Royal Assent on 23 March 1804, and the first Call of £4.12s. per share became due on 1 August. At the July 1804 Assembly, encouraged by the response to the new share issue, the proprietors resolved "That the Committee be empowered to contract for the making of the Reservoirs for the use of the Mills on the Rivers Rea and Arrow and for completing the Canal to the deep Cutting at the North end of Tardebigg Tunnel."

PREVIOUS WORK DONE ON THE
HOPWOOD TO TARDEBIGGE SECTION

The section of the canal between Hopwood and Tardebigge involved several major undertakings, a lengthy cutting through Bittell Hill, an embankment which was also the dam for Lower Bittell Reservoir, the aqueduct over the road between Cooper's Hill and the Lane House near Barnt Green, and Shortwood Tunnel.

Work on this part of the summit level had been going on sporadically since it was surveyed in detail by John Snape in 1792. Snape had modified his original line with a shorter, more direct, route between Shortwood Tunnel and Tardebigge Church, bringing it nearer to Hewell Grange, the Seat of the Earl of Plymouth. Hearing of this whilst in Italy, Lord Plymouth hastened back and requested "to be heard respecting the Line of the Canal under an apprehension that if carried where his Lordship understood it was intended to be done that it would materially injure his Seat and the Elegance of Situation and prospects of Hewell Grange and draw the Springs which supply a very fine Sheet of Water the formation of which had cost him a very large Sum." On 2 January 1793 the Committee, taking into consideration the part played by Lord Plymouth in promoting the Canal Bill and in assisting its passage through the House of Lords, received him courteously and offered to pay for further surveys by John Bull, Surveyor to the Birmingham Canal Company, on behalf of Lord Plymouth, and by Josiah Clowes on the part of the Company, to agree on a line that would be acceptable to his Lordship and yet not excessively costly. John Snape also undertook, on behalf of the Committee, to examine the line on Lord Plymouth's Estate, and in due course the more westerly and circuitous route with the tunnel under The Shaws was agreed upon.

In January 1794 Charles Carne contacted the Committee and offered to use his patent machine, using horses, to excavate cuttings, and in April he was advanced £600, under bond, to open the north end of Shortwood Tunnel, being lent the Company's barrows and spades, as many as he needed, for a fortnight. Unfortunately we have no report on the working and effectiveness of Mr Carne's machine. In April 1794 a local contractor, William Harrison, was allowed to have 12,000 bricks from the Company's brick kiln no.6 at Lea End, on condition that he replaced them at the Lanehouse Aqueduct "at Barn Green with Bricks as good and the same dimensions as the Company's Bricks." In May "Samuel Harris, owner of a piece of Wheat at the south end of Shortwood Tunnel through which the Canal is NOW cutting" was compensated at £10 per acre. In June, a proposal from the contractor, John Pixton, for cutting at Bittell Hill was considered and agreed and he began work at the northern end. In September the Committee ordered that the spoil banks on Bittell Hill should be levelled. In February 1795 the Committee resolved "That a Gang of 30 or 40 men be employed in opening the south Side of Bittell Hill." The Bittell Hill cutting was completed by Pixton early in 1796.

Work on Shortwood Tunnel began in January 1796 when the Committee ordered "That Shortwood Tunnel be bored in 3 places to the bottom of the intended Tunnel there to ascertain of what that Hill is composed." It was found to consist of clay soil and so would need a brick lining throughout. The approach cuttings had been made, and in October, as the West Hill Tunnel headway was nearly finished, it was resolved "That as soon as the Headway is done, Cottrell and his Men who are doing it begin the Headway at the North End of Shortwood Tunnel." At the same time it was ordered "That Clay be got ready for Brick-making at the North end of Shortwood Tunnel." By the time construction work ceased along the line of the canal in 1797, this tunnel must have been well under way.

A start was made on Tardebigge Tunnel in 1796 with the opening up of the south end by Mr Mollard, and the Committee decision, in January 1797, "That a shaft be sunk in Tardebigg Tunnel to the level of the bottom of the Canal to ascertain the nature of the Stone there".

COMPLETION OF THE CANAL FROM
HOPWOOD TO TARDEBIGGE OLD WHARF

More than seven years elapsed before work began again on this section of the canal. On the day following the July 1804 Assembly at which it was decided to go ahead and finish the canal as far as the cutting at the north end of Tardebigge Tunnel, Thomas Cartwright, having already done his homework, delivered to the Committee his estimates for doing all the necessary work, and it was resolved there and then "That he be contracted with for making the said Reservoirs and doing the Canal .... he giving Bonds himself in £950 and Surety in £500 for the Execution of the Work according to the said Specifications and Estimates and to compleat the same in 2 years from Michaelmas next. - In case of Mr. Cartwright's death before the Expiration of the said 2 years, the Contract to terminate on his death and the Committee to be at liberty to contract with another for finishing the Works."

We now see Cartwright, having foregone his salary as resident engineer since the end of 1799, free to act as contractor, and being engaged as such in view of his achievements in supervising the construction of the canal so far. Over the years he had gained much in knowledge and experience, so much so that the Company had not felt it necessary to replace Josiah Clowes following the latter's death in 1795.

On New Year's Day 1805 the General Assembly authorised the signing of the contract, already negotiated with Cartwright, "for finishing the Canal from Hopwood Wharf to the deep Cutting to Tardebigge Tunnel." This was done the following day and Cartwright was ordered to "prepare the Head of the Reservoir at Bittal Valley at the same time that the Canal is made across the said Valley." He was not expected to make the Reservoir, but part of it had to be excavated to provide material for the embankment, which incorporated a culvert for the River Arrow. Two other minor embankments were needed along this section of canal. One north of Shortwood Tunnel incorporated an arched aqueduct over a small brook running from Cobley Hill to join the River Arrow. The other, between Shortwood Tunnel and Tardebigge Old Wharf, contained a culvert near Farmer Harris's accommodation bridge for the stream through "The Puddles Meadow" which supplied water to the lake at Hewell Grange and the corn mills beyond.

Over local water supplies as the canal was completed south of Shortwood Tunnel there was some dispute. The 5th. Earl of Plymouth, Other Hickman, who had helped to promote the canal, had died in 1799. His son, Other Archer, the 6th. Earl, born in 1789, was only a teenager when the canal was constructed across his land, but his mother Lady Amherst (who had remarried), and his Agent, Francis Webb, soon complained to the Canal Company over the suspected loss of spring water supplying the Hewell Lake, caused, it was believed, by ground water draining into Shortwood Tunnel. A local farmer, Mr Hill, also complained that his well had run dry and a new well was sunk for him by the Canal Company. A clause was drafted by the Estate's solicitors, hopefully for insertion into the Canal Bill of 1808, for a reservoir to be created near to Shortwood Tunnel to boost the supply of water, on the lines of those prescribed for the Rivers Rea and Arrow. However, because of the difficulty of producing substantial evidence, steps to have the clause included in the Bill were abandoned. The Hewell Estate later acquired the right in an agreement of 1873 to draw off water from the canal, by a sluice, to feed the pools on the Estate providing it did not interfere with the navigation of the canal.

Because Cartwright was both engineer and contractor, responsible for the deployment of men and materials, the Canal Committee had few decisions to make and so, unfortunately, their minutes contain little reference to progress made during 1805 and 1806 with the construction work. They did, however, call in experts to survey and check the work as it progressed. In November 1805 Mr Parker was required "to write to Mr. Morris, Engineer to the West India Docks, London, to enquire if he can make it convenient to come and inspect and survey the works done by Mr. Cartwright under his present Contract and prepare a Report thereon against the next General Assembly." Mr Morris could not come and the inspection was, in fact, carried out by William and George Morecroft, who had been the contractors for earlier construction work at the Birmingham end of the canal. Later, in January 1807, Morecrofts were again instructed to survey the works done by Cartwright, as they were almost finished, to check that they were satisfactory.

As the completion of this section of the canal drew nearer, the Committee began to consider the wharves needed. The Act for the canal gave canalside landowners the right to set up their own wharves, so in October 1806 the Company's Clerk, Mr Hodgkinson, applied "to Mr. John Moore of Alvechurch to know his intentions respecting a Wharf on his land adjoining the Scarfields Farm there." Three months later, no satisfactory reply having been received, Mr Moore was given notice "as the Act directs, to make a wharf." So Scarfield Wharf, by the road bridge over the canal between Alvechurch and Cobley Hill, with its winding hole, stables, weighbridge and machine house, came into being, the weighbridge being that which had been at Hopwood Wharf until the canal opened to Tardebigge.

At Tardebigge the Company decided to establish a substantial public wharf with adequate accommodation for carriers and traders. In May 1806 it was ordered "That the Canal be made 15ft wider than Mr. Cartwright's Contract about 150 yards in length in Cherry Tree Valley and the Culver lengthened accordingly." Cartwright was asked to plan the wharf and estimate its cost, and was given the contract for making it, including the setting up of a weighing machine and the building of a house, for £800. The weighing machine, "all of iron", was supplied and installed by Mr Whitmore of Birmingham. In January 1807 the Committee ordered that a warehouse and crane be erected at the wharf at Tardebigge. The warehouse was to be built by Cartwright at an agreed cost of £103. A crane from the Stratford Canal Company was to be investigated, and may have been bought. The Committee directed that the old dirt flats used for the transport of materials on the summit level should be used in making a fence along the lower side of the wharf. Other features of the wharf were a winding hole at the north end of the basin and a wooden lift bridge also at that end for a lane between The Lower House and Brockhill Lane, which was later diverted. A similar wooden lift bridge had been constructed at Withybed Green near Alvechurch, operated by boatmen using a windlass.

To encourage a trade in coal from Tardebigge, the following advertisement was inserted in the press in August 1806:

"FRESH COAL TO TARDEBIG.
"The Navigation of the Worcester and Birmingham Canal being on the eve of opening from Birmingham to Tardebig, the Terms of Carriage of Coal per Ton from thence to Bromsgrove, Droitwich, Worcester, Redditch, Alcester, Evesham, &c. &c. &c. and the Quantities that can be carried per Week, or Month, by any Persons desirous of engaging in such Business, are desired to be forwarded, sealed up, and addressed to the Clerk, at the Office of the Worcester and Birmingham Canal Co. on or before the 1st Of October next."

As a result, a number of coal merchants and carriers applied for facilities at the wharf, such as permission to erect stables to accommodate their horses whilst carts and waggons were loaded there. Amongst these were John Rowlands of Dudley, William Cartwright of Kings Norton and William Harrison and John Jenkins of Alvechurch. On 6 March 1807 the Committee allocated six boat lengths for loading and unloading at the wharf to Messrs. William Cartwright & Co. of Kings Norton, Messrs. Thomas Dixon & Co. of Birmingham, Messrs. Cox and Co., John Rowlands of Dudley, The Windmill End Co., and Messrs. Wynn and Palmers. These carriers were allowed the use of the stacking ground adjacent to their wharf length, but it was forbidden for a boat to occupy a length for more than 48 hours if another trader was waiting to load or unload. Tonnages were fixed at 1½d. per ton per mile for grain, and 3d. for coal and other merchandise.

The opening of the Canal to Tardebigge was announced in the newspapers as follows:

"Worcester and Birmingham
CANAL NAVIGATION
NOTICE is hereby given, That this CANAL will be OPENED TO TARDEBIGG, on Monday the 30th. day of March inst.
A commodious Bason, Wharf, Weighing Machine, &c. are prepared at Tardebigg, for the accommodation of the Trade. By order of the Committee.
JOHN HODGKINSON, Accountant Clerk. Worcester and Birmingham Canal Navigation Office, 17th. March, 1807."

On 28 February the Committee ordered "That the Committee Barge be repaired", so it looks as if Thomas Carden, Chairman, and eight other Committee members used it on the opening day, 30 March, probably travelling by canal from Hopwood to Tardebigge, prior to their meeting held at the Cross Inn, Bromsgrove, later that day.

FACILITIES AND THE PROMOTION OF
TRADE AT TARDEBIGGE OLD WHARF

The Canal Committee was determined to do all it could to promote the use of the wharf and to encourage trade. Initially, coal stacked at Hopwood Wharf was allowed to be moved by canal to Tardebigge free of charge. A resident superintendent clerk was appointed to manage the wharf and operate the weighbridge, the first, John Busby, being replaced after three weeks by Thomas Richards, who was paid 18 shillings a week. To attract customers, the weighbridge was soon altered from "shortweight" (112 lb to the hundredweight) to "longweight" (120 lb to the cwt). From May 1807 farmers who bought coal from the wharf were allowed free carriage on wheat, barley, oats, beans, peas, flour, meal, malt and bran on boats returning to Birmingham, and tonnage on all merchandise except timber was reduced to 1d./ton/mile, that on timber remaining at 3d./ton/mile. On coal carried by road to Evesham a "drawback", or reduction, of 1s.5d. per ton was allowed; and for coal carted elsewhere a drawback of 1 shilling per ton.

The Committee, in May 1807, decided to invite proposals from parties interested in running a passenger boat daily from Birmingham to Tardebigge and return to meet coaches and other conveyances to and from Alcester and Evesham.

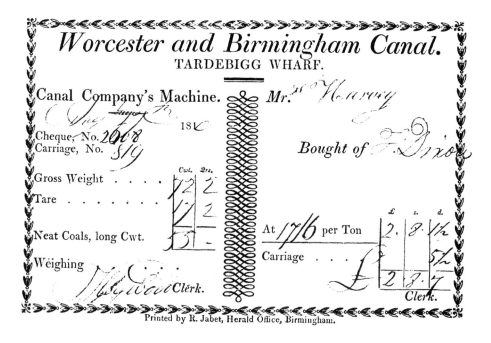

An 1810 weighbridge bill for the sale of coal at the Old Wharf, Tardebigge, issued by the machine clerk, J Heywood (Harry Thompson).

Lack of response led the Committee to try and run their own packet boat. In July two Committee members were deputed "to provide a Packet Boat, Horse, Driver and Steerer etc. to pass daily between Birmingham and Tardebigge and to arrange the Business and prices of Carriage and everything else relative to this Business." In January 1808 it was planned to have a packet boat specially built by Mr Taylor, a Birmingham boat-builder, for not more than £300. In the meanwhile it was ordered that "a trial be made of a Packet Boat now in the possession of Mr. Cartwright, who is agreeable to dispose of his Boat or let it out to hire." The fares for passengers were to be one shilling or more in the Principal Cabin, and 6d. for those in the Second Cabin. In the event, Cartwright decided to take in hand the packet boat business himself, but from Alvechurch and not Tardebigge. In August 1808 the Committee resolved that "Mr. Cartwright be charged twelve shillings a Trip for his Packet Boat between Birmingham and Alvechurch Wharf, and that if it goes more than three Miles an Hour then that the boat be not any longer permitted to pass on the Canal." The passenger and parcel service between Alvechurch and Birmingham seems to have been a commercial success, for the charge to Cartwright's successor was increased, it being ordered, in April 1813, "that Mr. Thomas Jenkins be charged twenty Shillings per Trip for his Packet from Alvechurch to Birmingham and back."

To cater for boatmen, traders and travellers, there was a pressing need for an inn at the wharf to supply food, drink and overnight accommodation. Meeting on 8 July 1807, the Canal Committee resolved "That a Petition be prepared and signed by this Committee to the Magistrates acting for that District that they will licence a House for that Place." And so the Navigation Inn was built on the corner of Brockhill Lane opposite to the wharf entrance. It was kept by John and Catherine Hunt until it closed after about thirty years, but they remained at the Old Wharf as farmers and coal dealers for many more years, the business being later carried on by their son Richard and his wife Emma until the early 1900s.

The roads near the wharf, subject to extra traffic, soon needed attention. The Surveyor of Highways was informed, and permission sought from Lord Plymouth's Steward for the felling of trees to allow for the widening and repair of the lane to the wharf from the directions of both Bromsgrove and Redditch (Brockhill Lane) during 1808.

Other early developments at the wharf included the sinking of a well, the building of a house for a clerk, providing a fenced garden for the wharfinger, and allowing traders to erect their own warehouses, up to 24ft by 15ft in area, at 5 shillings per annum ground rent, one such being built by William Ward of Oxford, and another by Mr Manton of Bromsgrove, a miller. Another business was soon set up on the wharf by Mr Steward of Bromsgrove, a timber merchant, who was allowed to rent land for a wharf and to "erect a Crane thereon at his own Expence," and he was later allowed to burn lime there.

The Wharf was soon a busy bustling place, but not on Sundays, for from August 1809 the wharfinger was directed to lock down the drawbridge north of the basin on Saturday nights and to unlock it again on Monday mornings. Perhaps it was sabotaged by the boatmen in due course, for in February 1819 it was reported to the Committee that it had fallen into the canal and required immediate attention. The Committee decided that it should be done away with, and applied to Lord Plymouth for permission to divert the road so that it would join Brockhill Lane by the canal bridge. This was soon done and there are now no visible traces of the original road.

Chapter 6

THROUGH TARDEBIGGE TUNNEL AND PREPARATIONS FOR THE FINAL THRUST, 1807-11

THE W/B CANAL ACT OF 1808

With the opening of the canal to what was soon to be known as the Old Wharf at Tardebigge, the proprietors must have been greatly heartened by the amount of traffic and income it soon generated. In July 1808 it was reported in Berrow's Worcester Journal that "Since the Canal has been opened to Tardebigg, being only 15 months, the tonnage has increased progressively, and that the last month's tonnage was upwards of £274. which is after the rate of £3,500. per annum, being treble the tonnage it produced before it was opened to Tardebigg." There was now a strong determination to press ahead with the completion of the canal to Worcester. At the same time there was the necessity of constructing the three remaining reservoirs for the mill-owners, at Lifford, Bittell and Cofton Hackett, the other two, Wychall and Harborne Reservoirs, having already been completed (see chapter 9). All the capital raised by the shares authorised by the 1804 Act had been spent and the Company was again in financial difficulties, with money owed and owing, so a Special Assembly was called for 17 November 1807 at which it was "Resolved unanimously that this Company apply to Parliament for Powers to raise Money to finish the Canal."

A Bill was drafted and presented to Parliament and "An Act to amend and enlarge the Powers of the several Acts relating to the Worcester and Birmingham Canal Navigation" received the Royal Assent on 27 May 1808. It empowered the Company to raise the further sum of £168,000, by the creation of 4,200 new shares of £40 each, or by granting annuities or mortgages of the tolls and rates; and, if necessary, to raise an additional sum of £40,000, by the creation of 1,000 new shares of £40 each; and it repealed that part of the 1798 Act which authorised money to be raised by the creation of half shares. The Company opted for the share issue, and by January 1809 all the 4,200 new shares had been subscribed for and the deposits of £1 per share paid.

REVIEWING PLANS FOR THE REMAINDER OF THE CANAL

There was now a need to review the plans made and the steps taken in earlier years towards constructing the canal from the summit level down to the River Severn. Little had been done so far along this section. During the early years of the canal's construction, when it was anticipated that it would all be finished in a few years' time, the whole line to Worcester had been surveyed in detail by John Snape, and the locations of the locks and steam pumping engines planned. This was done in late 1792. A year later, members of the Worcester Committee were ordered to "employ such Gentlemen as they think right in entreating for the land from the Summit to the Severn and at the same time entreat for what the Company shall pay each Occupier per Acre for spoilt Banks." As there were other more urgent priorities at that time, these negotiations made little progress. Early in 1796, with the West Hill Tunnel nearing completion, further planning of the southern section of the canal began with a resurvey of the line from Tardebigge to Worcester by Thomas Cartwright and James Jones. The Committee then decided that the wharf at Worcester should be on Wyld's Meadows to the south of Lowesmoor, and that the canal should be 30 yards wide from the Turnpike House at Lowesmoor as far as the first lock towards the Severn. It was also decided to purchase the buildings to be demolished to make way for the canal near Sidbury Gate in Worcester. Then, for ten years or more, little was done at the Worcester end.

THE APPOINTMENT OF ENGINEERS,
RENNIE, CARTWRIGHT AND WOODHOUSE

In the summer of 1808, following the passing of the Act to raise money for finishing the canal, the Committee was authorised to take all necessary steps to achieve this aim. Since the death of Josiah Clowes in 1796 the Canal Company had managed without an official consulting engineer, Cartwright having acted as both contractor and engineer in extending the waterway to the Tardebigge Old Wharf with little outside help or interference. Now, with the prospect of having to construct many locks, also engine houses and reservoirs to raise and store the water needed, it was clearly wise to enlist the help and advice of another experienced and reliable consulting engineer. So in July 1808 the Company's Clerk and Solicitor, Benjamin Parker, was instructed to write to John Rennie, Civil Engineer, of Stamford Street, London, to invite him to come and examine the line of the canal "when the Harvest is got in".

By this time, Rennie, aged 47, had acquired a considerable reputation as a civil engineer. Following three years at Edinburgh University, 1780-83, he had designed bridges, harbour works and drainage projects, installed a steam engine for James Watt in a London flour mill, and had been the Consulting Engineer for several broad canals including the Crinan Canal (Act 1793, opened 1801), the Rochdale Canal (first Act 1792, opened 1804), the Kennet and Avon Canal (first Act 1794, completed 1810), the Lancaster Canal (first Act 1792, finally completed 1819), and the Royal Canal of Ireland (from Dublin to the Shannon, first Act 1789, finally completed 1817).

Rennie accepted the W/B Company's invitation to come over, and on 21 September the Committee ordered Mr Hodgkinson to show him the line of the canal as surveyed by Mr Cartwright and ask him to suggest possible improvements to it; also to seek his advice on the construction of the locks and the materials needed, and to enquire his opinion on how the canal could best be supplied with water. Rennie, in his usual efficient way, submitted a written report and Hodgkinson was ordered to furnish Cartwright with a copy of it and instruct him to make the various surveys recommended by Rennie as soon as possible, and also to bore the ground to find clay suitable for brick-making and puddling along the line of the canal. By 18 November 1808 Cartwright had produced a profile and a ground plan of the line of the locks as proposed by Rennie, and these were sent for the latter's approval.

In January 1809, Thomas Cartwright, already involved with preparations for the completion of the canal, offered his services as official Resident Engineer, and on 1 March he was reappointed as such at a salary of 400 guineas per annum plus travelling expenses, to be paid as from 1 January, on condition that he worked whole time for the Company and employed a person at his own expense to assist him. Cartwright began work on several fronts, on the completion of Tardebigge Tunnel, on the location of brick-making sites and the supervision of brick-making, and on a survey of the works needed to raise water from the Severn to the summit. Unfortunately, in mid May, ill-health compelled him to send in his resignation. and the Committee instructed their Clerk, Mr Hodgkinson, to write to him "informing him that this Committee are sorry that his ill state of Health deprives the Company of his future Services." Cartwright was paid his salary up to midsummer and replaced as engineer by John Woodhouse, to whom he was directed to deliver all plans and papers belonging to the Company. Messrs. Lea and Startin of the Committee visited Cartwright and discovered that "there is a considerable Sum due from him to the Company." Cartwright offered the Company, in compensation, his canal materials stored at the barracks at Kings Norton. His death, about a year later, is not mentioned in the Canal Company's minutes, but Berrow's Journal of 21 June 1810 reported: "Monday died at Longbridge, in the Parish of Kings Norton, Mr Thomas Cartwright, formerly Engineer to the Worcester and Birmingham Canal." He had worked hard and with dedication for the Company over the years and deserved greater recognition of his efforts and achievements.

Cartwright's successor, John Woodhouse of Daventry, had been Engineer on the Grand Junction Canal and had been seconded to the W/B from January 1809 to erect his experimental boat lift at Tardebigge. A married man, he was appointed Resident Engineer by the Assembly on 4 July 1809 and he moved house to Barnt

Green, close to the canal and the reservoir at Bittell. He had a brother Jonathan at Overseal, who was instrumental in acquiring a boat for the use of the Committee in September 1810, and a son Thomas who replaced William Grey as the Company's Superintendent in January 1811 at a salary of 2 Guineas a week. Woodhouse served as engineer for two years, during which time he supervised the completion of Tardebigge Tunnel and the construction of Tardebigge New Wharf, worked on the completion of Bittell Reservoir and the planning of Lifford and Cofton Reservoirs, and organised supplies of bricks, stone and timber for the canal, as well as overseeing the construction and working of his lift and being involved with surveys and maintenance work on the summit level.

COMPLETION OF TARDEBIGGE TUNNEL AND THE NEW WHARF

The first construction task facing the Committee during the winter of 1808-9 was the finishing of the 580 yards long tunnel at Tardebigge. This, unlike the other four tunnels, had mostly to be cut out of solid rock. A start on it had been made in 1796 with the opening up of the south end and the sinking of a square brick-lined shaft, about 6 feet from side to side, about a third of the way from the south end in 1797. Work then ceased until January 1809 when Cartwright was asked to estimate the expense of finishing the tunnel and the time it would take. On 15 February he reported that 500 yards of the tunnel remained unfinished, and he was instructed to sink a shaft towards the north end, as soon as possible, "as marked on the Profile this day exhibited to the Committee by him." This shaft, a circular one, cut out of the rock, about one third of the way from the north end, remains unfilled, as does the other, and they can be viewed from inside the tunnel. They were eventually topped with convex brickwork caps.

The Committee advertised in the newspapers in February 1809 for "Persons willing to Contract for finishing the Tunnel in the Line of the Worcester and Birmingham Canal at Tardebigg", and on 12 April a contract was agreed with Joseph Smith of Occerhill, who had submitted the lowest tender of £14 per yard if bricked all round, and £11 per yard if bricked to six inches above top water. The Committee also approved an advertisement for "Persons willing to Contract for the Deep Cutting at the North and South Ends of Tardebigg Tunnel" which concluded "Security must be given for the Performance of the Contracts." In May 1809 contracts were awarded to Thomas Wilkins of Burbage, Wilts., for the deep cutting at the north end of the Tunnel, to be completed in 9 months at a cost of 8 pence per cubic yard (the lowest tender), and to Abraham Lees of Common Side, near Dudley, for the deep cutting at the south side at 7½ pence per cubic yard excavated. In March Cartwright had been instructed to employ two carpenters to make "Ranges" (the wooden formers for the brickwork arches) for the Tunnel. By December 1809 it had become evident that the job of cutting, and perhaps blasting with gunpowder, through the rock was more difficult and costly than anticipated, and Joseph Smith's offer to finish the tunnel by Midsummer 1810 for an extra £242.10s., to be forfeited if not completed by then, was accepted by the Committee. Smith was also, at the same meeting, given permission to draw 200,000 bricks from the Company's brickyard on Mr Webster's farm at Tardebigg, for lining the tunnel where necessary.

There is no further mention in the Assembly or Committee minutes of progress on the tunnel or the date of its completion, but an advertisement in Berrow's Journal of 17 January 1811, relating to the lift at Tardebigge, stated that at the July 1810 Assembly it was promised that the tunnel would be completed by Michaelmas, whereas it was not, in fact, filled with water until December, and no boat had, to date, unloaded at the new wharf south of the tunnel. So the tunnel was completed by December 1810, but was not in use until early in 1811. It was brick-lined at each end, and in parts between, with three thicknesses of brickwork, as can be seen today where the lining gives way to the rough-hewn solid rock.

Some 30 yards or so from the southern portal of the Tardebigge Tunnel, the line of the canal crossed the lane running from Tutnall to Webheath and on towards Alcester. To avoid building a bridge to take this road over the canal, it was decided, with the Earl of Plymouth's permission, to divert the road, or rather to build a new road above the tunnel mouth leading to the entrance gates of Hewell Park. In March

Picture post-card c.1900 of Tardebigge New Wharf, with a coal boat in the canal arm, before the new depot was built there (Doris Colledge).

Two of the old limekilns exposed at Tardebigge New Wharf in 2003. They had been filled with rubbish and hidden by a soil covering on top and by an embankment over the draw holes.

1810 the Committee gave instructions to Joseph Smith, the tunnel contractor, to make the new road under John Woodhouse's direction. The old road on the east side of the canal was ordered to be preserved; it could be accessed via the towpath but it ran steeply uphill and was soon disused since it was much easier for horse-drawn vehicles to use the new road and rejoin the old one where it crossed the lane between Hewell and Tardebigge Church. The line of the old road can still be seen beside the north side of the old warehouse and as it sweeps up the hillside in the hollow way on the east side of the canal.

South of the tunnel a wharf was planned on the west side of the canal with a 90 feet square basin and a warehouse, and in August 1810 a local "stone-getter", John Smith, was engaged to build the warehouse of stone with walls 2 feet thick up to the first floor and then 1ft 6in thick above. The stone came from Mr Field's quarry, just off Dusthouse Lane nearby, and Smith was paid 3s.6d. per cubic yard for his construction work.

The New Wharf, as it was called, complete with a weighing machine and machine house just inside the entrance, was ready for use early in 1811. Soon after the tunnel was completed. John Heywood was appointed machine clerk and wharfinger. When he was later moved to Lowesmoor in 1815, his place was taken by Benjamin Smith. A boy was appointed in 1813 to assist in supervising the warehouse and the charges for its use, he being paid 12 shillings a week. The New Wharf was immediately used by coal dealers Jenkins and Wright, soon to be joined by others, including Thomas Dixon. By 1814 lime-burning kilns were in use close to the basin, a special concession being made on the tonnage of coal used for this purpose. In February 1814 the weighing machine, which, to encourage customers, had initially been set to register 120 lb. per hundredweight, was altered to the normal 112 lb. per hundredweight. In August 1815 the Canal Committee lodged a complaint to the traders at the wharf that they were charging too high a price for coal. From such reports in the Committee minutes it is evident that the New Wharf was being well used by the time the canal was completed in 1815. It was certainly convenient for the supply of coal and other commodities to the Finstall and Bromsgrove areas.

LAYING IN STOCKS OF MATERIALS NEEDED TO FINISH THE CANAL
For the tunnels at Tardebigge and Dunhampstead and for the locks, bridges and other structures, many millions of good quality bricks were needed. Fortunately suitable clay for brick-making had been located by Cartwright at various places along the line of the canal. Early in 1809 advertisements were placed in newspapers seeking brick-makers "willing to contract for making Bricks in Moulds 10 inches long by 5 inches wide and 3 inches thick .... 5 million being wanted in the present year .... the bricks to be well burnt." Brick-making began in March 1809 on Dial House Meadow on Mr Webster's Farm off London Lane, Tardebigge. The initial contractors for this, Mansfield and Ross, proved unsatisfactory and they were soon dismissed and replaced by Thomas Price of Selly Oak, an experienced and reliable brick-maker. The contract price was 26 shillings per thousand. Huts were erected on site for the workmen. From this brickyard came, as has been mentioned, the bricks for Tardebigge Tunnel, and from it in 1811 Lord Plymouth's Agent was permitted to draw 200,000 bricks to build the Plymouth Arms Inn and its coach house and stable block, close to the entrance to the New Wharf. Thomas Price later, in 1813, contracted to make bricks towards the Worcester end of the canal at Offerton and at Blackpole Green at 34 shillings per thousand.

Another not very efficient brick-maker was John Foster. He was engaged in April 1809 to make one million bricks at Stoke Prior. In January 1810 the landowner, Mr Brettell of Stourbridge, complained to the Canal Company that clay had been dug up and bricks made without his permission or any agreement. In January 1811 Foster, now also making bricks at Tibberton Common, was threatened with non-payment for not stacking his bricks as directed, and a year later it was reported that out of 3 million bricks made by him many were totally unfit for lock-making and that he had been overpaid. In January 1813 Foster, owing money to the Company, disappeared; attempts to trace him were unsuccessful, and his bricks were later sold. Other brickmakers were William Howard and John Glover with sites at Hanbury and Oddingley. Bricks for locks and bridges from Lowesmoor to the Severn were supplied in 1814 by Messrs. Bromley and Dallow, local contractors.

Stone, in blocks of various sizes, needed for the footings of bridges, the coping of bridge parapets, the edging of wharves and lock sides, and for some warehouses, was mainly obtained from two sandstone quarries at Tardebigge. Berrow's Worcester Journal of 31 January 1810 carried an advertisement:

"TO GETTERS AND WORKERS OF STONE - A large Quantity of stone being wanted to be got and prepared for the Worcester and Birmingham Canal, at a Quarry near Tardebigg, Persons desirous to contract for getting and preparing the same are desired to apply to Mr. Woodhouse, the Company's Engineer, at Tardebigg..."

Three weeks later the Committee, having received proposals from Mr John Smith of Bristol "for getting Stone at Tardebigg Church for the use of the Canal", ordered "That Mr. Parker prepare a Contract with him for getting the Stone according to the following Specification: The Stone to be well bedded and jointed and Ashler faced and to be cut from one foot to six feet in length and from sixteen inches to three feet in breadth and from six inches to three feet in thickness, and to be conveyed by him from the Quarry to the Banks of the Canal at 4/6 per cube yard .... The Company to find four Railway Waggons and to put down the Railways with Cranes and other Machinery for conveying the Stone to the Banks of the Canal." This quarry was on the hillside just below Tardebigge Church and on Lord Plymouth's land, and it remained in use until October 1813 when the Company "having received Notice from Mr. Hunt on behalf of the Earl of Plymouth to desist from getting Stone at the Quarry near Tardebigge Church and it appearing to this Committee desirable that a small quantity more should be had for the purpose of completion of the Bridge over the Canal between the Parishes of Birmingham and Edgbaston - Ordered that Mr. Hodgkinson do apply to Mr. Hunt for permission to get a sufficient quantity of Stone to complete the said Bridge." The rails from the church quarry were removed about this time for use elsewhere on the line of the canal for transporting heavy materials. On the site of the quarry, later used as a tip, there is now a treelined depression below the boundary of the Churchyard.

The other quarry at Tardebigge was just off Dusthouse Lane about a quarter of a mile from the canal across fields and a small stream. It was reported in January 1810 that Mr Haynes of the Committee was negotiating with the owner, Mr Field, for the purchase or renting of this stone quarry. The following August agreements were made with William Hancock and others, and also with John Smith of Tardebigge, to get stone at different parts of Mr Field's quarry. Some of this stone was used by Smith to build the warehouse on the New Wharf in the Autumn of 1810, as already mentioned. Then in April 1811 Mr Haynes, who had been authorised to pay up to a thousand guineas for two acres of Mr Field's Quarry, this being Woodhouse's estimate of its value, reported to the Committee that "he had concluded a Bargain with Mr. Field for the two Acres for the Sum of £400, the same to be paid for on the Company commencing to work the said Quarry, and a further Condition that Mr. Field do return to the Company the Sum of Fifty Pounds whenever they have no further use for the said Quarry." A 3ft gauge railroad, constructed of one yard lengths of angle iron rail resting on stone blocks, was soon laid from the quarry in an arc up to a stone wharf made just below the site of the then recently constructed boat lift (later to be replaced by the present top lock). The Dusthouse Quarry and this horse tramway were used by the Canal Company, and also let out to other contractors from time to time, until 1869, when the rails were lifted. The quarry remained disused and overgrown until after World War 2 when it was used as a tip, filled in and levelled, so that there are now no visible signs of its existence.

Much of the timber needed for lock gates and other purposes was obtained locally in the latter part of 1809, some from Mr Green at Rednal and a large amount from Mr Brettell's land at Stoke Prior.

IMPORTANT DECISIONS CONCERNING
THE COMPLETION OF THE CANAL

By the Summer of 1810 the Canal Committee had decided to organise the construction of the final fifteen-mile stretch of the canal down to Worcester in three convenient five-mile sections. The first of these, from the lift at Tardebigge to where the canal crossed Body Brook in the Parish of Hanbury, would contain over 40 locks and lower the canal by some 300 feet. The second, from Body Brook to Offerton, to be known as the Five-mile Pound, contained no locks but included the tunnel at Dunhampstead. The third, from Offerton to the Severn at Diglis, descended in easy stages some 130 feet and would contain one or more basins at the Worcester end, with barge locks down to the River Severn.

Preparatory work on the Five-mile Pound began in 1810 but progress on the other two sections had to await the final outcome, in 1811, of the lifts versus locks controversy, as well as decisions about the dimensions of the locks. Back in January 1793, with a barge canal in mind, Clowes had advised that the locks should be 15ft 6in wide at the sides, 16ft wide at water level, and 80ft in length from sill to sill. In July 1795 the Committee resolved "That the locks be made 80ft in length from Heel to Heel, 15ft in width on the main Sill, and 5ft deep on the top Sill, - to pass Barges of 60 tons, or 2 common Canal Boats." It seems therefore that the protest following the economy plan for a boat canal in 1793 had been temporarily successful.

However, by 1809 the decision had been made that the canal should have narrow locks as far as the basin in Worcester and 4 broad locks from there down to the river at Diglis. But there was some apprehension concerning the legality of building mainly narrow locks on what had clearly been intended as a barge canal, and so legal advice was sought. Eventually, in April 1810, the Committee were reassured on receiving the following Opinion of Counsel:

"The Acts do not require that the Canal should be of any particular Size - The first Act supposes that Vessels of more than 35 Tons would be employed, the second supposes that Vessels of more than 46 Tons would be used - But neither of the two Acts requires that the Vessels should be confined to any particular Tonnage, and I therefore think that the Proprietors may with perfect Safety make the Canal of the Dimensions now proposed.

(signed) R.Richards, 19th. April 1810, Lincoln's Inn."

In was on 16 February 1811 that the Committee made several vital decisions. The line from the lift to Body Brook had been staked out, the work had just been advertised for contractors to send in their proposals, and Mr Callow was now instructed to value the land required and negotiate agreements with the various landowners. The engineer, John Woodhouse, had set forth his arguments and calculations to prove that locks of depth seven feet were, in use, simpler to operate and more economical of water and time than locks of ten feet depth with side ponds. Locks of six feet rise had previously been intended, but the decision was now made to construct seven feet rise locks.

The Committee also considered the route of the canal between London Barn and Stoke Court. Comparative costings of two alternative routes had been submitted by Woodhouse. The line that was rejected would have taken the canal about half-a-mile nearer to Bromsgrove at Aston Fields, thus making a possible canal branch to Bromsgrove cheaper to cut, but it posed greater constructional difficulties, being on a hillside, so the present line via Upper Gambolds was agreed.

With the summit level completed and in use to the New Wharf at Tardebigge, with surveys made and negotiations for land proceeding, with decisions made concerning the line of the canal, the use of locks and their dimensions, and with supplies of bricks, stone and timber etc. in hand, it was now possible to invite tenders from contractors for the remaining construction work onwards down to Worcester.

Chapter 7

THE TARDEBIGGE
BOAT LIFT, 1809-15

SOLVING THE WATER SUPPLY PROBLEM

At the beginning of 1809 the W/B Canal Company was poised to start the last stage of construction work on the canal from Tardebigge to the River Severn at Diglis. Locks were planned, and, to supply the water needed, steam pumping engines were to be obtained and installed in engine houses at strategic places, and storage reservoirs were to be made, so that water could be pumped up from the river in stages to the summit level at Tardebigge. This costly method of obtaining water had been envisaged in the 1791 Canal Act because of the Birmingham Canal Company's unwillingness to supply water and the Act's conditions that no reservoirs to supply the canal were to be constructed north of the Parish of Tardebigge. Towards the end of 1808 John Rennie, the consulting engineer, had expressed his opinion that the Birmingham Company did have sufficient surplus water to supply the W/B Canal. But in view of the continuing refusal of the Birmingham Company, in spite of several approaches, to part with any of its water, the W/B Company was now prepared to order the steam engines from Messrs. Boulton and Watt and to construct the engine houses and storage reservoirs.

There was, however, a possible way of avoiding the cost of pumping up water from the River Severn, and that was to use boat lifts instead of locks. Lifts cause little loss of water, and several had already been in experimental use elsewhere. A vertical lift designed and constructed by Robert Weldon on the Somersetshire Coal Canal at Combe Hay, near Bath, in 1796-7, using an enclosed caisson, had been tried out in 1797 and 1798, but, due to geological and other difficulties, had been abandoned in favour of locks. Another, patented in 1794 by Edward Rowland and Exuperious Pickering, had used a large water-tight empty chest beneath a caisson to float it in the lift chamber. This lift had been constructed on the Ellesmere Canal near Ruabon by 1796 and tried out, but, after critical reports on it in 1800 by Rennie and Jessop, it had been discarded. In 1798 James Fussell had patented his invention of a double vertical lift with two counterbalanced wooden caissons in parallel chambers separated by a wall, the caissons being connected by chains over large pulleys on top of the wall. Fussell's lift had been constructed on the Dorset and Somerset Canal in the neighbourhood of Mells, near Frome, in 1800, and successfully tried out, but it and four others, partially constructed, had been abandoned when work on the canal ceased in 1803, due to lack of money, and had never resumed. Then in 1806 John Woodhouse, an engineer on the Grand Junction Canal, obtained a patent for a double vertical lift similar in design to Fussell's but with minor differences of operation.

WOODHOUSE'S EXPERIMENTAL LIFT OFFER IS ACCEPTED

Woodhouse, realising that lifts might be the solution to the W/B Canal Company's problems, approached the Company and put his proposal to the Assembly at the Royal Hotel, Birmingham, on 3 January 1809. As reported in the minutes:

> "Mr. Woodhouse, an Engineer employed on the Grand Junction Canal, having produced a Model of a Machine for raising and lowering Boats in a Canal with thirty Tons weight on board, and having proposed to this Assembly to make such a Machine at his own Expence for a Trial, if this Company would be at the Expence of Digging and Masonry, in a proper Situation to be pointed out by Mr. Woodhouse and Mr. Cartwright on the line of the Canal, to try the Machine on a Fall of six Feet, and that the Grand Junction Canal Company be applied to for Leave for Mr. Woodhouse to do it, - Resolved that this Assembly accede to Mr. Woodhouse's Offer."

The experimental lift proposed by Woodhouse differed from his original patent in that it was to have only one caisson with balancing counterweights connected to it by chains passing over eight large pulleys mounted on a wall at one side of the lift chamber. The Committee decided to seek information about lifts already tried, and instructed the Company's Clerk, Mr Parker, in January 1809, to write to William Bennet of Bath, canal engineer, for information about Weldon's lift on the Somersetshire Coal Canal. By March Woodhouse was engaged in preliminary work on the lift site below Tardebigge Church. In May it was reported that Thomas Cartwright had sent in his resignation as engineer of the Company on account of ill-health and that Woodhouse had offered to replace him. At the Assembly on 4 July Woodhouse was appointed Engineer to the Company and it was resolved "That Mr. Woodhouse's Machine for raising and lowering Vessels be tried on a Fall of twelve Feet, instead of six Feet as resolved at the last general Assembly."

THE CONSTRUCTION AND LIMITED TRIAL OF THE LIFT

Construction of the lift continued during the remaining half of 1809, the various cast iron parts being obtained, and a building was erected around it to provide protection for the machinery and the men who would have to operate it in all weathers. By the end of November the work was so far advanced that the Clerk to the Company, Mr Parker, was instructed to write to ask Mr Rennie to witness "a Trial of Mr. Woodhouse's lifting Machine" at the end of December. However, there must have been unforeseen problems and delays, for it was reported to the Committee on 7 February 1810 that the lift would not be ready until 19 February. On 21 February it was reported to be ready and that trials would be made "as soon as the frost goes".

Although the lift was now finished, it could not be put to full working use by boats at that time because Tardebigge Tunnel was some months off completion and the canal at each end of the lift had not been excavated. However there must have been a short length of channel dug out and puddled at each end of the lift and filled with water, for a boat had been purchased by Woodhouse and evidently carted overland from Tardebigge Old Wharf to the site in order that the operation of the lift could be demonstrated. Berrow's Worcester Journal reported that on 26 February "Mr. Faraday and several engineers inspected Mr. Woodhouse's patent perpendicular lift, on the Worcester and Birmingham Canal, at Tardebigge, when it passed a boat the distance of twelve feet, in two minutes and a quarter, and was much approved by them and a number of other gentlemen present."

A PRINTED DESCRIPTION OF THE LIFT

A month later, on 29 March 1810, there appeared in Berrow's Worcester Journal the following advertisement:

> "PERPENDICULAR LIFT
> "This day is published, Price One Shilling, A Description of the Patent Perpendicular Lift, lately erected upon the Worcester and Birmingham Canal at Tardebig, in a letter to a Friend, by Edward Smith, Canal Agent, etc. Illustrated by Three Engravings from Drawings taken on the Spot by W. Hawkes Smith. Printed for W.H.Smith, No.4 Union-street, Birmingham; sold by Longman and Co., London and J.Tymbs and Son, Worcester."

There is a copy of this pamphlet in the library of the Institution of Civil Engineers in London. It contains, besides a perspective view of the lift and elevations with detailed dimensions and explanations, also an account of the visit made prior to 6 March by Smith and by his son who produced the drawings and details.

Smith's account relates how "a few days since, a party of us set off, on a very fine morning; and, to be on a certainty, we went to the residence of MR. WOODHOUSE,

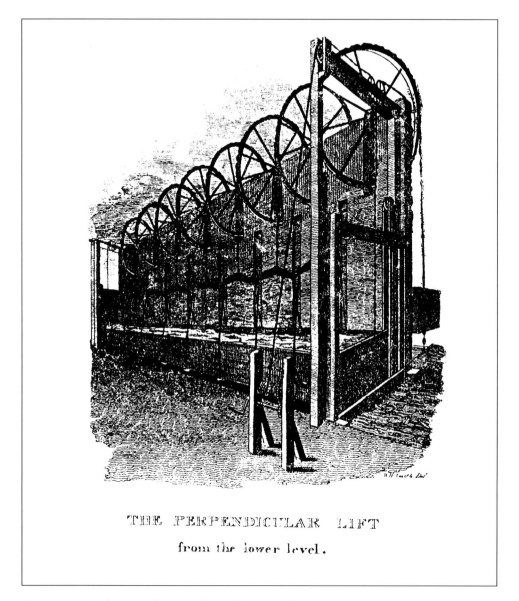

THE PERPENDICULAR LIFT

from the lower level.

Drawing of John Woodhouse's boat lift at Tardebigge from a booklet by Edward Smith, 1810 (Institute of Civil Engineers Library)

the Patentee and Engineer, at Barns Green, and procured a note to his foreman to show and explain to us the whole apparatus. By the time we arrived at Tardebig, we were much gratified by the arrival of MR. WOODHOUSE, who had followed us, and with great politeness attended us to the place, and gave us every information that we wished.

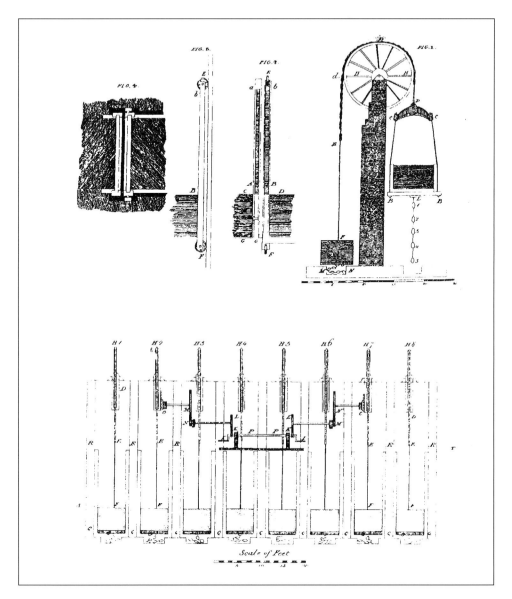

Diagrams in Edward Smith's booklet showing the working parts of the boat lift.

"On entering the building (for every part is under cover) at the lower level of the Canal, the appearance of a number of large wheels, rods, and chains, seen in perspective, had a very striking and pleasing effect; we walked by the side of an oblong trough or vessel, filled with water, large enough for a canal boat to float in. This reservoir of water with the canal boat weighs 64 tons, and is suspended by eight rods and chains over as many large cast-iron wheels or pullies, which are balanced on the other side of the wall by an equal number of square frames, loaded with brick-work, or other heavy materials. After examining the lower structure of the building and machine, we got into an empty boat, which floated in the reservoir, and were slowly raised to the upper level of the canal, without any noise or jarring in the machinery, by means of wheels and pinions on the other side, which were worked by two men with great ease, it took about three minutes to ascend twelve feet, the difference between the two levels. When the trough is thus raised to the necessary height, the paddles at the end, which are very ingeniously contrived for the purpose, being drawn up, a communication is made between the water in the trough and that in the canal, and the boat passes from the trough into the upper level of the canal, to pursue its course. In case a boat be ready in the upper level, it is in turn floated into the trough, the communication is stopped by letting down the paddles into their places, and the machine is made to descend by the same means to the lower level of the canal, where, by similar paddles, the boat is released to proceed on its journey. Whether the boat be loaded or empty it makes no difference in the weight, for as the machine is kept filled in a certain height with water, the boat, on its entrance, displaces just as much of this fluid as is equal to its own weight."

The account goes on to praise the simplicity of the lift and the strength and quality of its component parts, and to point out that "the machine may be adapted to raise twenty, thirty, or any number of feet, by greater length of chains, and adequate building to suit the levels, at a much less proportionate expence than in shorter lifts." An advantage of lifts, it is pointed out, is that as each lift is finished the canal may be used thus far, which is not the case with locks. On the other hand it is conceded that "the expence of erecting these Perpendicular Lifts must be, however, necessarily very great, besides the constant expence of two or more men stationed at each, to work it." Smith praises the Worcester and Birmingham Committee for patronising Woodhouse's plan, and speculates: "In the possibility of its not being adopted in the future progress of this canal, still it will remain as a model for all other canals, who of course may profit thereby."

In the description of the drawings, the outside measurements of the trough are given as length 72 feet, breadth 8 feet, depth 4 feet 6 inches, and it was constructed of 3 inch thick planking. The pulley wheels were 12 feet in diameter and the second and seventh were toothed around 12 feet of the circumference to engage the pinions of the two sets of geared mechanism worked by two winches mounted on a common spindle. The wall on which the pulley wheels were mounted was 30 feet high. The functioning of the paddles is described as follows:- "From the corners of the trough rise four strong posts, 12 feet high, in each of which is a groove, which receives the respective paddle. Parallel to these are similar posts in which slide the paddle of the canal. When a boat is to be introduced at the lower level, the narrow space between the paddle of the trough and that of the canal is first filled with water by opening a valve... ; the lateral pressure of the water against the paddles is thus removed. The chain, which hangs down between the upright posts, the lower part of which is double, is then linked to the hooks of both paddles, and, by means of the crane near the end, they are drawn up together, and the boat floats into the trough; the paddles are then dropped, and the trough raised to the upper level, when the boat is liberated by opening the paddles at the contrary end. A similar operation takes place when a boat is required to descend from the upper to the lower level." To prevent leakage at the paddles, there were strips of thick felt along the sides of the grooves against which the paddles pressed under the water pressure. Under the trough and also under the counterweights were hung lengths of chain which settled into shallow cavities as the trough or counterweights approached their lowest positions; the purpose of these was to prevent the imbalance which would otherwise occur as the chains connecting the trough and the counterweights moved round the pulley wheels as the lift was operated. To steady the trough and maintain its smooth vertical motion, small wheels attached to the top and bottom of each of its corner posts rolled against the vertical posts of the two fixed end frameworks which carried the paddle-lifting pulleys and chains.

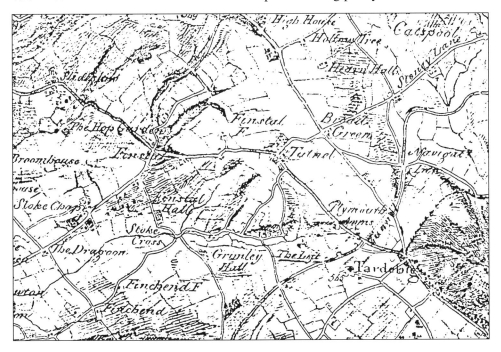

Part of a map c.1814 of the Tardebigge area showing the course of the canal and, marked, The Lift, the Navigation Inn at the Old Wharf and the Plymouth Arms. (Tim Brotherton Collection).

FURTHER TRIALS; OPERATIONAL PROBLEMS

Altogether, the lift was ingeniously contrived, but it needed to be operated with great care. So far, it is evident from the accounts given and the times quoted for the ascent or descent, that the boat had been confined to the caisson; this was because not enough of the canal had been dug and watered at each end for it to be floated out.

On 3 May 1810 the Committee ordered that Mr Woodhouse be paid £1,000 on account for his Lifting Machine; also that 30 yards of the canal above the machine and 40 yards below it should be finished immediately, and water put into the same so that trials could be carried out. At last two other boats were obtained and progress was such that, by the end of May, Rennie was invited to attend a trial of the lift. He came on 5 June and was attended by Woodhouse and several Committee members who feature in the Committee's report of the calamitous proceedings:

"That the Boat being in the lower Level, Mr. Francis and Mr. Haynes were in the Boat and Mr. Mabson, Mr. Shore and Mr. Woodhouse were on the Stage by the Side of the Boat on the lower Level - That the Paddle at one end of the Cradle in which the Boat was swimming was not let down when the Men employed in winding them up and down began winding up the Cradle with the Boat in it - That as soon as the Cradle began to rise above the level of the Water in which it was swimming, the Water began running out of the Cradle, whereby the Balance was lost and the Cradle precipitated to the upper Level almost instantaneously; that by the Velocity with which the Cradle fled upwards one of the Men at the Windlass was very much hurt by the Windlass striking him or whirling him about - That one of the Wheels was broken, so that the Machine could not be worked afterwards that day, and that a Beam at the Roof of the Building was displaced, but that no Injury was done to the Cradle or Boat or any of the Gentlemen above mentioned only by being a little sprinkled with the Water running out of the Cradle." We are not told of the reaction of Rennie or his opinion of Woodhouse for not properly supervising the working of the lift on this occasion. But the incident must have reinforced Rennie's doubts about the safety and reliability of this type of boat lift.

Further qualms were expressed by Messrs. Lea and Mabson of the Canal Committee who visited Tardebigge on 22 June to observe the passing of boats by the lift. They reported "That a Boat can be passed from the Upper Level and into the Lower Level in eight Minutes - That six Boats were passed in one Hour, including some little Stoppages, viz. three loaded Boats up and three loaded Boats down - That seventy two Boats may be passed by a twelve feet lift in twelve hours, but that in doing so, the two Men at the Windlasses and the one at the Paddles and at the Boats, have no time to take their Meals, unless relieved by another set of Men." They also stated that when one of the paddles was put down, while they were there, "a Rope got under it and occasioned much Leakage, the Cause of which could not be discovered 'til a person went into the Water and found the Rope - That afterwards a small piece of Board, about eight Inches by three, was swimming in the Canal, and that when the Paddle was put down, the Board was drawn under it by the Current of Water passing under it at the same time, which, by sticking under the Paddle, occasioned a Leakage in like manner as the Rope had done, and that it appeared to them that such Accidents are likely to happen. And they stated it as their Opinion that when the Ice breaks after a Frost, it will be equally detrimental to the working of the Paddles."

THE ASSEMBLY DECISION TO PROCEED WITH LOCKS

By the time of the Assembly of Shareholders on 3 July 1810 at the Hop Pole Inn, Worcester, John Rennie had paid another visit to inspect the lift and had submitted a written report, which was read to the Assembly. On the basis of this and other reports, the resolution was put that "this Assembly having weighed and considered the matter and the Estimates of the Expences of finishing the Canal with Lifts and Locks, and also the probable annual Expence which would be required to work them, are of Opinion that the said Lifts shall not be adopted nor any other Lifts instead of Locks." However, there were those present who felt that, with the canal not yet completed as far as the lift, it had not been adequately tested. So an amendment was proposed and carried, viz. "That the Trial of the Lifting Machine be continued until the General Assembly in January next, that in the mean time no Boat, except such as are specially authorised by the Committee, be loaded or unloaded until it had passed the said Machine into the lower Level, and that when the Canal and Machine are compleated and ready for passing Boats, Mr. Woodhouse be desired to give Notice thereof to the Committee, who shall, under his Recommendation, appoint persons to superintend the working of it." The following day, at the adjourned General Assembly, it was resolved that Rennie's report on the lift be printed and a copy sent to each proprietor.

In the event, Tardebigge Tunnel was not completed and in use until January 1811, after the Assembly held on 1 and 2 January at the Royal Hotel in Birmingham, so the lift had by then not been in operation with working boats as it had been hoped. There was at this Assembly a very large attendance. Those present were informed that a few days earlier, at a Committee meeting held on Boxing Day, Mr Woodhouse had expressed his opinion "that it will not be necessary to raise the water 428 feet from the Severn to the Summit .... and that the remainder of the Canal should be finished by Locks." By this time there were ideas afoot for a possible reservoir on the Body Brook in the Parish of Hanbury, east of the canal; also for other possible reservoirs in the Northfield area. In the light of these considerations, the Assembly this time passed unanimously the motion, as proposed six months

Worcester and Birmingham Canal Navigation,

ROYAL HOTEL, BIRMINGHAM.

AT A

Special General Meeting of the Committee

Of Proprietors of this Undertaking, holden the 22d of May inst. it was ordered that the following Statement should be signed by the Clerk of the Company, and printed and sent to all the Proprietors, viz.

THIS Committee having taken into their consideration the Resolution of the Special Assembly, holden at the Hop Pole Inn, in Worcester, on the 26th day of March last, stating, that *provided the Committee should be satisfied that a sufficient supply of Water could be procured on or near the Summit Level of the Canal, without a Recurrence to the River Severn, it would be the Interest of the Company to finish the Canal with Locks; and that the Committee should·be therefore impowered to proceed with the execution of the Canal, when the supply should be proved:*

And this Committee having examined and duly considered Mr. RENNIE's Reports, and Mr. BEVAN's Reports, dated the 26th March last, and 18th of May inst. and likewise the Report of a Select Committee, appointed to investigate the means of supplying the Canal with Water, without resorting to the River Severn, dated the 21st of May inst. and having examined and duly considered the testimony of various Surveyors, and other skilful Persons,

Do unanimously Resolve and Declare,

THAT IT IS PROVED, to the entire satisfaction of this Committee, that very considerable quantities of Water may be collected within the parish of Tardebigg, under the powers vested in the Company by the Act for making the Canal; independently of Water that may be procured *above its summit level,* and collected in reservoirs, abundantly more than sufficient for any trade that can ever be passed along it.—It is therefore

Resolved Unanimously,

That in pursuance of the power vested in the Committee, by the above-stated Resolution of the Special Assembly, the Canal shall be finished with Locks; and that Contracts for finishing the Canal with Locks be entered into without delay.

BENJAMIN PARKER,

Clerk of the Company of Proprietors.

Birmingham, June 5, 1811.

————ooo————

Printed by R. Jabet, Herald Office, High street, Birmingham.

The notice sent out to shareholders informing them of the decision of the Committee Meeting of 22 May 1811 that the canal should be completed with locks and not boat lifts. (WBCS archives)

earlier, that the canal should be completed with locks and not lifts. It was also agreed unanimously "That great Merit is due to Mr. Woodhouse for the Ingenuity he has shown in the Execution of the Lift and that the Thanks of this Assembly be given to Mr. Woodhouse for his Candor in advising the Adoption of Locks under the Circumstances in which the Company is now placed."

SUPPORTERS OF THE LIFT GET ORGANISED

If the Committee believed that, with Woodhouse supporting their view and that of Rennie that locks should be used, and having now got a unanimous vote in the Assembly for this policy, the issue was now finally settled, they were soon to be disillusioned. For a few days later, on 12 January, as reported in a lengthy advertisement in Berrow's Journal, an unofficial meeting of disgruntled proprietors of the Worcester and Birmingham Canal, resident in Kidderminster, took place in that town. The Chairman was H Perrin and the leading light was George Hallen, a Kidderminster Attorney and holder of new W/B Canal shares. The complaints expressed at the meeting were that, because of the delay in finishing Tardebigge tunnel and opening the new wharf, the lift had not been fully tested as promised at the July 1810 Assembly; that William Jessop, the canal engineer, had, at the request of Hallen, inspected the lift and reported favourably upon it and recommended its use along the canal, but the Canal Committee had declined to see Jessop or to consider his report; that various misrepresentations had been put about, such as that the lift had cost £10,000, whereas it had actually cost less than £4,000, and that it needed four men to work it. It was argued that it would in fact be cheaper to construct the relatively few lifts than the many locks; and that the passage of the canal by boats would take much less time by the fewer lifts than the many locks. The meeting passed resolutions that "a full trial should be had; and for that purpose that two boats should be provided, with horses, boatmen .... and that such boats be passed and repassed with as much Expedition as possible, for the space of one month"; also "that Mr. Jessop be employed to survey the country whence it is proposed to obtain water upon the summit of the Canal ... and that the Committee be requested to direct their Engineer to attend Mr. Jessop in such survey, and give him every assistance in making the same"; and that "the Committee be requested not to proceed with the Canal as for Locks until such trial of the lift can be had, and till it can be ascertained whether a sufficient quantity of water can be obtained on the summit without the aid of fire engines."

This report of the Kidderminster meeting also contained the suggestion that a local Society of Proprietors of the Canal Company might be formed at a subscription of 2s.6d. per share, paid into the Bank of Wakeman & Co., Kidderminster, and "that similar societies be formed in London, Worcester,

Birmingham, Bristol, Coventry, Bromsgrove, and other places where Proprietors reside", each society appointing a person to correspond with the others, Mr George Hallen acting as correspondent for Kidderminster and Mr William Ward Eagle for Coventry where he proposed to form a society. The report concluded with the signatures of sixteen Kidderminster shareholders.

A meeting was soon held in Coventry, convened by W W Eagle, who was a strong supporter of the Woodhouse lift, and resolutions were carried similar to those of the Kidderminster group. It is interesting that there was such strong feeling, almost affection, for the lift amongst some shareholders, spearheaded by Messrs. Hallen and Eagle who were prepared to put time, effort and money into organising meetings, compiling newspaper propaganda, commissioning surveys by such a prominent engineer as Jessop, and arranging and financing their own trial of the lift. It was suggested by some of their opponents that they were out to damage or delay the progress of the canal and that Mr Eagle had an interest in the patent of the lift, but these allegations were strongly denied. W W Eagle was, in fact, at that time a member of the Canal Committee, though not very active in that capacity.

By the time the Canal Committee met in Birmingham on 24 January they had received a letter from Hallen detailing the Kidderminster resolutions, together with a copy of Jessop's report. After considering these, the nine Committee members present resolved unanimously that whilst they were always prepared to consider information and recommendations "from any person friendly to this Concern", nevertheless "they cannot without a great Dereliction of Duty deviate in any respect from the Plan adopted unanimously at the last General Assembly for completing the Canal with Locks on the Recommendation of any Body of Proprietors, however respectable, unless they shall be so directed by a General or Special Assembly legally convened for that purpose." They also resolved that no benefit whatsoever could be derived by the Company in employing Mr Jessop, as the Company were fully satisfied with the ability, the integrity and the reports of their own Engineer Mr Rennie. It was also pointed out that, following improvements made to the lift by Woodhouse by 11 December last, trials of the lift had been carried out during the rest of that month "in the same manner as if the Wharf at Tardebigg had been completed." The Committee and other long-standing supporters of the W/B Canal no doubt remembered that Jessop had supported the opposition of the Staffordshire and Worcestershire Canal Company to their canal when it was being planned and Bills put before Parliament. Jessop had been no friend of the W/B Canal to date, and this was an added reason for rejecting his interference now.

Further advertisements and correspondence concerning the lift appeared in Berrow's Journal during January and February 1811. There was a notice and a report of a well-attended unofficial meeting of proprietors held in the Guildhall, Worcester, on 8 February at which they entirely approved "of the Committee having paid little attention to Mr. Jessop's report and for having recommended to the last General Assembly the Resolutions that were so unanimously adopted."

In Berrow's Journal dated 7 February 1811 the Canal Committee pointed out that Woodhouse had in the most candid and unequivocal manner, and entirely unsolicited, declared his opinion, that from the moment he had examined the situations, proposed by Mr Rennie, for making reservoirs on the summit for supplying water, he was satisfied a sufficient supply might be had and he advised the finishing of the canal with locks. The Committee also justifiably argued that "any proprietor not satisfied should have raised the matter at the General Assembly and have taken the opinion of the Assembly on whether Jessop's report should be considered." In the same issue, there was also a long report of a second meeting of Kidderminster supporters of the lift, held on 4 February, denying any wish on their part "to introduce confusion into the affairs of this public undertaking", suggesting that Rennie's plans for summit reservoirs needed further investigation which they were prepared to organise, and declaring "that although the Committee do not join us in our wish to have the Lift fairly tried, we shall, at our own expence, immediately proceed to carry that wish into effect (of which public notice will be given)".

INTENSIVE TRIALS OF THE LIFT

A fortnight later notice was duly given by the lift supporters that, in order to give a fair and impartial trial to Woodhouse's lift, it would be "constantly worked for one Month, from the 25th. day of February instant (Sundays excepted)", and it was hoped "that the Proprietors in general will inspect the working of it, or procure the opinion of some able Civil Engineer thereon, in order to enable them to give their Votes at the Special Assembly of Proprietors intended to be called for the adopting or rejecting it." This Special Assembly was called for 26 March 1811 in accordance with the rules, at the request of twelve proprietors, to follow the intended trials of the lift.

W W Eagle undertook to supervise these trials, but they had not been authorised by the Canal Committee, who at their meeting on 16 February, hearing that some of the Company's servants had been taken from their regular employment to look after and exhibit the lift, resolved that the lift "be locked up and the key delivered to Mr. Hodgkinson". When Eagle arrived to oversee the lift trial a day or two later he found that someone had entered the lift building and (as he reported in Berrow's Journal of 28 February) had "screwed the bosses of both the shafts which connect the first motion with the second and seventh wheels so tight that the machine could not be moved, with the intent, no doubt, to retard the working of the machine and cause injury thereto. I trust the committee will ... offer a reward for the discovery of the persons concerned, as it is evident no one but a mechanic well acquainted with every part of the construction of the machine would have thought of such an expedient. In future, proper care will be taken to prevent a recurrence by a night watchman for that purpose."

As already mentioned, W W Eagle was a Committee member, and after sending his complaint to the press, must have reached an understanding with other Committee members, for, as Berrow's Journal reported, the lift was in operation on Saturday 23 February, and trials began in earnest the following Monday and went on daily until Tuesday 19 March, except on Sundays and on Friday 8 March when "it being so very wet and the men not coming, the Lift was not worked." Statistics for the 19 days of operation were given, showing that the minimum number of boats passed was 37 in 5 hours 1 minute on 28 February, and the maximum 113 in 12 hours exactly on the last day. The time taken per boat varied from about 6½ minutes at best to around 8 minutes at worst.

In order to inform the shareholders before the Special Assembly called for 26 March, a Report of the Trials, dated 22 March and signed by W W Eagle and George Hallen, was posted to each one. The Report contained, besides the statistics of the 19 days' trials, also detailed comparative estimates of the total cost of constructing 72 locks of 6 feet rise, at £700 each, lock houses and summit reservoirs, £84,400, as against the total cost of 17 lifts with 25 feet rise, at £4,000 each and the extra amount of canal cutting, £69,000, saving £15,400. In the comparison of the annual working costs it is assumed that 72 men would be needed to work the locks night and day as against 34 to work the lifts and, with other assumptions concerning repairs and maintenance, a saving of about £4,000 per annum by using lifts is arrived at. The Report also refuted false allegations said to be circulating as to the motives of the lift supporters and suggested the following improvements to the structure of the lift: "The Conductor (trough) to be Six Inches deeper, to enable the Water to escape as the Boat comes in, and thereby lessen the Resistance; the Machinery to be brought on the same side as the Towing-path, that the Man who attends the Paddles, and the Regulators, may stand close to him at the Windlass, and if necessary assist him; the outward Paddle-gate to be made upon the the Plan of the Common Lockgate to open with a Beam, and the wide Part of the Canal to be brought nearer the Lift."

When Hallen and Eagle compiled their report and estimates, they were unaware of the fact that the Committee had, on 16 February, decided upon 7 feet rise locks to cut down on their number, construction costs, and passage time along the canal. The Committee's policy was deliberately to keep the opposition uninformed until the debate in the Special Assembly.

The Special Assembly on 26 March 1811 at the Hop Pole, Worcester, was well attended and, as reported, "lasted till a very late hour, and it was finally decided that, when the Committee were satisfied that water, sufficient for the supply of the Canal, could be procured at or near the summit level (without having recourse to the River Severn), they are then authorised to proceed with the locks, but in the mean time the Lift at Tardebigg (which appears to have given great satisfaction) should continue to work, as it was thought that a further trial might prove beneficial to the commercial interests of the country at large."

RENNIE'S REPORT ON THE LIFT
The decision of the Special Assembly must have been greatly influenced by a letter from John Rennie, dated 23 March 1811, addressed to Thomas Carden, Chairman of the Canal Committee. In it Rennie apologised for not being able to attend the Assembly due to Parliamentary business and criticised Jessop's Report and the report of the lift's performance and costings in the letter of Eagle and Hallen. Continuing, Rennie gave as his own considered opinion:

"The Lift does not in fact perform better than I expected it would, when worked for the short time and in the manner it has been done, and I doubt not, if carefully attended, it will work for a considerable time to come. My objections are that it is too complex, too delicate in its parts and requires much more attentive and careful management than can possibly be expected to be given when in general use on a Canal, that its parts are subject to frequent derangement, and the repairs consequent thereon will be very heavy, and the trade of the Canal frequently stopped.

"The Statements that have been given of the expence of erection and repairs are too low while the Statements of the Expence of Locks and the supply of Water by Steam Engines are exaggerated. .... Should the necessary powers be obtained from the Legislature to construct Reservoirs in the Situations I have seen and examined, I have no fear that an ample Supply of Water will be obtained with economy to the Company and advantage to the Mills."

The wise decision to finish the canal with locks was ratified at the following Assembly on 2 July 1811. By this time the Committee was quite satisfied that plans for three supply reservoirs, and possibly four more, submitted by Mr Bevan, Engineer to the Grand Junction and Union Canal Companies, were viable, as it had been reported that there was plenty of surplus flood water available on the River Rea, also much waste water flowing over the canal weirs on the summit at times, and "The summit of 14 miles, 6 feet deep, is of itself a Reservoir from which 1500 Locks may be drawn without impeding the Canal."

STORM DAMAGE TO THE LIFT
By the time of this July Assembly, William Ward Eagle had resigned from the Canal Committee and the lift had been struck by lightning and damaged. The latter event occurred at about 11.30 pm on 27 May and, as reported in Berrow's Journal, was

witnessed by Joseph Hughes, a brick-maker, who "was coming towards Tardebigg Wharf along the canal bank towards the lift building when, when he was 4 yards off and near the Strapping Post, he saw a flash of lightning in the building. This was followed by the clap of thunder and a violent crash in the building." He called to William Smith, a carpenter who was employed in working the lift and who slept in a room adjoining the lift building. When they entered the building they found the lift in a damaged state and a considerable smell of sulphur. Outside, water was seen to be flooding over the towpath and over the new embankment, so they ran beyond the Old Wharf to the drawbridge to shut the stop-gate to prevent the embankment being washed away. According to Smith, the lift had been in perfect order at 10 pm the same night. The Committee, on 5 June, ordered that "The Perpendicular Lift be not repaired", but they were overruled by the July Assembly which resolved "That the Lifting Machine now erected at Tardebigg be repaired under the direction of Mr. Woodhouse the Inventor, and that he be paid the Sum of Sixty Pounds and no more for repairing the same."

USE OF THE LIFT DURING CONSTRUCTION
OF THE TARDEBIGGE FLIGHT

Earlier, in February 1811, the contract for cutting the canal from the lift to Body Brook in the Parish of Hanbury, and for building the locks, bridges, culverts, etc. in that section, had been advertised, and Woodhouse, who had submitted the lowest tender, was awarded the contract. Because of this he was replaced as Engineer, in August 1811, by William Crosley. During the next four years he was busy on this stretch of the canal and the lift was used by him at times for moving materials to the pound below it. It was Crosley who reported to the Committee in July 1813 that the lift was "again broken and unserviceable." The damage this time had been caused through the ignorance and neglect of the man employed by Woodhouse to assist in passing boats through the lift. Through his mismanagement of the paddles, water had rushed through the lift and flooded over the banks of the Canal below it and threatened the canal works beyond. Only swift action by Crosley, who was nearby, averted a more serious disaster. Woodhouse was given permission to repair the lift at his own expense for the purpose of passing the materials he might want for the completion of his contract, but not until he had given the Company sufficient security to indemnify them against any damage which might occur to the canal works or to neighbouring property by any further accident to the lift. This event served to convince the Committee that the lift was too dangerous and unreliable to be retained and used on the completed canal, and Woodhouse was given notice that he would be required to give up the lift with all materials to the Company on or before 1 June 1814, to allow for its removal and other necessary works to replace it.

THE DEMOLITION OF THE LIFT AND DISPOSAL OF ITS PARTS

The following year, in August 1814, the Committee ordered the lift be dismantled, the roof to be brought to Birmingham to be used in roofing a warehouse to be built there, and the machinery also to be brought to Birmingham to be sold by auction. In September the Committee changed its mind and resolved "that the Roof of the Lift be conveyed to Worcester for a Warehouse intended to be built there instead of Birmingham as before directed." Apparently parts of the dismantled lift still lay around at Tardebigge, where the deep lock was made in its place, until June 1815, for on the 21st of that month the Committee resolved "That the Metal Materials of the Lift be brought to Birmingham without delay and deposited in the Company's Warehouse." Finally on 21 November 1815, a few days before the canal was officially opened, the Committee instructed one of their number, Mr Mabson, "to dispose of the Iron materials of the Lift upon the best terms he can."

So ended the saga of the Woodhouse Lift which, for four years, was in operation on the site of the present Top Lock at Tardebigge on the Worcester and Birmingham Canal. It had worked tolerably well, but it lacked the robustness, the simplicity and reliability of the common lock, which, with little change, still serves its purpose on the canal today.

Chapter 8

THE COMPLETION OF
THE CANAL, 1811-15

THE INVOLVEMENT OF JOHN WOODHOUSE AND WILLIAM CROSLEY

Following the unanimous decision of the January 1811 Assembly that the canal should be completed with locks and not lifts, the Committee was determined, despite the delaying tactics of some supporters of lifts, that construction work should go ahead forthwith. On 14 February 1811 the following advertisement appeared in Berrow's Worcester Journal:

> "TO CANAL CUTTERS AND LOCK BUILDERS.
> Persons willing to Contract for cutting the Worcester and Birmingham Canal, from near the Lifting Machine at Tardebigg to Body Brook in the Parish of Hanbury, and for Building the Locks, Bridges, Culverts, and other Masonry on that part of the Canal, are requested to deliver their Proposals, sealed up, at the Company's Offices in Birmingham by the 27th day of February instant, where a Plan and Specification of the Works may be seen; and also at Mr. Woodhouse's, the Company's Engineer at Tardebigg. To facilitate the Works, the Company have provided a quantity of Bricks, Stone, and Timber, which the Contractor must take at the Amount those Articles have cost the Company, or at a Price that may be agreed upon, and the Contractor must be prepared to find sufficient Security. The Works to be completed by the 1st day of March 1812, or any earlier or later period that may be agreed upon by the Contractor and the Committee."

For this five-mile section of the canal, with its many locks, the lowest tender received was from the resident engineer John Woodhouse. Like his predecessor, Thomas Cartwright, he had decided that it was perhaps more fulfilling and profitable to be responsible for the actual construction work, rather than just the supervision of it. On 27 February 1811 he was awarded the contract. His appointment was to take effect from July. However, the Committee decided that he could not, like Cartwright, continue also as engineer, and this was endorsed by the Assembly of 2 July. The Company now had to find another resident engineer, and John Rennie was asked to recommend one. Rennie's choice was William Crosley who was interviewed by the Committee and appointed on 7 August.

Crosley's father, also called William, of Brighouse in Yorkshire, had been assistant surveyor and resident engineer under Rennie for both the Lancaster and Rochdale Canals. He had died in 1796. Following in his father's footsteps, William Crosley junior was in 1802 appointed resident engineer to the Rochdale Canal which opened in 1804, and then to the Brecknock and Abergavenny Canal, during the latter stages of its construction. He came and supervised the completion of the W/B Canal from Tardebigge to Diglis until the Spring of 1815, living at Tutnall, not far from Tardebigge New Wharf. Later, from 1817 he worked on the Kendal Extension of the Lancaster Canal, became superintendent of the whole canal in 1820 and engineered the Glasson Branch (completed in 1825). From 1826 he was engineer to the Macclesfield Canal which opened in 1831. His 3½ years as resident engineer to the W/B Canal were not the happiest of his career as he faced delays, difficulties, and, towards the end, criticism from the Committee, but the detailed progress reports that he produced for the Assemblies of January and July 1814 and January 1815 showed great competence on his part.

The Committee must have had great confidence in John Woodhouse to have awarded him the contract for the whole five-mile stretch from Tardebigge to Hanbury with its many locks. That confidence soon began to evaporate, however, when he failed, in spite of repeated requests, to produce a report of the work he had done as engineer and an account of the materials he had purchased. At the July 1812 Assembly it was reported that nearly £2,000 had been lost due to "gross negligence" on his part through his failure to keep a proper check on the brick-makers and the quantity and quality of their bricks. As we shall see, as the work proceeded on this section, Woodhouse was taken to task for defects in the structure of locks and bridges, for his unwillingness to admit and put right these defects, and for slow progress. It is not surprising that he did not take kindly to his work being closely examined and criticised by Crosley, his successor as engineer, and this may have accounted, to some extent, for his obstinacy. The 1 March 1812 completion date in his contract was, of course, hopelessly unrealistic, but faults in the structures on his section were, in the end, largely responsible for the delayed opening of the canal in 1815. Unfortunately his experience and expertise as a contractor did not match up to his ability and ingenuity as an engineer. He ran into financial difficulties and, in the end, had to enter into arbitration with the Company over payment for his contract.

CONSTRUCTION WORK FROM TARDEBIGGE TO HANBURY

Construction work on the Tardebigge to Body Brook section began in the autumn of 1811, after the marking out of the line and the purchase of the land. In order to convey materials on this downhill section of the canal, the Committee, on 8 January 1812, ordered "That a Railway be forthwith laid by the side of the intended Line of Canal from a Wharf lately made for the purpose of loading Stone near the End of the Summit at Tardebigg down the Lockage to Sugar Brook, and that Cast Iron Rails and all other necessary Materials be provided for that Purpose where they can be had upon the best Terms." The Horseley Iron Works, Tipton, offered to deliver 150 tons of cast iron rails, each 3 feet long and weighing 40 lbs, at a total cost of £1387.10s. These would have been needed for a single track tramroad 2½ miles long from Tardebigge down to Stoke Pound. Lack of further reference to this tramroad in the Canal Company's minutes suggests that it was probably never constructed. (See Chap.13)

During 1812 Woodhouse was busy with the excavation work, starting from Tardebigge and continuing in the autumn through and beyond Stoke brickyard. Construction of locks and bridges began after the winter frosts in the spring of 1813. By the summer of 1813 the top seven locks were in use for work-boats, together with the lift. On 22 September 1813 it was reported to the Committee that Woodhouse had not been using Hey Head lime in the construction of the locks, as

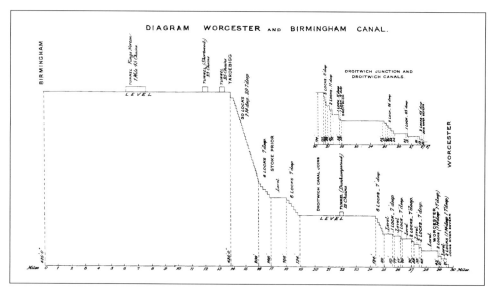

Profiles of the W/B and the Droitwich Canals produced by the SND Company. Strangely, the Edgbaston Tunnel is omitted and the figures given for the changes in level provided by the top lock at Tardebigge and the four bottom locks at Worcester are not correct.

per his contract, and he was ordered to rebuild them. A fortnight later Messrs. Francis, Lea and Mabson of the Committee reported that the bridges built and building by Woodhouse "are not according to Specification and that he be directed to pull down such Bridges and to erect others in all respects according to the Specifications annexed to his Contracts." Two months later, in December, the Committee, hearing that Woodhouse had not complied with the notice to pull down certain bridges over the locks but had been building other bridges similar to those directed to be pulled down, ordered Crosley to halt the work on Woodhouse's contract. Due to the severe winter, work ceased anyhow along the whole line of the canal. In January 1814 Crosley reported that "Between Tardebigg and Body Brook the Brickwork of twenty-nine Locks is finished except about 30,000 Bricks, the Gates are all in the Locks, but not yet fitted." Work had still to be started on the last mile which included the Astwood flight of locks. By April 1814 Woodhouse had been allowed to carry on, but was now forbidden to use the seven top locks for his work-boats because of damage that had been caused by them. To the July 1814 Assembly Crosley reported that "The Brickwork of 35 of the Locks agreed to be built by Mr. Woodhouse will be finished this Week and the Gates in their places, there will be 6 bridges finished and 4 more in a forward state; he will then have six Locks and 6 Bridges to begin; in these Locks and Bridges, including the 4 Bridges in progress, will be 1,600,000 Bricks to lay including the masonry; he has also 33,000 Cubic yards of Earth to remove; the Digging will require 60 Men and 10 Horses eleven weeks, and the Brickwork will require 50 Bricklayers. I found on the Work this morning 66 Diggers 7 Horses & 37 Bricklayers, Masons and Labourers, exclusive of those employed in hauling and providing Materials." The Committee now began to get more and more impatient of slow progress on this section of the canal and critical of the workmanship. Woodhouse was threatened with dismissal, and in October payment to him was suspended pending a thorough examination of his works. In December Crosley reported to the Committee that the locks, pounds and other works were far from complete and Woodhouse was urged to speed up the work.

Back in May 1814 the Committee had instructed Crosley to prepare a plan of a lock or locks to replace the boat lift. To have constructed two 6-feet locks and the pound between them would have required considerable earth moving and more expense than replacing the lift with a single 12-feet lock with a side pond. So Messrs. Spooner and Perkins of the Committee were deputed to go and inspect locks with side ponds on the Trent and Mersey Canal near Stone. As a result, the single deep lock was agreed on by the Committee on 19 July. The dismantling of the lift and the construction of the lock and side pond began in August and was completed in January 1815.

CREATING THE FIVE-MILE POUND

The line of the Five-mile Pound from Body Brook to Offerton had been staked out as early as May 1810, and Woodhouse had been instructed to sink one or more pits along the line of the tunnel at Dunhampstead Hill "to ascertain the strata". It was decided to advertise for contractors to cut this section in five lots each of length one mile. In July 1810 agreements were made in advance with Messrs. Heminsley, the contractors working on Bittell Reservoir, to cut lots 1 and 2, (i.e. the two-mile length at the Hanbury end), with Joseph Smith, who was then finishing the Tardebigge Tunnel, to cut lot 3 which included Dunhampstead Tunnel, and with Charles Holland to cut lots 4 and 5 (i.e. the two-mile length at the Offerton end). In September and October 1810 a detailed survey was made and a plan produced with the names of the owners and occupiers of the land needed. The chief landowners were Mr Phillips of Hanbury Hall, Mr Amphlett of Hadzor and the Dean and Chapter of Worcester Cathedral. Negotiations began with these in November 1810 and continued well into 1811. There is no record of work carried out on the Five-mile Pound in 1811, but some preparatory work, including the approach cuttings to the tunnel, must have been done, for on 24 January 1812 proposals by Joseph Smith for finishing Dunhampstead Tunnel were

Near the north end of the Five-mile Pound the W/B Canal crosses Body Brook. Top: On the off-side of the canal the overflow into Body Brook. Below: Body Brook culvert and the overflow waterfall.

received by the Committee, and Crosley was instructed to prepare the necessary contract. In February an agreement was made with George Rew for building the bridges and culverts on the Five-mile Pound. Smith did some work on the tunnel, but in May it was reported in the Committee minutes that "George Rew, having laid before the Committee proposals for finishing the work lately undertaken by Joseph Smith and abandoned by him", it was resolved that Rew's offer be accepted and a contract made with him. George Rew was a competent and experienced bricklayer who had worked on the construction of the lift at Tardebigge in 1809 and had been employed by the Company in 1811 to oversee the brickmakers and check the quality of their bricks and then, later, to report on the brickwork of Woodhouse's locks. He finished the brickwork lining of Dunhampstead Tunnel in about two months, it being reported on 4 July 1812 that the tunnel was almost completed.

Other developments on this section in 1812 included the takeover by William Tredwell of Messrs. Heminsley's contract for lots 1 and 2, agreement with the Commissioners of the Turnpike Road between Droitwich and Hanbury for diverting the road temporarily whilst the canal bridge was constructed, and instructions to Charles Holland to raise the banks to a height of 7 feet on the towpath side between Trench Lane and Offerton. In July 1813 Crosley reported that the whole of the Five-mile Pound was nearly completed and almost ready to be made navigable, but in January 1814 work still remained to be done south of Dunhampstead Tunnel, and Samuel Frost & Company's proposals to complete the embankment and puddling between Trench Lane and Offerton for £359 was accepted. By July 1814 this had been done and three boats were being built by James Taylor alongside the canal near the Droitwich to Hanbury Road for conveying materials from there to Offerton for work on the canal between Offerton and Blackpole Green. But two bridges north of the Hanbury Road still remained to be finished by Richard Jones, who had been a contractor on the West Hill Tunnel. The Company was saved from building a third accommodation bridge when Mr Phillips of Hanbury Hall accepted £80 in lieu. The last bridge to be built on this section was put in hand as late as 21 June 1815 when the Committee resolved "That a Bridge for foot passengers be forthwith erected over the Canal in the Parish of Hadzor in the line of the Footpath leading from Huntingdrop to Droitwich." This is the so-called "Coffin Bridge", the only original brick-built narrow foot-bridge on the canal.

FROM OFFERTON TO DIGLIS

The line from Offerton to Diglis had been staked out by Woodhouse in May 1811, and plans and sections prepared by him. Negotiations with landowners were entrusted to Messrs. Carden and Wall of the Worcester Committee. In July 1811 the late Mr Dent's land at The Blockhouse came up for sale and they immediately stepped in and bought the part needed there for the canal and wharves. In August Samuel Hodgkinson, Engineer of the Birmingham Canal Company and brother of

John Hodgkinson the W/B Canal Company's Clerk, was asked to mark out the canal through Sansome Fields to the River Severn, including the proposed wharf at Lowesmoor. He had been given leave by the Birmingham Company to assist with the surveying of the W/B Canal in 1810 and he continued to do so from time to time. Whilst negotiations with other landowners were proceeding, work began on Dent's land already acquired, as reported in Berrow's Journal of 30 April 1812:

> "On Wednesday last workmen began cutting that part of the line of this Canal which runs in the neighbourhood of this City; the spot on which they have commenced is a piece of land which adjoins the Commandery."

No contractor had yet been engaged for this section of canal, so the work undertaken was probably a propaganda measure of limited scope, intended to provide visual evidence to Worcester citizens that the canal was arriving at long last.

By the middle of April 1813 Crosley had produced detailed plans and sections of the four lots into which this section from Offerton to Diglis had been divided for cutting the canal, and an advertisement addressed "TO CANAL CUTTERS, LOCK AND BRIDGE BUILDERS &c." appeared in Berrow's Journal of 22 April informing would-be contractors that "The Length from Offerton to the Severn is about five Miles three Furlongs, in which there are intended to be twelve Boat and four Barge Locks, about twenty Road and Occupation Bridges, several Culverts &c." Plans, specifications and conditions could be inspected either at the Company's office in Birmingham or at Mr Crosley's at Tutnall near Tardebigge, and proposals, on printed forms provided, were to be in by 10 May. On 10 May the Committee met and awarded only two contracts, one to William Tredwell for cutting lot 4 from Blockhouse Fields to the Severn, and the other to Charles Holland for building the four barge locks, one turnpike bridge, two occupation bridges and one culvert in lot 4. In order that work on this lot might proceed, the Committee set to work immediately to buy the required land as well as the houses and other buildings to be taken down in crossing Sidbury Street. It was not until 15 September 1813 that contracts for lots 1, 2 and 3 were awarded after further advertisements, Charles Holland to do the cutting and bridge building in lot 1 at the Offerton end and also the building work in lots 2 and 3, William Tredwell to cut lot 2, and Samuel Frost & Co. to cut lot 3. It appears that there were not at that time many willing contractors to choose from.

On 15 September 1813 the Committee made important decisions concerning the locks and the location of basins in Worcester. The original plan had been for four barge locks from the River Severn up to basins and wharves on Inglethorpe's Meadows on the south side of Lowesmoor. But in April 1811 Woodhouse had been ordered to "ascertain the greatest height to which the Water has ever been known to rise in time of Floods from the River Severn over Diglis Meadows" and to report on "the practicability of making a Bason and Wharf out of Floods way in Diglis Meadows .... in case the whole of the Transhipments between Boats and Barges were to be made there." No decision was then made, but two years later Crosley was asked to investigate further the feasibility of basins at Diglis. Following his favourable report, the Committee now decided that two barge locks only should be constructed between the river and two basins to be made at Diglis, each basin to be two acres in extent, one intended for coal and the other for merchandise. The other two locks up to Lowesmoor were to be narrow boat locks.

This was not quite the end of the matter, for early in 1814 negotiations with Mr Tymbs, the owner of Inglethorpe's Meadows, over the proposed basin ran into difficulties and in March Mr Knapp's land on the north side of Lowesmoor was viewed as a possible alternative. In June plans for the basin and wharf on this new site were drawn up and the necessary land acquired, and in July applications from contractors were invited "for the Completion of the Basons, Wharves and other Works" at Lowesmoor.

As to progress on this section, Crosley reported to the Assembly on 4 January 1814 that "From Offerton to Blockhouse Field the Cutting is about one fourth of it done, and Bricks, Stone, Timber and other Materials are providing upon the Ground for the purpose of forwarding the Locks when the building season commences. From Blockhouse field to the Severn the Work is about one half of it finished." It was then confidently predicted by Crosley and the Committee that the canal would be completed by Michaelmas that year. But this was not to be. On 5 July 1814 Crosley reported that, of Charles Holland's contract from Gregory's Mill to the Severn, the two barge locks and only one of the four boat locks and two of the bridges were nearly finished. The digging between Offerton and the Severn was in a forward state but, due to the severity of the winter (in January and February the Severn had been so thickly frozen that dancing and tea-parties had taken place on it) and the wetness of the spring, the brickwork had been much retarded. Charles Holland had run into difficulties with money, manpower and materials, and in May had asked to be released from his contract; he was allowed more money and urged to employ more workmen. And, as we have seen, there were delays on other sections, especially with Woodhouse's contract.

In June and July 1814 advertisements appeared in the press for contractors to undertake the making of the wharves and basins at Diglis and Lowesmoor. Samuel Frost & Co. were awarded the contract in June for building a wharf and puddling a basin at Diglis. The name of the Lowesmoor contractor is not recorded, but it was probably George Rew. In September, the Committee ordered that a start should be made on building the wharves, machine houses and lock houses from Tardebigge to Worcester and, in particular, at Lowesmoor a weighing machine and machine house with dwelling attached. After the usual lull in bricklaying in the winter months, work on these resumed in the spring, and in May 1815 the Committee resolved "That the Wharfs, Machine Houses and Warehouses between Tardebigg and Worcester be completed without delay and that seven Lock Houses be built."

FINANCIAL PROBLEMS AND EVENTS IN THE EARLY MONTHS OF 1815

At the Assembly on 3 January 1815 Crosley reported: "The Lock substituted for the lift is finished except the Paddles for the Side Pond. The Pond between this Lock and Mr Woodhouse's first Lock is not yet finished and will require three Weeks longer with the same strength as is now employed. The Brickwork and Masonry of the whole of his Locks and Bridges are finished, but there wants some of the Racks for drawing the Paddles and some of the Forebays to be repaired. A number of his Locks and Ponds also require cleaning and some of the Banks raising and strengthening, and the greatest part of his gravelling and fencing is also unfinished." Crosley also reported that between Body Brook and Offerton the embankment of some of the valleys needed raising and strengthening and the towing path needed gravelling. From Offerton to the Severn the locks and bridges were practically finished but 800 lineal feet of towing path coping and 1100 feet of parapet coping remained to be done. The wharf walls were finished, except the coping at Stoke and Hanbury Wharves, and the machine house at the latter was ready for its roof. The walls of the basins at Lowesmoor and Diglis were ready for coping.

Although the canal was evidently nearing completion, the Committee wisely sounded a note of caution, advising that the opening should be delayed a few months to allow recent work sufficient time to settle and to enable adequate provision of wharves, warehouses and other amenities to be made. The Committee had great pleasure in informing the Assembly that, after much discussion, agreements had been reached with the Birmingham Canal Company for a "Navigable Communication" across the Bar and for a supply of water from them "at a moderate expence", and a Bill would be presented to Parliament by the Birmingham Company for these measures. On the financial front, however, there was bad news. In spite of raising an extra £40,000 by 1000 debentures of £40 each early in 1813, as permitted by the 1808 Canal Act, the W/B Company now owed its Treasurers John Startin and William Smith, bankers of Birmingham, £27,000, others £5,000, and needed £7,000 more to finish the canal and provide for the traders. It was proposed that application should be made to Parliament for a Bill to permit the raising of further money sufficient to pay off the debts and finish the canal, also to authorise the construction of two reservoirs near Wychall Reservoir in Birmingham to supply the canal with water, and to fix the tolls on cargoes from the River Severn to parts of Worcester.

Due to the financial situation, final construction work on wharves, basins, warehouses etc. was slowed down during the early part of 1815 whilst the Bill to raise more money was passing through Parliament. To enable essential work to continue, ten prominent shareholders, including Thomas Carden, lent the Company £300 each at the January Assembly, on condition that the money would be repaid with interest out of the first monies raised by the intended Act.

Crosley's task of supervising the completion of the canal from Tardebigge to the Severn was now almost at an end, and he departed early in 1815, whether voluntarily or compulsorily, as an economy measure, is not recorded. His salary was in arrears and he had to wait for payment until June the following year. On 18 January the Committee ordered "that Mr. Crosley be required to deliver into the Company's Offices all Plans, Sections, Specifications, Books and Papers in his possession belonging to the Company." His last recorded duty was in February when he and George Rew were asked to report separately in what respects Woodhouse had broken his contract. In the following months of 1815, after Crosley's departure, Samuel Hodgkinson, the Birmingham Company's Engineer, was called in, from time to time, to advise and report on the final work being done on the canal.

In February 1815 the Committee began to put pressure on Woodhouse to speed up work on his section. The Company's solicitors were instructed to warn him that "unless he do immediately employ an additional number of Workmen and use greater Exertions than he has yet done for completing his Contract, the Company must take legal proceedings against him and his Sureties without delay." In April the solicitors again wrote listing all his works not yet completed. At last, on 10 May, the Committee hearing that the whole of the canal from Tardebigge to Diglis was navigable, applied for Samuel Hodgkinson to come and survey Woodhouse's section, especially the locks, and they resolved "That the Committee go in their Boat on Friday morning next at Six o'Clock to view the Work."

THE FIRST RECORDED PASSAGE OF THE CANAL TO WORCESTER

On Friday 12 May, two days after their meeting, members of the Committee set out early, as planned, and made the first recorded passage along the canal from Tardebigge to Worcester. As reported in Berrow's Journal of 18 May:

> "The first boat that has completed the trip by the Canal from Birmingham reached this City on Friday evening last; several Gentlemen belonging to the Committee were on board; and the voyage was completed within the space of eight hours. We understand that, from the arrangement now nearly completed, the most sanguine expectations are formed that this undertaking will be open, for the conveyance of goods, merchandise, &c. about Midsummer."

As it would have been impossible for a horse-drawn boat to have travelled all the way from Birmingham in eight hours, the point of departure was evidently Tardebigge. The Committee boat probably brought some members of the Committee from Birmingham the previous day, and they and others who made the trip to Worcester stayed overnight at the Plymouth Arms, Tardebigge, ready for the 6.00 am start. A Bill for £105.0.4½d. received from the Plymouth Arms was, a few months later, ordered by the Committee to be examined, and what was owing to be paid "in due course."

THE STOP-LOCK AGREED ACROSS THE WORCESTER BAR

On the same day as the epic voyage to Worcester took place, 12 May, another long-awaited and welcome event took place, as reported in the same newspaper:

> "The Act for establishing a navigable communication between the Birmingham Canal Navigation and the Worcester and Birmingham Canal received the Royal Assent on Friday last."

It had been a long struggle, for from 1792 onwards applications had been made from time to time to the Birmingham Canal Company for an agreement to breach the Bar, and for a supply of water. Final negotiations began in the summer of 1814 over compensation tolls to the Birmingham Company and the cost of water and, as the agreed Bill went before Parliament in February 1815, various proprietors of the W/B Company organised petitions in favour of it on the streets of Birmingham. The stop-lock across the Bar was to be constructed by the Birmingham Company at an estimated cost of £2,300, and it would be owned and maintained by that Company. It would have four gates, two at each end, to prevent the flow of water through the lock whichever canal had a higher level than the other. If the difference in levels should be more than 6 inches, then the water lost by one company to the other due to the passage of boats had to be measured and paid for, the rate being three shillings per 4,000 cubic feet of water passing through the lock. The additional tolls to be paid in compensation to the Birmingham Company were to be 4d. per ton on coal and other merchandise passing through the lock either way, and a further 4d. per ton on coal and coke passing from the W/B Canal into the Digbeth Branch of the Birmingham Canal; also wharfage rates of 2d. per ton on coal and coke from the W/B Canal landed at any of the wharves of the Birmingham Canal, and 4d. extra per ton on coal or coke conveyed more than five miles along the Birmingham and Fazeley Canal. Construction of the Bar lock began straight away and it was ready for use by August. Messrs. Boulton and Watt were approached in July to supply apparatus for measuring the amount of water passing through it.

THE 1815 W/B CANAL ACT

The next piece of good news for the W/B Canal Company was the passing of their own Parliamentary Act for authority to raise enough money to pay off their debts and to complete the canal with wharves, warehouses, weighing machines, cranes and lock houses ready for the trade. The Act received the Royal Assent on 7 June 1815 and gave the Company powers to raise up to £90,000, either from the existing proprietors by creating up to 2,250 new shares of £40 each, or by granting annuities, or by mortgage of the tolls and rates. The Act also gave permission for the construction of two reservoirs in the parishes of Northfield and Kings Norton for supplying the canal with water, and it returned to the Company land for these reservoirs which had been purchased prematurely, and therefore illegally, in April and had been forfeited to the Crown, with the proviso that if the debt of £27,096.10.4d due to their Treasurers was not paid by 29 September 1815, the land for the reservoirs would be sold to discharge the debt. Another provision of the Act was the fixing of new tolls, consequent upon the decision to make basins at Diglis and Lowesmoor instead of, as originally intended, just one basin in Worcester at Inglethorpe's Meadows. The tolls were to be 4d. per ton between Sidbury and the Severn and 6d. per ton between Lowesmoor and the Severn.

In view of the urgency of raising the necessary money as soon as possible, the Assembly of 4 July endorsed the Committee's recommendation "that the Sum of £36,000 be raised by Annuities at the rate of £10 per Cent upon every hundred Pounds advanced for 99 Years payable half yearly and redeemable by the Company after the expiration of three years'. To the probable dismay of many impatient shareholders, the Committee sounded a note of caution, stating that they were not prepared to declare the canal open until "the Works were tried and found to be properly executed" and all preparations had been made for the accommodation of the traders. The Committee also reported to the Assembly their belief that the Birmingham Canal Company had sufficient surplus water to be able to provide an adequate supply to the W/B Canal and that reasonable terms could be agreed between the two Companies. There was therefore no urgent necessity for the construction of the supply reservoirs in the Northfield area.

FINAL PREPARATIONS FOR THE OPENING OF THE CANAL

As the high-interest annuities attracted new money, so the final work on the canal was put in hand and the Company's debts paid. The Committee obtained permission from the Birmingham Company in July for Samuel Hodgkinson to survey the canal works from Tardebigge to Worcester. He was evidently not happy with some of Woodhouse's locks, and in August John Rennie was invited to come and examine them, but he declined to do so, possibly because of Crosley's involvement and premature departure. Mr Potter of Lichfield was then called in. Some of the locks were found to be defective, and by October three of them, nos. 15, 20 and 27 (numbered from the

Birmingham end and now numbered 44, 39 and 32), had given way, and needed to be rebuilt. Various modifications were ordered to be made, the size of paddles reduced to 15 inches square, Gornal stone was to be used "at the Coins and Forbays", and two sills made at the head of each lock instead of one. The barge locks at Diglis in Charles Holland's contract were not finished until September with the installation of the paddle gear and paddles, but in October some defects in these locks were found and ordered to be put right. It was a good thing the Committee had taken the precaution of not allowing the canal to be opened until it was judged to be entirely safe.

Not anticipating these constructional delays, the Company advertised in the press, at the and of June and the beginning of July, as follows:

"WORCESTER AND BIRMINGHAM CANAL NAVIGATION.
To Canal Carriers, Traders, &c.

The above CANAL will be OPENED for the purpose of Navigation in a very short time. Any Carriers or Traders intending to come upon the Line may be accommodated with Warehouse Room, to a certain extent, in the public Warehouse belonging to the Company either at Birmingham or at Worcester; or should they prefer building private Warehouses, may be accommodated with Land for that purpose, and for Wharfs adjoining the Basins of the Canal, by application to Mr. Hodgkinson at the Company's Office at Birmingham. N.B. The Basin at Worcester is immediately adjacent to the deep Water of the River Severn."

At Worcester the Company was constructing two warehouses of its own on the east side of the inner basin at Diglis, and one similar warehouse at Lowesmoor. Applications were soon received from Messrs. Skey, Small & Co., Mr George Ryder Bird and Messrs. Crowley, Hicklin & Co. for accommodation in the Diglis warehouses, and their tenancy was agreed at a rent per annum of 7½ per cent of the building costs. Messrs. Pickfords were to be accommodated on the same terms in the Lowesmoor Warehouse until a warehouse of their own was built there. Their own premises were ready before the delayed opening of the canal, and by then G R Bird was renting part of the Lowesmoor warehouse. Boat lengths and stacking ground for coal had also been allotted to various coal dealers both at Diglis and Lowesmoor Basins by this time. At Hanbury Wharf, in reply to an application in October from a Mr Horseley of Droitwich for a private wharf, the Company made it clear that the wharf there was to be a public one.

Other work carried out ready for the opening of the canal included the provision of cranes, two of wooden construction from Mr Nickolls of Birmingham for the warehouses at Diglis Basin, and two iron cranes from the Eagle Foundry, Broad Street, Birmingham, one of 5 tons SWL (Safe Working Load) for the Lowesmoor warehouse, the other of 10 tons SWL for the south-west corner of the Diglis Basin. These cranes were transported by canal to Tardebigge and from there overland to Worcester. Walls, fencing and gates were erected for protection at Lowesmoor and Diglis.

In November the Committee ordered seven lock houses to be built, under the direction of Samuel Hodgkinson, at various locations, also a temporary house at Diglis for the ticket clerk and lock-keeper. In March of the previous year Crosley had been directed to report to the Committee the number and situations of the lock houses necessary to be built between Tardebigge and Worcester and to provide specifications for the design of a lock house. The decision was made that there should be one lock-keeper for every six locks along the canal, with the exception of the four locks at the Worcester end.

Appointments of lock-keepers, machine clerks and toll clerks, were made in November 1815. They included John Hunt to attend the Blockhouse and Sidbury Locks, Richard Rowlands to attend Gregory's Mill and Astwood Locks, and John Gilbert the six Offerton Locks. The wharf weighing machines at Hanbury and Stoke Wharves were put in charge of John Bolding and William Blount. Francis Cocks was appointed ticket clerk at Diglis, with orders to keep account of vessels passing between the river and the basin, their weights and loading, and to issue tickets with the name of the owner, the steerer, the load, where loaded, and the distance travelled on the W/B Canal; and he was to make a return weekly to the Company's office in Birmingham. Many of the men appointed as lock-keepers, weighing machine and toll clerks were probably chosen from those who had given good service in connection with the recent construction work on the canal.

At long last, the Company was able to announce in the newspapers, in a notice dated 4 November 1815, that "The Worcester and Birmingham Canal will be OPENED, for the purposes of Navigation, from Birmingham into the River Severn below Worcester, on MONDAY the 4th DECEMBER next." and that "There is a commodious Basin near the Junction with the River at Diglis below Worcester, where Severn Vessels and Canal Boats may tranship their Cargoes; and a navigable Communication with the Birmingham Canal is now open."

THE CANAL OPENS TO TRAFFIC

Of the opening of the canal on 4 December 1815, Berrow's Worcester Journal gave, perhaps due to lack of space, only brief details:

> "OPENING OF THE WORCESTER AND BIRMINGHAM CANAL.
> This event took place on Monday. About half past 10 in the morning of that day several boats started from Tardebigg, and between 5 and 6 in the evening the first of them arrived at a wharf near Sidbury, adjoining this city. Several boats afterwards arrived; among others was one of Messrs Pickfords, with a cargo of goods, and which has already started again with another cargo for Manchester."

The Worcester Herald was rather more informative, giving an impression of the enthusiasm with which many of the citizens of Worcester greeted the first boats to arrive:

"Monday being the day fixed by public advertisement for the opening of the Worcester and Birmingham Canal, a large concourse of people assembled at the different locks and bridges, near this city, for the purpose of witnessing the ceremony of the first passage of the various boats. Several of these vessels started from Tardebigg between the hours of ten and eleven on that morning, and the first, which was Mr. Vaughan's, in Sidbury, laden with coals, arrived at its destined wharf, a little before six in the evening. This was followed by some others, shortly afterwards, amongst which was one with a cargo of goods, and which has since departed again, with a fresh cargo for Manchester. There was a band of music, a profusion of shouting, and a discharge of cannon and small arms, and the scene altogether was as lively as could be desired."

Home News.

FRIDAY EVENING, DECEMBER 8.

Monday being the day fixed by public advertisement, for the opening of the Worcester and Birmingham Canal, a large concourse of people assembled at the different locks and bridges, near this city, for the purpose of witnessing the ceremony of the first passage of the various boats. Several of these vessels started from Tardebigg between the hours of ten and eleven on that morning, and the first, which was Mr. Vaughan's, in Sidbury, laden with coals, arrived at its destined wharf, a little before six in the evening. This was followed by some others, shortly afterwards, amongst which, was one with a cargo of goods, and which has since departed again with a fresh cargo, for Manchester. There was a band of music, a profusion of shouting, and a discharge of cannon and small arms, and the scene altogether was as lively as could be desired.—We may now congratulate our readers on the completion of this stupendous work, and we anticipate, with much pleasure, the numerous benefits which it is calculated to entail off this city and its neighbourhood. A direct water communication is thus opened from the north of England to Bristol and other parts of the west, and we need not dilate upon the important consequences of such a communication to the commerce of the divers towns within the reach of its influence. That this canal will prove an accommodation of great consequence to the public, it will be unnecessary to state, and we therefore earnestly hope that it will at last amply reward those who have embarked their capital in an undertaking of such national importance.—The first act for the cutting of this canal was passed on the 9th of June, 1791.

The report in the Worcester Herald of the opening of the canal to Worcester on 4 December 1815. (WRO)

The owner of the first boat, Thomas Vaughan, was the landlord of the King's Head Inn, Sidbury, situated next to the road bridge and lock and with a small farm adjoining, stabling, and a large yard able to receive up to 300 coaches, gigs, waggons or carts; he had a coal business and his own canal wharf. With regard to the "band of music", an elderly lady, Mrs Footman of Worcester, widow of a boatman whose forebears had been boatmen on the canal, told me she had heard that, on the day the canal opened, the Worcester Brass Band played from Tibberton to Worcester.

The general euphoria consequent upon the opening of the canal continued and, a fortnight later, crowds gathered to welcome the first Severn trow to enter Diglis Basin. As reported in the Worcester Herald of 23 December:

"The advantages of the new Canal begin already to be sensibly felt by the public, and there is an appearance of bustle and activity in the basins, wharfs, &c. that presents a favourable idea of the extent of commerce which this grand undertaking has produced. It will be seen by the advertisements that Messrs Bird, Barnett, Meaby, and Barnett, have established a warehouse at Diglis for the reception of every species of property, which they immediately forward to all parts of the kingdom; and other wharfingers are also using all possible exertions to complete the requisite buildings for the same purpose. There will be a competition, therefore, highly favourable to the public, and we trust that ample compensation will redound to the parties thus busily engaged. - The first boat that came down from Birmingham was Mr G.R.Bird's, which delivered a cargo of goods to Messrs. Barnett, Meaby and Co.'s trows for Bristol and the West of England. Yesterday evening the Neptune, registering 90 tons burthen, belonging to Mr. J.Soule, of this city, arrived from Bristol with a full cargo of merchandize for the North, (being the first trow that has entered the basin at Diglis since the opening of the Canal,) under a salute of cannon and music, and amidst the congratulations of an immense concourse of the inhabitants."

Thus, within two or three weeks of the opening of the canal, the interchange of cargoes between canal and river boats at Diglis Basin was taking place, and the canal was set to transform the business and commercial fortunes of Worcester and improve the transport of coal and other goods between Birmingham and the North and Worcester and the South West, as its promoters, a quarter of a century earlier, had anticipated. Of these promoters, Thomas Carden had been a tireless supporter and Committee Chairman throughout the long years, and it must have been a great satisfaction to him in particular to see the canal at last completed and in use. Other promoters, amongst them Thomas Hooper and Wilson Aylesbury Roberts, did not live to see this happen, and the man who surveyed the canal, John Snape, died a few days after its opening, on 1 January 1816.

Chapter 9

RESERVOIRS AND
WATER SUPPLIES

ACTION BY THE RIVER REA MILLOWNERS

The Act of Parliament for the W/B Canal had stipulated that immediately after the waterway was made over the River Rea the Canal Company should make three reservoirs for the sole use of the owners and occupiers of the mills on this river and its tributary the Bourn Brook. Similarly, as soon as the canal was made over the River Arrow, two reservoirs for the use of the mills on that river were to be made. The canal was actually made and in use over the River Rea at Kings Norton in 1796, but there was no attempt on the part of the Canal Company to make the required reservoirs at that time, partly because the first priority was to finish the West Hill Tunnel and the canal as far as Hopwood, and partly because there was no money then available for the making of any of the reservoirs. The millowners were no doubt aware of the financial difficulties of the Canal Company which held up further construction work on the canal from 1797 for several years, but by 1803 their patience was exhausted and they threatened to take legal action.

Faced with this threat, the Assembly of 5 July 1803 proposed to apply to Parliament for powers to raise money for making the reservoirs as well as for extending the canal to Tardebigge, A Special Assembly held on 29 July ratified the decision to apply for the Act of Parliament and agreed "That the Reservoir on Mrs. Hankins's Estate, mentioned in the original Act, be made without delay and that the Clerk do send Mr. Bedford, the Solicitor for the Mill Owners, a Copy of this Order." Thomas Cartwright had been instructed to estimate the cost of constructing this reservoir at Wychall. His estimate of £949.19s.9d. was considered and approved by members of the Committee on 30 July and they ordered "That the Clerk do prepare an Article with Mr. Cartwright for making such Reservoir at the sum of £950 to be finished by next Lady Day." The clerk was also instructed to negotiate with the agent of Mrs Hankins for the purchase of the land.

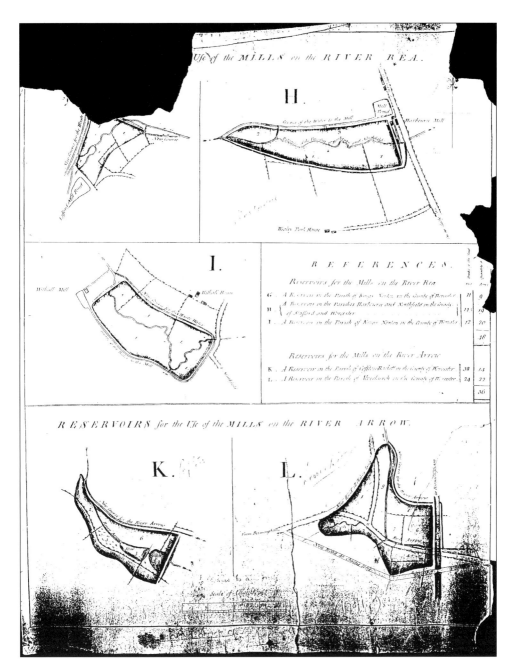

John Snape's original 1804 plans of the five reservoirs to be made for the millowners on the Rivers Rea and Arrow, top left Lifford, H Harborne, I Wychall, K Cofton, L Lower Bittell. (NWMT)

However, negotiations for the 20 acres of land needed, which had been occupied by John Green, took some time; the money for Cartwright to pay for labour and materials was not available; and it was not until February and March 1804 that copies of the plans of the reservoirs were obtained from John Snape for an agreed £3.13s.6d. The millowners, impatient at this delay and with the prospect, so far, of only one of the reservoirs being made, obtained through their solicitor a Writ of Mandamus (i.e. a High Court Order) from Westminster. This, dated 8 February 1804, quoted the clauses in the 1791 Act relating to the reservoirs, admonished the Canal Company for neglecting and refusing to make them despite divers applications having been made by the millowners, and commanded the Company to make and complete forthwith all three reservoirs with the necessary pipes, leaders, gutters and weirs,

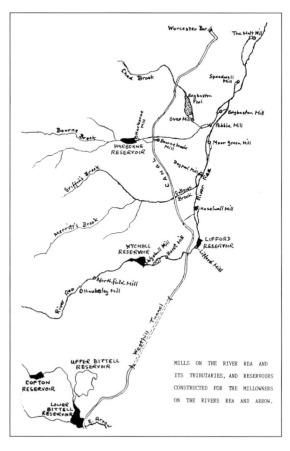

Outline map showing mills and reservoirs constructed for the benefit of mill-owners on the Rivers Rea and Arrow.

so that water could be fed into the River Rea, as and when required. The Company would default in their duty at their peril. The legal costs of the Mandamus, amounting to £101.3s.6½d, were later charged to the Canal Company.

ACTION BY THE CANAL COMPANY:
WYCHALL RESERVOIR CONSTRUCTED

Following the publication of the Mandamus, the Canal Committee on 8 March 1804 ordered that "As the Reservoirs for the Mills on the River Rea must be made with all possible dispatch, and the Application to Parliament for powers to raise Money for payment of the Company's Debts and making the said Reservoirs will be attended with considerable Expence, and there being very little money in the Treasurer's hands,

- That the Treasurer discontinue the Payment of the 5/- in the Pound to the Company's Creditors 'til further Orders." Following the Royal Assent to the Act on 23 March and the receipt of income from Calls on the shares authorised, work on Wychall Reservoir accelerated and it was probably completed by the end of the year. As with all these reservoirs for the millowners, the river was diverted to one side of the reservoir, and pipes, leaders, gutters and weirs were installed so that flood water could be diverted into the reservoir and water let out when the millowners, at meetings called for the purpose, decided by a majority vote that it should be done. In the case of the River Rea mills, all the millowners from Wychall Mill to Lloyds Slitting Mill in Birmingham, inclusive, were entitled to vote.

At the Assembly on 3 July 1804 it was resolved "That the Committee be empowered to contract for the making of the Reservoirs for the use of the Mills on the Rivers Rea and Arrow and for completing the Canal to the deep Cutting at the north End of Tardebigg Tunnel." The following day Cartwright, having, in anticipation, already prepared estimates for these works, delivered them to the Committee and it was decided that he should be contracted with to make the reservoirs and to complete the canal to the north end of Tardebigge Tunnel.

HARBORNE RESERVOIR

A draft agreement was made with Cartwright in October 1804 for making the reservoir at Harborne Mill, and in January 1805 the contract was signed and the 19 acres of land bought from the landowner, Jervoise Clarke Jervoise Esq. who had shares in the canal, for £760.10s. Cartwright was not to be charged tonnage on materials for the reservoir transported along the canal. Although there is no minute to the effect, it is likely that Harborne Reservoir was completed in 1806. There is no record in the minutes of the amount paid to Cartwright for executing this contract.

LOWER BITTELL RESERVOIR

The next reservoir to be started was at Bittell for the River Arrow mills. On 2 January 1805 the Committee ordered "That Mr. Cartwright prepare the head of the Reservoir at Bittell Valley at the same time that the Canal is made across the said Valley." This Reservoir, on the estates of John Waldron, Thomas Horton, Philemon Baylis and Michael Biddulph, was to cover 22 acres when completed. Part of it was excavated to provide the earth for the canal embankment across the valley which must have been completed in 1806. In July 1807, three months after the opening of the canal to the Old Wharf at Tardebigge, it was reported to the Committee that three-quarters of Bittell Reservoir had been made, but in the light of events this was probably a gross over-estimate. It was intended that the remainder should be tackled when the harvest was over. However, due to lack of money, this was not done, and it was not until November 1808, following the Act to raise more money, that the Committee decided that the making of the reservoirs on the River Arrow should be recommenced in the following March. On 15 March 1809 John Woodhouse was asked to value the work already done by Cartwright at Bittell Reservoir and advertisements were put in newspapers for contractors to submit proposals for completing this work. On 10 May the offer of John Heminsley of Cheslyn Hay, Cannock, to complete Bittell Reservoir in one year for £540 was accepted. Heminsley and Sons began work at the beginning of November following a survey and the staking out of the reservoir by John Woodhouse and John Hodgkinson. A request was received from River Arrow millowners that the river should flow through the reservoir and not round it, but the Committee ruled on 6 December 1809 that the watercourse should be made beside the reservoir as the 1791 Act had directed. The following June it was reported that Heminsley and Sons were behind schedule in their contract for the reservoir. In September Woodhouse was instructed to complete the new course of the River Arrow from where it emerged from under the canal on the east side of the embankment at Bittell to communicate with the original course of the river. It was not until 24 April 1811 that Bittell Reservoir was reported to be finished.

A recent aerial photograph of Lower Bittell Reservoir showing the canal embankment and Jacob's Cut with, at the junction, the lengthsman's cottage. (Andrew Stumpf, BW)

LIFFORD RESERVOIR

Steps to construct the third of the reservoirs for the River Rea millowners at Lifford in the Parish of Kings Norton, partly on land belonging to Thomas Dobbs and beside his Metal Rolling Mill, were not taken until 1809, probably because of the Company's longstanding dispute with Dobbs over land encroachment and avoidance of tolls. In May 1809 Woodhouse was requested to set out the reservoir as soon as possible. This request was repeated in July. It appears that Dobbs had refused to allow any work to begin on his land until it was paid for. In September, on being asked the price of the five acres or so of his land needed, he demanded £230 per acre for the meadowland and £120 per acre for the rest. He was offered £150 per acre regardless. Mr Tomkins who owned the rest of the nine acres needed was offered and accepted £130 per acre. On 1 January 1810 the Committee ordered "That Mr. Snape be applied to go with Mr. Woodhouse with his, Mr. Snape's, original Plan of the Reservoir at Kings Norton near Mr. Dobbs, and that the said Reservoir and the Watercourse be staked out according to such Plan exactly." Dobbs was not prepared to accept the Company's offer for his land and therefore obstructed the marking out of the reservoir. However the Committee persisted and in March asked the Company's accountant clerk, Mr Hodgkinson, to assist Snape in staking out the reservoir and in providing a plan for those who wished to tender. Dobbs remained obstructive, and in May an intended advertisement for contractors to tender for the work had to be postponed because Dobbs still refused to accept the Company's offer and he elected to argue his case before the Commissioners who were duly summoned to meet on 28 June at the Shakespeare Tavern in Birmingham. In October the Committee again ordered Woodhouse, with Snape's assistance, to mark out the reservoir. This may have been achieved, but the contract was not advertised because of the legal wrangle between Dobbs and the Company which was not settled until 7 December 1810, when a jury of the Commissioners met in Bromsgrove at the dwelling house of George Healey and gave a ruling in favour of the Company, which was also granted legal expenses. These expenses were disputed by Dobbs and it took two more years for them to be settled by the Commissioners.

The members of the Canal Committee were probably relieved at having to wait for over a year until asking Woodhouse's successor, William Crosley, in February 1812, to negotiate for the making of the reservoir at Lifford. No outside contractor was engaged, and the reservoir was apparently constructed under Crosley's direct supervision. In July 1812 good progress was reported. By April 1813 flood gates had been installed by the side of the reservoir to allow Dobbs to flood his meadow. In January 1814 Crosley reported to the Assembly that the reservoir was finished "except a part of the leaders for supplying it with water, and this may be done in about six weeks."

COFTON RESERVOIR

The last of the five reservoirs for the millowners to be completed was at Cofton Hackett, on the River Arrow upstream from Bittell. It was to cover 14 acres of land formerly owned by Rebecca Lowe and Edward Seager at the time of the 1791 Act, but now belonging to Michael Biddulph of Cofton Hall. The water was to be contained by a straight embankment, and the Arrow diverted round the reservoir so that Cofton Mill and other mills downstream would receive as much water from the rivulet and a spring as before. In March 1810 Woodhouse was ordered to make a survey of the reservoir and estimate its cost. It was staked out and an advertisement for contractors to deliver their proposals appeared in the newspapers in mid-April. On 25 April Woodhouse reported to the Committee that great difficulty was anticipated in making the embankment at Cofton because of the sandiness of the soil there, and the millowners were to be informed and consulted about the problem. No further action was reported for almost two years. Then in February 1812 Crosley was asked to re-survey the reservoir and he must have proposed some solution such as heavy piling for the embankment. In January 1813 proposals by William Bassett for making the reservoir were accepted, but by June he had not made a start and the Committee ordered the contract to be re-let on the same terms. There was no re-advertisement of the contract, so it seems likely that Crosley took on the supervision of work on the reservoir, as he had done at Lifford. He reported to the Assembly of 4 January 1814 that "The Embankment of the Reservoir at Cofton is finished and the Fencing will be done in the course of the Spring. It is probable that the face of the Bank will require stouring, as it is composed entirely of Sand, but this will be best seen after it has been filled with water." In April 1814 the Committee ordered the brickwork at Cofton Reservoir to be completed forthwith. So the reservoir was evidently finished that year, and before Crosley's departure early in 1815. However, there seems to have been some dispute with the landowner over the size of the reservoir, and some ancillary work remained to be done, for in March 1816 the Committee ordered that Cofton Reservoir was to be reduced to the size required by the 1791 Canal Act, the head was to be reduced and strengthened with ling, and leaders and gutters were to be completed without delay.

WATER SUPPLIES FOR THE CANAL

The construction of reservoirs for the millowners, as required by the 1791 Act, had been done reluctantly and at considerable cost, whilst the Company was continually short of money and anxious about its own water supplies and how they could be obtained. Although, as the first sections of the summit level were completed in 1793, water had been obtained from the Birmingham Canal to fill it, the Birmingham Company continued to be against the provision of supplies to the W/B Canal for the eventual working of its locks, and for this reason dragged its feet over allowing a lock across the Worcester Bar. However, following negotiations with neighbouring canal companies, a Bill was eventually presented to Parliament in 1806 by the Birmingham Company for the removal of the Bar. The W/B had submitted a scheme in the Bill for an engine, worked by manpower, horses or steam, to raise in 12 hours from the canal with the lower level the water required for passing boats through a Bar stop-lock in 24 hours, the water being stored in a reservoir at a slightly higher level nearby. The Bill was opposed by the Dudley Canal Company and by Birmingham merchants and manufacturers, fearing it would cause an increase in the price of coal, and it failed.

The Birmingham Company obtained most of its water by pumping from disused coal pits alongside its canal and had more than it needed, as John Rennie soon found when he was called upon to survey and report on the Birmingham Canal and its water supplies. He was also consulted by the W/B Company in September 1808 over its water supply situation and gave it as his opinion that the Birmingham Canal Company could supply the W/B with water on much more reasonable terms than it could be pumped from the Severn by steam engines, provided that the Birmingham Company was agreeable. At that time the Birmingham Company was not agreeable, so the W/B Company had to face the trouble and expense of having to pump water up in stages from the River Severn.

In January 1809, with the last part of the construction of the canal hopefully about to begin, the W/B Committee ordered Thomas Cartwright "to investigate the Tunnels needed and the heights Water is to be raised by Steam Engines and the possibility of a Reservoir on the Shell Brook for the long level." In the following October the Committee ordered one of its members, Mr Haynes, to apply to different engineers to enquire "on what terms they will erect Engines to raise water out of the Severn to supply the Canal, and the Expense of working the Engines." A letter dated 16 October 1809, written by John Hodgkinson to Messrs. Boulton and Watt of Soho, near Birmingham, outlines the plan to raise water 428 feet from the Severn to the summit level of the canal in three stages by steam engines at a rate of 60, or alternatively 80, locks of water per day, and asks for estimates of the cost of supplying and installing the engines and the running cost per year, the engines to be erected at locations 14 miles, 16 miles and 20 miles from Birmingham. This letter, now preserved in the Boulton and Watt Collection in Birmingham Reference library, has superimposed notes, made by the recipients, calculating the number of cubic feet of water to be raised per stroke of each engine at 12 strokes per minute and with an 8 feet stroke. A year later, in October 1810 the Committee gave their approval to the proposals and estimates of Boulton and Watt. Of the three engines to be used, one was to be situated at North Claines to raise water 130 feet from the River Severn nearby to the level of the Five-mile Pound, one at Hanbury to raise the water 149 feet to a reservoir at the level of the pound between the locks now numbered 37 and 38 (the second pound below the Halfway lock cottage), and one at Tardebigge to raise water the final 149 feet to the summit level. However, the contract was not proceeded with, for, no doubt deterred by the estimated great expense of creating, maintaining and fuelling this pumping scheme with its system of channels and subterranean culverts, the Committee were relieved to consider a viable alternative put forward by Rennie and supported by Woodhouse. This was to obtain an Act of Parliament authorising the making of reservoirs in the parishes of Northfield and Kings Norton in Birmingham. With the hope of achieving this, and also of getting an agreement with the Birmingham Company for water, the scheme to pump water up from the Severn was shelved, together with the idea of using boat lifts instead of locks.

The W/B Company was now anxious to put pressure upon the Birmingham Canal Company over the Bar and water supplies, and at the January 1811 Assembly it was resolved that the Committee should apply to Parliament for its own Act "to enable the Company of Proprietors of this Canal to open a navigable Communication between the Birmingham and the Worcester and Birmingham Canals", and they were given power to add the Company's common seal to any petition in favour of the application. In March various carriers, traders and manufacturers were being approached to organise and sign petitions in favour of the Bill. However, due to lack of support, the Bill was soon dropped. This abortive attempt to breach the Bar must have soured relationships with the Birmingham Company, for three years elapsed before further negotiations between the two companies were reported. Eventually in February 1814 a letter from John Houghton of the Birmingham Canal Company gave news of two powerful steam engines being erected upon a pond at Cappenfield near Bilston which would provide a large supply of water and might produce a surplus. In April 1814 negotiations over the Bar and water supplies were resumed and focussed mainly on the tolls to be charged on goods passing from one canal to the other and on charges for water. By the end of the year a compromise had been reached, and early in 1815 the Birmingham Company's Bill for "Establishing a navigable Communication between the Birmingham Canal Navigations and the Worcester and Birmingham Canal, and amending certain Acts relating thereto", was presented to Parliament. The Bill was passed and it received the Royal Assent on 12 May 1815. The Act included conditions that the Bar Lock connecting the two canals should be constructed, owned and managed by the Birmingham Canal Company; it prescribed the tolls payable to the B.C.N. by boats passing either way through the lock; and it stipulated that if the level of one of the canals was six inches or more above that of the other then it would be entitled to claim compensation for loss of water when boats passed through the lock at a rate of 3 shillings per 4,000 cubic feet. (For further details see chapter 8).

Four years earlier, in 1811, B Bevan, engineer to the Grand Junction and Union Canal Companies, had been commissioned to draw up plans for three supply reservoirs, and possibly four more, in the Northfield and Kings Norton areas, as proposed by Rennie. In May 1811 he submitted these plans, and it was reported that even that old antagonist Thomas Dobbs of Lifford, now described as "an intelligent Mill Owner", had admitted that there was plenty of surplus flood water available in that region. Also, James Wolfindale, the lengthsman, reported that a great deal of water from the canal flowed to waste through weirs in wet weather, and it was stressed that "the Summit of 14 miles, 6 feet deep, is of itself a Reservoir from which about 1500 Locks may be drawn without impeding the canal."

Nothing more was done about the proposed reservoirs until August 1814 when the Committee invited Bevan to accompany them to inspect their locations and to explain how they would get their water. In January 1815 the Assembly took the Committee's advice that it would not be wise to rely entirely upon the Birmingham Company for water supplies in future, and that therefore permission to construct reservoirs should be sought in their intended Parliamentary Bill. In their case in support of the Bill, it was stated that "In the Vale of King's Norton, immense quantities of flood water are collected at times, which greatly obstruct the working of the Mills on the River Rea, and which, if diverted for the use of the Canal, would supply the same, and benefit the Mills." It was proposed therefore "to enlarge and appropriate the present Reservoir at Witchall, made for the use of the Mills, to the use of the Canal; to make another Reservoir near to Witchall Reservoir for the use of the Mills, containing as much water, capable of being drawn off, as Witchall Reservoir will supply; and to make an additional Reservoir near to Witchall, for the use also of the Canal."

Unfortunately, well before their Act was passed and received the Royal Assent on 7 June 1815, the Company in April went ahead and bought the land needed for the extra two reservoirs, paying £3,500 to Mr Attwood for 29 acres and £1,850 to Mr Shorthouse for 14 acres. As this was in contravention of the 1791 Act, the land was forfeit to the Crown. The new Act, which authorised and prescribed the reservoirs, as well as permitting the raising of new money and the adjustment of tolls, also stated that his Majesty had remitted the forfeiture, and the Company was empowered to retain the land in question provided that their debt owing to their treasurers was repaid by 29 September next, otherwise the land would be sold to pay that debt. By the time of the Assembly on 4 July, three weeks after the passing of the Act, the Committee reported that they had "every reason to believe that the surplus Water of the Birmingham Canal Company will be amply sufficient to supply this Canal with Water". So there was no need to construct the proposed new reservoirs, at least for the time being. By January 1818, three years after the canal's completion, it had been decided that the reservoirs were not needed and the land acquired for them was sold by auction.

MAINTAINING THE WATER LEVEL AT DIGLIS BASINS

Once the canal was open there was a problem at the Worcester end since the two barge locks passed a large volume of water from the Diglis basins into the river. Normally enough water flowed over the weirs, as well as through the locks, higher up the canal to supply the Diglis basins, but not in time of drought. To deal with such an emergency the Committee in 1817 decided to obtain a steam pumping engine for Diglis and, after inspecting several elsewhere, they resolved in October "that a patent pump equal to raise 700 gallons per minute be ordered. That Mr. Beale be requested to order the same and that he require it to be delivered without delay." The building of an engine house began in November, and in January Messrs. Percival Jones of Bilston were paid £200 for a Whimsey Engine. This engine was situated on the south side of the pound between the two barge locks and used, when needed, to pump water up from the river into the basins. In July 1819 the Assembly was informed that, as there had been much rain, the Diglis engine had been little worked. In July 1820 an engineer, Daniel Greenway, was engaged to work the engine at Diglis and maintain it at 3s.6d. per day of 12 hours, Joseph Nicklin the lock-keeper to keep him informed when water was required. In 1821, to save water, it was decided to equip the barge locks with side ponds, and in April William Tredwell was instructed to complete the excavation and puddling of these side ponds for £400. The use of the ponds must have saved almost 50% of the water previously passing through the locks and have greatly reduced the need for working the pumping engine.

AGREEMENT FOR WATER SUPPLIES FROM WYCHALL RESERVOIR

When the W/B Company sold its land intended for reservoirs in the Vale of Kings Norton in 1818, the canal's water supply seemed more than adequate, it having been reported at the July 1817 Assembly that, in spite of three months drought, "the supply of water was equal to the Trade of the Canal." However, as trade increased by about 10% per year and more and more water was needed, the Birmingham Company began to be awkward, as was reported to the January 1821 Assembly. The Company now looked for ways and means of minimising their dependence upon the B.C.N. for water. One way would be to construct their own supply reservoirs. Another would be to try and persuade the millowners to relinquish their exclusive rights to water from their reservoirs and allow surplus flood water to feed into the canal; the two most suitable reservoirs for this being Wychall and Cofton, both above the level of the canal.

Early in 1821 the millowners on the River Rea were approached, and on 9 August "A Meeting of Proprietors and lessees of Mills and Lands upon the River Rea" was held at the Public Office in Birmingham, attended by Mr Samuel Tertius Galton, Mr Dobbs, Mr Bedford on behalf of Heneage Legge Esq., and Mr Chance on behalf of

James Taylor Esq. They considered a report from their surveyor, Mr Francis Giles, concerning the abundance of surplus flood water flowing over the weirs and head level of Wychall Reservoir and the proposed line of a feeder from the head level of the reservoir to the canal, nearly one mile in length and with a fall of 16ft 6in. They agreed this feeder on condition that there should be a locked floodgate under the control of a servant of the millowners, to be called the "Weir Keeper", paid for by the Canal Company; that the Canal Company should pay for the construction of the feeder under the supervision of Francis Giles; that a committee of five of the millowners should give directions to the weir keeper; and that the agreement could be ended by a majority vote of a meeting of the proprietors and lessees of the mills. On the following day, 10 August 1821, the Canal Committee met and accepted these proposals. But in view, no doubt, of the expense and the conditions imposed, the feeder was not actually made until many years later, in 1836.

TARDEBIGGE RESERVOIR

During 1821 the former plan for reservoirs in the Vale of Kings Norton was resurrected, but this, besides needing the re-purchase of the land, also required an Act of Parliament, as it would otherwise have again contravened the 1791 Act. By January 1822 this idea had been dropped in favour of making a reservoir at Tardebigge, complete with an engine to pump water up to the summit level, and this needed no Parliamentary sanction.

The Tardebigge Reservoir, to be made on the site of the claypit and brick-kilns near Dial House Farm, used in making the canal, was intended to hold 5,000 locks of water and was estimated to cost £5,000. Across the middle of the site there was a small stream which marked the boundary between the parishes of Tardebigge and Stoke Prior. By July 1822 the land had been purchased from Mr Brettell and others, a contract entered into, and work had begun. The contractor for the reservoir and the embankment was Mr McIntosh. In September another contract was made with Jonathan Heaton for making the engine pit and headways. In October the Committee resolved "That the Horseley Iron Company's offer for erecting an Engine at Tardebigg for £2052 for the use of the Company agreeable to Mr. Batham's Specification be accepted." The engine was to be of 50 HP and was to be installed by the end of March 1823. It and its boiler would have been transported, in parts, by canal from the Horseley Works at Tipton. In February 1823 the Committee ordered that the brick culvert, 3 feet in diameter, from the engine to the summit level beyond the top lock should be completed without loss of time. By March 1823 the reservoir was ready to receive 30 to 34 feet depth of water and hold about 1,000 locks. By the following July it was reported nearly finished and containing plenty of water, and by the end of 1823 it held 3,500 locks and the engine was performing well. However, after a period of heavy rainfall there was some anxiety over the safety of the embankment, so it was ordered to be strengthened at a further cost of £1,500.

During 1824 the reservoir was deepened to increase its capacity and the dam was strengthened after the extra land required was obtained from the Earl of Plymouth who now owned it. By January 1825 the reservoir and the engine were in use, and this must have reduced appreciably the demand for water from the B.C.N. However there was still work to be done on the reservoir to raise its capacity to around 5,000 locks by strengthening and raising the embankment still further. McIntosh now seemed very reluctant to complete his contract but, after about twelve months delay and much exasperation on the part of the Committee, he did so. By the end of 1826 the work was completed, including the repair of culverts through the base of the embankment which had given way.

A recent aerial photograph of Tardebigge Reservoir and part of the Tardebigge Flight of locks down from the New Wharf with, in the foreground, Patchett's Farm (Andrew Stumpf, BW)

More water was still needed. In November 1826 George Rew, now Clerk of Works, was asked to examine the possibility of a second reservoir "below the present one at Tardebigg sufficient to hold 5,000 Locks of Water, with an Embankment sufficiently strong to be raised to allow from 1,000 to 10,000 Lockfuls more if the Trade requires it." A month later this idea had been abandoned in favour of raising the embankment of the existing reservoir by a further 20 feet. In April 1827 Mr Jacob, a Birmingham surveyor, was engaged to draw up a plan of the extra land needed, but no further steps were taken as problems soon arose with the embankment which, by April 1828, had subsided 2 feet 7½ inches, as reported by

George Rew. McIntosh was now summoned to meet the Committee of Works at the reservoir, but failed to turn up; he was traced to the Plymouth Arms Inn, whence, because of an eye infection, he refused to go to the reservoir. At a later meeting he was told "to put right the embankment". Following remedial work, pits were sunk in August, by George Rew, below the embankment to check for any leakages of water. At that time Rew was paid £50 "for his great exertions and the accuracy of his estimates and surveys, leading to a very material saving on the expenditure of the works in supplying the canal with water."

Finally, in December 1831 the Committee decided upon a feeder from Tardebigge Reservoir linking an existing culvert through the base of the embankment, which was originally intended to discharge surplus water into the stream which had been dammed to make the reservoir, with the canal. This brick culvert, of the same cross section, followed the contour, curving round the hill, to feed into the canal under the wing wall below the bottom gates of the lock now numbered 43, by the "Halfway House". Water could be let out of the reservoir through the base culvert by a valve which was operated from the top of the embankment by rotating a long spindle running down the dam face. Another valve in a manhole at the end of the base culvert was operated to divert the outflow either into the stream, or via the culvert into the canal.

Tardebigge Engine House before its conversion into licensed premises.

All the reservoir culverts had a series of brick-lined access pits, some of them 3 feet square, others 5 feet in diameter, with manhole covers, to allow maintenance; and some of them had valves to control the flow. The pit in the engine house was about 100 feet deep, this being the maximum height the water needed to be raised by the steam engine when the level of water in the reservoir was very low.

ENLARGEMENT OF LOWER BITTELL RESERVOIR

As plans to raise the level of Tardebigge Reservoir were being considered and rejected in 1827, another idea, to extend and raise the level of the existing Bittell Reservoir, was also under consideration, and on 30 April the Committee decided to ask Mr Jacob to draw up plans for this and of the land needed. The go-ahead was given and by September 1827, under George Rew, the work was reported as making progress and the workmen involved were to be given £5 each "as a Mark of the Committee's approbation of their Conduct and Exertions." The January 1829 Assembly heard that the Bittell extension had earlier been completed at a cost of £200. This enlargement of the reservoir was obviously done not just to benefit the River Arrow millowners, but it must have been carried out with their approval, either to compensate them for the intended use of Cofton Reservoir as a canal feeder, or with a view to pumping surplus water up from the reservoir to the canal when needed. The enlargement of the reservoir involved raising the water level and the creation on the opposite side of the road near Bittell Farm of a new small reservoir known as the Mill Shrub linked to Lower Bittell by a valve and channel under the road.

UPPER BITTELL RESERVOIR

In 1829, with trade on the canal continually on the increase and more and more water needed, a new location for a reservoir was suggested behind the existing Bittell Reservoir. This was to be above the summit level of the canal and would therefore not require pumping to deliver its supplies. In November 1829 an experienced engineer, Edward Boddington, was paid £50 for attending at Bittell and Tardebigge Reservoirs, presumably to advise the Company and to survey this new reservoir. On 6 July 1830 the Assembly heard that a treaty had nearly been concluded to make this reservoir extending over 80 acres of land. It would be fed by three small streams which drained surrounding farmland and by a culvert conveying water, as needed, from Cofton Reservoir. It would contain about 10,000 locks of water and cost about £2,000. The Assembly agreed that work should start on it as soon as possible.

On 27 August the Committee of Works approved a "Section and Specification for raising an Embankment for making a Reservoir in Bittal Back Valley". Instead of advertising for a contractor, it was decided to invite tenders from Mr Paddington of Stockton, Mr John Wolfindale and Mr Edward Gale. Of these, John Wolfindale had been long employed by the Canal Company as a contractor for general works and maintenance. In September, Boddington himself submitted a tender to complete the work for £2,790.14s.9d. and this was accepted and a contract signed. John Wolfindale and Edward Gale who had also tendered were each given £5 in compensation for their trouble in preparing estimates.

Boddington lost no time in commencing the work. In November he was paid £250, the first of many such instalments, for work done and for materials. On 24 December he promised to have the reservoir ready to hold 1,000 locks by the following 1 March, provided barrows could be used, instead of carts, in unfavourable weather. Work proceeded apace and the July 1831 Assembly heard that the reservoir was "in a state of forwardness". It had been in use in the spring, and the contractor was praised for his efforts. In May the reservoir had been fenced by William Shippey at a cost of £21.8s.9d. By January 1832 it contained 6,000 locks of water and the embankment was still being raised. The whole work was successfully completed in November 1832, with a 30ft depth of water, having taken just two years, and it was to be the main source of supply for the canal in the future. The following April, 1833, a cottage was ordered to be built on the south-west bank of the reservoir for a resident attendant.

Because Upper Bittell Reservoir, as it came to be called, tended to get low in time of drought, whilst Lower Bittell often had a surfeit of floodwater, a decision was made in 1835, evidently with the agreement of millowners on the River Arrow, to install a steam engine to pump water up from Lower Bittell to Upper Bittell, as and when required. A large Boulton and Watt engine was chosen, costing £3,270, and a contract signed in November 1835. There is little information about its installation in the Canal Company's minutes, but letters from the Company's Clerk, John Hodgkinson, to Mr Hamilton of the Boulton and Watt Company (now in the Boulton and Watt Collection at Birmingham Reference Library) provide interesting details. In January 1836 Mr Hamilton came over "to set out the Engine House" and the location of the pit, or well, that was to be sunk. It turned out to be a wet spring, and this hampered construction work, but ensured sufficient water in the Upper Reservoir for the summer, so building work on the engine house could await longer daylight hours and more favourable weather. By April 1836 a branch canal "as far as the level of the land extends" was almost finished, enabling bricks and other materials and coal for the steam pumping engine to be delivered by boat. This canal arm came to be known as Jacob's Cut, having been surveyed by Henry Jacob of Birmingham who was also engaged by the Canal Company on other surveys about this time. Where the road from Barnt Green to Hopwood crossed this canal arm a wharf was made and used for the unloading of coal for neighbouring farms and dwellings as well as for the pumping engine. In October 1836 Messrs Boulton, Watt & Co. were sent a cheque for £1,500 on account of the engine furnished, but it had not been assembled and set up by then, and various parts were still needed in December. On 21 March 1837 Hodgkinson wrote to

Upper Bittell Reservoir and Engine House. Sluicegates in a chamber at the end of Jacob's Cut enabled water to be pumped up either from Lower Bittell Reservoir or from the canal via a culvert to the base of the pumping well. (Ian Hayes)

Hamilton saying that bad weather was indicated "by the Glass" and urging him to send Wilkinson over to complete the engine house as soon as possible, so that pumping could begin from Lower Bittell to raise 1,000 locks, and, if enough flood water should be available, to fill the Upper Reservoir. The engine was evidently completed and used that Spring, but by October that year there were problems, so Wilkinson was again sent for to examine and work the engine, and it was found that the foundation of the pumps had given way and they were no longer working perpendicularly. Wilkinson was blamed for not seeing that they had been fixed upon a perfectly firm and solid foundation.

The engine and pumps at Bittell were only worked occasionally when the need arose, and it was usual for an engineer from Boulton and Watt to be sent for to service the machinery and work the engine. Thus, a letter from John Hodgkinson to the Boulton and Watt Company, dated 27 November 1838, requests "a proper man" be sent to Bittell as soon as possible to set the engine to work to pump about 3,000 locks of water up from the lower reservoir; coal had been provided and the Company's workmen were ready to assist; the lower reservoir was nearly full and from the appearance of the weather a further supply was expected shortly. A more urgent letter was sent to Mr Hamilton on 31 July 1839: "Please send someone to Bittal Engine to put it in working order immediately". One of the embankments of the canal had given way and Lower Bittell had not enough room to let the water off the canal fast enough. (This disaster happened at what is now known as the Bournville Embankment, which, following torrential rain, had given way; there was a month's stoppage of traffic on the canal whilst repairs were carried out under the direction of Edward Boddington.)

In 1842 a decision was made to raise the embankment and to increase the capacity of Bittell Back Reservoir. This work was carried out by a contractor, John Beck, during the latter part of 1842 and on into the summer of 1843 at a cost of £280. Two years later, in 1845, a new detached chimney stack was built to replace the original chimney at Bittell engine house

REGULATIONS FOR THE WATER
MANAGEMENT OF BITTELL RESERVOIRS

The two Bittell reservoirs, together with the Mill Shrub, Jacob's Cut, the pumping station and the River Arrow with associated streams and culverts, weirs and controlling valves, formed a complex flexible water supply system which could be regulated for the benefit of both the canal and the Arrow mills. In 1883 an agreement was reached between the SND Company and the millowners that (1) No water from Cofton Reservoir or from streams supplying the River Arrow was to be directed into the canal or into Upper Bittell Reservoir except when the water level of Lower Bittell was less than 8 feet below weir level, (2) The watercourses into Lower Bittell were to be kept clear, (3) Floodgates were to be kept locked in position, (4) Valves in the weir were to be lifted to supply the mills from 6 am to 5 pm each day but not on Sundays, but when Lower Bittell was full the valve would be lifted 3 inches, (5) When Lower Bittell was low in water it would be supplied from Cofton Reservoir, (6) If for any reason there was yet insufficient water in Lower Bittell to supply the mills, then water would be released from Upper Bittell to supply the mills through convenient watercourses.

These regulations were issued to Wm Barfleet & Sons representing the millowners and to the reservoir attendants at Bittell.

SUPPLEMENTARY WATER SUPPLIES

With the completion of Tardebigge and Upper Bittell Reservoirs and their associated pumping engines, adequate water supplies for the canal were assured for the foreseeable future. These supplies were supplemented by drainage and the release of floodwater into the canal at various locations. At Upper Gambolds halfway down the Tardebigge Flight of locks, a small reservoir was excavated to hold up to 150 lockfuls of surplus water running over lock weirs above it and it was used to top up, when necessary, the levels in pounds below it.

Eventually the Wychall Reservoir floodwater feeder, originally agreed with the River Rea millowners in 1821, came into use in 1836. This was after a survey for the feeder channel by George Rew in 1826 and the decision by the Canal Committee ten years later, in 1836, to carry out the work. Thomas Dobbs of Lifford had, in the meanwhile, died in 1827, leaving other River Rea millowners perhaps more cooperative than he had been.

THE REMAINING ENGINE HOUSES

As time went on, competition from the railways caused a reduction in canal traffic on the W/B and other canals in the latter part on the nineteenth century. As a result the pumping engines, especially the one at Tardebigge, needed to be used only on rare occasions. The last working of the Tardebigge beam engine was on a four-hour maintenance run in January 1914, the engineman being George Waring from the lengthsman's cottage by Lower Bittell Reservoir. It was dismantled, the engine and boiler broken up, and the metal taken for munitions in the winter of 1915/16 during the First World War. The Bittell engine was in use until about 1902, the last man to work it from 1897 being Henry Melley, a labourer from Parsonage Farm. It was eventually dismantled and scrapped by Thomas Ward of Sheffield in the 1930s. The remaining chimney stacks of both the Tardebigge and Bittell engines were demolished at about the same time in the winter of 1937/8. A proposal that the Bittell engine be replaced by an electric motor to work the pump was dropped due to the rapid decline in commercial traffic on the canal at the time. The two engine houses still stand, that at Tardebigge having been converted into a licensed restaurant, the Bittell one remaining as a ruin which, hopefully, may be preserved.

THE RESERVOIRS IN RECENT TIMES

Of the five reservoirs made by the W/B Company for the millowners two, Wychall and Harborne, were done away with in the 1950s. Water was let out of Wychall Reservoir permanently about 1958 and the site is now tree covered. However the canal can still be supplied with water from the rivulet there via a valve and the canal feeder through Kings Norton Park. For many years Harborne Reservoir was used for pleasure boating and fishing, but around 1957 this came to an end as the embankment was breached and water let out. Soon the south side of the reservoir was tipped over, and in 1973 a primary school, "Water Mill School", was built there, in addition to residential development. Much of the original dam of the reservoir survives behind a scrapyard on Harborne Lane, and a footpath runs beside the Bourn Brook, now back along its old course.

Lifford Reservoir remains intact. Now in the ownership of Birmingham City Council, it is open to the public and fishing permits are available.

In the early part of the nineteenth century the leases of Cofton, Upper and Lower Bittell and Tardebigge Reservoirs, with the ownership of the surrounding land, were acquired by the Hewell Estates. Much of this land, which included most of Barnt

Green, was sold by auction in September 1919. Cofton Reservoir was then leased to the West Midlands Transport Fishing Club. In 2004 local residents formed a company, Cofton Lake Conservation Ltd., to purchase the lease and prevent the surrounding area of the reservoir being built on by developers. British Waterways continue to maintain the headbank and valves of the reservoir and retain the right to run water from it straight to the canal or to replenish Upper Bittell. Upper Bittell, Lower Bittell and Tardebigge Reservoirs are also owned by British Waterways. All are used for fishing and Upper Bittell is used by a sailing club (see chapter 22). Tardebigge Reservoir can still supply water to the canal near the Halfway House via the brick culvert which was strengthened with a polyethylene pipe inside it in 1987. The flow of water to the reservoir from the canal is controlled by paddlegear beside the towpath above the reservoir lock cottage which allows water to cascade down into a stream below.

THE WATER MANAGEMENT OF THE CANAL

Following nationalisation and the disuse of the stop-locks at Gas Street Basin and Kings Norton, the summit level of the W/B Canal together with the Northern Stratford Canal and the main line of the B.C.N. comprise some 40 miles of waterway on the level which contain altogether a vast quantity of water and form a considerable reservoir shared by these three canals. This is kept topped up by a number of water supplies. These include water pumped from old mine shafts at Bradley and Bilston, the Chasewater and Rotten Park Reservoirs, Earlswood Lakes on the Stratford Canal and, feeding into the W/B Canal, water from Cofton and Upper Bittell Reservoirs and the Wychall feeder. On the W/B Canal water supplies are further supplemented by drainage into the canal, especially from adjacent Birmingham suburbs, also by releasing stored water from Tardebigge Reservoir, and by back-pumping, when necessary, from the Severn to Diglis basins and using pumps installed at the deep Sidbury and Blockhouse Locks.

The water management of the W/B Canal also includes the means of disposing of surplus flood water after prolonged heavy rain. At times this is more than the lock weirs can take. From the summit level much can be released into Lower Bittell Reservoir via the overflow weir at the Jacob's Cut end of the embankment. In addition there are valves and overflows at various places along the canal to allow quantities to escape into local streams.

The monitoring of the water levels of canals and reservoirs and control of the flow of water is being increasingly achieved by telemetric and remote control systems. On the W/B Canal these measures include the introduction of apparatus to operate remotely the electric pumps at the Sidbury and Blockhouse Locks and the storm paddles by Lower Bittell Reservoir.

Chapter 10

CONSTRUCTION WORK FROM 1815, INCLUDING THE DROITWICH JUNCTION CANAL

O ver the years a number of modifications and additions to the waterway and its structures have been planned and the work carried out. However several major schemes to construct linked canals or to convert the W/B Canal into a ship canal were abandoned for various reasons. Details of the plans for these are included as being, like the original project for a Stourbridge to Worcester canal, of historical interest.

INITIAL WORKS ALONG THE WATERWAY

Following the opening of the canal early in December 1815, the Committee met frequently to deal with initial problems, to monitor the state of the structures and to provide for the needs of the growing number of carriers. In the first few months of 1816 it was decided to erect further stables at both ends of the West Hill Tunnel and at various other locations, to build extra lock houses located at the Blockhouse in Worcester, at Bilford, Offerton and Gas Street Basin, and to consolidate the towpath at various places with gravel or with broken limestone from Dunhampstead. Padlocks were supplied to lock-keepers to prevent the use of the locks between 8.00 pm and 5.00 am, except by boats with special permits. To deter would-be vandals, fences were erected and watchmen were recruited to protect the wharves and the merchandise on them, especially at the Birmingham and Worcester ends of the canal. Every few months members of the Committee travelled the length of the canal to inspect and report on its state and its usage.

In January 1816 the Committee decided that the length of the canal should be accurately measured and that posts or stones with cast iron plates showing the distance from the Bar in Birmingham should be sited along the canal at intervals of one furlong (i.e. every one-eighth of a mile). In May this task was entrusted to

George Rew. These distance markers were necessary to prevent disputes over the tolls to be charged between places along the canal. The tolls were based on the mileage covered as well as upon the nature and weight of the merchandise carried.

In July 1817 the decision was made that all bridges should be numbered over the centre of the arches using white figures on a black ground, also that the locks should be similarly numbered, the numbering being from the Birmingham end. The renumbering of bridges and locks, as they are now from the Worcester end, took place some time after the SND Company took over. From references to bridges and locks in the half-yearly chief engineer's reports to SND shareholders, it appears that the renumbering took place around 1890. In the early 1900s some of the bridges and locks had their new numbers set into the masonry on precast concrete blocks, each digit being on a separate block. In the case of the locks, these blocks can be seen set into the wing wall below the mitre gates on the off-side.

One of the original stones with its metal plate marking the distance, 23 miles 4 furlongs, along the canal from Worcester Bar, Birmingham, to the location, later, of Grove's Hanbury Brickworks beside the canal. It was found in the canal and it is now displayed in the Waterways Museum at Gloucester. (NWMT)

DEVELOPMENTS AT DIGLIS

A few days after the canal was open, one enterprising boat-building firm, Charles Bird and Son of Stourport, applied to the W/B Canal Committee for permission to build a dry dock for an extension of their business at Diglis. Samuel Hodgkinson was instructed to meet Charles Bird to agree a location, and in March 1816 the Committee decided that he should have land adjacent to the upper barge lock at a rent of £7.10s. for twenty-one years. Work began on the construction of the dock, but in April 1817 it came to a halt because the Committee was not satisfied with it. In May the work went ahead under close scrutiny and with the proviso that water should not be let in until the Company's engineer gave the go-ahead. The dock was completed later in 1817 and it was used by Birds until 1847, and then by succeeding boat-builders. It was built large enough to accommodate sizeable river boats and it is still in use.

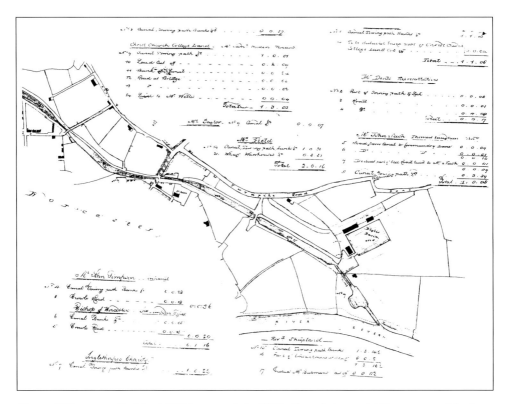

*Part of Ebenezer Robins' 1817 map of the W/B Canal through Worcester with the
names of the landowners and the area of their land acquired for the canal. At this
time the small outer basin had not been enlarged and the New Basin, boat dock
and side ponds to the locks had not yet been created. (WRO)*

Initially Diglis outer basin above the barge locks was quite small and there was
a stop lock at the entrance to it from the canal. In 1818 it was decided to enlarge this
basin to its present size and to do away with the stop lock. The plan and
specification were produced by Joseph Nicklin who was the Diglis lock-keeper at
the time. Extra land was bought from the Revd. Shapland early in 1819; the
contractor was Charles Holland; and from Thursday 21 October to Sunday 24
October 1819 the canal was stopped and emptied below Sidbury Lock for the
purpose of completing the enlarged basin and cleaning the pound up to Sidbury.
Many navvies must have been employed and the canal was probably open again to
traffic, as was intended, on the Monday following.

Of the making of the long sluice, or arm, off the outer basin parallel to the canal
between the river and the basin, there is, curiously, little mention in the minute
books of the W/B Company. It is not shown on Ebenezer Robins' detailed large-

scale map of the canal in Worcester of 1817. It seems to have been made soon after the outer basin was enlarged in 1819 to provide much-needed extra moorings and wharfage. It is shown on D Dempsey's map of 1821 as the "New Basin". In the late 1850s it was incorporated into Webb's chemical manure factory. After the chemical works closed down early in the 20th century, the arm was used by boat builders, including Evertons.

Other early construction work at Diglis included the strengthening of the barge locks, and the making, in 1821, of a side pond to each barge lock. To replace a temporary lock house, a new one was built in 1816. Around the basins warehouses, cranes and stables were constructed, and by the mid 1820s Diglis was a busy place, as cargoes were transferred between river vessels and canal boats, and traders in coal, timber, building materials, farm produce etc. occupied the wharves and nearby stacking grounds.

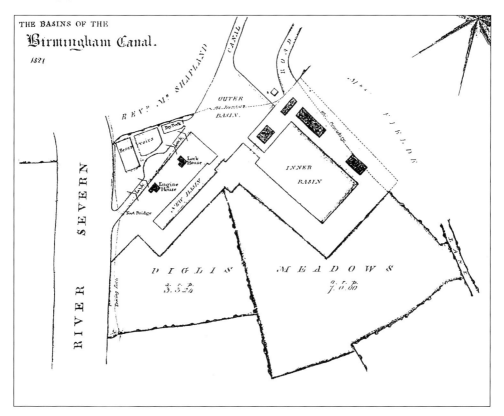

1821 plan of Diglis Basins showing the enlarged Outer Basin, the New Basin, four warehouse buildings, the lock-keeper's house, engine house for the pump, the dry dock and the side ponds (labelled reservoirs) of the two barge locks. (WCCHC)

DEVELOPMENTS AT WORCESTER WHARF, BIRMINGHAM

At the Birmingham end, increased facilities soon became necessary. The B.C.N. and the W/B each had a sluice (or arm) running under Gas Street at their end of the Bar Lock. The W/B sluice, originally used by the Dudley Coal Company, was taken over by the new Gas Works, erected in 1817, and enlarged to make a square basin. At the south end of the Worcester Wharf, on the outside of the right-angled turn, a short basin had been made by 1810 (shown on Kempson's map of that date). This basin was extended to four boats length in 1824 by the contractor William Tredwell. Known as the Severn Street Basin, since road access to it was from Severn Street, it remained in use until the 1920s when it was filled in and the site occupied by the Post Office Transport Depot. Across the entrance to Severn Street Basin a vertical wooden lift bridge was erected in 1878 to provide access to Worcester Wharf from Commercial Street. In his memoirs, George Bate recorded that "The heave-up bridge on the Worcester Wharf that was geared up four pillars was dismantled in my time about 1927. It had not been used for years."

In 1829 Messrs. Pickfords extended their occupation of the Worcester Wharf, purchased a crane, warehouse and stable already there and were allowed to make a sluice 50 yards long and 5 yards wide. This part of the Worcester Wharf with its facilities near to the Bar was in later years taken over by the Severn and Canal Carrying Company whose disused wharves and warehouses were eventually demolished in 1972 and the site later occupied by the James Brindley Hotel.

Around 1880, following the development of Commercial Street, another short canal arm was cut at the corner where the canal turns right out of Gas Street Basin. This arm, known as the Commercial Street Basin, was used for many years by boats delivering Morelands matches from Gloucester and Noakes salt from Droitwich to their own warehouses there. Following the end of this traffic the basin was filled in around 1960.

The Canal Company's Office was at first at the corner of Bridge Street and Wharf Street opposite the entrance to the Worcester Wharf. By 1820 new offices had been built on land rented and later bought from Sir Thomas Gooch to the south-east of the Wharf and facing the Severn Street Basin constructed a few years later. These offices were abandoned in 1864 in favour of new offices in Gas Street over the canal arm at the W/B end of the Bar Lock, and the disused office premises, by this time fronting Commercial Street, were sold in 1871 for £2,700.

As trade increased on the W/B Canal in the early decades of the nineteenth century, the Worcester Wharf at Birmingham became an ever busier and more bustling place. Stables were built for 14 horses and 10 donkeys on the Gas Street side, and others were located on the Worcester Wharf and in neighbouring streets. Weighing machines, cranes, warehouses, a sawmill, lime kilns, stacking grounds, cottages for wharfingers and toll collectors, etc. covered the area; and wharves extended round the corner up to Granville Street Bridge on both sides of this wide section of the canal. The latter part of the nineteenth century saw the area that had been fields and orchards to the south and west of Gas Street Basin transformed with the creation of new streets, factories, and crowded dwellings.

THE SLUICES AT TARDEBIGGE AND HANBURY

Elsewhere along the canal minor developments took place from time to time. In December 1830 it was decided to cut a sluice at Tardebigge New Wharf from one corner of the basin, two boats in length and two boats in width, to provide extra wharfage for local traders, mainly in coal, and this was done in 1831. Part of this sluice was eventually used in the construction of the present dry dock in 1924. At Hanbury Wharf too, there was a demand for boat lengths and wharfage for carriers of coal and salt between there and Droitwich, transport being by horse and cart before the making of the Droitwich Junction Canal. The sluice or basin was constructed there during 1834 at a cost of £519, and it still remains in use.

BRIDGES

Over the years it became necessary to replace many of the original bridges over the canal by wider and stronger ones to take, first, increasing horse-drawn traffic, then, later, steam-powered vehicles and motor vehicles. Some new bridges also became necessary. In December 1811 the Canal Committee considered a request for "a commodious bridge over the Canal at the boundary of the Parishes of Birmingham and Edgbaston". Kempson's map of 1810 does not show a bridge at this point on what had been a quiet country lane when the canal was cut there in 1792. There may have been a drawbridge there but carts and waggons could easily have done a slight detour and have used the nearby Bath Row Bridge. Almost twenty years later, as development was taking place near Five Ways, the lane was about to become a busy thoroughfare and a substantial brick bridge was needed. The bridge was planned in 1812 and built in 1813. There was a stoppage of traffic on the canal from 16 to 23 August 1813 whilst the brick arch of the new bridge was turned. Stone for the coping of the parapets came from Tardebigge Quarry. The country lane soon developed into New Bridge Street, but it was later rechristened Lee Bank Road with the coming of the Railway and the nearby Five Ways Station and yet a further reconstruction of the canal bridge.

Mention has already been made in chapter 4 of two accommodation drawbridges which were soon replaced by brick bridges, one at Leay House Farm (now Mary Vale Road) in the parish of Kings Norton in 1810, the other at "Lot's Hole" in the Parish of Edgbaston, replaced in 1818. Another at Withybed Green, Alvechurch, lasted some 70 years. In May 1816 the Committee ordered "That a brick Bridge be built over the Canal at Witheby Green in Alvechurch in lieu of the draw Bridge there now in a most ruinous state." However, two months later it was ordered that this bridge should be repaired and not taken down. It was not until October 1839 that the Canal Committee decided "That the Company's Surveyor be directed to prepare and lay before this Committee of Works an Estimate of the Expence of erecting a flat-topped Cast Iron Bridge with Brick Abutments over the Canal at Witheby Green". However, perhaps because the estimated cost was too high, the drawbridge survived a further forty years. It was not until April 1880 that the SND Committee minutes recorded the building of "a new fixed bridge at Alvechurch to replace the decayed lifting bridge." There are local tales of the old "heave-up" bridge which lifted vertically by gears up four posts and was operated by a lock windlass. Boatmen, southbound, were in the habit of hastily dropping the bridge behind them in order to delay the following boats making for the Tardebigge Top Lock. Both the bridge and the tempers of following boatmen must have suffered in the process.

Amongst other original bridges demolished and replaced were Rainbow Hill Bridge in 1834; the Granville Street Bridge (formerly known as the Jews Bridge because the Jews Burial Ground had earlier been located there) in 1856-7; the bridge over the Turnpike road at Selly Oak in 1885 with the introduction of horse trams; Wharf Street Bridge, Kings Norton, in 1904; Whitford Bridge, Stoke Pound, in 1911; and Hopwood Bridge in 1913. On some of the remaining brick bridges there can still be seen on the outside of the parapets the bases of the iron posts which used to carry a diamond-shaped cast-iron notice prohibiting the use of the bridge by heavy vehicles. Unfortunately, as ageing bridge parapets are renewed, these rusting remains are being removed, as has happened at London Lane bridge, Tardebigge.

An instance of the damage to bridges caused by heavy traffic occurred at Shernal Green in September 1913. A heavy threshing machine passed over the bridge there and caused severe structural damage. The bridge was closed for a time, then repaired by the canal company, the owners of the threshing machine having agreed to pay £50 in compensation.

One interesting bridge which was erected over the canal privately without the permission of the Canal Company was at Stoke Works. In September 1828 the Canal Committee issued an order to Mr Guise, who owned land and property on both sides of the canal south of Shaw Lane Bridge (including the Boat Inn), "to take down within one week the Bridge erected by him over the Canal at Stoke Prior without leave from this Company, or an action for trespass will be taken out against him." The bridge in question was a suspension bridge giving pedestrian access between his large house in Shaw Lane, with canal frontage, a wharf and adjoining malthouse and warehouse, and a cottage on the other side of the canal. Following the death of Charles Guise, his land and property were sold by auction in June 1849 at the Golden Cross Hotel in Bromsgrove. Lot 6 in the sale catalogue is described as extensive premises including a messuage lately converted into two houses with garden, wharf and suspension bridge over the canal, in the occupation of William

Harper. So Mr Guise must have reached an agreement with the Canal Company to keep his bridge. It seems likely that, once the properties on opposite sides of the canal came into different ownership following the auction, the bridge, which could not have been very substantial, would have been taken down. However it remained a canal feature for some twenty years.

Soon after its takeover of the W/B Canal, the SND Company came under increasing pressure to repair and strengthen some existing road bridges to take heavier traffic and to replace a number of the original narrow humped-back bridges over main roads by wider ones with longer and less-steep approaches. Whilst the Canal Company accepted its obligation to carry out and pay for repairs to its bridges as originally constructed, it was not prepared to finance the construction of the more substantial replacement road bridges. A long legal battle between the SND Canal Company and the Worcestershire County Council over the liability for the construction, upkeep and repair of replacement bridges including those at Hanbury Wharf, Stoke Wharf, Hopwood Wharf and Selly Oak (Bristol Road) was eventually resolved in favour of the Canal Company in the House of Lords in 1915. Other canal companies faced with the same problem followed the litigation with interest and contributed to the costs incurred by the SND Company.

New bridges had to be constructed over the canal at various times to take the railways, main lines as well as factory sidings, as mentioned in chapter 13. Recent years have seen the construction of two motorway bridges, one for the M5 near Tibberton, the other for the M42 between Alvechurch and Barnt Green. The latter necessitated the construction of a new canal cutting across Coopers Hill under the Motorway, as described later in this chapter.

Six other new bridges over the canal have been constructed in recent times. Across the Bar Lock at Gas Street Basin a cast-iron footbridge in traditional style was erected in 1988 to connect Gas Street with the Worcester Bar and the new James Brindley Hotel. In 1990 a brick-built footbridge in traditional style was built at The Vale near the University Halls of Residence in Edgbaston and a nearby winding hole and canal lay-by created with a view to passenger boats operating between the University and the International Convention Centre. In 1994 the original narrow Masshouse Lane Bridge carrying what had been a country lane over the cutting north of the West Hill Tunnel was replaced to take modern suburban traffic. In 1999 a non-traditional utility footbridge was constructed just below the mitre gates of the Offerton Flight bottom lock no.11 by Worcester Rugby Football Club to provide access between their two playing fields on opposite sides of the canal. Early in 2001 a new modern-style footbridge was built to connect the towpath at "Salvage Turn", where the canal does a right-hand turn at the end of Gas Street Basin, with Commercial Street and the Mailbox development. In 2002 the George Street Bridge in Worcester, built in 1936 to replace the original hump-backed bridge, was replaced by a modern wide concrete-arched bridge to create an easier and more imposing approach from the city centre to the new Shrub Hill Retail Park.

Unfortunately a number of brick accommodation bridges have been demolished over the years. They include Husbandry Road Bridge at Astwood near Wychbold, Hill Farm Bridge just below lock no.47 above the Upper Halfway Lock House, Nine Elms Bridge between Breedon Cross and Bournville, and in recent years one at Alvechurch just south of Callow Hill Bridge in 1984 and another, the nearest of two accommodation bridges along the canal east of Blackpole, in 1988. Others have been threatened, but now that most of the canal is included in conservation areas, they are, to some extent, protected and less likely to be demolished. Since the year 2000 several accommodation bridges needing urgent repairs have been saved and restored by British Waterways or by outside contractors, some with the help of financial grants and volunteers from the W/B Canal Society. These include bridges no.50 below Upper Gambolds and no.58 above Tardebigge Old Wharf, both restored in 2001.

THE PROPOSED HIMBLETON BRANCH CANAL

From the time that the W/B Canal was first planned a number of proposals for branch canals came up at various times. Two of these, the Netherton and the Stratford Canals were made and were completed in 1798 and 1816. In October 1825 the Committee of Works discussed an idea for a branch canal from the W/B just north of Dunhampstead Tunnel to serve limestone workings in the Parish of

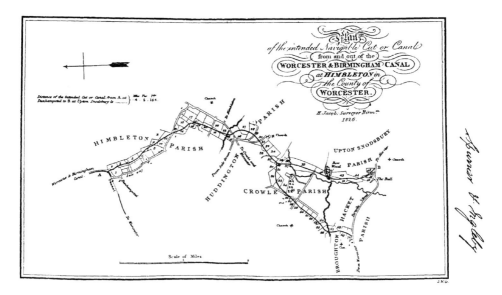

Henry Jacob's 1826 plan of the intended Himbleton Branch Canal. Spurrier & Ingleby were the Canal Company's solicitors. (WRO)

Himbleton. There was a great demand for lime for building and agricultural purposes at many places along the W/B Canal, and there was an abundance of limestone in the Himbleton area and also customers for coal, so the proposed branch canal was an attractive proposition. The W/B Canal's own engineer George Rew was instructed to investigate and survey a possible line. Four weeks later Rew produced a plan and estimate of the proposed branch canal terminating at Broughton Hackett. It was to be 4 miles 6 furlongs 10 yards in length, with two locks to lower the level by 10ft and then by 6ft, and the estimated cost was £9,429.17s. The January 1826 Assembly agreed the proposals, and accordingly a detailed survey was made by the Birmingham surveyor Henry Jacob to accompany the necessary Parliamentary Bill. Various amendments were made to the Bill in Parliament which would have affected the liability of the W/B to pay rates on its property. As a result, at the beginning of May, the Bill was withdrawn. A Tramway was later constructed instead.

THE PROPOSED WORCESTER AND GLOUCESTER UNION CANAL

Another proposal which could have benefited the W/B Canal Company was for a canal to link the Gloucester and Berkeley Canal at Gloucester with the W/B Canal at Diglis, and thus bypass the River Severn between Sharpness and Worcester which, in time of drought, was difficult, if not impossible, to navigate. On 1 January 1825, as the Gloucester and Berkeley Ship Canal was nearing completion, a meeting was held at the Royal Hotel, Birmingham, at which it was unanimously resolved "That a Company to be called the Worcester and Gloucester Union Canal Company be established, and that £100,000, or such other sum as shall, when surveys and estimates have been prepared, appear to be necessary, be raised for the purpose of cutting the Canal." Shares were to be of £50 each, and a deposit of £2 was required towards the initial expenses of surveys etc. The shares, limited in number to 2,000, were initially allotted and reserved until 1 February as follows:- to proprietors of the Gloucester and Berkeley Canal, 300; of the W/B, 300; of the B.C.N., 600; inhabitants of Worcester, 200; of Gloucester, 200; of Tewkesbury, 100; and landowners through which the Canal may pass, 300. No person could hold more than 50 shares. As soon as 500 shares had been subscribed for, Thomas Telford, or his nominee, would be employed to survey the line of the canal; and as soon as 1,500 shares had been taken up, a General Meeting would be called to elect a Treasurer and permanent Committee.

The provisional Committee appointed to promote the canal included five persons from Gloucester, the remaining nine being from Worcester and Birmingham. From the composition of this Committee and the fact that its Chairman, Isaac Spooner, was also Chairman of the W/B Canal Committee, it appears that the initiative and demand for the canal came mainly from the W/B Canal Company. Enough support was immediately forthcoming for Telford to be commissioned to report by 3 February on the feasibility and the estimated cost of the canal, which he put at £200,000. It may have been this sum, double the initial estimate, together with the threat of a projected Bristol to Worcester railroad, which deterred further subscribers and caused the promoters to postpone indefinitely the presentation of a Parliamentary Bill, as reported in Berrow's Journal of 24 November 1825.

It so happened that the summer of 1825 was a dry one and the need for the projected canal was, as reported in the Gloucester Journal, shown "by the case of a Birmingham merchant unable to get nearly 600 tons of slates from the Gloucester/Cheltenham area to Birmingham, due to lack of water in the River Severn." The proposed canal would also have been useful in the summer of 1826 which was excessively dry, causing navigation on the Severn to be interrupted during July and August. However, at other times when the river, a free navigation, had been navigable, the planned canal with its inevitable tolls could have been little used and have been a financial disaster. This realisation must also have contributed to the failure of its promotion.

CONSTRUCTION OF THE DROITWICH JUNCTION CANAL

In July 1851, as the Oxford, Worcester and Wolverhampton Railway Company was constructing a loop line to Worcester from a junction with the Birmingham and Gloucester Railway at Stoke Prior, the W/B Canal Committee recommended to the Assembly of Proprietors that a branch canal should be made to link the W/B Canal at Hanbury Wharf with the Droitwich Canal. The need for such a junction canal had long been realised, and, over the years, several abortive attempts had been made to gain authorisation for its construction. As early as January 1786, as the Parliamentary Bill for a canal between Stourbridge and Worcester was being prepared, the Droitwich Canal Company had insisted that the new canal should be linked to their own, and petitioned that provision for such a junction canal should be included in the Bill. The same demand was made when, in 1790 and 1791, Bills were before Parliament for the W/B Canal, and John Snape included this junction on his 1789 plan. It was certainly intended that the Droitwich Junction Canal should be made as soon as possible, but as it was difficult enough to get the Bill for the W/B Canal through Parliament, it was decided to make the Junction Canal the subject of a separate Bill. On 5 July 1792 the W/B Committee resolved that a survey should be made by Mr Snape for the Droitwich Junction Canal and that Messrs. Roberts, Hooper and others should take steps to obtain an Act of Parliament for it. Snape was evidently too busy at the time to take on this survey, and three months later the Committee again resolved that he should survey the line of the Droitwich Junction Canal, this time assisted by Cartwright. The survey was made and a plan produced by Snape by early November. On this plan the line of the canal from its junction with the W/B lies on the south side

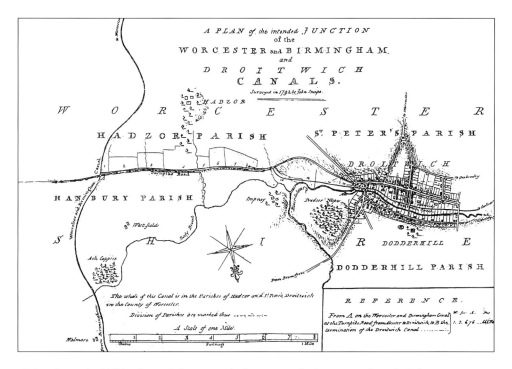

John Snape's 1792 plan of the intended Droitwich Junction Canal. When it was completed sixty-two years later its course was in Hanbury Parish, north of the turnpike road and not, as shown here, on the south side in Hadzor Parish. (WRO)

of the Hanbury to Droitwich Turnpike Road, in the Parish of Hadzor, for almost a mile, before turning under a bridge and running adjacent to the River Salwarpe to join the Droitwich Canal by Chapel Bridge. On 2 January 1793 it was reported to the Committee that objections had been received to the proposed line of the canal from representatives of the Hadzor Estates. Because of this and the preoccupation of the W/B Company with the prolonged construction of their own canal, nothing more was done about the Junction Canal for 21 years.

In September 1814, as the W/B Canal was nearing completion, a new survey for the Junction Canal was made by Thomas Allen, this time showing the line of the canal on the north side of the Turnpike Road and in the Parish of Hanbury. It was evidently intended to include clauses in the 1815 W/B Parliamentary Bill to sanction the construction of the Junction Canal, but there must have been objections on the part of Lord Somers who owned much of the required land at the Droitwich end, for on 18 January 1815 the Committee directed that "Lord Somers be given a copy of the Petition to be presented to the House of Commons to satisfy him that they do not propose a canal branch through his estate." So, in order not to risk jeopardising their Act, which was primarily to raise money for the completion of their canal, the W/B Company again abandoned plans for the Junction Canal.

Five years later, another attempt was made by the W/B Company to obtain agreement for this canal link. The Assembly of 4 July 1820 resolved that a deputation from the Company should confer with the Committee of the Droitwich Company on this matter. At the next Assembly on 3 January 1821 it was reported that a joint approach by the two companies had been made to Lord Somers via their solicitors, but that he was determined to oppose any Parliamentary Bill. The hope was expressed that the inhabitants of Droitwich would try to persuade his Lordship to change his mind. However, his Lordship's mind was not to be changed, and no further action was then contemplated.

Lack of this canal link continued to be a great inconvenience for many years, as coal and salt between Hanbury Wharf and the salt works in Droitwich had to be transported by horse and cart. In February 1834, in desperation, the W/B Committee ordered "That the Committee of Works be requested to ascertain the practicability and probable expence of constructing a Railway from this Canal at or near Hanbury Wharf to the Salt Works at Droitwich and report to this Committee." Probably due to objections from landowners nothing came of this proposed railway.

It was the construction of the Oxford, Worcester and Wolverhampton Railway Company's track from Stoke Works Junction to Droitwich and Worcester during 1851 which galvanised the W/B Company into action again. The railway was a direct threat to the carriage of coal and salt by canal to and from the salt works at both Stoke Prior

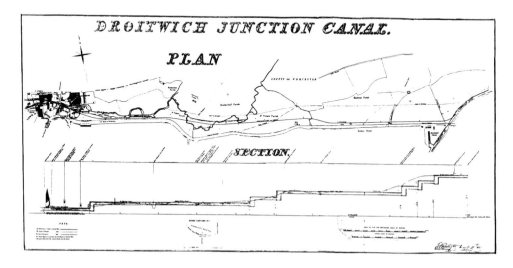

Richard Boddington's plan and section of the Droitwich Junction Canal, signed by him and dated November 12th. 1851. (WRO)

and Droitwich. W/B Canal shareholders, at their Assembly on 1 July 1851 were encouraged to support a Parliamentary Bill for a Junction Canal and the Committee were empowered to proceed. It was decided to set up another Company separate from the W/B, and to make an independent application to Parliament, though members of the Committee of the new Company were mostly shareholders and Committee members of the W/B, including the chairman William Mabson. It was proposed that the new undertaking should be leased to the W/B Canal Company. The W/B Company's engineer, Richard Boddington, was engaged and paid to superintend the construction of the canal, and he produced a plan and section of it, dated 12 November 1851. It was to be a narrow canal, just over one and a quarter miles in length, with six locks to give a fall of 66 feet from Hanbury Wharf to the River Salwarpe at Droitwich, and with a barge lock between the river and the end of the Droitwich Barge Canal. This barge lock was to be constructed by the Droitwich Company and would have four pairs of gates so that vessels could lock up or down between the canal and river, depending on the level of water in the river. To cut down on the loss of water from the W/B Canal, each of the deep narrow locks would have a side pond.

Each of the landowners and tenants to be affected by the new canal was notified of the proposals by a printed communication, dated 5 December 1851, from the solicitors, Messrs Chaplin, Richards and Stubbin of Birmingham and Messrs. Curtler and Holyoake of Droitwich. The Somers family (John Earl Somers and the Revd. James Somers Cox) still owned land needed in the Parish of St. Peter, Droitwich, but this time there was no obstruction from them, nor from the Vernon family of Hanbury Hall who owned the land in the Parish of Hanbury. However there was strong pressure for various measures to be included in the Droitwich Junction Canal Bill, chiefly from the proprietors of salt works in Droitwich. Petitioners who submitted written Briefs to be placed before the Parliamentary Select Committee, due to meet on 18 March 1852, included William Clay and fellow trustees of the Droitwich Patent Salt Works, Thomas Harrison who had been an employee for 40 years of Clay and Newman and had managed vessels engaged in the Droitwich salt trade for 19 years, and John Henry Bradley, salt manufacturer. There were complaints about the run-down state of the Droitwich Canal, the high tolls (1s.6d. per ton on coal and salt for all or part of the six-mile length), and no horse towing path. The barge locks, 66 feet long, were too short by 5 feet to take canal boats around 71 feet long. The Patent Salt Company, some of whose land was to be taken, wanted clauses to prohibit the proprietors of a rival company, Elkins, from laying pipes to carry brine along the canal or towing path, and to direct that any parts of their land taken but not used for the canal should be offered back to them. There were objections to the fact that the Droitwich Junction Company was not really an independent company and that it would be controlled by the W/B Company; also complaints that there was a lack of provision of accommodation bridges in the plans.

The Droitwich Junction Canal Bill was presented to Parliament on 4 February 1852 and read for the first and second times on 5 and 10 February. It was then referred to the Select Committee, which met on 18 March and took into account petitions for and against the Bill together with various proposed amendments. The amended Bill received its Third Reading and was passed by the Commons on 1 April. The Lords added further minor amendments before passing the Bill, and it received the Royal Assent on 28 May 1852.

The Droitwich Junction Canal Act empowered the Company to raise the capital sum of £24,000 divided into 1,200 shares of £20 each. Calls of not more than £4 per share were to be made at not less than three-monthly intervals. In addition the Company was allowed to borrow on mortgage or bond up to £2,000 provided all 1,200 shares had been subscribed for and half the share capital had been received. In accordance with the Companies Clauses Consolidation Act of 1845, there were to be initially seven directors of the Company, named as John Brearley Payn, William Mabson, Howard Luckcock, Joseph Gibbins, Frederick Isaac Welch, Isaac Lea and Thomas Wells Blakeway. Their remuneration was to be fixed by a General Meeting of the Company. As usual the Act authorised the compulsory purchase of the land needed and the construction of the canal and ancillary works including bridges, culverts, locks and side-ponds, wharves and towing paths. Water to supply the canal was not to be taken from Body Brook or the River Salwarpe or their tributaries, nor indirectly from the Birmingham canals. Occupation bridges were to have the roadway at least 15 feet wide, the approaches were to have a maximum gradient of 1 in 15 and fences at least 4 feet high were to be provided. Maximum tolls were prescribed for the length of the canal, which also covered wharfage and the use of the Barge Canal as far as the new railway bridge over that canal on the west side of Droitwich. These tolls were 2d. per ton on lime and limestone; 3d. per ton on coal, salt, iron, stone, bricks and timber; 6d. per ton on grain, flour and other goods; and six shillings on boats with less than 20 tons load except those returning empty. Powers were granted to make bye-laws and impose penalties subject to the approval of the Justices. The Company was given powers to lease or to sell the canal to the W/B Canal Company provided at least three-fifths of the shareholders of each Company agreed the terms. Finally, the Act conceded the demands of the Droitwich Patent Salt Company, in their petition to Parliament, that any of their land taken for the canal and unused should be offered back to them and that no brine should be conveyed alongside the canal or over canal land.

By the time of the passing of the Act, £17,700 had been subscribed towards the cost of the canal. Berrow's Journal of 17 June 1852 reported that work on the canal had started. At the first Assembly of the Droitwich Junction proprietors on 2 July, it was agreed that, in accordance with the Act, the W/B Company could lease the canal, and the W/B at their Assembly four days later decided that this should be done. During the following months of 1852 progress on the Droitwich Junction Canal was held up because of negotiations between the W/B Company and the Birmingham Canal Company over a proposed amalgamation of the two Companies. Following the failure and termination of these negotiations at the end of October, the construction of the Droitwich Junction Canal was put out to tender. On 28 January 1853 the Board of Directors considered four tenders ranging from £1,875.11s.10d. to £2,551.7s.0d. The lowest tender by John Beck was at first approved, but the contract was actually made on 24 February with Messrs. Jennings & Yates, for the sum of £1,940.0s.0d.

During January and February 1853 agreements were made with the Droitwich Salt Company and Lord Somers for their land needed in the Parish of St. Peter, and in May with Mr Vernon's trustees for the Hanbury Estate land. The July Assembly was informed that all the land needed had been acquired and that the works were in rapid progress. Minutes of the monthly meetings of the Board of Directors for ensuing months report payments on account to the contractors and also sums paid to the engineer, Richard Boddington, to John Knight and William Brookes for bricks, and to Thomas Chambers for lime. Work on the canal was hindered by bad weather towards the end of 1853, but at the Assembly of 4 July 1854 the Directors reported that the works were rapidly nearing completion and that they expected the canal to be open by 1 September. Nearly all the shares had been taken up by proprietors of the W/B Canal and most Calls had been paid. A dividend of £5 per share was to be paid for the last half year.

Meanwhile, following the Act, tolls on the Droitwich Canal were reduced from 1s.6d. to 6d. per ton for the length of the canal from June 1852. The W/B Company had agreed to lease the Droitwich Barge Canal for 21 years from 24 June 1853, and at their Assembly of 3 January 1854 decided that the locks on this canal should be lengthened. This alteration to the barge locks was completed by July 1854.

The Junction Canal was complete and officially opened for traffic on Monday 9 October 1854, when, as reported in the Worcester Herald, "several laden barges, preceded by a boat, containing Mr. Boddington, the engineer, and a number of friends, made the passage down from Hanbury Wharf out of the Birmingham and Worcester Canal through the newly constructed branch to the old canal." This link, the Newspaper added, "should be hailed with pleasurable satisfaction .... for although Droitwich is now extremely well off for railway accommodation, the transit by canal is also of the utmost importance."

Oversight of the Droitwich Junction Canal and the collection of tolls was undertaken by a lock-keeper at the Droitwich end. For him a lock-house (recently demolished) was built on the Hanbury Road near to the Town Mill Lock, where boats locked down into the river Salwarpe.

The canal was well used at first, but, with the decline of the salt industry in Droitwich in the early l900s, traffic dwindled and by 1917 it had practically ceased. Together with the Barge Canal, the Droitwich Junction Canal was abandoned by Act of Parliament in 1939, parts being subsequently sold off, filled in and built over.

In the 1960s, with the "New Town" development of Droitwich, the restoration of both Droitwich Canals was mooted. The Droitwich Canals Trust was formed in 1973 and since then mostly voluntary work has restored the Barge Canal from Vines Park in Droitwich to Ladywood and the top three locks of the Junction Canal. Depending on funding, the two canals should soon provide a through waterway again via Droitwich between the W/B Canal and the River Severn.

MODIFICATIONS TO THE W/B CANAL LOCKS AND WEIRS

In the absence of early plans with details of the locks as originally constructed it tends to be assumed that they were built essentially as they are today. However, over the years the locks have not only been repaired and their gates replaced when necessary, but they have also been to some extent structurally altered and rebuilt. As a result, today there are variations in the locks along the canal, both in their appearance and in the way they function.

In an article published in December 1971 in the W/B Canal magazine "Fifty Eight", George Bate wrote: "At one time there were no paddles in the mitre gates, all bottom end paddles being ground paddles in the wall, and a culvert to the outside of the lock wall; many of these culverts have been blocked up at both ends and a few still only at the entrance where the paddle was; some of these blocked up culverts have the date marked on them in the cement when they were done away with in the 1880s."

Most of the structural alterations and improvements to the locks were evidently instigated and supervised by the W/B Canal engineer, W F Hobrough, in the years following the 1874 SND takeover. They included, beside the change to gate paddles in the mitre gates, also the construction of most of the overflow weirs at the locks between Tardebigge and the Five-mile Pound. In this section in most cases the surplus water flows on the off-side above the lock, either under the bank (as at locks 55-57 and those of the Astwood Flight) or over an open cill, into an open culvert for a short distance before descending and either joining the old lower offside ground paddle culvert to pass into the pound below, or else entering the pound through a separate subterranean culvert. In the case of a few locks located just above road bridges, as at Whitford Bridge and Stoke Wharf Bridge, the overflow goes under the towpath into a short walled open culvert and then underground to outflow below the lock. Between the Five-mile pound and Diglis the overflow water at the locks is culverted around the lock gates under the bank.

There are variations also in the ground paddle structures at the top end of the locks, some set into the side of the canal wall with the paddle gear at the edge of the canal, others set into a side chamber and with the gear a distance from the bank.

In fairly recent times many of the mitre gates have been fitted with hydraulic paddle gear, but British Waterways policy is now to replace it, when gates are changed, with the so-called "traditional" gate paddle gear designed and introduced, it is believed, by Mr Hobrough. However, an under-water innovation is the replacement of wooden paddles by coplastic ones which are easier to operate and are more durable.

THE BIRMINGHAM SHIP CANAL AND OTHER PROJECTS

In the 1880s various schemes were proposed for ship canals to link inland cities with the sea. These arose out of Mr Salt's Committee of 1883 which had reported that the only successful canal systems in Europe were those where the waterway had been widened and deepened to permit steam traction and the use of large craft. The Manchester Ship Canal was authorised in 1885 and was soon under construction. Birmingham was not to be outdone. The vision of a Birmingham Ship Canal, bringing sea-going vessels up from the Bristol Channel to the Worcester Wharf in Birmingham, inspired such doggerel as this which appeared in March 1886 in "The Town Crier":

> "I sing a song of Birmingham,
> Of Birmingham-on-Sea,
> For that they say is what she is
> In days to come to be.
> The times are bad, the riddle is
> When better shall we see?
> Canal locks have been picked, and so
> Let's hope we get a 'quay'."

In 1887 a pamphlet was published outlining plans for "The Birmingham and Bristol Channel Improved Navigation". The idea was to dredge and deepen parts of the River Severn, to ease the curves at places on the Gloucester and Berkeley Ship Canal, and to deepen and widen the W/B Canal, so that lighters carrying 200 to 250 tons could ply between Sharpness and Birmingham. A provisional committee of 31 people, including local industrialists, was set up in Birmingham. Evidence was heard from people such as Mr Morton of Messrs. Fellows and Morton (then running steam narrowboats between Birmingham and London) who advised that, whereas it needed a crew of four on a steam narrowboat together with three on the butty to carry some 40 tons, it would need only five men to man one boat to carry 80 tons; and if vessels carrying 200 tons were used there could be a saving of 50 per cent in transport costs.

The vessels envisaged for the proposed Improved Navigation were to be of special design to economise on space and headway, being about 100 feet long, 18 feet wide and with 6 feet draught. They would have bilge keels or sliding keels to let down when on the River Severn or in the Bristol Channel below Sharpness. Such ships would require locks on the W/B Canal at least 110 feet long, 20 feet wide, 8 feet in depth over cills, each to provide a change in level of at least 14 feet. The long Tardebigge Flight would be replaced by a hydraulic incline similar to that operating on the Monkland Canal in Scotland where two caissons on rails conveyed ships, one ascending and the other descending a 1 in 10 incline. The canal would be deepened throughout from 5 feet 6 inches to 9 feet, widened to 66 feet, straightened in places, and the sides protected with dwarf walls or piling. Road bridges would have to be widened and raised, tunnels enlarged and partly cut open. There would also need to be considerable improvements in space and facilities at the Worcester Wharf in Birmingham to accommodate the larger vessels and their cargoes. The estimated cost of thus transforming the W/B Canal was put at £690,000, slightly more than the canal had cost to build in the first place.

These proposals, favoured by the Chambers of Commerce of Birmingham, Worcester and Wolverhampton, were duly considered by the Birmingham Corporation from which much of the financial backing would have had to come, but in March 1888 it decided instead to support improvements to the canal route between Birmingham and London. So, whilst Manchester's ship canal went ahead and was completed in 1894, Birmingham's Ship Canal project was abandoned.

During the promotion of the ship canal scheme the SND Company had shown little enthusiasm for it, but some years later, in 1900, it did consider the possibility of widening the W/B Canal to take larger vessels, However, due to lack of interest and financial support from civic and business interests the idea was soon dropped.

In 1923 there was renewed interest in improving Birmingham's waterway links with the sea, this time only for vessels to carry up to 100 tons. On 5 June 1923 a Special Canals Committee of Birmingham City Council was appointed to consider the matter. On the basis of a report produced by Howard Humphrey, who had been associated with the Manchester Ship Canal, the Bristol Channel route was favoured rather than routes to the Mersey, the Trent or the Thames, on the basis of the cost involved. Again, the main task would have been the widening and deepening of the W/B Canal from Birmingham to Hanbury Wharf and the Droitwich Canals from there to Hawford, this being the proposed route to the Severn, also the replacement of the existing locks by 34 deeper ones and one boat lift, and the necessary alterations to bridges and other structures. The cost was estimated at two and a half million pounds. During 1924 there were meetings of interested parties including local authorities and an appeal for financial funding from the Government. Then in 1925 there was a change of plan as the Birmingham to Mersey scheme was favoured. But by the end of 1925 Governmental hedging and doubts concerning the economic return on the capital expenditure needed led to the abandonment of plans to upgrade either the W/B Canal or the waterways between Birmingham and the Mersey.

THE NEW CUT UNDER THE M42 MOTORWAY

The last major civil engineering project on the W/B Canal was the making of the New Cut across Cooper's Hill, near Alvechurch, in connection with the construction of the M42 Motorway. The original line of the canal followed the contour round the hill, but to enable the motorway to cross over the canal without a costly elevation, it was decided to reroute the canal with a deep cutting through the hill and to block off the original channel at the Lanehouse end to take the motorway over it at a low level. Work on the cutting and the motorway bridge across it took place throughout 1984. The New Cut was officially opened on 9 March 1985 by Dr Alan Robertson, vice-chairman of the British Waterways Board; a tape was cut at the southern end and a flotilla of pleasure boats made its way to the northern end where a second tape was cut. At the southern end of the New Cut a new footbridge takes the towpath over the old canal, which is now a waterway cul-de-sac.

Chapter 11

THE FINANCES AND FORTUNES OF THE WORCESTER AND BIRMINGHAM CANAL COMPANY

THE COST OF MAKING THE CANAL

The original estimate of the cost of making the canal had been £180,000, with a further £70,000 permitted by the 1791 Act to be raised, if necessary, from the shareholders. As we have seen, this combined amount of £250,000 was exhausted by the time the canal reached Hopwood in 1797, and further substantial amounts had to be sought under four more Acts in 1798, 1804, 1808 and 1815. No itemised record of the total cost of the undertaking on its completion is available. It is, however, possible to estimate the final cost from the amounts authorised to be raised by the five Acts of Parliament during its construction, bearing in mind the fact that not all the permitted amounts were received. In the 1815 W/B Canal Act the following figures are quoted:

	Amount Raised	Amount Authorised
Under the 1st. Act (1791)	£250,000	£250,000
2nd. Act (1798)	4,000	149,929
3rd. Act (1804)	49,680	49,680
4th. Act (1808) shares	168,000	168,000
annuities	40,000	40,000

According to these figures a total of £511.680 had so far been raised under the provisions of the previous Acts. Of the £90,000 permitted to be raised by the 1815 Act only £36,000 was asked for and obtained by high interest 10% annuities. A month after the opening of the canal, the January 1816 Assembly heard that debts of £31,215 remained outstanding. In the meanwhile some of the income from

GENERAL STATEMENT *of the Worcester and Birmingham Canal Navigation to June 27, 1795.*

Dr.

		£.	s.	d.	£.	s.	d.
	The several Calls made to June 27, 1795, in the Whole 80 per Cent. with the Payments of several of the Proprietors in full, amount to the Sum of				148824	12	0
Deduct	Act of Parliament	13658	17	5			
Deduct	Interest on the Calls up to Christmas, 1794 . . £10889 17 7; Interest not paid to Defaulters . . . 121. 15 2	10768	2	5			
	Paid for purchase of 51 Shares, at 20 Guineas Premium	1836	0	0			
	Paid Mr. Pratt as a Compensation for 5 Shares resigned to Mr. Ingram	100	0	0			
	Paid Mrs. Hopper	15	0	0			
	Defaulters	4505	0	0			
	Balance in the Treasurer's Hands	9172	2	0			
					40055	1	10
					108769	10	2
Add	Debts owing by the Company				1171	4	1¼
	Amount actually expended on the Work				£ 109940	14	3¼

Cr.

	£.	s.	d.
By Land, Leases and Rents	4295	19	10½
By Cutting	56070	5	6½
By Masonry, Aqueducts, Culvers, Bridges, and Stop-Gates	10344	1	9¼
By Tunnels	12541	8	9½
By Houses purchased, Wharfs, and Salaries	4194	11	7
By Utensils, viz. Boats, Barrows, Team, Rail Roads, Waggon, Centers, &c.	3600	9	1¼
By General Expences, not reducible under any particular Head, Committee Meeting, Commissions on Land and Law Expences	4187	12	9¼
By Surveying	761	5	6½
By Sundry Materials	4023	2	9¼
By Rent of Farm, Levies and Taxes, and temporary Damages	1008	19	6½
By Roads	574	6	6¼
By making Spoil Banks and Back-cutting into Land	837	16	1½
By Timber Account for Stop-Gates, Trunks, Cutting, &c. in a State not completed	4412	17	11¼
By Fences	560	17	8
By Engine	261	19	5½
By Cash advanced in part of Work not completed	2254	19	1¼
	£ 109940	14	3¼

The 1795 Statement of Accounts giving details of expenditure to date, including the cost of obtaining the Act of Parliament for the canal. (WRO)

tonnages received on traffic on the summit level over the twenty years from 1795 to 1815 must have contributed towards the construction costs. Taking these figures and considerations into account, together with a statement in a published Case for the proposed Worcester and Birmingham Canal Bill of 1815 that "The whole line of the Canal is now cut, and £500,000 and upwards has been expended therein", it would seem that the total cost of constructing the canal must have been in the region of £600,000. In his book "Canals of the West Midlands" Charles Hadfield put the figure at around £610,000, his estimate being based on an unspecified source of information stating that "Up to 27 May 1815, £597,394 had been spent". Had a barge canal been constructed throughout, as originally intended, the cost would have been considerably higher. As already noted in Chapter 5, the main cause of the delays in the canal's construction, its completion with mainly narrow locks, and its high cost, was inflation, due partly to the War with France and partly to competition for skilled engineers and labourers at a time when many canals were under construction. At an average cost of approximately £20,000 per mile, the W/B Canal was one of the most expensive to make; but this figure does, of course, include the cost of the construction of the five reservoirs for the millowners, also the money expended in obtaining the several Acts of Parliament. The considerable cost of gaining the 1791 Act was listed in a Statement of Accounts up to 27 June 1795 as £13,658.17s.5d.

SHARE VALUES AND DIVIDENDS IN THE EARLY YEARS

Those people who were listed in the 1791 Act for the W/B Canal as the original shareholders in the Company must have had high hopes of financial benefit from their investment. Other local canals already completed were doing well; their shares were at a premium, worth far more than their original face value, and dividends of 5% and more (17% by the Birmingham Canal Company) were being paid. There were hopes that the W/B Canal would he completed in a few years time and be as successful as its neighbouring competitors. However this was not to be. At first the value of the shares rose during the "Canal Mania" of 1792-4, some being reportedly sold in 1792 at a premium of £294. But as the years passed by and it seemed at times as if the canal would never be completed, the original investors must have become increasingly frustrated and depressed as they saw the value of their shares, which with extra Calls had cost them nearly £140 each, fall to below £50 by 1807 and new shares, created by the 1808 Act, available for only £40 each. Some defaulted on their Calls and their shares were forfeited and sold by the Company. No interest, apart from the original 5% on paid-up shares as stipulated in the Act, was paid until well after the opening of the canal in 1815.

Once the canal was opened throughout in December 1815, prospects were much rosier. But at first, outstanding debts had to be honoured, especially the interest to be paid on the £40,000 borrowed upon debentures in 1813 and on the £36,000 raised by annuities in 1815. To obtain the necessary money initially, the Assembly of 2 January 1816 decided not to borrow more, but to raise £30.000 by making a Call of £5 upon every share in the undertaking. Also, to encourage trade, tonnages on coal and coke were reduced from 3 January 1816 to 2s.6d. between Birmingham and Tardebigge on the summit level, and to 3 shillings if passing to any place between the top lock and the Severn. At the July 1816 Assembly it was reported that many improvements had been made and work done on locks, bridges, warehouses, wharves and towpaths; that six lock houses and two stables had been built; and that income from trade had averaged £900 per month in the first six months. Thereafter, the tonnage income increased from just over £10,000 per year in 1816, to just over £14,000 in 1818. A saving of £1,800 per annum was achieved when the high interest annuities of 1815 had been redeemed by the time of the January 1819 Assembly, as permitted by the 1815 Act. But debts on mortgages, debentures, etc., were reported to be around £80,000 in July 1919. However, the January 1820 Assembly agreed the first half-yearly dividend of £1 per share, and thereafter dividends were declared at each half-yearly Assembly of shareholders. Tonnages continued to increase steadily, reaching £18,707 in 1821, £27,875 in 1829, around £34,000 in 1830, £40,000 in 1837, reaching a peak of over £44,000 in 1840. At the same time dividends gradually rose from £2 a year per share in 1820-24, to £3 in 1825-27, reaching £4 in 1828-40. Share values, however, tended to fluctuate, for example between £36 and £50 in 1824, between £54 and £60 in 1828, and reaching a peak of £105 in 1830. As reported in Berrow's Journal of 3 June 1830: "Shares in this improving Concern have been sold, within the last few days for £100 each, the price now asked is £105. A few years ago they were as low as £25." By October of 1830, however, the price of W/B Shares had fallen to £75, probably because in that month plans were made public of two proposed railways, one from Bristol to Gloucester, the other between Birmingham and Bristol via Worcester and Gloucester. Both of these plans were soon dropped, and shares rallied to around £90 in value in the early 1830s. However, when the Birmingham and Gloucester Railway plans took shape in 1835 and its construction began following its Act in 1836, share values began steadily to plummet.

TRAFFIC ON THE CANAL

Until the Birmingham and Gloucester Railway was completed in 1841, traffic on the W/B Canal continued to increase steadily. Initially mainly in coal, timber and agricultural produce, markets in these expanded. Additional cargoes came through the advent of the Birmingham and the Worcester Gas Works, the opening of the Gloucester and Berkeley Ship Canal in 1827, the establishment of Salt and Alkali Works at Stoke Prior around 1830, and intensive limestone quarrying near Dunhampstead mainly between about 1830 and 1850. Efforts were made by the W/B Canal Company itself to promote increased trade. These included the attempt in 1820 to resurrect plans for a Droitwich Junction Canal, only to be frustrated by the opposition of the landowner, Lord Somers; and the plan in 1834 to build a railway between Hanbury Wharf and Droitwich which failed for the same reason. In 1825-6 the Company tried unsuccessfully to promote a four-mile branch canal from just north of Dunhampstead Tunnel to serve the limestone quarries east of the W/B Canal, but in 1832 it did succeed in establishing a horse tramroad system instead (see chapter 13).

On 15 December 1837 a Special Assembly of the proprietors authorised its Committee to apply to Parliament for an Act to borrow up to £40,000 to improve the navigation of the River Severn between Worcester and Gloucester and take tolls on the river, but this plan was withdrawn in the light of other Severn improvement schemes mooted between 1838 and 1842, when an Act was passed creating the Severn Commission and authorising locks to be constructed on the river. But the W/B Company undertook some dredging of the river meanwhile.

THE LEASE OF THE COOMBE HILL CANAL

From 1825 until 1850 the W/B Canal Company was involved with the Coombe Hill Canal. This short barge canal, two and three-quarters of a mile long, linked the River Severn, about five miles south of Tewkesbury, with Coombe Hill where the road to Cheltenham branches off the main road between Tewkesbury and Gloucester. It joined the River through two locks and terminated in the Coombe Hill Basin. It had been constructed in the 1790s to provide a short route for the transport of coal from the River Severn by water and road to Cheltenham. It was never very busy, but it contributed indirectly to trade along the W/B Canal and seemed to offer reasonable financial prospects. In 1822 John Mabson and several other committee men and shareholders of the W/B Canal took it upon themselves to acquire a seven years' lease of the Coombe Hill Canal at £250 per annum. In 1825 the W/B Canal Company took over this lease for the remaining four years of its term and carried out maintenance work on it involving, amongst others, John Wolfindale and the contractor William Tredwell. In 1829 the W/B Company renewed its lease for a further 21 years at £500 per annum.

At the W/B Assembly of Proprietors on 1 January 1845 it was reported that the Committee had advertised a project for extending the Coombe Hill Canal to Cheltenham on the grounds that there was a need to connect the collieries of Staffordshire with the town of Cheltenham. Negotiations had taken place to purchase the canal from its owners. But the scheme had been dropped because of legal advice that the W/B Company was not justified in financing it. In 1850 as the lease expired, and with the Birmingham and Gloucester Railway now serving Cheltenham, the W/B Company was, in the event, fortunate that the Staffs. & Worcs. Canal Company gained the lease of what had become a growing liability. Due to declining use and disrepair the Coombe Hill Canal closed in 1876. To what extent the operation of the Coombe Hill Canal benefited the trade and finances of the W/B Canal Company during its 25 years' involvement with it is uncertain.

THE LEASE OF THE LOWER AVON NAVIGATION
As the financial prospects of the W/B Company continued to improve, it had the resources to take another step to encourage more traffic, especially in coal from the Staffordshire collieries to Pershore and Evesham, via the W/B canal to Worcester, down the River Severn to Tewkesbury and then up the River Avon. This involved taking on the lease of the Lower Avon Navigation in 1830 for 21 years from its owners, members of the Perrott family, at a cost of £880 per annum. Control by the W/B Company of the River Avon with its seven locks between Tewkesbury and Evesham must have proved well worth while, since in 1851 the lease was renewed for a further 21 years at £850 per annum. This second period, however, saw the opening of the railway from Ashchurch to Evesham in 1864, which caused a great reduction in the river traffic to Evesham. The lease now became a liability rather than an asset and, with the agreement of the Midland Railway Company by whom the Canal Company was expecting to be taken over at the time, it was not renewed when it terminated in 1872. During its 42 years control of the Lower Avon, the W/B

Canal Company was, by the terms of the lease, obliged to keep the locks and buildings of the navigation in good repair, and there are references in the W/B Committee minutes to various repair works being undertaken.

THE STRUGGLE FOR SURVIVAL

With the opening of the Birmingham and Gloucester Railway throughout in 1841, the fortunes of the W/B Canal began to decline. There was fierce competition for goods, and tonnages had to be reduced. Stoppages on the canal and river during some severe winters drove more goods onto the railway. In July 1842 the W/B Assembly reported a general depression of trade and receipts during the past half year down by over £2,000 from £22,028 the previous year to £19,878. There was a miners' strike and further depression in 1843. The January 1845 Assembly reported trade again down by £5,782 in the year 1844. 1846 and 1847 were better years, but thereafter the downward trend continued.

In 1847 the Company decided to take advantage of Parliamentary legislation permitting canal companies to manage their own carrying trade. Given the go-ahead by the Assembly of January 1848, a Carrying Company had been started by July. Its first Manager, Mr Bass, was soon replaced, due to illness, by Mr F H Needham, who had a business in hay and corn at Lowesmoor, Worcester. This W/B Canal Carrying Company was reconstituted in 1861 and eventually sold in 1868 for £350 to a Midland carrier, Mr Joshua Fellows (later partner in the carrying company Fellows, Morton and Clayton, founded in 1889), he promising to do all he could to promote the traffic of the canal.

The construction of the Oxford, Worcester and Wolverhampton Railway Company's branch line from Stoke Prior to Droitwich, connecting to Worcester, which opened in 1851, was another blow to the W/B Company's business, as it creamed off trade in salt from Stoke Works. In an attempt to compete, the W/B Company was at last able to construct the Droitwich Junction Canal, 1852-4. Although nominally promoted by a separate Company, the new canal was leased immediately to the W/B Company and run by them. But it was never a very great asset in terms of increased trade.

As railway mania gathered momentum in the mid 1840s, the W/B Canal Committee, concerned for the future survival of their canal, considered possible lines of action. They had a valuable asset in the line of their canal, the land corridor 30 yards wide, and wider where there were embankments and cuttings, on the level, out of Birmingham. Why not join the bandwagon and construct their own railway alongside the canal? As described in Chapter 13, the Birmingham and Worcester Direct Railway was surveyed by the canal's engineer, Richard Boddington, in 1845 to link the Worcester Wharf, Birmingham, with the proposed branch line of the O.W.& W. Railway from Stoke Prior to Worcester. This scheme died a natural death when the railway investment bubble burst at the end of 1845. A later more modest plan in 1864 for a railway beside the canal from Birmingham to the Midland main line at Kings Norton, likewise came to nought.

Other possible ways of salvation adopted by some canal companies were agreement and cooperation with a railway company as happened with the B.C.N. and the London and North Western Railway Company, or a takeover by a railway company as occurred in the case of the Stratford-on-Avon Canal, taken over by the Oxford, Worcester and Wolverhampton Railway in 1856. In such cases the railway company guaranteed to the canal shareholders a modest, but none-the-less welcome, dividend in the region of 1 or 2 per cent per annum. In 1852 the W/B Company was offered terms for an amalgamation with the B.C.N. in which W/B shares would have been converted into Birmingham Canal shares, with a dividend guaranteed by the London and North Western Railway Company, but the terms were considered unacceptable and negotiations were terminated. At their July 1858 Assembly W/B Canal shareholders learnt that an agreement had been reached between their Company and the Oxford, Worcester and Wolverhampton Railway whereby the Railway Company, as owners of the Stratford-on-Avon Canal, would lease the W/B for 21 years, the W/B Company to receive a rent equal to 9% of the gross annual income of both companies, such rent not to fall short of 10 shillings per share, nor be greater than £1 per share, and an application would be made to Parliament within five years for the amalgamation of the two companies. By January 1859 this agreement had been cancelled, it was said, due to legal difficulties.

By 1865 the W/B Company's debts amounted to around £100,000 and receipts had fallen to about 60% of their peak around 1840. In this desperate financial predicament, following the failure of their own West Birmingham Railway plans of 1864, the shareholders at a Special Assembly on 16 June 1865 decided to accept the offer of the London railway contractors, McClean, Brassey and Elliott, to purchase the W/B and the Droitwich Junction Canal for railway conversion. Whilst the Bill for this takeover was before Parliament, where it was vigorously opposed by the Gloucester and Berkeley and other canal companies and defeated, a Special Meeting of the W/B Assembly on 15 June 1866 set up a committee of eight people to investigate the affairs of the Canal Company, its books, papers, letters and documents, and report back. Their report was duly printed and circulated to the shareholders, but it does not appear in the Company's minutes. A year later, at the July 1867 Assembly, the Committee reported a half yearly income of £9053.15s. from tonnage, wharfage, weighing and rents, to be set against "the usual and ordinary expences of the Canal", £7515.10s.2d., plus the half year's guaranteed dividend on the Droitwich Junction Canal shares amounting to £600. The slight excess of income over expenditure went not on any dividend to W/B shareholders, but to the Company's former and existing bankers in part payment of debts. The last recorded half-yearly dividend had been 10 shillings per share for the latter part of 1863. From 1840 to 1863 dividends had been gradually falling, from £3 per annum in the later 1840s, to £2.50s. in 1851-2, £2 in 1853-4, and £1 or l0s. in subsequent years to the end of 1863.

The W/B Canal Company went into liquidation in 1868. As reported to the July Assembly, there had been proceedings in the Court of Chancery by several mortgagees, praying for an injunction against the payment of further dividends and for the appointment of a Receiver to receive the whole surplus revenue of the Company. The injunction had been granted, and the Receivers were to apply any surplus revenue to the repayment of the mortgage debt. The canal continued to be managed by its Committee of shareholders as before, but with this financial oversight and restriction.

A little light amidst the financial gloom was shed in 1871 with the passing of the Act for the Birmingham West Suburban Railway, to run beside the canal from Birmingham to Kings Norton. The Railway Company agreed to pay the Canal Company a rent of £1,400 per annum for the land needed for the railway.

Towards the end of 1871 the Midland Railway with the cooperation of the Canal Company drafted an agreement for the railway company to take over the canal. The agreement was intended to be signed and to come into effect on 19 December 1871. There is a copy of the agreement, a comprehensive document in copperplate handwriting and dated 5.12.71, in the Waterways Museum, Gloucester. Under it the undertaking, property and rights of the Canal Company would be transferred to the Railway Company. The transfer would include the interests of the Canal Company in the Lower Avon Navigation, the Droitwich Canal and the Droitwich Junction Canal. The Railway Company would pay the mortgage and debenture debt of the Canal Company amounting to £100,473.5s.8d, together with all its other debts and liabilities. The registered shareholders of the 6,000 shares in the Canal Company would each receive £1 per share per annum in perpetuity. This takeover agreement was delayed and eventually abandoned due to opposition in some quarters and ongoing debates in Parliament about the pros and cons of railway and canal amalgamations.

SALVATION

Whilst construction work on the Birmingham West Suburban Railway was proceeding in 1873, negotiations were taking place between the W/B Company and the Gloucester and Berkeley Canal Company on the terms and conditions of a takeover by the latter. A Special Assembly of the W/B Company, held on 17 September 1873 heard that the Seal of the Company had been affixed to a proposed agreement. The January 1874 Assembly learnt that a Bill was being put forward in

Parliament for the transfer of the Company's undertaking to the Gloucester and Berkeley Canal Company in consideration of the payment of £1 per annum per share to be paid in perpetuity to the W/B shareholders. The last Assembly of the W/B Canal Company was held on 14 July 1874, when it was announced that "Notwithstanding very strenuous opposition in both Houses of Parliament, the Bill awaits its 3rd. Reading and the Royal Assent." The Bill received the Royal Assent on 30 July 1874. On 1 August the solicitors and the secretary of the Gloucester and Berkeley Company travelled to Birmingham and took possession of the Seal, minute books, registers of shares and mortgages, bank pass-books and other documents of importance, and brought them back to their office in Gloucester. So the Worcester and Birmingham Canal Company came to an end, its assets and its debts taken over and its shareholders assured of at least a small guaranteed dividend. Their canal was now in safe hands and it was in the interests of the new owners to continue to maintain it as a commercial waterway.

Chapter 12

FROM 1874 UNDER THE SHARPNESS NEW DOCKS COMPANY AND BRITISH WATERWAYS

THE GLOUCESTER AND BERKELEY CANAL ACT 1874

From the point of view of the Gloucester and Berkeley Canal Company, closure of the W/B Canal and its replacement by a railway would have caused a loss of much of its trade and revenue. It had therefore opposed attempted railway takeovers of the W/B Canal (see Chapter 11) and, following the Midland Railway's abortive attempt initiated in 1871, it decided the time had come to take over the W/B Canal itself. During 1873 a sub-committee of the directors of the G & B Company entered into negotiations with the W/B Company. The directors commissioned a survey of the W/B Canal and its finances by Messrs. Wilton and Riddiford in June 1873 and subsequently decided to put forward a Parliamentary Bill for its takeover.

The Gloucester and Berkeley Canal Act, which received the Royal Assent on 30 July 1874, was a costly undertaking and not without financial risk. It involved at the same time taking over the Droitwich and the Droitwich Junction Canals. Some of its liabilities followed the terms of the Midland Railway's proposed takeover. The W/B's debts of £100,473.5s.8d on mortgages and debentures were to be paid off within twelve months, together with any interest due. The G & B Company would honour all the existing agreements entered into by the W/B Company. It guaranteed to pay the W/B shareholders on the 6,000 shares they held a dividend of £1 per share per annum to be paid half-yearly on 1 January and 1 July. But the G & B Company were given powers to redeem the shares, giving six months notice, at £25 per share.

The Act stated that "The Name of the Company shall from and after the passing of this Act be 'The Sharpness New Docks and Gloucester and Birmingham Navigation Company'". This long-winded title was soon for most purposes abbreviated to "The Sharpness New Docks Company" and known by the initials

SND which were later to be seen on single cast-metal bricks included in the brickwork of some of its buildings.

The Act gave the G & B Company power to raise up to £120,000 by new shares or stock. It included the stipulation that the W/B Canal would not be converted into a railway. Powers were given to alter tolls on the W/B Canal and new maximum tolls were laid down as follows:

First Class. Lime and limestone per ton, per mile, one penny.

Second Class. Salt, bricks, building and paving stones, gravel, sand, ashes, and manure per ton, per mile, one penny.

Third Class. All other minerals, goods, merchandise, and things except those in the fourth class, per ton, per mile, one penny halfpenny.

Fourth Class. Gunpowder, dynamite, petroleum, and all kinds of explosive articles, per ton, per mile, threepence.

Maximum tolls for the use of all or any part of the W/B Canal: in the First Class, one shilling and two pence per ton; in the Second Class, one shilling and sixpence per ton; in the Third Class, two shillings per ton; in the Fourth Class, three shillings and sixpence per ton.

Concessionary tolls allowed on salt from Stoke Works or Hanbury Wharf to the Stratford Canal, 9 pence, or 6 pence if destined for foreign shipment at London; to Worcester, 9 pence; to Birmingham or the Netherton Canal, 18 pence. On slack coal for use in the manufacture of salt, from Birmingham to the Stoke Works or Hanbury Wharf, thirty shillings per boat load.

These concessionary tolls were a continuance of previous arrangements negotiated by John Corbett with the W/B Canal Company of which he had been a leading shareholder. It helped, no doubt, that he had also been a director of the G & B Canal Company and remained a director of its successor, the SND Company, for many years.

THE SND ADMINISTRATION OF THE W/B CANAL

Following the takeover of the W/B Canal, control of its affairs passed from its Assembly of Proprietors meeting in January and July each year to the Board of Directors of the SND Company which issued reports in April/May and October/December for its half-yearly meetings of shareholders. At the time of the takeover in 1874 and for some years following, the Chairman of the Directors was W C Lucy, and their Secretary was Henry Waddy. The Company's Engineer and Superintendent was W B Clegram; he was in charge of the day-to-day management of its canals. He had served the G & B Canal Company since 1829, and when he resigned in 1885 due to ill health after 56 years service, he was granted a pension of £500 a year and allowed to continue to occupy the company's house, Saul Lodge, for the rest of his life.

The SND Company decided to administer its waterways in two sections; the Gloucester and Berkeley Section comprising the Sharpness New Docks, the G & B Canal and Gloucester Docks; and the Worcester and Birmingham Section comprising the W/B Canal and the two Droitwich Canals. The records and finances of the two Sections were kept separately. Following the resignation of W B Clegram in 1885, George William Keeling C.E. was appointed Consulting Engineer to the SND Company. F A Jones became local engineer of the G & B Section and W F Hobrough continued as local engineer of the W/B Section, having succeeded Richard Boddington in 1875. Details of the career and achievements of Francis Hobrough are given in chapter 14.

INITIAL DREDGING AND OTHER IMPROVEMENTS

By the terms of the 1874 Act the SND Company was required "to keep, support, and maintain the Worcester Canal and the several reservoirs, lock-gates, towing-paths, and other works belonging thereto, well and sufficiently repaired, dredged, cleansed, scoured and supplied with water." Accordingly, soon after the takeover, there began a programme of dredging and improvement of the canal which had suffered neglect through lack of finance in previous years. Early in 1875 a new steam dredger for the W/B Canal was tried out on the Stroudwater Canal. It worked to a depth of 6 feet. It began work between Kings Norton and Birmingham in November 1875, moving, on average, about 625 tons of mud per week. A year later it was reported that "since the steam dredger has been employed, nearly 30,000 tons of mud have been removed between Birmingham and Kings Norton." In 1877 the canal between Kings Norton and Tardebigge was dredged, and also the basins and canal at Worcester, removing another 30,000 tons of mud. Following this the steam dredger worked on the Droitwich Canals from which some 73,000 tons of mud were removed. So within a few years the W/B section canals had been cleared and deepened, thus easing the passage of laden boats and enabling them to carry heavier loads.

THE PROVISION OF DONKEYS FOR HIRE

In 1875 Mr Clegram purchased ten donkeys for letting out to canal traders on the W/B Canal. The use of donkeys, working in pairs usually side by side to haul boats, had certain advantages over horses. They worked hard and mostly lived long lives. They were hardy and stood up well to to rough weather, and they were less fussy than horses about food and drink. They could be taken on board a boat passing through a tunnel not having a towpath. They were sure-footed and had hard hooves; some were never shod and this was a saving of money. Their main disadvantage was impulsive stubbornness; they would sometimes come to a halt and refuse to budge for no apparent reason, even if beaten or coaxed with oats or carrots. Along with horses and, for a time, mules they were used mainly on the W/B Canal until the 1920s.

Following the successful introduction of the first ten donkeys, the Diglis toll clerk, Edward Waldron, was instructed to purchase others fit for work on the canal and he did so. An existing stable at Diglis was taken over. George Smith of Worcester was the supplier of the hay, straw, chaff, bran and oats which were sold to the traders for the animals. A uniform harness was ordered bearing the Company's initials "G & B N Co" and each was numbered to correspond with the number of the donkey which was branded on the forehoof. Hire charges were fixed at 7 shillings for a salt voyage and 9 shillings for a coal voyage. By the end of 1875 there were 30 donkeys available.

In June 1876 the Canal Company decided to privatise its tracking business (i.e. the loan of animals for boat haulage) and it entered into an agreement with Mr Smith for him to keep and let out on loan a sufficient number of animals, not less than 40 at any time, he to purchase at fair valuation the whole of the Company's animals, harness, provender and machinery, and to have free use of the stables for 12 months but then to pay rent for them.

THE INTRODUCTION OF TUGS

Steam tugs had been in use for towing barges and narrowboats on the River Severn since about 1830, and on some canals since the 1840s. The SND Company soon decided to introduce tugs on the W/B Canal to replace the leggers and tow trains of boats through Tardebigge and Shortwood Tunnels and through the West Hill Tunnel. In June 1875 trials took place with a steam boat from Wolverhampton. In February 1876 an order was placed with Messrs. Stothert of Bristol for three steam tugs at a cost of £1,150 each. One tug was for towing through Tardebigge and Shortwood Tunnels and along the canal between, another for towing through West Hill Tunnel, and a third was to be on standby, for use when one of the other tugs was out of use being repaired or serviced. These tugs had wrought iron hulls, were 45 feet long, had 6ft 9in beam and a draught of 4ft 6in. They had condensing engines rather than simple high pressure engines, and Messrs. Stothert guaranteed that this would give a 40 per cent saving in the consumption of coal and less "wear and tear".

Two of the tugs were ready for use later that year, and in November Mr Clegram submitted tunnel-tug timetables and byelaws to the SND Company. The timetables were in operation for many years. In the summer months tugs left Tardebigge and Kings Norton on the even hour from 4.00 am to 8.00 pm, and returned on the odd hour from 5.00 am to 9.00 pm. In the winter the tugs ran between 6.00 am and 6.00 pm. The bye-laws were displayed on large enamelled metal plates fixed on pairs of tall timber posts at the ends of the tunnels. They included instructions that no boats should traverse the tunnels except in the tow of the Company's tug, that all cabin fires were to be extinguished, and that every boat should be in charge of a capable steerer. With the bye-laws were also listed the timetable and the charges, and the notices were signed by H Waddy, Secretary of the SND Company, and dated 1876.

During 1876 the SND Company recruited tug crews. Each crew of two consisted of an engineer and a steerer, engineers being paid 30 shillings per week and steerers 25 shillings per week. Two shifts a day were to be worked, so two engineers, Frank Rowles and Isaac Bolton, and two steerers, John Millard and William Veale, were appointed to the Tardebigge Station; and two engineers, Henry Doggett and Alfred Bolton, and two steerers, Henry Norman and John Fisher, were appointed to the Kings Norton Station. These appointments were reported to the 24 November 1876 meeting of the SND W/B section Committee. In the event, two or three of the newly appointed tugmen backed down and were replaced, including John Millard at Tardebigge whose place was taken by William Hawkins. Most of the tug crew members came from the Gloucester area, young men, who settled down in the Tardebigge and Kings Norton areas, and most of them got married and had families. In due course some of their sons found employment with the Canal Company, and there are descendants of some of the tugmen still around in the areas.

The steam tug Birmingham *towing a train of boats out of the northern end of the West Hill Tunnel, August 1936, with the horses waiting on the towpath and repairs to the tunnel portal under way on the off-side of the canal. (NWMT, J Greene)*

For instance, William Hawkins' son Percy became a tug steerer and fitter, and Percy's son became a tug engineer. At Tardebigge some tugmen and other canal workers joined the choir at Tardebigge Church. Frank Rowles eventually became Section Inspector at Tardebigge and his son Morton Rowles taught at Bentley School in the parish.

Of the two members of a tug crew the engineer was responsible for the upkeep and operation of the steam engine, firing the boiler, replenishing the coal bunker, ash disposal and keeping the engine room clean and tidy. To prevent filling the tunnels with smoke and choking the crew of the boats being towed, the engineer had to ensure that his tug entered a tunnel with a full head of steam and a clear fire under the boiler. The steerer, besides steering the tug, had first to go round the boatmen to inspect and stamp their toll passes and check the condition of their tow ropes. He saw to the paraffin head-lamp needed to illuminate the tunnel ahead. He had to keep records, in a log book which each tug carried, of the boats towed. He was also responsible for keeping the outside decking and housing clean and helping to coal the bunkers.

At first the tugmen were housed in two rented houses at Tardebigge and Kings Norton. Two years later in 1878 the Canal Company built for the tugmen and their families the terrace of four split-level cottages (known as Tug Row) on the road outside New Wharf at Tardebigge and the two pairs of semi-detached cottages at the north end of the West Hill Tunnel, one pair on the hill above the portal, the other above the cutting by the Masshouse Lane/Primrose Hill high bridge.

At its 26 January 1877 meeting the SND W/B Committee was given a report of the first three weeks of the tug workings. In this period, January 1-21, 638 boats had been towed, 472 of them loaded, 166 empty. Towing charges were 3 shillings loaded, 2 shillings unloaded, through all three tunnels; 1s.6d. and 1 shilling respectively through West Hill only. There had been no major problems and the third tug from Messrs. Stothert of Bristol was expected to arrive in May.

One consequence of the use of the steam tugs was the necessity of opening up two new shafts at the West Hill Tunnel, a quarter of the way from each end, to improve ventilation and provide an outlet for smoke and steam from the tugs. This was done in 1877/8. Though tug crews were under instruction to damp down the engine fires before entering tunnels, the extra shafts were found to be necessary. Only one shaft in the centre of the tunnel had been left open when the tunnel was first constructed.

There were accidents in the West Hill Tunnel in 1879, 1882 and 1890 when boats, too heavily loaded and too top-heavy, sank in the tunnel and traffic was held up from one to two days whilst these boats were raised and removed. A contributory cause was, apparently, that the tugs tended to travel too fast and so the tugmen were warned against speeding.

Of the first two tugs, one named *Worcester* was originally based at Tardebigge New Wharf to work through to the far end of Shortwood Tunnel where there was a winding hole. The other tug *Birmingham* was based at the north end of the West Hill Tunnel where there was a coal store. The third spare steam tug *Gloucester* arrived on the canal in May 1877. In 1890 it was reported that the engine of this tug together with those of *Birmingham* and *Worcester*, was to be replaced with a compound engine to give a 25 per cent saving in fuel. Work on the tugs was undertaken under the supervision of the canal's engineer Francis Hobrough in the dry dock at Stoke Depot.

In 1895-6 a new steam tug was built at the Stoke Prior workshops; it was named *Stoke*. Because the steam tugs needed boiler and other repairs from time to time, it was necessary for the canal company to have four tugs so that when one tug was undergoing repairs there was another in working order in reserve. The hull of *Stoke* was made of heavy steel plating. This, it was found, did not last like the wrought iron plating of the other tugs. *Stoke* was eventually broken up in 1944.

TELECOMMUNICATIONS ALONG THE CANAL

One of the assets of the W/B Canal Company which was inherited by the SND Company was a telegraph system alongside the canal. The electric telegraph had been invented and developed in America in the 1840s and introduced into this country in the 1850s. In 1862 Elliott's Metal Works beside the canal at Selly Oak were the first to be granted permission to erect telegraph poles along the towpath between their Works and Birmingham. Elliotts erected the poles and they were charged a rental of £1 per annum per mile of wire. A condition was that other parties might be allowed the use of the same poles by agreement. In 1870 Nettlefolds, screw manufacturers at Breedon Cross, were granted the same facilities on the same terms. In 1872 the Post Office in Worcester was similarly allowed to erect poles and telegraph wires between Rainbow Hill and Diglis. As more users and wires were added the Canal Company increasingly benefitted financially.

The SND Company was able to add to this income as the telephone was invented and developed and began to replace the telegraph in the late 1870s. In 1881 the National Telephone Company Limited was allowed to run its wires from Birmingham to Lifford Mill using the existing poles and adding others as needed, the charge still being £1 per annum per mile of wire. The same year, Cadburys, recently established at Bournville, were given the same facility. In 1883 a wire was permitted from Birmingham to Bittell en route to Blackwell through the West Hill Tunnel, and this is when the brackets and insulators, many still remaining on the roof of the tunnel, were first installed. By the turn of the century, telegraph poles along the line of the canal were carrying many telephone lines and the Canal Company was allowed a free telephone service.

A horse-drawn working boat travelling towards Worcester on the Five-mile Pound, and, by the bridge, a telegraph pole carrying wires of the Canal Company's own telephone system. (Birmingham Museum and Art Gallery)

However the substantial financial benefits to the SND Company soon came to an end when the telephone company in 1907 refused to continue to pay the high rental charges based on the length of its wires and, instead, requested a charge based only upon the number of poles. Also the Canal Company was informed that in future it would have to pay for its telephone service. The Canal Company refused to accept these new conditions, so in 1909 the Post Office, which now ran the telephone service, removed all its wires including those of the Canal Company. The Canal Company then decided to set up its own telephone system, and in 1910 a tender of

One of the many remaining telephone line brackets, with insulators, attached to the roof of the West Hill Tunnel.

£488 from the Walsall Electrical Company was accepted and the system was installed between March and August that year.

The Canal Company's private telephone system was in use until the early 1930s. It was then dismantled and the poles removed. Jack Merrell and Wilf Colledge, who carried salt from Stoke Works to Birmingham on the narrow boat *Medway* twice a week in the 1930s, remembered collecting the poles on some of their return journeys and delivering them to the Tardebigge Depot for the section inspector Edgar Spiers. The only items that remain of the canal's former telecommunications system are the many metal brackets, with or without their insulators, which can be seen in the tunnels and also under the accommodation bridge no.56 below the top lock at Tardebigge.

Now, after more than fifty years, British Waterways have a new interest in telecommunications along the line of the W/B Canal as they benefit from the laying of fibreoptic cables below the towpath in 1997.

THE CONTINUING USE OF TUGS ON THE CANAL

In 1907 the SND Company decided to introduce tug towing along the whole summit level of the canal. Charges for this were 5 shillings for a loaded boat and 4 shillings for an empty boat between Tardebigge and Birmingham, whilst the option remained of using the tugs only through the tunnels, the charge for this remaining at 3 shillings and 2 shillings for loaded and empty boats respectively. Accommodation was arranged for tugmen at Worcester Wharf in Birmingham, and oilskins were provided for steerers to protect them from the weather. With the introduction of tug towage on the summit level came the need for animals to be left at Tardebigge New Wharf by boats travelling on from there to Birmingham and return. So a stable block was built there close to the wharf in 1907.

In 1910 there was a new tug timetable with a daily service of five tows each way along the summit level. For this at least three tugs, possibly four, would have been in use each day. To provide this service there was a need for additional tugs. In 1908 a new oil-powered motor tug called *Sharpness* was purchased. It was built by boatbuilders Abdella & Mitchell of Brimscombe. In the following year, 1909, it was decided to convert the Company's committee boat *Harriet*, which had an iron hull and had been used at times for ice-breaking, into a tug. It was adapted and fitted with a new steam engine and boiler by Abdella & Mitchell and rechristened *Droitwich*.

The oil-powered tug *Sharpness* had its exhaust pipe close to the water line and this caused problems with its noxious exhaust in the tunnels and it was never popular. To mitigate the problem of smoke and exhaust fumes in the West Hill Tunnel a gas engine was installed in 1911 in a brick-built engine house above the central ventilation shaft. The gas main was laid by Birmingham Corporation. The gas engine was maintained by a canal workman based at Hopwood.

By 1911 the steam tugs *Worcester* and *Birmingham* had been in use for 35 years and were reported to be worn out. As the ventilation problem in the West Hill Tunnel had been dealt with, it was decided in December 1911 to order two motor tugs to be built, at a cost of £766 each, by Abdella & Mitchell in collaboration with Messrs Perman & Co. These new motor tugs were built at Queensferry on the River Dee near Chester. They were given the same names as their predecessors and were known, to distinguish them, as *Worcester Oil* and *Birmingham Oil*. They had round-bottomed iron hulls; they were 45 feet long with 7ft beam and 3ft 9in draught; they had 28 HP oil engines; and they could tow up to twelve loaded boats.

Following the arrival of the motor tugs *Worcester* and *Birmingham* in 1912, the old steam tug *Worcester* went down to Gloucester Docks to be broken up. The steam tug *Gloucester* was soon scrapped, her boiler being used in the tug *Droitwich*. But the old steam tug *Birmingham* was kept and it remained in use on the W/B Canal for many years, being used mainly through the West Hill Tunnel. In July 1927 a violent thunderstorm at Bittell caused the canal to overflow its banks and this tug, being keel bottomed, turned over on her side in the shallower water near the canal bank as the flood subsided. The steam tug last saw service in the West Hill Tunnel in 1928.

Towage along the summit level was discontinued in 1911, presumably because by then it was not economically viable. But the original service of two tugs, one through Tardebigge and Shortwood Tunnels and one through West Hill Tunnel continued to operate. Records show that in 1905 about 800 boats per month used

The tunnel tug Sharpness, *with headlamp and canopy, towing boats out of the south end of Tardebigge Tunnel. ("The Motor Boat" magazine, 4 November 1909)*

An early photograph, probably c.1930, of a steam tug at Tardebigge new Wharf with, behind, Plymouth House and, by the old warehouse, a horse and working boat. (Phillip Coventry).

the tugs. From 1907 to 1911 it was between 600 and 700 boats per month. By 1916 the number had fallen to around 350 boats per month and the Committee was told that the number of boats passing barely paid the wages of the tug crews. It was decided to discontinue the first turn in the morning and the last turn in the evening and to reduce the number of tugmen employed from four to three working in alternate shifts at both Tardebigge and Kings Norton.

In March 1917 the new motor tug *Birmingham*, now surplus to requirements, was sold to the Borough Council of Marylebone, London, for £950. It was renamed *Tyburn* and was used for transporting rubbish along the Regent's Canal from Paddington Basin to various canalside tips until 1950, then used for maintenance work and ice-breaking on the Grand Union Canal. In 1957 the boat was fitted out by Wyvern Shipping of Leighton Buzzard as a hire boat and renamed *Perseverance*. In this guise she was purchased for use by a school and then, in succession passed to three private owners. Eventually, in the late 1980s she was rescued from dereliction on the canal at Uxbridge by BW and now, after treatment to prevent further deterioration, she has returned to Tardebigge where, on the New Wharf, back as *Birmingham*, she awaits her turn for restoration by the "Friends of the Working Boats" organisation.

In the 1920s and 1930s the tugs continued to operate, despite the gradual diminution in trade and the replacement of many animal-drawn boats by motor boats usually with a butty boat in tow. During World War 2 (1939-45) the four tugs in use were *Stoke*, *Droitwich*, *Sharpness* and *Worcester*, though *Stoke*, whose steel hull was badly pitted and worn by 1944, was broken up that year. A few horse-drawn working boats continued in use until the 1950s, the last ones being those of Charles Ballinger, so a tug still had to be available. The steam tug *Droitwich* remained in use until after World War 2. She was moored in the basin at Tardebigge for several years awaiting the retubing of her boiler, but this never got done and she was eventually stripped of her engine and fittings and her sound empty hull was used as a platform raft on maintenance work in the 1950s.

The last remaining tugs in use following the War were *Worcester* and *Sharpness*. *Worcester*, which had been fitted with a Bolinder engine in 1930, was last used as a tunnel tug in 1955. It then continued in occasional use as an ice-breaker until and after being purchased, together with the tug *Sharpness*, by Precision Dies & Tools Ltd of Tardebigge in 1959. Four years later it was sold to Philip Murray for use as a holiday boat on the Macclesfield canal. Eventually, after several years of neglect and Mr Murray's death, it was donated by a nephew, who now owned the boat, to the then newly formed organisation which we now know as the Boat Museum at Ellesmere Port, where it has been twice restored. *Sharpness*, mainly used on maintenance work and for ice-breaking, was also sold and has had several private owners. It was located on the Shropshire Canal for many years and has recently been restored by Mr and Mrs Paillin of Melton Mowbray.

The last tug crews were John Colledge (steerer) and Charles Hawkins (engineer) at Tardebigge; and Billy Greaves (steerer) and Percy Bolton (engineer) at Kings Norton.

THE MAINTENANCE DEPOT MOVES TO TARDEBIGGE

Soon after the W/B Canal was completed to Worcester in 1815, a maintenance depot was established at Stoke Prior. It was built on the off-side of the canal on the opposite side of the Hanbury Road Bridge to Stoke Wharf. It comprised a dry dock, alongside the canal, which could be drained into the nearby brook, a carpenter's shop, fitter's shop, blacksmith's shop and stores. To house some of the craftsmen employed there and also a lock keeper the row of five terraced houses was built in 1849 along the road nearby.

Francis Hobrough, who was appointed Engineer of the W/B Canal soon after its takeover by the SND Company in 1874, lived in the Bridge House, which was (and still is) a quite imposing building, with various outhouses including a stable and coach house. When tugs were introduced in 1876 and based at Tardebigge New Wharf there was good reason for moving the maintenance depot of the canal to Tardebigge, but while Mr Hobrough was firmly established at Stoke Wharf and in charge of the canal the move was resisted. However when he retired in 1908 the SND Company decided

The motor tug Worcester *in British Waterways blue and yellow livery berthed alongside the Tardebigge New Wharf maintenance depot. (Doris Colledge)*

that the move was overdue and set about implementing it. In October of that year the removal of stores and plant began and new buildings began to be erected at Tardebigge New Wharf. By 1911 the move was complete and the Bridge House and the workshops at Stoke Prior were available to other tenants.

THE CANAL DURING AND BETWEEN THE TWO WORLD WARS

During World War 1 (1914-18) the value of canal transport was recognised by the Government, but there was increasing concern that the canals, through lack of money and manpower, were in need of maintenance and subsidy. The Ministry of Munitions sought greater use of the waterways, and at the beginning of 1917 the canals were taken over by the Government under a Board of Trade order and grouped in regions. The W/B Canal was included in the Midlands group. In September 1917 it was inspected by government officials who, concerned about the impediment of the Tardebigge flight of locks, went to inspect the Foxton Canal Incline, with a view to installing a similar system alongside the Tardebigge flight. Nothing came of this as the War soon ended. Other measures to boost canal carrying were the exemption of some older canal employees from military service, the use of some service personnel, and a war bonus of 15 shillings per week for each working boat in use from 1 January 1918. As with other canals, the W/B Canal returned from government to private control on 31 August 1920.

In the 1920s and 1930s, as road transport using heavy lorries increased, trade on the W/B Canal steadily declined, being by 1939 about half of what it had been in

The hole in the centre of the aqueduct over Bournville Lane caused by a German bomb on 3 December 1940. The wharf canopy and the dwelling house of Sparrey's Wharf are seen in the photograph taken on 31 December 1940. (BW)

1920. Closure of the canal became increasingly likely as its trading losses mounted. Around 1926, George Cadbury, chairman of the Severn and Canal Carrying Company, a River Severn Commissioner and with other canal interests, set up a guarantee fund, supported by various firms in Birmingham and Bristol, to offset, by a subsidy of some £1,600 a year, a trading loss of over £3,500 per annum. This support lasted five years, after which the SND Company continued to bear the losses to enable the canal to survive. However, the Droitwich Canals, which by 1939 had been disused for some years, were by Act of Parliament abandoned that year.

World War 2 (1939-45) brought the threat of air raids and a possible breach of the canal with loss of water and damage by flooding to people and nearby properties. To minimise this risk, the stop-gates at the ends of aqueducts and embankments were ordered to be closed whenever air-raid sirens sounded. It was fortunate that the stop gates at each end of the Bournville embankment were closed when, at about 10.00 pm on the night of 3 December 1940, a high explosive bomb hit and blew a large hole in the bed of the canal and the masonry arch of the aqueduct over Bournville Lane. There was damage to Cadbury's factory basement due to flooding and the house on nearby Sparrey's Wharf was

Aerial view of Tardebigge Church and the maintenance depot at the New Wharf, Tardebigge, built 1909-11. (Aero Pictorial Ltd)

severely damaged. It took several weeks to clear the debris, rebuild the aqueduct and retaining walls and to repuddle the canal bed with clay brought by canal from Alvechurch Brick Works.

FROM 1948 UNDER THE TRANSPORT COMMISSION AND BRITISH WATERWAYS

On 1 January 1948, in common with the railways and remaining navigable waterways, the W/B Canal, having during World War 2 been under Government control, was taken over by the British Transport Commission. Thus nationalised, the canal became the responsibility of the Docks and Inland Waterways Executive and it was administered as one of the Midland Region Group of waterways based at Gloucester. In 1962 the British Waterways Board was set up as an independent body, free from the previous competition with road and railway interests under the Transport Commission. Under the Board the waterways were divided into three regions, Southern, Northern and Scottish, and the W/B Canal was one section of the Southern Region which had its central office at Gloucester. In charge of the W/B Canal during this period were section inspectors Leslie Thompson (1949-59), George Colledge (1959-74) and Stuart Perry (1974-89).

In 1988 British Waterways decided upon a countrywide reorganisation of its regions under which the W/B Canal became one of six divisions of the Midland Region, the other five divisions being Birmingham and the Black Country, Coventry and Ashby, Trent and Mersey, Stratford and the Grand Union from Birmingham to Napton, and the Shropshire Union together with the Staffs. and Worcs. Canal. The Midland Regional Manager was Stewart Sim and the Regional Office was located at Auchinleck House, Five Ways, Birmingham. The reorganisation became operational on 1 April 1989, when Glyn Phillips took up his appointment as Waterway Manager of the W/B division.

Glyn Phillips did not reside at the New Wharf, Tardebigge; he administered the canal from a portacabin behind the old office building. One consequence of the new organisation was that Stuart Perry's job title was changed from Section Inspector to Engineering Supervisor. He did not take kindly to this effective reduction in his status and responsibility.

In 1993, under further reorganisation, the W/B Canal Division and the Stratford and Grand Union Division were united and the three canals were then administered from headquarters at Lapworth. Because of this change, in April 1993 Glyn Phillips moved on and Andrew Stumpf was appointed Waterway Manager of this new area, to be followed by Jonathan Green. Following the 1993 reorganisation Stuart Perry retired and the house at the wharf entrance which he and his predecessors had occupied was then let to non-waterway tenants, as has been the case with other British Waterways properties no longer needed for its employees.

Since 2003 a yet further restructuring of British Waterways organisation has meant that the northern section of the W/B Canal on the Birmingham side of its junction with the Stratford Canal at Kings Norton is now in a new West Midlands Waterway area, whilst the remainder of the W/B Canal, from Kings Norton Junction through the West Hill Tunnel and on down to Worcester, is in the new Central Shires Waterway area.

Chapter 13

THE RAILWAY HISTORY
OF THE CANAL

HORSE TRAMWAYS

From time to time during the nineteenth century the W/B Canal Company found itself involved with railways, some planned but not constructed, others built. Some were opposed, others tolerated or approved of, and some actually planned by the Canal Company itself. Before the advent of steam locomotives, horses were usually used for pulling waggons along railroads, constructed at first with hardwood flanged timber rails, later with cast iron rails. Most of these horse tramroads were made in the latter part of the 18th century and the early years of the 19th century. Iron railroads were usually constructed of short lengths of cast iron L-shaped flanged rail secured to stone blocks. The waggons had wheels without flanges and could therefore also run on hard flat ground.

Benjamin Outram, partner with William Jessop and others in the Butterley Iron Works founded in 1790, was an ardent advocate of this type of tramway. Those he designed and manufactured in the 1790s, and until his death at the early age of 41 in 1805, used 3 feet long cast iron rails with the flanges on the inside. The rails were secured at each end by metal spikes which were driven into hardwood cylindrical plugs fitted into holes drilled into the top of heavy stone blocks. These blocks with flat bases usually weighed from 150 to 200 lbs and formed a firm foundation for the tramroad.

It was in November 1798, when the W/B Canal had been completed only as far as Hopwood and the Company was in financial difficulties, that Joseph Wilkes, an enterprising agent of the Butterley Works, came and persuaded the Canal Committee to consider constructing a horse tramway from the summit level at Tardebigge down to Worcester. Outram was invited to survey this possible tramway and, as already described in chapter 5, provided estimates of the cost of a double line and also of a single line. In recommending such a railroad, Outram pointed out that if the railroad were only a temporary expedient, it would be exceedingly useful in the construction of the remainder of the canal alongside it. He also invited shareholders in the canal, in the printed prospectus which was sent to each of them, to go and inspect one of his already successful railroads, especially the Peak Forest Tramway which had been completed three years earlier at Chapel-en-le-Frith in Derbyshire to convey limestone from quarries to the Peak Forest Canal. This railroad had a gauge of 3ft 6in as, presumably, the Tardebigge to Worcester tramway would have had if it had been made. Although in 1800, and later in 1802, the W/B Company agreed that a temporary single line railway should be made down to Worcester as soon as the canal was completed to Tardebigge, this project had apparently been abandoned by the time the canal was open to Tardebigge Old Wharf in 1807.

There is, however, a surprise resolution in the Canal Assembly minutes of 4 July 1810 "That Mr. Woodhouse prepare an Estimate of the Expence of laying down an Iron Railway from the building erected for trying the Lift at Tardebigg along the Line of Canal to opposite Droitwich, and that he prepare another Estimate of the Expence of laying down an Iron Railway from opposite Droitwich down to the nearest point of the Droitwich Canal", and "That Mr. Eagle be requested to apply to Mr. Harvey the Manager for the Grand Junction Canal Company to know on what Terms they will sell their old Iron Rails that have been taken up, sufficient for ten Miles of Road, with a proportionate number of Wheels." News that these rails were available to be disposed of cheaply may have tempted the W/B Company to try and obtain and use them for a temporary railroad to link the canal at Tardebigge with the Droitwich Canal. If a bid was made it must have been unsuccessful for there is no further mention of this project.

When work on the Tardebigge Flight of locks down to Stoke Wharf was initiated in January 1812, the Canal Committee did realise the advantage of a temporary tramway to convey materials up and down this inclined section and they ordered one to be constructed. Two weeks later an offer of 150 tons of cast iron rails at £9.5s. per ton, each rail being 3 feet long and weighing 40 lb, was received from the Horseley Iron Works, Tipton, and the canal's engineer, William Crosley, was ordered to get a pattern for such rails made. We are not told the intended gauge nor whether this railroad would have stone or wooden sleepers; in fact it is not entirely certain that it was ever made since orders of the Canal Committee were not always carried out and there is no minute to record its actual construction or eventual removal. The contractor for this section, John Woodhouse, may have decided he could manage without the tramway. We do however know that George Rew, when he was working on Dunhampstead Tunnel, was lent by the Company some iron rails from Tardebigge in May 1812, so Rew evidently laid down a tramway, possibly to convey bricks from Oddingley or Hanbury brickyard for lining the tunnel or possibly to fetch limestone from nearby quarries.

THE TARDEBIGGE QUARRIES' TRAMROADS

There were two old sandstone quarries at Tardebigge, one just below the church, stone from which had probably been used in the reconstruction of the church in 1776-7, the other, known as Dusthouse Quarry, adjacent to Dusthouse Lane and about half a mile north west of the church. Both had been worked long before the canal was completed to Tardebigge. Both were used as a source of stone by the Canal Company, and tramways were constructed from each of them to the bank of the canal. As described in Chapter 6, a contract was made with John Smith of Bristol, early in 1810, for getting stone from the Church Quarry, and the Canal Company provided a tramway from the quarry down to the canal with four waggons and cranes etc. It would have been too steep an incline and too dangerous to connect the quarry with the canal immediately below it, so the tramway ran on a longer gentler slope towards the accommodation bridge south of the site of the Top Lock. Evidence for this is provided by remaining earthworks and by local people's memories of parts of a tramroad being unearthed at various times. The Church Quarry was relatively small and after 1813, by order of its owner the Earl of Plymouth, only limited amounts of stone were allowed to be obtained from it. The last known extraction was in 1827, when, under Lord Plymouth's mine rights, the Canal Company was paying him 6d. per ton for stone from his quarry.

Realising, no doubt, the limitations of the Church Quarry, the Canal Company, early in 1811, negotiated for the purchase of two acres of Mr Field's Dusthouse Quarry. From this quarry a tramway was constructed to cross a small stream, which was culverted, and then to wind its way in a shallow S-shaped curve up to a stone wharf by the canal, just below the Woodhouse lift which had recently been completed. It seems that Woodhouse, who at the end of February 1811 had become the contractor for the canal from Tardebigge to the bottom of the Astwood Flight of locks, was responsible for creating this tramway as part of his contract, for, as the canal was nearing completion, in February 1815, the Canal Committee ordered that "Mr. Woodhouse's cast iron railroad from Tardebigge Stone Quarry be taken to at a fair valuation to be agreed." Thereafter the Canal Company instructed and allowed various stone-getters from time to time to use the quarry, and the tramway was let out to private operators. There are references to the quarry in the Canal Committee minutes, e.g. in 1819 to a stone horse trough produced at Dusthouse for use at Stoke Prior, in 1825 to Thomas Wycherley, stonemason, allowed stone from the quarry, in 1827 to stone obtained by Thomas Higgins from Dusthouse for building a wall at Lower Bittell Reservoir, in 1829 to the quarry being fenced along its boundary, and in 1830 to stone permitted to be obtained by Mr McAllister for a wharf at his Stoke Prior Salt Works. In February 1857 the canal's Committee of Works resolved that the "Tram way to the Stone Quarry and the Crane way at Tardebigg be let to Mr. William Griffin." Two months later an agreement was confirmed between the

Company and William Griffin and James Bennett "for the use and occupation of the Tramway, Waggons and Crane at Tardebigg at a rental of £20 per Annum." By 1869 the rent for the use of the tramway had been reduced to £5 per annum as the quarry was evidently little used. Finally on 24 December 1869 "The Engineer was instructed to take up the Tramway at Tardebigg and restore the land." This was done, and in April 1870 the Canal Committee resolved "That the old rails at Tardebigg be disposed of as suggested in exchange for new guard castings" (these presumably to protect bridge abutments).

The only known map showing the Dusthouse Tramway is that of the proposed Birmingham to Worcester Direct Railway produced by the canal's engineer, Richard Boddington, in 1845. The tramway could not have been thoroughly lifted in 1869-70 since broken rails have been unearthed at various times by ploughing, and old rails were discovered by Ian Hayes, some in 1953 and another a year or two later. The first rails found were in situ at the top end of the tramroad by the side of the canal about 2 feet below the surface. They were 3 feet long lightweight edge rails with a spike at each end, laid 3ft 3in apart between inside edges, and had probably been supported on longitudinal timber baulks. This could have been part of the crane-way above-mentioned, rails for a travelling crane used to lift stone from waggons to canal boats. The later discovery was part of a tramplate of L-section, weighing approximately 40 lbs per yard length, at the quarry end of the tramway. A square iron lug cast on at the end of each plate would have slotted into a hole in the stone sleeper block. This quarry tramway could have been constructed under Woodhouse's supervision from some of the cast iron rails which the Horseley Iron Works offered to supply to the Canal Company early in 1812.

THE HIMBLETON LIMESTONE QUARRIES' TRAMROADS

During the 19th century, there was a considerable amount of limestone quarrying in the parish of Himbleton and much limestone was carried along the W/B Canal to various wharves where some was burnt in lime kilns to produce lime for mortar and for use on the land. In November 1819, just four years after the completion of the canal, the Canal Committee considered a letter from Mr Edward Presdee, a proprietor of limestone near the canal in the parish of Himbleton, producing 150 tons of limestone per week, offering to pay the Company 3d./ton/mile for the use of a railway to be laid between the canal and his limeworks and kept in repair at the expense of the Company. This proposed horse tramroad was needed to convey coal to his limeworks as well as limestone to the canal. Its route was apparently to be along or beside Trench Lane. A survey was soon made and two Committee members deputed to carry the railway into effect. Agreement was sought from the Dean and Chapter of Worcester, Lords of the Manor, in April 1820 for the railroad on their land. However, when enquiries revealed that Mr Presdee's lease of the

quarry had only three more years to run and that the tramway would cost £800 to
£900 to make, it was decided to seek a longer term agreement with the owner of the
quarry; so in January 1821 the Canal Committee resolved "That it appears advisable
for the Company to enter into an agreement with Lord Shrewsbury for laying down
a rail road for the purpose of conveying Lime and Limestone from his Lordship's
Quarries in the Parishes of Himbleton and Huddington to the Canal near to the
Bridge in Trench Lane." It was hoped to make an arrangement with Lord
Shrewsbury via his solicitor. There is no mention in the Company's minutes of the
actual making of this tramway, but there still exists a narrow hedged strip of land
for some way along Trench Lane beyond the railway level-crossing, which suggests
that the tramway was constructed, perhaps at Lord Shrewsbury's expense and
owned by him, to a wharf at Dunhampstead opposite the present boat-hire business.
This tramway would have been severed by the construction of the Birmingham and
Gloucester Railway in 1840 and was probably disused by then.

In 1825 plans were drawn up for a branch canal from a wharf on the bend of the
canal just north of the Dunhampstead Tunnel to run for some 4 miles and to serve
limestone quarries and convey coal along its route. Details of this, and the reasons
why the project was abandoned, are given in chapter 10. A few years later, it was
proposed to construct a tramway instead to run from the same wharf. In August
1831 the Company's surveyor and clerk of works, George Rew, laid before the
Canal Committee an estimate for a railway from the canal to Mr Chambers'
limestone quarry in the parish of Himbleton, amounting to £218, and also an
estimate for making a basin for the convenience of loading boats with limestone for
£90. He was asked to produce a specification and to obtain tenders for the work, the
Committee having decided that the basin should be 25 yards long and 10 yards wide
(large enough to accommodate 4 narrowboats at a time). In October, William
Tredwell's tender for the basin and railway, including turnouts, through the land of
the Revd. R A Amphlett was accepted, he to find all the materials and to keep the
railway in repair for seven years. Mr Amphlett was paid £100 per acre for his land,
and the charge for the use of the railway was to be 1s./ton/mile. £200 per acre was
charged by Mr Amphlett for the right to the limestone under his land. The railway
was to run across two fields to Dean Brook. In March 1832 Messrs. Eagle and Beale
of the Canal Committee were deputed to confer with the Company's solicitor, Mr
Spurrier, over further land needed for the railway from the trustees of the estate of
Mrs Chamberlain. In the meanwhile George Rew had bought some quarry rights,
for it is recorded in July that a lease had been agreed "for land for a Railway to
certain Limestone Quarries lately purchased by George Rew, until such mines shall
be worked out." On 1 January 1833 the Canal Company's assembly of shareholders
was told "Your Committee have completed the Railway for bringing the produce of
the Lime Quarries to the Banks of the Canal." So the tramway was made and

extended as required, and plans of 1836 for the Birmingham and Gloucester Railway show where a bridge had to be constructed over it, this bridge remaining until the main line was realigned in recent times to take high-speed trains.

This Himbleton limeworks tramway system remained in use during the 1840s. In 1847 the Canal Company demanded a rental of £15 per annum from Mr Davenport for his use of the railway, failing which the rails would be taken up and the land restored to the owners thereof. He negotiated a reduced rent of £10 in January 1848. At the same time William Wild was informed that he would be charged £5 per annum for the railway over his land unless the rent paid to him by the Company for the land acquired for the track was cancelled. It seems that the quarries on his land were practically exhausted, for in 1850 Wild requested that the tramway across his land should be taken up and the land restored. This was allowed to be done by Wild himself under the supervision of the Canal

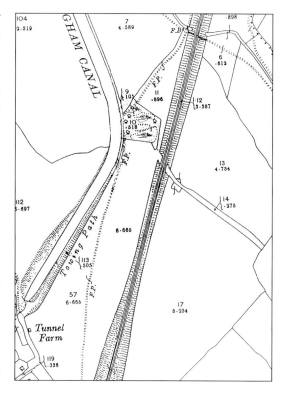

Part of a 1902 map of the canal north of the Dunhampstead Tunnel showing the overgrown site of the old basin for boats loading limestone and the track-bed of the former tramway through a tunnel under the Birmingham and Gloucester Railway to the limestone quarries. (WRO)

Company's engineer, Richard Boddington, and Wild was paid £10 for so doing. Other sections of the tramway must have continued in use into the 1850s, for in 1859 it was reported in the Canal Committee minutes that "Mr. Wall having attended this meeting in reference to his claim for Rails taken up from the tram way at Himbleton - Resolved that Mr. Wall be paid £16.16.4d. being his agreed proportion of the value of the Rails so taken up." During the 1830s and 1840s the limestone workings and the tramway had brought welcome revenue to the Canal Company, but this evidently diminished as the quarries were worked out and the tramways were lifted.

THE BIRMINGHAM AND GLOUCESTER RAILWAY

The first recorded apprehensions on the part of the W/B Canal Committee of an impending railway threat to their business occur in the minutes of their meeting on 10 December 1824. This followed the advertisement of a meeting to be held in Bristol three days later to consider proposals for a railway line from Bristol to Birmingham via Gloucester and Worcester. The matter was raised at the January 1825 Assembly and it was resolved to resist this and other railroads. However, after an extensive survey, this Bristol to Birmingham railway scheme was abandoned in 1826 in the face of financial and engineering difficulties.

In 1827 the Gloucester and Berkeley Canal was completed, and soon business interests in Birmingham and Gloucester began to consider the possibility of a railway between these two places. A Birmingham group paid Isambard Kingdom Brunel £100 to survey an indirect route avoiding steep gradients and towns where land was expensive. His route, which would have skirted Redditch and Evesham, was rejected on the grounds of expense, and eventually another engineer, Captain W S Moorsom, was engaged to survey a more direct and less costly route. His plan, which included the two mile long Lickey Incline with its 1 in 37½ gradient, was ready by 1835. The route bypassed towns such as Bromsgrove, Droitwich, Worcester, Tewkesbury and Cheltenham, and it was planned to join the Birmingham and London Railway at Garrison Lane and use that railway's Curzon St Station. There were to be two railway bridges over the W/B Canal, one at Breedon Cross, the other at Tibberton. Between these bridges the railway would have run west of the canal, but opposition from the Hadzor Estate near Droitwich caused Moorsom to revise his plan and locate the second crossing north of the Hanbury to Droitwich Road.

The W/B Canal Company was inevitably concerned about this direct threat of competition for freight transport between Birmingham and the new Port of Gloucester and its January 1836 Assembly authorised the Committee to be vigilant and "to take such measures as may be necessary to guard the interests of this Canal". A few weeks later approaches were received from the Birmingham and Gloucester Railway Committee for the construction of the bridges to cross the canal. Copies of the plans and sections of the railway were obtained by the Canal Committee and advice sought from the Grand Junction Canal Company re their earlier experience with the London and Birmingham Railway. In February it was decided to raise a petition to oppose the Birmingham and Gloucester Railway Bill, but, if unsuccessful, to insist on the best possible terms. At the 1836 July Assembly a deputation was appointed to monitor the progress of the Bill and insist that clauses were included in it to protect the works of the canal from injury and to secure financial compensation. In October 1836 the Committee applied to the Birmingham and Gloucester Railway Company for £6,500 surety against possible damage and obstruction of the canal, and at the January 1837 Assembly it was reported that this sum had been received from the Railway Company.

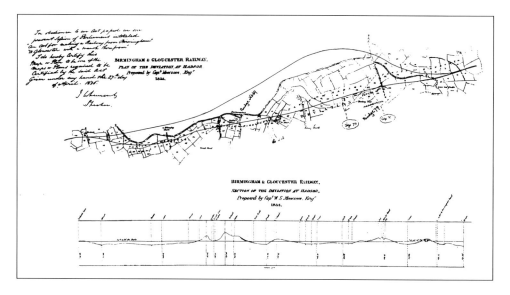

Part of the 1835 revised plan of the Birmingham and Gloucester Railway between Tibberton (left) and Hanbury (right) showing the abandoned route through Hadzor Estate land west of the canal and the adopted route on the east side with references to the landowners and occupiers affected. (WRO)

The Birmingham and Gloucester Railway was finally open to traffic into Curzon Street Terminus, Birmingham, in August 1841, but it had been in use as far as Camp Hill the previous December. Its effect on the trade of the W/B Canal began to be felt in the early months of 1841, for, as reported in the Assembly minutes of July 1841, there had been two months of continuous frost from mid-December to mid-February and "a considerable portion of those Goods and Merchandise which would otherwise have waited for the breaking up of the frost and the re-opening of the Canal were, during the continuance of the frost, forwarded by the Railroad." Over £1,000 of tonnage was thereby lost. The Railway continued to cream off traffic from the W/B Canal and to contribute to the Canal Company's financial difficulties in the years ahead.

RAIL LINKS TO WORCESTER AND TO BREEDON CROSS WHARF

The nearest point to Worcester on the Birmingham and Gloucester Railway was Spetchley, and in response to pressure from Worcester interests, Robert Stephenson, in 1844, surveyed a branch line to run from the main line at Spetchley to the Albion Inn at Worcester together with a spur to Diglis Basin. Two versions were produced of the planned railroad into Diglis, but the Spetchley Branch idea was abandoned in 1845 when the Oxford, Worcester and Wolverhampton Railway Company's plan for a branch line to Worcester from the Birmingham and Gloucester Railway at Abbott's Wood, south of Worcester, was adopted instead. So Diglis missed having a canal-railway interchange. However, a spur from the Birmingham and Gloucester line was constructed in 1843 to a siding alongside the W/B Canal at Breedon Cross Wharf, and this freight interchange was in use for many years. The Midland Railway, which absorbed the Birmingham and Gloucester in 1845, eventually had its own canal boats and Breedon Cross was one of many points of interchange of freight on the Midlands canal system, parts of which passed into railway ownership.

THE PROPOSED BIRMINGHAM AND WORCESTER DIRECT RAILWAY

The year 1845 saw the peak of the "Railway Mania". A great many railway schemes were mooted and companies formed to promote them. The W/B Canal Company decided to join the bandwagon by proposing to construct a "Birmingham and Worcester Direct Railway". In August 1845 the Canal Committee rejected an offer from the directors of the Great Eastern and Western Railway to buy the canal with a view to converting it into a railway. A similar offer from the Midland Railway was also turned down. In September the W/B Company set up a provisional committee to plan its own railway to follow the canal, with slight deviations, from its wharf in Birmingham to join the O.W.& W. Railway at Worcester. However, the O.W.& W. Railway Company had already in its Act of 4 August 1845 obtained planning consent for a line from Stoke Prior to Worcester, so the W/B Canal Company quickly realised the wisdom of restricting its own plans to a railroad linking its Birmingham Wharf with this O.W.& W. link at Stoke Prior, and it also included in these plans a branch from Scarfields, Alvechurch, to Redditch. A survey was carried out and a plan of the railway made by the Canal Company's engineer, Richard Boddington.

Throughout October 1845 a prospectus appeared in seven newspapers for this "BIRMINGHAM AND WORCESTER DIRECT RAILWAY WITH A BRANCH TO REDDITCH". An independent company was to be formed with powers to incorporate the W/B Canal Navigation. The capital needed, £500,000, was to be raised in 25,000 shares of £20 each. The names of fifty-eight W/B proprietors were listed as the provisional committee. The engineer was to be Richard Boddington and the secretary W Hodgkinson. It was stated that there would be easy gradients on the railway and that a considerable portion of the tunnelling that had been necessary for the canal would be avoided. Share applications were to be received by 24 October. On 30 October the provisional committee met and decided to go ahead with the scheme. On 27 November a notice appeared of the intention to apply to Parliament for a Bill in the next session early in 1846 and to deposit the plans with the Clerks of the Peace for Warwick and Worcester, as required, by 31 December 1845.

From the fourteen-feet-long plan of the proposed Birmingham and Worcester Direct Railway, 1845. Top: the line at the Birmingham end with (added) the suggested location of a Lucy's Mill Station. Bottom: the railway line at Tardebigge through a tunnel (dotted) with the permitted extent of deviation, and features which include, on the left, the course of the tramway from Dusthouse Quarry to the canal between the accommodation bridge and top lock and, on the right, the line crossing the Old Wharf and (dotted) the necessary deviation of the canal alongside. (BWMT)

Unfortunately, by the end of November 1845, the general financial situation had deteriorated and the business world was seized with panic. Many deposits for shares were withdrawn and on 12 December the provisional committee decided to postpone any approach to Parliament for the time being and to return the deposits paid on shares to the subscribers. All the plans and documents were to be preserved, ready for a future application. All this was explained at the January 1846 Assembly of the Canal Company, and it was agreed that the expenses so far incurred, about £1,700, would be borne by the Company.

In 1989 Richard Boddington's plan of the railway was discovered in the store at Icknield Port Yard in Birmingham and it is now in the keeping of the Waterways Museum at Gloucester. This large scale plan, about 14 feet long, shows the proposed line, including the branch to Redditch and many interesting local map details. The sites of seven stations are pencilled in; they are at Lucy's Mill (Bridge St.), Church Road, Edgbaston Hall, Selly Oak, The Leys Farm (Stirchley Street), Lifford, and Reachill's Wharf (Kings Norton). The track of the Dusthouse Quarry tramroad at Tardebigge is shown and also many canalside features existing in 1845. In order to avoid sharp curves the railway deviated from the line of the canal in many places, requiring the purchase of much extra land. Between Tardebigge Tunnel and Stoke Pound, the descent of around 190 feet in just over 2 miles would have meant a gradient of something like 1 in 60, not as severe as the 1 in 37½ of the Lickey Incline, but nevertheless a potential problem. A long tunnel parallel to the West Hill Canal Tunnel would have been needed, as well as other tunnels or deep cuttings at Shortwood and Tardebigge. These factors would have contributed significantly to the difficulties of constructing and operating the railway.

OTHER RAILWAYS AFFECTING THE CANAL

Towards the end of 1845 the canal's engineer, Richard Boddington, was asked to produce a report on "the various Railways calculated in any way to interfere with the Works or Interests of this Canal". His report, dated 22 January 1846, listed as many as seventeen such projected railways, plans for which had been deposited with the Clerk of the Peace for the County of Worcester. Of these, twelve would have required bridges over the canal, and most of them could well have taken away some of its trade. In the event only two of these planned railways went ahead, the Hereford to Gloucester and the Ashchurch to Malvern, both distant from the W/B Canal. The others, like the canal's own Birmingham to Worcester Direct Railway, came to nought.

In the 1850s three railways were built each of which required a bridge to be constructed to cross the canal. The first of these was the Oxford, Worcester and Wolverhampton Railway Company's link between Worcester and Stoke Works via Droitwich, opened on 18 February 1852. This involved a bridge over the canal at

Blackpole, north-west of Worcester; it also meant the loss of some freight, especially salt from Stoke Works as well as from Droitwich, from the canal to the railways. The second was the Redditch Railway, authorised in 1858 and opened to passengers between Redditch and its junction with the Midland Railway at Barnt Green on 19 September 1859. Concerning the building of the Redditch Railway Company's bridge across the canal at Withybed Green, the Canal Company's minutes mention two problems which arose. One was over a request to sink piles in the bed of the canal and the other was over the dimensions of a temporary bridge which differed from those specified in the Act. The third Railway, the Worcester and Hereford Railway, was authorised in 1853 to link the O.W.&W. Railway at Worcester with the Newport, Abergavenny & Hereford Railway at Hereford. It involved major engineering works, including a bridge over the River Severn and two long tunnels, one through the Malvern Hills and the other through a ridge near Ledbury, 1567 and 1323 yards long respectively. There were also the lofty brick-built Rainbow Hill Bridge crossing the canal at Lowesmoor and the cast-iron one over Foregate Street in Worcester made at Hardy and Padmore's canalside foundry. Plans for Rainbow Hill Bridge were approved by the canal's engineer, Richard Boddington, in July 1858, and £50 was received from the railway company in compensation for land taken for the building of the bridge. Open first between Malvern Link and Henwick in July 1859, the section over the canal and the River Severn was not in use until May 1860, and the whole line was opened on 13 September 1861.

TWO 1860s SCHEMES FOR A RAILWAY ALONGSIDE THE CANAL

On 23 March 1864, a special meeting of the Assembly of the W/B Canal Company was called to consider a proposal for the construction by the Company of "a Railway from New Street Station in Birmingham along the Banks of the Canal to a Junction with the Midland Railway at Kings Norton or Northfield and with a Branch through Harborne to a Junction with the West Midland near to Halesowen." The Assembly agreed to the financing of a survey which was carried out by George Lea, Engineer, and Richard Clarke, Surveyor, for £250. In May provisional directors were appointed of a new company to be known as "The West Birmingham Railway and Canal Company". These directors were mainly Birmingham bankers and industrialists, with, as Chairman, Major-general Studd. The W/B Assembly of 5 July endorsed the flotation of the new company and the arrangements by which it would, on the completion of the railway, absorb the Canal Company and convert W/B Canal shares into £25 preference shares in the new company with a guaranteed interest of 4% in perpetuity.

A prospectus of the railway appeared in the newspapers in July with an application form for shares. The estimated £400,000 capital needed was to be raised by 16,000 shares of £25 each. There was mention of an extensive goods depot to be located near to the Worcester Wharf in Birmingham, and the advantages of the railway for both passengers and freight were extolled. By September the Parliamentary Bill had been drafted and it included clauses permitting the necessary narrowing of the canal, the new width of canal and towing path to be 37 feet. Unfortunately the project failed to get adequate financial support, and at the January 1865 Assembly the Committee had to announce its abandonment, due mainly "to the exceptional state of the money market, which defeated many other attempts to raise Capital for similar purposes."

Where the Canal Company itself had failed, others were soon to step in. At a well-attended special meeting of the Assembly of shareholders held on 16 June 1865 it was announced that a consortium comprising Messrs. John Robinson McClean, Thomas Brassey and George Elliott, all of Great George Street, Westminster, had offered to purchase the W/B and the Droitwich Junction Canals. The normal July Assembly three weeks later heard the financial proposals. The consortium would pay £3,000 per annum for 2 years, then £4,500 for 2 years, then £6,000 per annum in perpetuity, or a lump sum of £135,000, the intention being to use parts of the canal land for a railway. In view of the parlous state of the canal's finances and diminishing income, the Assembly agreed to negotiate a deal. But this required an Act of Parliament; so a Bill was presented in January 1866. This met with vigorous opposition and the promoters were required by clauses inserted into their Bill to maintain the canal as a water highway in perpetuity. The Bill failed, but another attempt was made in 1867. Again the Bill was opposed by interests such as the Gloucester and Berkeley Canal Company and by various canal carriers, and when the same condition that the canal be retained and not converted to a railway was required of the promoters, they withdrew their Bill. So the canal was safe from closure and conversion, at least for the time being.

THE BIRMINGHAM AND WEST SUBURBAN RAILWAY

A railway alongside the W/B Canal from Birmingham to Kings Norton was seen increasingly to be a desirable and useful addition to the passenger transport facilities in that developing area. The Canal Company's failure to raise the necessary money for the project in 1864 was possibly due to lack of confidence caused by its own financial problems. When, early in 1870, the Company was approached by an independent group wishing to promote the same scheme there was a better prospect of success. The July Assembly of the Canal Company agreed in principle to cooperate with the promoters and laid down conditions safeguarding the property and working of the canal during and following the railway's construction. The Canal Company was to be adequately recompensed financially and to be represented on the Board of Directors of the Railway Company.

It was reported to the January 1871 Assembly of the Canal Company that "The Birmingham and West Suburban Railway Company" had been set up and their Bill prepared for Parliament. The seal of the Canal Company had been added to an agreement with the Railway Company over the sale of land and other conditions.

The Act for the railway was passed and received the Royal Assent on 31 July 1871. There was to be a single track between the Canal Company's Albion Wharf at Bridge Street in Birmingham to a junction with the Midland Railway at Lifford. The original 1871 plans of the railway show a tunnel under the turnpike road at Selly Oak and a great 275 yards long viaduct to take the railway over the Worcester Wharf of the canal. This viaduct would have necessitated a 1 in 20 ascending gradient from Granville Street with 20 arches of varying sizes, and the radius of curvature of the track as it swept up and over the canal round to the Albion Wharf terminus would have been about 220 yards. A branch to Harborne was planned from Metchley Park Road curve. The surveyors of the railway were Alexander & Littlewood; the engineers were Lawford & Haughton.

Construction work on the railway began in the spring of 1872. At the beginning of the usual Whit week stoppage of the canal the Edgbaston embankment section was drained between the stop-gates at each end. A million bricks had been deposited ready beside the canal and a wall eighteen inches thick was built along the middle of the waterway. Earth dug out on the east side to widen the bed of the canal on that side was transferred over the wall to fill in the west side to make the foundation for a new towing path and the trackbed of the railway. This work, undertaken by a great many navvies, was completed within the week on the Saturday, apart from the stone coping of the brick wall in places, and it was intended to rewater the canal and reopen it for navigation on the Monday. The dramatic events which followed were reported in Aris's Birmingham Gazette of Monday 27 May. Water was apparently let in slowly over the Saturday night through a 12 inch square valve in the southern stop-gate, but at about 7.00 am on the Sunday morning the gate was opened (by whom is not stated) and water from the ten-mile stretch of canal to Tardebigge rushed in towards Birmingham, advancing "like a great tidal wave", and soon the canal was full and in some places washing over the embankment, and a breach occurred. Navvies tried to repair the breach at first and a canal boat was placed across the gap, but to no avail; the boat was carried through the breach and landed a complete wreck in the field below. A number of other canal boats were damaged by colliding together violently. Sturge's Fields became a sea up to 3 feet deep. Nearby in Packenham Road, the lowest level, the waters formed "a great lake", rushing into basements and the ground floors of some 8 to 10 villa residences. The water spent itself in Charlotte Road where the culverts carried away an immense quantity. A strong force of police was soon on the scene; thousands of people turned up to witness the devastation; fire engines arrived to pump water from homes. Navvies set to work on the Sunday to repair the breach with a brick wall several feet thick, banked up with earth behind. This was completed on Monday. The damaged boats were lifted by crane and sawn up. Repairs and the clearing of mud and sand etc. from the affected areas continued on subsequent days and the canal was not open to traffic until Saturday 15 June.

Fortunately there was no loss of life in this disaster, but there was, as described by a local resident in another newspaper, "much damage and distress, gardens inundated and shrubs and plants uprooted, brickwork of some houses dislodged, furniture and carpets ruined, as the current of muddy water pursued its career of destruction and devastation". Graphic artists from the "Illustrated London News" arrived post-haste to depict the scene at the breach for that publication. The W/B Canal Committee, through its engineer, Richard Boddington, protested strongly to the railway contractors, Messrs. Aird and Sons, at the way the breach was being repaired, and he was soon authorised to superintend the work. John Lloyd, engineer to the Warwick Canal Company, was appointed to assess the damages to be awarded to the W/B Company for loss of income due to the extra three weeks' stoppage.

The breach in the canal embankment at Edgbaston which had occurred on Sunday 26 May 1872. (Illustrated London News, 8 June 1872)

During 1872, with some work in progress, a revised plan of the railway was produced in which the tunnel at Selly Oak was replaced by a viaduct and bridge over the main road, and the planned viaduct over the canal in Birmingham was modified to reduce the gradients involved by increasing its length to 460 yards and the number of arches to 32. Also an agreement was reached with the Canal Company for the narrowing and deepening of the waterway under the two skew railway bridges to be constructed over the canal at Selly Oak, thereby restricting the summit pound henceforth to narrowboats. The Bill authorising these modifications passed through Parliament in 1873.

Construction of the railway, single track with passing loops, continued, the canal being used by the contractors for the carriage of materials. Narrowing of the canal for the bridges at Selly Oak took place during and after the Whit week stoppage, the Railway Company paying £50 a day, after 7 days, to the canal company which in turn compensated carriers for having to travel between Birmingham and Kings Norton via Warwick and the Stratford-on-Avon Canal. The railway was opened in due course on 3 April 1876. By this time the costly and awkward viaduct at the Birmingham end had been abandoned and the terminus was at Granville Street. There were stations at Church Road, Somerset Road, Selly Oak (passing loop), Stirchley Street (now Bournville), and the line from there continued alongside the canal to Breedon Cross wharf where it then joined the siding previously constructed by the Midland Railway in 1867 from Kings Norton Station round under the main line of the former Birmingham and Gloucester Railway to the wharf. On this last section from Breedon Cross Wharf to Kings Norton Station which, with the siding, was now double track, a station was opened at Lifford on 1 June 1876. Passenger services ran between Granville Street and Kings Norton.

Meanwhile the Midland Railway Company had, towards the end of 1871, offered to take over the W/B Canal Company, and in January 1872 the W/B Assembly agreed to try and negotiate a deal. In the Spring of 1872, however, a joint committee of both Houses of Parliament was set up to consider canal and railway amalgamations, so negotiations with the M.R. were deferred. The Assembly of January 1873 was informed of further delays following Parliamentary decisions, and the Midland Railway's bid was foiled by the Gloucester and Berkeley Canal Company's successful takeover, completed in 1874.

By the time it opened to traffic the Birmingham West Suburban Railway had been taken over (on 1 July 1875) by the Midland Railway Company which soon had plans to develop it. In 1881 an Act was obtained for doubling the track and running into New Street Station in Birmingham. Work on this began in 1883 and the SND Birmingham Committee gave permission for the contractor, Joseph Firbank, to use the canal for transporting bricks, of which some 30 million were to be used to line the deep cuttings and the three tunnels at the approach to New Street Station. As the tunnel works got under way there was evidence of subsidence, the weighbridge house on the wharf being seriously affected, and work was suspended. To enable tunnelling to proceed whilst at the same time allowing the canal to remain open safely and steps to be taken to strengthen and stabilise the embankment and wharf area, a 70-feet long timber trough was constructed to the design of Francis Hobrough, the W/B Canal engineer. This trough, wide enough and deep enough to allow the passage of boats, was strongly constructed of stout timbers and caulked. It was installed on the canal bed between dams across the basin, with guard rails at each end, in January 1884 during two stoppages of five and three days. As a precaution, there were night and day watchmen at the Granville Street Bridge stop-gate, and the stop-gate at the south end of the Edgbaston Valley was closed after each boat, until the tunnelling was completed and the risk removed. There were two short stoppages of the canal between the Bar Lock and Granville Street in July and November following accidents to the Midland Railway works, and compensation was agreed for boats unable to use the alternative Netherton and Lapal Tunnel route. The trough was removed and the works completed during a stoppage in February 1885 which, planned to last six days, actually lasted six and a half days longer, and claims totalling £220 had to be paid to boat owners in compensation in respect of the 167 vessels involved.

Because the railway tunnel under the canal ran, at a lower level, adjacent to the Holliday Street tunnel, it was necessary to replace the old brick aqueduct by the present sturdy cast-iron framed one. At the same time what had been little more than a passage (known as "The Gullet") from the corner of Holliday Street and Gas Street under the canal and wharf to Foredraught Street was widened as a continuation of Holliday Street and diverted to skirt the deep railway cutting and the entry to the final tunnel into New Street Station. The canal bed and wharf are upheld by brick vaults between girders supported by cross-girders resting on decorated cast-iron columns along the pavement edge on both sides of the road. The imposing metal bridge parapets have coloured diamond-patterned panels.

At Selly Oak a new bridge with a new embankment was built over the main road on the Birmingham side of the existing bridge which remained in situ for some time. Part of the old embankment still remains. The two railway bridges over the canal also had to be rebuilt to take the double track. To bear the extra load, four piers were sunk each side of the canal, between 40 and 50 feet in depth, under Mr Hobrough's supervision. Because of the realignment of track, Selly Oak Station was moved a little further away from the canal. To bypass the devious route via Breedon Cross and Lifford a new more direct section of track was built between Bournville and Kings Norton Stations.

THE MIDLAND RAILWAY CENTRAL GOODS DEPOT

Following completion of the railway between Kings Norton and New Street in 1885, the line began to be used for main line express passenger services as well as for local trains. A new station had been established at Five Ways and plans had been made for the old line from Five Ways to Granville Street to be extended by a large tunnel under Worcester Wharf to a new Midland Railway goods depot. Following the completion of this work, "Worcester Wharf Goods Depot" opened on 1 July 1887. From Granville Street the railway was double track, descending an incline of 1 in 80 towards and within the tunnel. Again the wooden trough was used as a safety measure during tunnelling. Through the tunnel the depot sidings gradually spread over an area of ten acres between the Worcester Canal Wharf and Suffolk Street, some rails entering a large busy warehouse lit by electricity. The depot, latterly known as "Suffolk Street Goods Depot", closed in March 1967 and the rails were then soon lifted. Part of the site became a car park before its subsequent development and part is now occupied by the "Mailbox" development of shops and other facilities created out of the post-office administrative building built there. The trackbed of the goods line from Five Ways through the road bridges and the tunnel remains in place and has been used by some road vehicles.

FACTORY SIDINGS ACROSS THE CANAL

There have been no further public railway developments affecting the structure of the canal, but a number of canalside factories were allowed to build bridges over the canal at various times to gain rail access into their works for traffic to and from the railways. One such bridge was constructed for the British Alkali Works at Stoke Prior (see Chapter 17), another for Hill Evans and Company's Vinegar Works at Worcester. The Hill Evans Company's branch line, some 900 yards long, was opened in 1872. It connected the vinegar works west of the canal with the railway main line near the Worcester locomotive works. Besides crossing the canal, it also crossed several roads where the traffic was controlled by standard Great Western Railway signals. There were four semaphores on a signal post in Pheasant Street, two for the railway, two for road vehicles. Another railway bridge over the canal was built for Cadbury's of Bournville. It was a skew bridge which allowed a railway connection between their works sidings and their Waterside canal wharf. These private railway branches no longer exist, and the "vinegar bridge" in Worcester has long gone, but the bridges which carried the railway across the canal at Stoke Prior and Bournville remain in situ.

LOSS OF THE LIFFORD LOOP

In addition to the loss of canalside industrial railways, another casualty was the eventual disappearance of the Midland Railway's loop line from Bournville via the canal wharf at Breedon Cross and round to join the old Birmingham and Gloucester

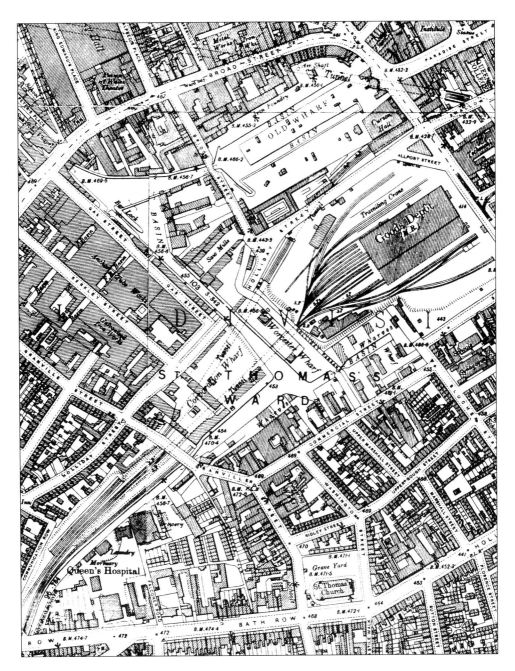

1902 O.S. map showing Gas Street Basin, the Old Wharf of the B.C.N., the Midland Railway's Goods Depot, railway tunnels under the Worcester Wharf and other features. (BRL)

line towards Kings Norton Station. This section of track became redundant as far as passenger traffic was concerned when the double-track main-line route between New Street Station and Kings Norton opened in 1885. As a result Lifford Station on the loop line was moved back to its original location on the Birmingham and Gloucester line west of the canal bridge. There, following the creation of the rail link curve in a cutting between the two main lines in 1892, the station served the circular route thus available for suburban passenger trains travelling one way out from, and the other way into, Birmingham New Street Station.

The Lifford loop continued to be used for the interchange of goods between railway and canal until the 1930s, and sidings from the loop served the Kings Norton Metal Works, established there c.1890, for many years. Today part of the trackbed northwards through the main-road bridge at Breedon Cross is now a road. The arch through which the Lifford loop passed under the Birmingham and Gloucester Railway remains adjoining the canal bridge No.74, but most of the trackbed south of Breedon Cross has been built over.

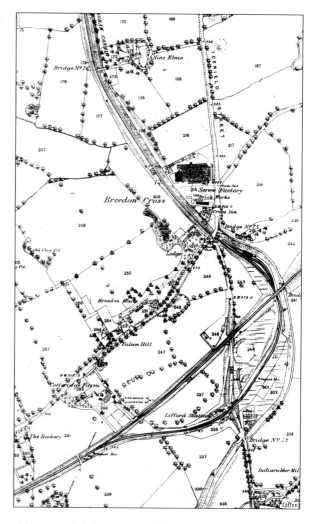

Above and right: maps of the Lifford and Breedon Cross area. Above: 1882 showing the original Birmingham and West Suburban Railway route between Bournville and Kings Norton Stations following the canal and curving round to join the Birmingham and Gloucester Railways; also Nettleford's Screw Factory. Right: 1904 showing the more direct route opened in 1885 and the link curve from it to the Birmingham and Gloucester railway; also the newly-erected Kings Norton metal Works with its railway sidings and canal basin.

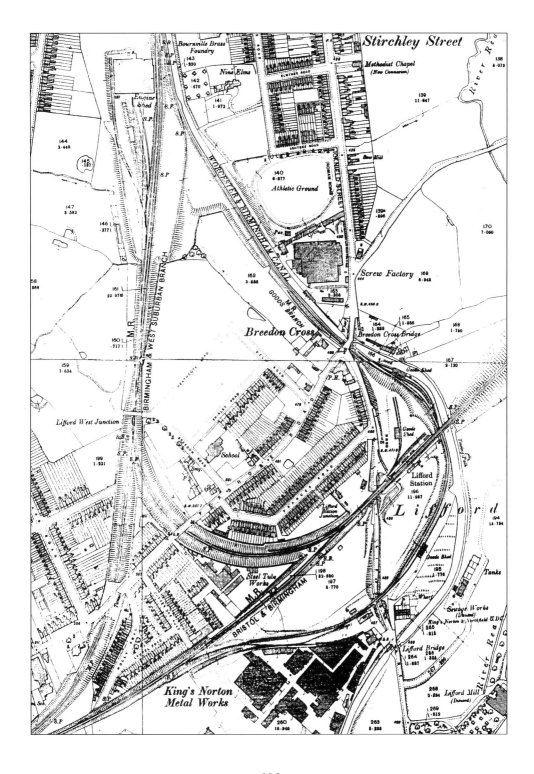

Chapter 14

THOSE WHO MANAGED AND MAINTAINED THE CANAL

Over the years a great many people have been involved in the management and maintenance of the W/B Canal. They include the Company's secretaries, clerks, treasurers and bankers; prominent shareholders and Committee members; engineers and surveyors; lock-keepers and lengthsmen, carpenters, fitters, bricklayers and other maintenance staff. The names and deeds of many of these are forgotten because most of the early office records have been lost or destroyed. But we do know of many devoted employees of the Canal Company who gave long and faithful service, including, in some cases, several generations of the same family. Information about them has been derived from the minute books of the Company's Assemblies and Committee meetings, from newspaper reports and obituaries, and from the memories of those who knew them.

MANAGEMENT OF THE W/B CANAL COMPANY

When the canal was completed in 1815, a number of those who had been involved in the administration of the Company during the period of its construction continued to serve. In particular, Benjamin Parker, a Birmingham attorney, having helped to promote the canal and having been elected Clerk of the Company at its first Assembly in July 1791, remained in office until 1825, when he retired due to ill-health. As Company Clerk, he had been responsible for organising, advertising and sending out notices of Assembly meetings, advertising for contractors, keeping the Register of Shareholders, and dealing with the overall administration of the Company's business. He was succeeded by John Hodgkinson who had also served during the canal's construction since 1793. The Assembly minutes of January 1840 recorded his death "after upwards of 46 years of faithful service" and praised him for his "integrity and exertions". His brother Samuel Hodgkinson, Engineer to the B.C.N., had assisted the W/B Company with advice as the canal was being completed following William Crosley's departure early in 1815, and in subsequent months he was involved in designing lock-keepers' cottages, warehouses and other structures. John's son William Hodgkinson, who had already for ten years assisted his father, was appointed Accountant Clerk in his place and served in this capacity for many years until his resignation at the end of 1868 after having worked for the Company for 42 years. He was awarded the substantial pension of £250 per annum on condition that he would continue to give the Company the benefit of his services and information, when required, and not engage in other employment. He, in turn, was succeeded by Henry Parry at a salary of £350. The Company was fortunate in the calibre, integrity and length of service of these Chief Accountant Clerks into whose hands its day-to-day financial affairs were entrusted.

THE W/B CANAL COMMITTEE

Unlike later companies, the W/B Canal Company's constitution included no Board of Directors. In accordance with the 1791 W/B Canal Act, an Assembly of shareholders was held in January and July each year at which fifteen of its members were elected to serve on its Committee, to carry out its instructions, to oversee the day-to-day running of the canal, and to deal with problems and emergencies and the appointment of the workforce. At each Assembly the Committee reported on its activities and made recommendations. It met regularly and, at times, travelled the length of the canal on its Committee Boat to inspect the condition of the waterway. There was no salary attached, only the receipt of expenses for travel and meals. Some Committee members were birds-of-passage, serving for short periods only; others were repeatedly re-elected and gave long and devoted service. Three of the latter were Thomas Carden, William Mabson and William Beale. Thomas Cardon, besides being an original promoter of the canal, was on the Committee during the whole of the time it was under construction, being for most of the time its chairman, and he continued to deal actively with the affairs of the waterway at the Worcester end at least until 1827. William Mabson, another prominent and long-serving Committee member, was a Birmingham business-man who had been on the Committee well before the completion of the canal and who had much to do with proposals relating to railways and other developments in the mid 19th century. William Beale's long service was also greatly valued. Following his death, the Committee of Works in September 1848 resolved to convey deep sympathy to the wife and family of "their late most highly and deservedly respected Friend and Colleague William Beale Esq." who had given almost 40 years service and who had been a highly regarded and most zealous and useful member of the Committee and frequently its chairman.

EARLY W/B CANAL ENGINEERS

In charge of the maintenance of the waterway and its structures, including locks, bridges, tunnels, warehouses, wharves, and dwelling houses, were the resident engineers and surveyors. Following the departure of William Crosley in the early summer of 1815, the last stages in the completion of the canal were supervised by Samuel Hodgkinson of the B.C.N., as already mentioned, assisted by William Shore of the Canal Committee. In January 1816 Shore was officially appointed Engineer to the Company for one year at a salary of £350 per year backdated to 17 July 1815. In July 1816 he was reappointed as Superintendent of the canal with a salary of £300 plus £100 expenses. In January 1818 the Assembly praised Mr Shore for his work but agreed that he should be replaced at less expense. The advertisement for his successor stipulated that "The person most wanted is a working Engineer, one practically conversant in a Masonry Carpenter's work, cutting, puddling, fencing and measuring; in fact a Man who will be competent to superintend the Works of the Company, and, if necessary, work himself." The man who fitted this description, and who was appointed, was George Rew.

GEORGE REW

George Rew was first mentioned in the Canal Committee minutes of 29 December 1809, having been paid £45 for work done on the Caisson Lock, or Lift, at Tardebigge. Early in 1811 we find him involved in brick-making near Tardebigge and towards the end of the year inspecting the bricks made by other contractors. In February 1812 Crosley signed an agreement with Rew to build the bridges, make the culverts and undertake other brickwork on parts of the Five-mile Pound. In May 1812 "George Rew, having laid before the Committee proposals for finishing the work lately undertaken by Joseph Smith and abandoned by him, resolved that his offer be accepted." This was the completion of the brickwork of Dunhampstead Tunnel, which, with the other work in hand, must have been satisfactorily done, for in the summer of 1814 Rew was negotiating with Holland, the contractor, over carts, barrows and planks etc. needed to excavate Lowesmoor Basin. In February 1815 Rew was instructed by the Committee to report on ways in which John Woodhouse had broken his contract in the Stoke Prior area. George Rew was evidently a man who had proved his worth by the success of the works he had undertaken, a competent practical man who, like Thomas Cartwright before him, had progressively gained in experience, and in whom the Company had the confidence to appoint as Superintendent of the canal in January 1818. Rew continued to serve until 1837, being frequently mentioned in the minutes, producing estimates for proposed works such as side ponds at Sidbury and Blockhouse locks and a possible second reservoir at Tardebigge, supervising general repairs, fencing, bridge works, including the construction in 1828 of the cantilever foot bridge at the bottom end of lock 33 (Tardebigge Flight), and the planning of the Himbleton quarries railroad system. In 1828 he was, as already mentioned, especially commended and financially rewarded for his estimates, surveys and work in connection with the construction of Tardebigge Reservoir. But, as time went on the Committee did, on two occasions in 1833 and 1835, find fault with Rew and threatened his dismissal. However he continued to serve until 1837 when the July Assembly was informed that "The sudden death of Mr. George Rew, the Company's Surveyor, to whose care the Works of the Canal had been entrusted for upwards of 20 years, has rendered it necessary to place another of the Company's Servants in that Department until a competent Surveyor can be appointed."

RICHARD BODDINGTON

In caring for the works of the canal, Rew had shown great practical ability, but he was not a professional engineer, able to plan and execute major works, as was his successor, Richard Boddington, appointed in 1840. Richard was the son of Edward Boddington who had been engaged by the Canal Company in 1829 to plan and survey Upper Bittell Reservoir and who, as the chosen contractor, had completed the work efficiently by 1832. Edward Boddington had also been summoned urgently on 31 July 1839 to survey a major breach, 50 yards long, in the Gallows Brook Embankment between Selly Oak and Breedon Cross, caused by heavy rain and flooding in the Rea Valley. He was then asked to undertake the necessary repair work, assisted by his son. The repair took over a month, about 150 labourers being employed, and it seems probable that Edward, committed elsewhere in the north-east of the country, left much of the oversight to his son Richard. At any rate officials of the Canal Company were so well impressed by Richard's capabilities that he was soon appointed to be their Engineer and Surveyor.

In October 1839, to prevent any similar disaster in the future, Mr Boddington senior was asked to accompany the Committee of Works on a survey of the summit level to consider what weirs it might be expedient to make and what cottages to erect near stop gates so that they could be quickly closed in an emergency. In December he was paid £150 for so doing. Then in January 1840 his son Richard took up his appointment with the Canal Company. He was to serve, with distinction, for some 35 years. During this time, besides seeing to the normal routine maintenance of the canal, he undertook several major tasks. In 1845 he produced, on behalf of the W/B Canal Company, a detailed survey of the route, between Birmingham and Stoke Works, of the proposed Birmingham and Worcester Direct Railway and he was listed in the Prospectus as its Engineer (see chapter 13). In 1851 he produced a plan and section of the Droitwich Junction Canal and, as engineer, he supervised its construction 1852-4 (see chapter 10). During his term of office he was expected to keep abreast of the many plans and proposals for railways which would need to cross the canal or which could affect its business, and to report on these to the Canal Committee. He came to live beside the canal at Stoke Wharf near the maintenance depot, which was equipped with a dry dock, carpenters and fitters shops, stores and a smithy. In 1849 the "Navigation Row" of five cottages for Company employees was built, and a skilled workforce recruited to man the depot. Of Richard's personal and family details we know that he was in his mid twenties when appointed in 1840, his first wife Salina died in 1843, he married again and his second wife Maria died in 1863. He saw the Canal Company taken over by the Sharpness Company in 1874, and his last recorded duties were in June 1875.

W F HOBROUGH

Boddington's successor, who took his place immediately, was William Francis Hobrough (1828-1912), an experienced professional engineer. Starting out as a boat-builder with his father at Huddiscoe, Norfolk, he joined the Royal Navy and spent several years as ship's carpenter on H.M.S. *Howe*. He then set up as a contractor in Norwich and carried out work for the Yarmouth Harbour Commissioners, dealing with local rivers and drains, during which time he invented a mud-carrier for transporting dredged material from dredger to river bank, which cut the cost of dredging by a half. He then carried out extensive works at Lydney Harbour on the Severn Estuary, making a new entrance to the docks, erecting several self-acting coal tips and removing considerable quantities of rock by means of submarine blasting with dynamite exploded by electricity. It was following this contract that he was chosen by the SND Company to be Engineer in charge of the W/B and the two Droitwich Canals. He came and lived in the Bridge House at Stoke Wharf adjacent to the Maintenance Depot, where, with his family and household servants, he lived the life of a gentleman. He was a big, well-made man with a beard. He owned a brougham and a waggonette and kept stables and a smallholding. He took an active interest in local affairs, serving sometime as Churchwarden of St. Michael's Parish Church and as a member of the Stoke Prior and Dodderhill School Board. He was greatly respected and looked-up-to by the canal employees, many of whom earned extra money from time to time by doing gardening and other jobs for him.

During his time as Engineer he exercised a firm grip on the maintenance of the canal and the Company's workforce. On taking over, his first tasks were to improve the canal by extensive dredging and to introduce the tug-haulage of boats through Tardebigge and Shortwood Tunnels and through the West Hill Tunnel. When in 1884 the Midland Railway began tunnelling under the Worcester Wharf in Birmingham to gain access to New Street Station and to their new goods depot being built, there was a danger of the subsidence of the canal and the prospect of a long stoppage of the waterway traffic. To minimise the danger and the delays, Hobrough had a substantial watertight wooden trough constructed and located over the line of each of the tunnels as they were being made so that boats could pass. The trough was 70ft in length, 4ft deep inside and 7ft 6in wide, and the tradesmen from several boat docks, including Farrin's Dock at Stoke Prior, were employed to caulk the joints and seams of this massive structure to make it watertight. Many civil engineers from around the country came to inspect this contrivance, and Hobrough received the congratulations of both the Railway and the Canal Companies for his achievement. Another notable success was the steam bucket dredger, constructed by Hobrough in 1885-6, together with his invention and use of a new method of shifting the material dredged from the canal bed by means of iron boxes, or skips, fitted into boats and lifted and discharged by steam cranes, thus effecting a considerable saving in labour costs. The dredger had an iron hull fitted with an elevator chain of buckets and was worked by a mobile steam engine which could be lifted out of the dredger and used for other purposes. This dredger remained in use, together with several work boats and twenty iron skips, until 1912, when it sank and overturned just above lock 16 at Offerton. It was not used again and was eventually scrapped in 1917.

When W F Hobrough retired in 1908 after over 33 years service for the SND Company he received various souvenirs and an illuminated address from its employees and officials.

W T GRIFFITHS

Hobrough's successor, W T Griffiths, served for only 5 years, 1908-13. He lived on Stoke Wharf in the Wharf House, which had been for many years a shop, and he added the present glass verandah. During his time he was kept busy as the Maintenance Depot was moved in stages from Stoke to new premises on Tardebigge New Wharf. To help in his travels up and down the canal he was provided with a motorcycle and sidecar by the canal company.

SECTION INSPECTORS 1913-1989

The men who followed W T Griffiths in charge of the maintenance of the canal were given the title of Section Inspector. Those who served successively in this capacity were Frank Rowles (1913-30), Edgar Spiers (1931-49), Leslie Thompson (1949-59), George Colledge (1959-74), and Stuart Perry (1974-89).

Besides having the expertise and experience to organise and oversee the maintenance work on locks, weirs, bridges and buildings etc., the SND engineers and section inspectors needed also to have a working knowledge of steam and other engines used as motive power for the tugs and for the machinery used in the workshops, sawmill, and in dredging and pumping.

Frank Rowles had been one of the original tugmen transferred from Gloucester in 1876. He became involved in local affairs, he was respected in the community and by his fellow workmen, and he merited his promotion.

Edgar Spiers had been in the employ of Bellis and Morcom, steam engine manufacturers in Birmingham. He was described by L T C Rolt as a shy, soft-spoken, gentle man who appreciated the dedication and workmanship of his staff and rarely interfered with their work.

Leslie Thompson, a carpenter by trade, did not get on too well with his workforce and they were not sorry when he moved on to Gloucester. He had the distinction of being the first of several car drivers who, in recent years, returning from an evening out, have managed to cause their vehicle to demolish part of the parapet above the south portal of Tardebigge tunnel, and in one case to have finished up in the canal.

George Colledge, a member of the Colledge family who lived on the New Wharf for many years, was a skilled bricklayer. He was a man of great strength, very popular, and knew how to get the best from his fellow workmen.

Stuart Perry, who came from Cheshire and retired there, was a volatile character. A very practical man, he was soon on the scene with his foreman, David James, when a roof fall occurred during repairs at the north end of the West Hill Tunnel in November 1979, killing two workmen. They commandeered a holiday boat and went through the tunnel from the south end to look for any workmen who might have been injured or trapped.

SOME EARLY LOCK-KEEPERS, CLERKS AND MAINTENANCE MEN

When the canal opened in December 1815, some of those who had been employed in its construction and had given good service were given jobs as lock-keepers, clerks and maintenance men. They included John Hunt appointed as the lock-keeper of Blockhouse and Sidbury Locks, Richard Rowlands as lock-keeper of the locks at Gregory's Mill and Astwood, Worcester, John Gilbert as lock-keeper of Offerton Locks, Francis Cocks as ticket clerk at Diglis, John Bolding as superintendent of the wharf weighing machine at Hanbury, and William Blount as the superintendent at Stoke Wharf. Other positions were filled by already-experienced employees such as John Heywood, machine clerk, who was moved from Tardebigge to Lowesmoor, his place being filled by his assistant, Benjamin Smith.

LOCK-KEEPERS AND LENGTHSMEN

In the early years there was a lock-keeper for every six locks of the canal down to Worcester. On the top thirty there were lock-keepers' cottages at the Top Lock, Tardebigge Reservoir, Upper Halfway, The Halfway, and Stoke Flight. For the six locks between the Queen's Head and Stoke Wharf there was one of the three canalside cottages near Whitford Bridge, Stoke Pound; for the Astwood Flight of six locks the cottage by lock 18; and for the Offerton Flight of six locks the cottage by lock 15. Covering the more scattered six locks down to Lowesmoor there were lock cottages at Claines (Tolladine), at Bilford, and at Gregory's Mill. The lock-keeper at the Blockhouse was toll-clerk and minder of Blockhouse and Sidbury locks and the canal from Lowesmoor to Diglis. Finally there was the Diglis lockhouse and toll office. When the Droitwich Junction Canal was opened in 1854, cottages were provided for two lock-keepers, one at Hanbury Wharf, the other on the Hanbury Road near the Town Mill. Also at that time, an additional toll office was built beside lock 17 (Lower Astwood Lock Cottage); this was vacated, vandalised and then demolished in the 1950s, as were also the lock cottages at Tolladine and Gregory's Mill. As, in the latter part of the 20th. century, commercial traffic was replaced by pleasure cruising, many of the lock cottages were sold or rented to people unconnected with canal maintenance. Fortunately most of the remaining cottages and structures of the canal are now "listed buildings", and many have been restored.

Besides supervising the use of the locks, the lock-keepers were expected to keep them in good order, to lubricate the lock paddle-gear and to padlock it at night to prevent locks being used then, also to trim hedges and keep the towpath on their

A group of W/B Canal workmen at the repair of one of the Tardebigge flight of locks in 1894. From left to right: Harry Colley and, in front, a son of James Waldron, James Waldron, Edward Crumpton, James Bishop, George Woodward, Philip Vale, Fred Warren, William Harris (seated), Nathan Blunn, John Tallis (WRO)

The replacement of a lock gate probably c.1950, at Brassington Bridge, Stoke Prior, George Bate, kneeling, on the right. (F. Lewis)

stretch of canal in good repair. Damage to locks and other structures had to be reported and also the boats and names of persons breaking the Company's bye-laws. Many of the lock-keepers cultivated the patch of ground across the lock opposite to their cottage, producing flowers and vegetables, some of which they sold to passing boatmen or bartered for items of "surplus" cargo such as coal or sugar. They also usually kept pigs and poultry and brewed their own liquor. Their wives sold pots of tea and refreshments to fishermen usually at 3d. or 6d. a time.

In recent times there have been just four full-time lock-keepers to cover the 58 locks. Around the year 2000, Roger Hatchard at Diglis, together with a part-time relief, was looking after the canal from lock 1 to lock 8, Brian Parker at Offerton from lock 9 to lock 16, Allan Troth at Astwood from lock 17 to lock 37; and Mick Handford at Tardebigge from lock 38 to lock 58. Together with one lengthsman, Ken Mitchell at Lower Bittell, they were responsible for the day to day oversight of the whole length of the canal.

With its 58 locks the W/B Canal Company has had, over the years, a great many lock-keepers, as well as lengthsmen, craftsmen and others involved in repair and maintenance. Many of these men spent all their working life on the canal and many were members of families of which several generations were canal employees. Many were related by marriage, for canal workers and their families, together with working boat families, were members of a close-knit waterway community.

From Tardebigge Tunnel to Diglis the lock-keepers acted as lengthsmen, keeping a watchful eye upon their section of canal and dealing with problems. On the summit level between Gas Street Basin and Tardebigge Tunnel there were, when the canal was busy with working boats, several lengthsmen whose duties included policing their section, undertaking towpath and hedge maintenance and being ready, if needs be, to close stop gates to protect the embankments at various times. There was a lengthsman's house at Kings Norton as well as the one at Bittell at the entrance to Jacob's Cut.

TOLL CLERKS

The collection of tolls was an important and essential operation on all canals, being the main source of income. Toll houses were situated at strategic locations where working boats had to stop to be examined and records kept of their movements and the type and weight of the cargoes on board. The toll payable was based on the distance travelled along the canal and also on what was being carried. Each toll-house keeper had the gauging details of all boats passing his station. Most of the boats using the W/B Canal had been gauged and registered on the B.C.N. at either Tipton or Smethwick. A boat being gauged would be progressively loaded, one ton at a time up to its maximum load. At each stage the amount of freeboard ("dry inches" in the records) would be recorded as the average of four measurements taken each side of the boat at the bow and stern with a gauging rod. Copies, made by hand, of pages of the B.C.N. gauging registers were deposited at the toll offices of canals on the routes travelled. Then from the gauging table for the particular boat a toll clerk, using his gauging rod to ascertain the average freeboard, could work out the toll to be levied. This was either paid on the spot or booked to the boat's owners if they had an account with the canal company.

Whilst the canal was busy with working boats there were up to ten toll offices along its length. These were at the Bar Lock in Birmingham, Selly Oak, Bittell, Tardebigge Top Lock, Stoke Wharf, Hanbury Wharf, Lowesmoor Basin, Blockhouse Lock, and Diglis, and also, following the opening of the Droitwich Junction Canal, by lock 17 at the bottom of the Astwood Flight to cater for traffic to or from that canal. Tolls were collected by lock-keepers or weighbridge clerks at some locations such as Tardebigge, Stoke Wharf, Hanbury Wharf, The Blockhouse and Diglis.

At Selly Oak the toll office was at first on the wharf there, but following the narrowing of the canal where the Midland Railway crosses it near Raddlebarn Road, a new cottage and office was built on the towpath side around 1875 for the toll clerk

W J Parish. Three years later a second adjoining cottage was added for assistant toll clerk J Miles, it being noted in the Committee minutes that Mr Parish was of a nervous disposition and had not been well. It was a lonely and potentially dangerous spot, especially at night, and Parish, with toll money on the premises, was, no doubt, glad to have the company and protection of his new neighbour. Designated by the Canal Company as Fieldings Lane Station, the toll office was known to canal people as Selly Oak Stop. It was conveniently situated to catch traffic passing between the canal's two junctions one with the Stratford Canal at Kings Norton and the other with the Netherton Canal at Selly Oak. The two cottages have long since been demolished.

THE WOLFINDALES

Over the years several generations of Wolfindales were involved in the maintenance of the canal. Tardebigge parish registers record the baptisms in 1814 of John, son of Mary and John Wolfindale, boatman at the Lift, and of Thomas, son of Nancy and James Wolfindale, labourer. Of the two fathers, the second may have been the James Wolfindale who had been appointed by the Canal Company in the summer of 1807 as its "Walking Surveyor", to reside in the machine house at Hopwood and to go over the new works (from Hopwood to Tardebigge) every day and over the old works to Stratford Junction twice a week, as recommended by Mr Cartwright, and to report to the Office on the state of the works every Saturday. In May 1809 he was instructed in future to walk to Birmingham three days a week and to Tardebigge three days a week. He reported in August 1809 on repairs needed at Tardebigge Wharf and to the road over the bridge at Alvechurch. In May 1810 he was ordered to report any boatmen using spiked shafts to facilitate their passage through the tunnels, contrary to bye-law no.10. He continued in this post as lengthsman on the summit pound, keeping a watchful eye upon the works of the canal until 1824, when, perhaps tired or incapable of so much walking, he resigned and was succeeded by James Price. He was then engaged as machine clerk at Hanbury Wharf. His son, James Wolfindale junior, was, in March 1824, appointed as a lock-keeper, but not for long, for he was replaced in November 1825 and we hear no more of him.

As for John Wolfindale, boatman at the Lift in 1814, records show that, after the completion of the canal, he was employed from time to time as "resident contractor" for minor works, such as in 1823 removing a fall of stone in Tardebigge Tunnel, in 1825 delivering gravel at Coombe Hill on the leased Coombe Hill Canal, in 1827 constructing roads and a feeder at Bittell, in 1830 tendering, unsuccessfully, for the contract to construct Back Bittell Reservoir, and in 1843 dredging the Droitwich Canal at 5d. a yard. His namesake relative, John Wolfindale, born in 1832, whose home was at Withybed Green, became a boatman and then worked on canal maintenance, dredging etc. He married Ann and one of their sons, Tom Wolfindale, followed in his father's footsteps as dredgerman and worked for 54 years on the canal, from about 1886 to 1940. Tom's daughter has told of the long periods he would be away, sometimes working at Gloucester and sleeping on the cabin floor of a workboat, and that it was at Gloucester that he met his wife, Margaret. When working in Worcester, he would set off at 4.00 am and walk there along the towpath, a journey of some 15 miles in addition to a day's work. Along with other canal employees, he was expected to lend a hand with lock repairs, ice-breaking, and other jobs. Because Hobrough's steam dredger, until its demise in 1912, could only be successfully operated on the summit and other long pounds, Tom Wolfindale's dredging was mostly done with an old-fashioned spoon dredger, the operation of which, and the disposal of the spoil using wheel-barrows, was really heavy work. In 1930 Tom had the end of his thumb scrubbed off on the side of the West Hill Tunnel whilst steering a boat through it, with his hand on the end of the tiller, his experience being talked of for many years as a warning against this danger.

THE WARINGS

In 1825 James Wolfindale the elder was replaced as machine clerk at Hanbury Wharf by John Waring. The Warings were another family of long-serving canal servants. There were two John Warings on the payroll in 1825, the elder at Hanbury Wharf, and his son, lock-keeper at Stoke Prior. The latter became the first tenant of the Reservoir House at the entrance to Jacob's Cut at Lower Bittell about 1840, when weirs were made and attendants' houses constructed at several places on the canal to prevent flood damage. John Waring and his wife Sarah remained at the Reservoir House until his retirement in 1865, when one of his sons, James, took over. Unfortunately, that same year James's six-year-old son was drowned and four years later, perhaps fearful for the safety of other members of his family in that dangerous location, he left and was succeeded there in 1869 by his elder brother Richard, who, following his father, had been lock-keeper at Stoke Prior. Richard and his wife Sarah remained at Bittell for 14 years. They moved to Astwood Lock in 1883 and he died there, aged 74, in 1894. One of their sons, also named Richard, succeeded his father at Bittell and remained there for 37 years until his retirement in 1920. Another son, Jack Waring, was lock-keeper at Offerton around the turn of the century, 1900.

At Bittell, the Warings acted as lengthsmen from Hopwood to Tardebigge Tunnel as well as being available for general maintenance work. They had to keep weekly records of the water levels at Cofton, Upper and Lower Bittell Reservoirs, and also of the canal; and they were responsible, in conjunction with the water bailiff resident at Upper Bittell, for controlling the flow of water from the reservoirs into the canal and into the River Arrow; also for taking any necessary action to prevent flooding.

Repairs to lock 28, Stoke Pound, in 1952. Left to right: Peter Woodward, Ray Maries, Tom Brown, George Bate. (Paul Denning Bate)

THE WALDRONS

Between 1835 and 1853, the lock-keeper at the Blockhouse in Worcester was John Waldron. He and his wife Harriet had a large family. One son, George, born 1832, became lock-keeper and machine clerk at the Round House for the Droitwich Junction Canal; son Edward, born 1835, was toll-collector at Diglis in the 1870s; another son James, born 1843, was lock-keeper at Stoke Flight for many years until he was accidentally drowned in the nearby lock in 1909. The three sons of George Waldron all worked on the canal, Leonard succeeded his father at the Round House, Harry was a labourer at Hopwood, and Harold, after spending 20 years as donkeyman at Stoke, followed his uncle James as lock-keeper at Stoke Flight. Harold's daughter Kathleen married George Collins who became lock-keeper at Astwood in Wychbold Parish. So at least seven members of the Waldron family were employed at various times by the Canal Company.

THE WARNERS

In her book "Lock Keeper's Daughter" Pat Warner has given a fascinating account of life in the 1920s and 1930s, living at the Reservoir Lock Cottage where her father Jack Warner was lock-keeper from 1909 until he died in 1952. He had previously been lock-keeper at the Blockhouse, Worcester, where Pat's five older sisters had been born, and he followed his father at the Reservoir Lock Cottage. His wife Agnes was a daughter of Edward Crumpton who was lock-keeper at the Upper Halfway Cottage in the early 1900s until his retirement about 1915, and her sister Alice was the wife of Dennis Watton who was toll clerk at Diglis from 1924-49. Jack Warner's grandfather had worked on canals, and Jack proudly used his grandfather's windlass inscribed with the initials F.W. Two of Jack's five brothers also worked on the canal. One, William ("Joe") Warner, was toll clerk and lock-keeper at the Top Lock, Tardebigge, from about 1920 to 1955. His duties included being in charge of stores and the Company's stables at the New Wharf. He had been born at the Reservoir Lock Cottage in 1878 and had previously worked with the Tardebigge maintenance gang. Jack's other brother, Fred, also began as a labourer at the New Wharf, became lock-keeper on the Droitwich Junction Canal and ended up as the Lower Astwood lock-keeper.

Jack Warner's only son John died at the age of 6 months, so there was no one to follow in his footsteps. But of William's sons, Arthur worked for a time at the Worcester Wharf in Birmingham, William as a bricklayer and storeman at Tardebigge living at no.1 Tug Cottages, and Jack was the last tugman with Percy Bolton at the West Hill Tunnel. Fred's only son Dick followed his father as lock-keeper at the Lower Astwood lock cottage before it was demolished. He was a cripple and he kept ducks on the canal; the Five-mile Pound was his duck pond and he would ride his bike along the towpath in the evenings and crack a whip and the ducks would then return home. Lock no.17 there was long known as Warner's Lock; previously it had been known as Colley's Lock, George Colley having been lock-keeper there for many years in the latter part of the 19th century. Dick Warner moved to Stoke Flight Cottage around 1955, married Ruth Teale, daughter of Fred Teale the last lock-keeper at the Halfway Lock Cottage, in 1958 and died in 1966. Ruth lived on alone at Stoke Flight until 1986.

THE BISHOPS

Two brothers, Jim and Tom Bishop, of a Belbroughton farming family, became lock-keepers about 1880. Jim and his wife Sally were at the Halfway Lock Cottage for over 50 years until he retired in 1934 at the age of 70, when Fred Teale took over. Jim, who was clean-shaven, had never been to school and had started work as a ploughboy. He and Sally kept hens and pigs, the pigsty being across the lock, and they cultivated the land around the lock and cottage. Rain off the roof was fed into a tank below the brewhouse (washhouse) and, being soft. was used for washing. A pump in front of the brewhouse supplied drinking water. Sally used to make tea for the fishermen in jugs at 3d. a pint and 6d. a quart. Jim kept an eye on Brazier's Wharf near the Halfway House, for which he was paid an annual gratuity. He used to boast that he was the first in that area to have a wireless set with valves and batteries. Jim's son Bill Bishop was steerer on the tunnel tug *Sharpness* from 1916-24, with Percy Hawkins who was engineer, before becoming a farm labourer.

Tom Bishop and his wife Jessie lived at the third of the three canalside cottages below Whitford Bridge, Stoke Pound. He had a black beard and was always referred to by his brother as "our kid of the whiskers". Sadly, Jessie drowned trying in vain to save two of her children from drowning, and Tom then married Mrs Woodward, widow of a canal employee. Tom's surviving son Albert was a bricklayer and he and his wife Alice lived from 1906 at the Gregory's Mill Lock Cottage in Worcester, celebrating their Golden Wedding there in 1956, when he recalled how in those 50 years traffic had fallen from more than 40 boats a day to an average of only one. Whilst Albert was away on war service 1914-18, Alice did the lock-keeping including the locking of the gates each night.

THE PARKERS

Since 1920 three generations of Parkers have served as lock-keepers at Offerton, living in the lock house opposite lock 15. William Parker started work as a lengthsman on the canal in 1915. He and his wife lived at Hanbury Wharf and from there moved with their son William to Offerton in 1920. When William senior died in 1937 his son succeeded him and was lock-keeper until his retirement in 1980, with breaks due to war service and later to ill-health. During William junior's time as lock-keeper at Offerton thirteen people were drowned there including some experienced boatmen who, he said, "used to stop off and slip between the boat and the side. They got drawn under the boat and that was it". On one occasion he had to rescue his own daughter after she tripped into the lock; he lifted her out, unconscious, by her clothing with a boathook.

Following William Parker's retirement in 1980 his son Brian has continued there as lock-keeper.

MAINTENANCE MEN

Besides the lock-keepers there were men who did good service as skilled craftsmen, blacksmiths, carpenters, fitters, bricklayers, etc. As the canal was completed in 1815 its maintenance depot was established on the off-side of the canal south of the road bridge at Stoke Wharf. The blacksmith's and carpenter's shops there are mentioned in 1817 in the Committee minutes, and in 1819 James Wolfindale was ordered to make an inventory of the timber and tools in the shops and yard there. John Tallis, who died in 1862, and his son John, who retired in 1908 after 65 years service, lived in canalside cottages at Stoke Pound and spent most of their working lives as carpenters at the Stoke depot. Of three generations of Woodwards, who also lived alongside the canal at Stoke Pound, George was a carpenter at Stoke depot, his son Alfred was a bricklayer, and Alfred's son Peter became George Bate's assistant at

Winter 1957. A new lock gate for one of Diglis barge locks outside the carpenters' shop, New Wharf, Tardebigge. It went by canal, the water level of the Five-mile Pound having to be lowered to pass through Dunhampstead Tunnel. As can be seen, some of the brickwork at the entrance to the shop had to removed to get the gate out. (David James)

the Tardebigge depot until his early death in 1955 at the age of 33. Amongst others who were based at the Stoke Wharf depot around 1900, having given long service there, were Thomas Rammill the blacksmith, Herbert Goodyere the fitter, and Reuben White, carpenter, whose two daughters taught at Stoke Prior School and who had to retire when he went blind.

GEORGE BATE

After the new maintenance depot was established at the New Wharf, Tardebigge, from 1809 to 1913, a new generation of craftsmen soon took over. One of these was George Bate. George began work in the carpenters' shop at Tardebigge in December 1915 at the age of 14 as assistant to his father, Herbert Bate, who was the foreman carpenter. It was during the 1914-18 War; Herbert's mate, Charlie Wright, had enlisted in the army, so young George was kept busy. He soon learnt the skills and was retained when the war was over. He succeeded his father when he retired in

Repairs to Diglis Barge Lock No.2, date unknown. (Doris Colledge)

1932 and continued full-time until 1968, making, repairing and fitting lock gates and stop-gates, making and repairing doors and windows for the Company's lock houses and other buildings, fences, timber bridges, etc. and repairing the hulls of wooden boats. From 1968-76 he worked part-time as lock-keeper and lengthsman on the Tardebigge Flight.

George lived beside the canal all his life. His childhood was spent with his parents and many brothers and sisters in a cottage beside the canal at Stoke Pound. From there he had attended Stoke Prior School until the then leaving age of thirteen and had spent a year working at the nearby salt works. Then in 1917 the family moved to the cottage beside the canal and Tardebigge Reservoir where George lived until his marriage in 1928. Then after four years residence at the Upper Halfway canal cottage, he returned to the Reservoir Cottage, taking over the tenancy from his parents. His final move was in 1976 to Tardebigge New Wharf to the little cottage (since demolished) at the back of the warehouse. He died a year later.

George Bate was proud of his long family links with the canal. His great grandfather Charles Bate was a blacksmith at Hanbury and he had been employed during the final years of the construction of the canal to sharpen and harden the masons' and bricklayers' tools and to shoe the horses used to transport materials. One of his sons, John, at one time kept "The Red Lion" at Bradley Green, being at the same time a blacksmith and agent for local farmers with the Canal Company. In 1869 he moved to "The Queen's Head", Stoke Pound, where he had a blacksmith's shop and a wharf built, known for many years as Bate's Wharf. There, until 1901, besides running the public house and blacksmithing for local farmers, he shoed canal horses and also employed a wheelwright who taught his son Herbert this craft. In 1894 Herbert started work as a carpenter at the canal depot at Stoke and eventually moved, with the depot, to Tardebigge, becoming Foreman Carpenter there.

George Bate was one of the family of nine children of Herbert and Jane Bate. The family lived in the middle of the row of three canalside cottages just below Whitford Bridge at Stoke Pound, and young George took a great interest in the canal and in the many commercial boats then passing daily and their crews, an interest which continued throughout his life as he kept a diary of events. This diary and his memory were the source of a series of thirteen articles which appeared in Tardebigge Parish Magazine from June 1969 to November 1970 and also of many contributions to the W/B Canal Society's magazine "Fifty-Eight" from November 1969 until April 1977. His writings form an invaluable record of the happenings on the canal during and before his time, since in his younger days he tapped the memories of many old long-serving canal employees. He was awarded the B.E.M. in 1967, and he was for many years a vice-president of the W/B Canal Society.

AT TARDEBIGGE NEW WHARF DEPOT

From 1941 to 1946, during and just after World War 2, the late Tom Rolt lived on his converted flyboat *Cressy* moored just above the Top Lock at Tardebigge. In his books "Worcestershire" and "Landscape with Canals" he describes the maintenance depot at the New Wharf and the craftsmen who worked there at that time. Besides George Bate, still using tools like the adze, plough and shell-augur, making and installing lock gates, there was Tom Insull, the burly blacksmith, getting on in years and rather deaf, who, besides shoeing the boat-horses, also forged guard irons and spikes for the boats, and ironwork for the lock-gates. Then there was Percy Hawkins, son of one of the first tugmen, William Hawkins; he was the fitter, highly

Canals Sometimes Leak

They're getting down to things at the Worcester Wharf, Bridge-street, Birmingham—right down to the bed, in fact. This section of the canal has been isolated and the water taken away so that repairs can be carried out. At this point the canal runs over the railway line, and it was because it was found that water was seeping through to the tunnel that the present work was put into operation. Above you see workmen engaged in making the new bed; and (right) a collection of some of the odd things that had found their way into the canal.

Birmingham Gazette photographs.

A report in the Birmingham Gazette of 15 April 1939 showing Gas Street Basin drained and work in hand to repair and make watertight the bed of the canal following seepage of water into the railway tunnel below. Also shown are some of the items found when the basin was emptied.

skilled and able, for instance, to bore with great accuracy a tapered hole in the boss of a new propeller casting. Also there was Tommy Hodges from Farrin's Stoke Prior boatyard which had closed some years earlier and who now repaired the Company's workboats as well as those of some of the canal carriers including Charles Ballinger. He was a short, thickset, jovial man, who could remember the time when twenty boatbuilders were at work on the banks of the W/B Canal. He died in 1945. It is regrettable that as the Tardebigge Depot has been run down under British Waterways, the workshops have closed and many of the old skills are no longer practised there.

THE JONES'S

Besides the skilled craftsmen, including carpenters, smiths, and fitters, based at the depots, there have been, over the years, many other men, stonemasons, bricklayers and general labourers who have helped to maintain the canal, and some of them have given long service. In 1935 James Jones died after almost 60 years as master stonemason and bricklayer on the canal. He came from Worcester where his parents had lived at Gregory's Mill Lock, his father having worked for 50 years on the maintenance staff of the Company. His uncle, Richard Jones, had also worked on the canal as a bricklayer/stonemason, and his grave, with crumbling headstone depicting seven of the tools of his trade, is in the old Finstall Cemetery, for he lived in the Reservoir Cottage, Tardebigge, where the Bate family later lived. James Jones's grandfather, Richard Jones's father, was the Richard Jones who had been appointed contractor assisting Thomas Cartwright in the construction of the West Hill Tunnel from 1894 until its completion. This was indeed a long family involvement with the canal.

RECENT LEVELS OF MAINTENANCE

Whilst the canal was busy with working boats until the early decades of the twentieth century, many men were employed in its management and maintenance. According to George Bate there were still in 1901 some 86 men employed by the SND Company on the W/B and Droitwich Canals. These included toll-clerks, weighing machine clerks, staff at the Birmingham Offices (46 Gas Street), eight tugmen, lengthsmen, stablemen, wharfingers, dredgermen, bricklayers (three gangs, six men to a gang), four carpenters, a fitter, blacksmith and saddler, and eleven lock-keepers, plus two lock-keepers and a toll clerk on the Droitwich Canals. During the 1914-18 War manpower was depleted and by 1920 there were about 50 men employed. By the end of the 1939-45 War there had been a further reduction to around 26. But until 1961 all lock-gates were still made and repaired at the Tardebigge Depot and repairs and maintenance work were undertaken by the W/B's own employees. Since 1965 gates have been made at Bradley and elsewhere, and outside contractors have been increasingly brought in to carry out major repairs.

After nationalisation, and with dwindling commercial use, maintenance work on the canal was greatly reduced. In the 1960s, 1970s and 1980s towpaths were allowed to become eroded and overgrown and, in places, impassable, as along Bittell Cutting (restored in 1993) and in the neighbourhood of Hanbury. Dredging was neglected and it was not uncommon for some of the larger pleasure boats to be grounded on the mud. Leaking lock gates added to this problem by reducing water levels in some of the pounds.

With the support of Local Authorities and Conservation Groups and with more efficient management by British Waterways, there has been since the early 1990s a great improvement in the condition of the canal and its environs, making it much more attractive as a recreational amenity. Progress is, as ever, dependent upon the limited money and manpower available. The various users of the canal today do owe much to the small but dedicated team of those who do their best to maintain the waterway, its towpaths, locks and lock-surroundings in good order.

Chapter 15

CARRIERS ON THE CANAL

EARLY CARRIERS

It is clear from the terms of the 1791 Act for the W/B Canal that it was intended to be a barge canal and its summit level was constructed as such, the width being 40 feet and the depth 5ft 6in. The tunnels were constructed 16 feet wide to take barge traffic. The Stratford Canal, too, was constructed as far as Hockley Heath as a barge canal, with Brandwood Tunnel 16 feet wide, and as late as June 1796 its Committee was minded to build broad locks as far as Kingswood. The narrow guillotine stop-lock at the Kings Norton junction had then, apparently, not yet been built.

At first the W/B Company supplied its own boats for hire to encourage the coal trade from Birmingham to Selly Port from 1795, and to Kings Norton and along the Stratford Canal to Hockley Port from 1796. These boats were apparently about 9 feet wide and could carry 60 to 80 tons of coal. Vessels carrying these amounts were reported to have passed through the West Hill Tunnel to Hopwood at its opening in 1797. Such boats continued to be used on the summit level to convey coal and farm produce long after the decision in 1809 to build narrow locks down to Worcester. In May 1816 three of these W/B Canal Company's boats were ordered by the Committee to be repaired.

Once the stop-lock had been installed across the Worcester Bar in Birmingham and the canal was open to the Severn at Worcester, there was a through route for narrowboats from the north to the south west, avoiding the river with its problems between Stourport and Worcester. Established canal carriers were quick to make use of this new route. Amongst the boats arriving at Worcester on 4 December 1815, the day the canal was opened, was one belonging to Thomas & Matthew Pickford and Co. It delivered a cargo of goods and soon set off back with a cargo bound for Manchester. Another carrier initially on the scene was George Ryder Bird of Birmingham. One of his boats was reported to be the first to deliver a cargo of goods from Birmingham, destined for Bristol and the West of England, which was loaded onto a trow in Diglis Basin. Soon to follow and also become established carriers along the canal were S Danks and Co., Robinson Corbet and Co., Crowley Hicklin and Co., James Bromley, Joseph Smith and Sons, John Whitehouse and Sons, and Worthington & Co. These firms rented or purchased warehouses at Diglis or Lowesmoor and appointed local agents. In addition to slow boats carrying heavy materials such as coal, timber, bricks and stone, most of these carriers had a fleet of fly-boats, working day and night with changes of crew and horses, to provide an express delivery of goods. The fly-boats worked mostly to a published weekly timetable and they delivered far and wide over the existing canal network.

In January 1816 the W/B Canal Committee decided on regulations allowing fly-boats to pass along the canal at all hours and to have preference over other boats at locks. Also, to assist boats to catch the spring tides on the River Severn, laden boats were to be allowed to pass through the locks at all hours for three days before any spring tide. Otherwise, coal boats were not permitted to use the canal at night between the hours of 9.00 pm and 5.00 am. Lock-keepers were issued with padlocks to prevent the locks being used by unauthorised boats at night.

T & M PICKFORD

T & M Pickford were busy carriers on the W/B Canal in its early years. Thomas and Matthew were sons of James Pickford of Poynton, Cheshire, who was a waggoner to London in the mid eighteenth century. His sons joined and succeeded him in the business and they began to make use of the canals as they came into being. In 1795 Pickfords had only 10 boats registered, in 1803 they had 28 boats, but by 1838 at the peak of their canal business, before they began transferring carriage to the new railways, they had a fleet of 116 boats and 398 horses to pull them. They established depots and bought or rented warehouses at strategic points on the canal system. From 1816 Worcester was an important outpost of their business. In November 1817 they bought the warehouse they had already been renting at Lowesmoor for £830. Extra wharfage and warehouse space was rented at Lowesmoor and Diglis as their business increased. They were established on the Worcester Wharf in Birmingham and in 1829 they bought a crane, warehouse and stable from the canal company for £2,000. They were also given permission to construct a sluice (canal arm) there 50 yards long and 15 feet wide. This covered arm would have provided sheltered accommodation for up to four narrowboats.

In their haste to expand, Pickfords seem to have employed some unreliable crew. One, steerer James Cox, in January 1816 caused his boat to sink in the 34th lock (now numbered 25); he was reported to have drawn the paddle of the upper gate without having shut the paddle of the lower gate. Later that year he was prosecuted for damaging the stop-lock at the Jews Burial Ground near Granville Street Bridge in Birmingham. In 1819 William King, lock-keeper at Astwood, reported steerer Wildsmith of Pickfords fly-boat no.4 for doing considerable damage to the lower gate of lock 40 (now 19) of the Astwood Flight. In 1820 Ambrose Fidoe, keeper of the stop gates at the Birmingham basin reported Pickfords boatman Walker for running a boat with such violence into the gates that they were broken and the stone quoins were displaced. Pickfords were charged for all the damage done except in the case of the sunken boat where the Canal Company agreed to pay half the loss of £465 sustained by Pickfords because "Messrs Pickfords have certainly entitled themselves to the consideration of this Company by the Exertions they have made to bring Trade to this Canal."

Following the completion of the Birmingham and Gloucester Railway in 1840, Pickfords began to use the railway and reduce their reliance upon the waterway route to the south west. A prolonged freezeup of the canal early in 1841 hastened this process. In 1843 Pickfords sold their Lowesmoor warehouse for £700, but they retained their rented accommodation at Diglis and Lowesmoor until March 1848, by which time their carrying by canal was virtually at an end.

GEORGE RYDER BIRD

George Ryder Bird was the well-to-do proprietor of an extensive canal-carrying business based from 1814 at the Three Cranes Crescent Wharf in Birmingham. Previously he had been a barge and boat builder in partnership with R S Skey, and their premises had been in Broad Street. He built up a fleet of fly-boats, many of which plied between Birmingham and London where he had agents at the various basins. As already mentioned, he was one of the first enterprising carriers to make use of the W/B Canal and he arranged for the transfer of cargoes at Diglis between his boats and the Severn trows of Barnett, Meaby & Co. He rented one of the first two warehouses to be built at Diglis ready for the opening of the canal. He remained a regular carrier on the W/B Canal until his death in 1837.

We know a good deal about the business and family life of Ryder Bird from a most interesting personal diary which he kept from 1820 until 1830 and which is in Birmingham Reference Library. The diary gives details of his family and personal engagements, his travels, his health, the weather and its effect upon the movement of his boats, and items of national and local news. He was a landowner whose property included a house, cottages, and the Lower Mills near Stourport. He kept sheep which he sheared himself; he had apple orchards; he grew wheat and barley and harvested hay. He was married twice and had sons George Ryder, William and James, and daughters Mary and Caroline. He was afflicted with the gout which recurred from time to time. He recorded exceptional weather conditions, droughts, heat waves, floods and long frosts which froze the canals and held up traffic on them. He enjoyed entertaining and days at the races, and he travelled at times to London and the Continent with members of his family. Some typical entries in his diary:

9 June 1822. "About 7 in the evening a most tremendous storm of Rain fall which put our Stable and Wharf under water."

1 Jan. 1823. "All the canals fast (frozen); Chomly with a Cargo of goods from Worcester stopped near Hanbury."

13 Oct. 1823. "A Quarter before three o'clock Mr Sadler Junr went up in a fine Balloon from the Crescent accompanied by James Busby - was seen for 20 minutes, took the direction to Hagley and landed safe in a field nr Kinfair or Ewell." (The balloon was filled with coal gas from the nearby Gas Works beside the W/B Canal, and G R Bird charged admission to his property to witness the ascent, making over £200 after expenses had been paid.)

3 Dec. 1824. "Henry Fauntleroy was executed at the Old Bailey on Tuesday 30 Novemr 1824."

12 & 13 May 1825. "Continued Rain very heavy for 26 hours - the Worcs & Birmm Canal over-ran its Banks and did some damage to the Houses in Wharf Street - a very great Blossom on the Fruit Trees and every prospect of much Fruit."

30 Aug. 1826. "I dined at the Bean Club this day."

27 Aug. 1827. "My Son G R Bird married to Miss Sarah Walton this day at Lichfield."

4 Mar. 1828. "Mr Partridge took from me 12 ounces of Blood."

16 Nov. 1829. "I took possession of Pew No 15 in Edgbaston Church on Sunday November 3rd 1829." (Ryder Bird and family had moved in 1827 to live at The Cottage, Edgbaston.)

George Ryder Bird took into partnership his namesake eldest son and it is as G R Bird & Son that the business is referred to in the W/B Canal Committee minutes in 1824 when they claimed compensation from the Canal Company for tea alleged to have been pilfered whilst in the Company's warehouse at Tardebigge; also when in 1831 they asked for cast iron beams and other repairs to their warehouse at Diglis, and when in 1835 they were refused a request for a drawback (reduction in tonnage) on the carriage of spelter. G R Bird senior must have been disappointed that his son George was more interested in social engagements, such as exercising and dining with his Troop at Barr and going off to the races, than in helping to run the business, which was wound up soon after his death in 1837.

CROWLEY, HICKLIN & COMPANY

Another busy user of the W/B Canal, with wharves at Diglis and Lowesmoor and a daily fly-boat service, was Crowley, Hicklin & Co. based at the Crescent Wharf in Birmingham. They advertised in Birmingham Commercial Directory: "N.B. Lock-up boats provided for wine and spirits." They ran a stage-boat service on the

Breedon Cross Wharf c.1900. Here merchandise was transferred between rail and canal transport. Standing on the Midland Railway boat in the foreground is Mr Millward. (Birmingham Museum & Art Gallery)

Birmingham Canal between Birmingham and Wolverhampton. In the W/B Canal Committee minutes one of their boatmen was reported in 1822 for damaging a stop-gate at the basin in Birmingham; another in 1836 for breaking the padlock on the Blockhouse lock gate when it was locked on a Sunday at church-service time. In 1824 it was at the request of Crowley & Co. that the General Assembly of the W/B Canal Company agreed to a bye-law requiring slow boats to allow fly-boats to pass them in descending the locks to Worcester. Crowley & Co. were still using the canals in the 1870s, but on a much reduced scale, having, like many of the other firms, transferred much of their business to the railways.

INDUSTRIAL USERS OF THE CANAL

Besides the general carrying companies using the W/B Canal, there were local businesses located beside or near to the canal with their own boats for bringing in coal and other supplies and for carrying their produce to their customers. These

A working boat pulled by two donkeys at Masshouse Lane Bridge which crosses the approach cutting north of the West Hill Tunnel. (BRL)

included many of the industries which grew up beside the canal, as described in chapters 17 and 18 of this book. In addition there were, at various times and in various places along the canal, a number of farmers, shopkeepers, coal dealers and others with their own boats and boatmen.

T & M DIXON

One local business which extended over five generations and made extensive use of the canal for over 130 years was that of Dixons of Tardebigge. Thomas Dixon, a Birmingham canal carrier and coal dealer, whose business, Thomas Dixon and Co., had been established in 1790, was one of six applicants who were each allotted a boat length and stacking ground at Tardebigge Old Wharf when the canal opened to there in March 1807. In 1809 the tenancy of the Lower House Farm nearby, having just been acquired by the Hewell Estates, was available, and Thomas Dixon acquired the lease of the property, including 77 acres of farmland, and came out to live there with his wife Rebecca and twin sons William and Thomas. Their aim was to expand their carrying and coal business and also to begin farming and convey farm produce by canal into Birmingham. This was an attractive prospect in the light of the W/B Canal Company's decision in May 1807 that farmers who bought coal from the recently opened wharf at Tardebigge would be allowed carriage, free of charge, on wheat, barley, oats, beans, peas, flour, meal, malt and bran on boats returning to Birmingham. At first the Dixons had a struggle financially to find the capital for extra boats, waggons and horses for an expanding carrying and coal business and also livestock and equipment for the farming side. Between 1809 and 1816 the Canal Committee minutes record six occasions when T Dixon & Co. were threatened with legal action unless their three-monthly accounts, £165 in 1809, increasing, as their business expanded, to over £300, were paid.

Of Thomas Dixon's two sons, William married Mary Lane of Rous Lench near Evesham and moved to Horns Hall across the fields from the Lower House for a few years before returning to Birmingham. His brother Thomas in 1813 contracted a runaway marriage with Mary Harvey of Weethley near Alcester, whose widowed mother was a coal customer. This created a rift and started a long and acrimonious correspondence between the newlyweds and Mrs Harvey which only came to an end when the first child was on the way. In the meanwhile Mrs Harvey made a point of transferring her coal custom to Jenkins & Wright on the New Wharf.

Thomas and Mary continued to live at the Lower house and they produced a family of five daughters and two sons. Following the death of his father in 1838 Thomas carried on the business, and when he in turn died in 1856 he was succeeded by his two sons Thomas and Matthew, then aged 38 and 26. Their business partnership was thereafter known as T & M Dixon. The two brothers worked together for 40 years, during which time their business expanded and diversified, extra farms were taken over, depots and agencies established in various places, and a large coal and timber business was set up at the railway goods yard in Redditch. Thomas died in 1896 without issue, but his brother Matthew lived until 1924 and had a family of five sons and five daughters. Three of his sons, Matthew, Hugh and Ralph continued the business until their deaths in the 1930s and then two of Ralph's sons and several other relatives were involved in the final years up to and immediately following World War 2.

Over the years T & M Dixon's business and farming empire grew and included, besides coal, milk, meat, eggs, poultry, grain, fruit, vegetables, also timber, building materials and lime burnt in kilns beside the canal at the Old and New Wharves, and animal and poultry feeds produced in the old warehouse, rented from the Canal Company, on the New Wharf. From general carrying, their fleet of canal boats came to be mainly used for their own business. In the latter part of the 19th century their fleet of some 50 boats, including many day boats based in Birmingham for their coal trade there, was managed by Thomas Colledge who lived on the New Wharf where his wife ran a shop and post office. By the 1920s and 1930s only four or five of these horse-drawn boats remained in use. In 1905 a special motor boat *Enterprise* was constructed for Dixons at Farrin's boatyard at Stoke Prior. It was designed by the W/B Canal Company's Engineer, Francis Hobrough, and it was the first motor canal boat in the country, being driven by a Wolseley car engine. It could carry 15 tons and was able to make the journey into Birmingham in 3½ hours, half the time taken by horse-drawn boats. It left Tardebigge Old Wharf early each morning, and stopped to pick up at Harris's Bridge, to carry milk, fruit, vegetables, eggs and poultry into the City, returning in the afternoon with various commodities. The *Enterprise* ran for many years on into the early 1930s until being superseded by road transport.

THE WORCESTER AND BIRMINGHAM CANAL CARRYING COMPANY

Following the decline in trade along the canal in the 1840s due to the transference of goods to the railways, the W/B Canal Company decided to avail itself of the 1840 Parliamentary legislation which permitted canal companies to set up their own carrying businesses. Previously, canal companies, as the providers of water highways, had been forbidden to compete with canal carriers on their canals. At its Assembly on 4 January 1848 the W/B Canal Company reported that "in September last, Messrs Pickford & Co having given your Committee notice that they should on 25th March next give up possession of the Warehouses they hold on the Canal" it was necessary for the Canal Company to provide their own carrying business. At the following Assembly of 4 July it was reported that this carrying business had been started and that Mr F H Needham (who was in business at Lowesmoor Basin) had been appointed as its manager. Boats were bought from Pickfords and elsewhere and the business continued with limited success for 20 years until 1868 when it was taken over by J Fellows & Co. This latter firm had been established by James Fellows in 1837 and had built up a successful carrying business mainly between the Midlands, London and Manchester. Joshua Fellows, son of the founder, wishing to extend the business to the Severn and the south west, seized the chance to buy both the W/B and the Staffordshire and Worcestershire Canal Companies' carrying businesses which neither Company was keen to continue.

THE SEVERN AND CANAL CARRYING COMPANY

For five years, from 1868 to 1873, J Fellows & Co. were in competition with their main rivals, Danks and Sanders, for trade on the W/B Canal and the River Severn. Samuel Danks & Co. of Stourport had been carriers on the W/B canal from the beginning. Over the years the business was carried on by members of the family with various partners at various times. By the early 1860s the partnership was between Benjamin Danks of Stourport and John Sanders, a barge owner and carrier on the Severn, and they were leading carriers on the Severn and down from Gloucester to the Bristol Channel. In 1873 a new company "The Severn & Canal Carrying, Shipping and Steam Towing Company Limited" was formed by the

The Severn and Canal Company's warehouse and boats in Gas Street Basin c.1933. From the warehouse side, in order:- on Wilden, *Bill Brown, his wife and dog; and standing just to the right of them Tom Mayo; on* Motor No.2, *Jack Mayo and, halfway along the boat, his son Charlie; standing on the horse boat, Lionel Tonks; on* Motor No.7, *Henry Tonks, his wife Martha and two sons; on* Wulfruna, *Sid Hopkins and son and, on the left of the group on the back of the boat, Eddie Birch. (Tom Mayo)*

merger of Danks & Sanders and J Fellows & Co. The Company's name was soon abbreviated to "The Severn & Canal Carrying Company", and it remained a major operator on the River Severn and the W/B Canal for a great many years.

Besides owning river craft, tugs, barges and trows, the S&CC Company had a large fleet of horse-drawn narrowboats, there being over 80 of them just before World War 1. They were mostly built in the Company's own boatyard at Stourport Basin, stronger and with higher sides than most other wooden narrowboats to withstand the rigours of working on the River Severn. Having been towed by tug from Gloucester to Worcester, the crew of a S&CC Company's narrowboat, in order to work up the W/B Canal, would pick up a horse from the Company's own stables at Diglis Basin. Northbound along the canal they would mostly be carrying timber, wheat, sugar, cocoa beans, and chocolate crumb for Cadbury's, Bournville. Southbound they would return mainly with coal from Cannock, some to be

The Severn and Canal Company's boat Lenchford *delivering Typhoo Tea at the Company's Gas Street Basin Warehouse (Stanley Holland Collection)*

delivered to customers, including houses and farms, along the canal, some destined for Worcester and Gloucester.

In the 1920s the S&CC Company's use of horse-drawn boats began to decline rapidly, partly due to the increasing use of quicker road transport, partly due to inadequate dredging and maintenance of the canal. Following the purchase of the first of a series of motor narrowboats in 1927, the use of horse-drawn boats by the Company came to an end in 1929, many being sold to other carriers. From around eight motor boats in use in 1929 others were added to reach a maximum of eighteen by 1935. S&CC Company traffic continued along the canal during World War 2, but finally came to an end with nationalisation of the canals in 1948, when the carrying company's boats were sold and its head office and warehouses in Birmingham closed down.

For many years S&CC Company boats were a familiar sight on the W/B Canal. They were mostly named after places in the West Midland and Severn region. Their tarpaulin cargo covers carried the Company's name in large white letters and, for some unaccountable reason, their boatmen were widely known as "toe-rags".

TARDEBIGGE LOCK HOUSE LEDGERS

Information about the passage of boats along the W/B Canal in the latter part of the nineteenth century is contained in four ledgers recovered some time ago from the top lock house at Tardebigge by Alan Picken and kept at his Canal Museum at Llanfrynach on the Brecon and Abergavenny Canal. One ledger relates to local traffic from, or passing through, Tardebigge New Wharf and dates from November 1859 to May 1902. Each entry gives the date, the owner and steerer of the vessel, origin and destination and nature of the cargo and the tonnage carried. Throughout there are many entries for the boats of Thomas Dixon formerly, and T & M Dixon latterly, carrying mostly grain. In the earlier years the boats of P Robinson and James Bennett and Son carried stone, probably from Dusthouse Quarry, and rough timber. Later from 1878 the boats of W H Wynn's canalside brickworks at Alvechurch, and from 1899 the boat of Samuel Frisby's brickworks beside the canal at Tardebigge, carried bricks to various canalside locations. From Bate's Wharf, Stoke Pound, George Beck and T Clayton carried uncut timber at various times.

The three other ledgers all belonging to the Sharpness New Docks and Birmingham Navigation Co. give complete records of boats passing Tardebigge top Lock (1) from January 1882 to May 1883, (2) from June 1883 to October 1884, and (3) March 1890 to August 1891. The information recorded includes the date, hour of arrival, when ticketed, ticket number, owner, steerer, origin, destination, type of cargo, weight of cargo in tons, cwt and quarters, and weight if gauged. Over this

At Cadbury's Waterside Wharf, S&CC Co's Motor No.6 *with, on board, Mr and Mrs Charlie Mann, Auntie and baby. (NWMT)*

period the number of boats passing per day varied from around 20 to around 35, Cargoes included coal, coke, gas tar and gas water, salt, bricks, pipes, lime, hay, grain, potatoes, chemicals (including manganese and phosphate), road stone, logs, poles, pitch, flour, sugar, matches, ale and petroleum.

THE RECORDS OF GEORGE BATE

When George Bate, who worked as carpenter at the W/B Canal depot at Tardebigge for many years, lived as a lad with his parents in one of the three canalside cottages near Whitford Bridge at Stoke Pound, he kept notes of working canal boats in the early 1900s before World War 1. Of the companies using the canal he listed:

The Severn and Canal Carrying Company	around 100 boats
Jacob Rice and Son of Gloucester	around 60 boats
Healings Flour Mill, Tewkesbury	2 boats
James Smart and Son	6 boats
Chadborn, Son and Taylor	6 boats
James Waldron	6 boats
T & M Dixon	20 boats
Cadbury Brothers Ltd	12 boats
Salt Union Ltd (Stoke Works)	8 boats
Townshends Flour Mill, Worcester	2 boats

Working these company boats were a number of boating families remembered by George Bate and listed, with, in brackets, the number of families related to each other as: Mann (4 to 6), Manley (3), Stokes (4), Lees (2), Tonks (4), Brown (5), Worrell (2), Birch (4), Helm (3), Parrot (2), Maysey (3), Bourne (3), Wright (2), Coleman (2), Merrell (2), Dyer (2), Pittaway (2), Footman (2).

"NUMBER ONE" CARRIERS

Individual carriers who owned and worked their own boats were known as "Number ones". Many of these were members of family businesses, farmers, brick and tile makers, dealers in coal, timber, lime, hay and straw. Some worked from the larger public wharves and basins, others had permission to use private canalside wharves alongside their premises or with nearby road access. Some of the licensees of public houses alongside the canal used to have, as a side line, a coal business, using their own boat to fetch supplies from collieries, one example of this being Thomas Vaughan of the Kings Head, Worcester, whose coal boat was the first to traverse the newly opened canal in 1815.

At Worcester, in the early 1900s, coal merchants having their own canalside wharves and boats included George Weaver between George Street Bridge and the

Blockhouse, John Greenaway at the Blockhouse, and the licensee of the Mason's Arms in Portland Street. John Smith, the licensee of the "Elephant and Castle" public house at Lowesmoor Basin, had a boat which took hay and timber up the canal and brought back coal. Also at Lowesmoor, Ernest Jackson who dealt in scrap iron and coal at the Basin operated two boats.

Amongst the number ones, using the W/B Canal from outside, was Tom Ball of Tewkesbury, a tall man with grey whiskers who always wore a bowler hat; he, with his mate, carried mostly sawn timber and bales of hay. Also from Tewkesbury were the brothers Bill and Tom Pitt who carried hay for Wheatleys, undertakers, of Birmingham, which they unloaded at Holliday Street Wharf.

From Gloucester came William Giddins, an elderly broad-built Salvation Army man. He had two boats *William Caleb* and *Savona*, one skippered by Dick Perks. With his young mate Billy Male he took "England's Glory" Matches from Moreland's Gloucester factory to their Commercial Street warehouse off Gas Street Basin in Birmingham. He also carried salt from Stoke Works, and whilst tied up there used to play his accordion and, with another boatman, Charlie Tonks, lead a sing-song. His son Bill Giddins also bought a boat and worked for Healings Flour Mill, Tewkesbury, for some time, taking flour up to Graham's Wharf, Bridge Street, Birmingham. When William Giddins died he left his boat *Savona* to his nephew Charles Ballinger, who renamed it *Energy*.

CHARLES BALLINGER

Charles Ballinger came of a canal-carrying family. In 1879 James Ballinger of Deerhurst, near Tewkesbury, registered his boat *Thomas no.1* with Birmingham Sanitary Authority. From 1892 *Thomas* was owned by Sarah Ballinger, probably his widow. According to the records of the Droitwich Inspector of Canal Boats, the masters of the boat in the 1890s were C and M Ballinger, probably sons of James. By 1928 Charles Ballinger, whose home address was in Gloucester, had taken over the business of his uncle William Giddins and was operating, with his wife Frances and with the help of his married sister Olive and her husband (Mr and Mrs Phipps), two horse narrowboats, *Thomas* which had been built in 1906 and *Edna Grace* named after his daughter who sometimes accompanied her parents on trips. During World War 2 and up to 1947, he was working two more ex-S&CC Company horse-drawn boats, four in all. One of these was *Frances* (previously *Hanbury* built by George Farrin in 1924), the other was *Energy* (previously *Savona*, built in 1910 and owned by William Giddins). For the repair of all his boats Ballinger made use of the dry dock at Tardebigge New Wharf, the work being carried out up to 1945 by Tom Hodges, master boat-builder, who had been employed by Farrins of Stoke Prior until it closed in the mid 1930s, and then by George Bate. Amongst those who worked Ballinger's horse-drawn boats over the years were C Tonks, H Brown, R Jones, G Harris and H Birch.

Charles Ballinger and his wife on their horse boat Frances *below Tardebigge top lock. (Angela Rolt)*

Charles Ballinger's motorboat Bridget *entering lock 23, Stoke Wharf, Whitsuntide 1961. Behind is the Bridge House, formerly the residence of the Canal Engineer, Francis Hobrough. On the left-hand side is the brick surround of the under-towpath overflow weir. On the right-hand side is the former weighbridge house and, now with verandah, the former shop. (NWMT, Arthur Watts Collection)*

In 1949 Ballinger acquired two former S&CC Company motor narrowboats *Fir* and *Beech*, renaming them *Bridget* and *Olive*. In 1953 a further motor boat *Kimberley*, formerly FMC owned, was added and renamed *Susan*. By this time the three motors had taken over from the horse-drawn boats. Ballinger and his wife were usually on *Olive*, Lionel Tonks and his wife and family on *Bridget*, and George Page on *Susan*. During his thirty or more years of canal carrying, Ballinger worked mainly on the Severn below Worcester and up the W/B Canal to Birmingham and onto the B.C.N., carrying Moreland's "England's Glory" matches from Gloucester to their Commercial Street warehouse in Birmingham, chocolate crumb from Frampton to Cadbury's, Bournville, coal from Cannock to lock houses and other canalside premises, and many other items.

Ballinger was a tall slim man and in his youth he had helped his father on *Thomas*. He was deeply religious, a man of principle, and he would not allow anyone to swear in front of his wife. When he died in 1962 regular canal carrying on the W/B Canal came to an end. Of his horse-drawn boats, *Edna Grace* was bought by Alan Picken and *Thomas*, the last remaining, was taken over by Ray White in 1952. Ray used it to carry coal from Cannock to Townshend's Mill, Diglis, until May 1955. It was the last horse-drawn commercial boat using the canal, and following its withdrawal, the tunnel tug *Worcester*, which had towed it through Tardebigge, Shortwood and West Hill Tunnels, also ceased working.

THOMAS RICE AND SONS

In July 1927 Thomas Rice, his wife Florence, and their six children moved house by canal boat from 29 Robin Hood Street, Gloucester, to 30 George Street, Worcester. At Gloucester, Tom had worked with his father in a business which included trading in horses, timber and general goods, and carrying on the River Severn and canals. Tom and Florence had worked boats together during the 1914-18 War. During the 1926 General Strike Tom was placed under military control and was paid £1 per day to move food by boat. He and his father were reputed to be the last persons to work a horse-drawn boat from Gloucester to Stourport. The move to Worcester was because Tom already had business in the area and the house, situated on the city side of George Street canal bridge, had land around it which bordered the canal and included a two boats' length wharf, stables and an orchard. When the Rice family arrived from Gloucester, they brought with them by boat, besides furniture, two donkeys, goats, chickens, ducks, pigeons and pigs. At Gloucester the donkeys had been used for boat haulage because the only access from the street to the back yard and stables was through the house. They were used at Worcester for some time and then replaced by a horse. At Worcester Tom, helped by his older sons, ran a business in coal, firewood, household paraffin, candles and poultry. From Gloucester Tom brought his two canal boats *Regina* and *Adelade*, so-named because two of his wife's sisters had emigrated, one to Canada, the other to Australia. One of these was broken up and its planks used for fencing in 1932, it being replaced by *Elsie* bought from the S&CC Company. The boats carried mainly timber, coal, sand, bricks and flour.

In 1931 the general business was disrupted as Tom became ill and was unable to work for over two years, but his two canal boats were kept working by four of his sons, one boat usually by Sidney aged 16 and Eric aged 8, the other by Edwin aged 14 and Thomas aged 12 in 1931. Sidney, Edwin and Thomas had had adequate schooling, but from now on Eric was to attend school only occasionally when the School Inspector called and threatened to take his father to court. Sidney often gave lessons to his young brother on their boat in the evenings.

Tom Rice and his sons had several oft-repeated carrying trips. One was to load tree trunks from Sale Green at Dunhampstead Wharf and take them to Corbett's timberyard at Selly oak; then to go on to one of the collieries, Cannock, Littleton or Brownhills, to load coal for the Severn Commission; proceed to Stourport from where one of the crew rode the horse back to Worcester, whilst the other took the boat down river, being rejoined by his mate, who had hitched a lift upriver, at Lincomb Lock where coal was being unloaded by barrow with the help of men of the Commission. Further coal was delivered at Holt, Camp and Diglis River locks.

Another trip meant taking a boat by tug to Gloucester and then on to Sharpness to load timber; then return to Gloucester and be towed upriver to Stourport; then, as there was no horse, the boat was bow-hauled from the Severn lock up the Staffs. and Worcs. Canal and the River Stour to Baldwin's iron and steel works at Wilden. To bow-haul, a special leather harness was worn over the shoulder attached to the tow rope. Having unloaded the timber the boat was loaded with sand using tipper waggons at the nearby sand quarry and bow-hauled back to the river to be towed back to Diglis and then bow-hauled again up the W/B Canal to Hardy and Padmore's Foundry above the Blockhouse Lock, to be laboriously unloaded with shovels into the "sand hole".

Sometimes timber was brought from Sharpness by lashing two already-loaded boats together side by side and laying timber across both to make a platform on which to load more timber. This way about four normal boat-loads of timber were carried at a time to Aston's at the Worcester River Dock. Rices also delivered bricks from Barker's Brick Works, Gregory's Bank, Worcester, to various canalside wharves.

By 1934 Tom Rice had recovered from his illness; his sons Sidney and Edwin had left the boats to get married, son Tom was working for the Severn and Canal Company, and he and son Eric began to work for Townshend's Flour Mill, situated beside the canal at Diglis, Worcester, using the mill's own boat *Violet*. From 1934 to 1940 the two Rices, father and son, worked this boat, taking flour up to Townshend's canalside depot at Tipton, and bringing coal back from Littleton Colliery to the mill. This was a weekly trip, taking the best part of seven days to complete and some 90 hours work; only Sunday and Monday nights were spent at home in Worcester. This came to an end when *Violet*, trapped in the ice at Tardebigge during the long freezeup of January/February 1940, was damaged beyond repair and its cargo of coal had to be retrieved by lorry. Tom then worked in the munitions factory beside the canal at Blackpole, and Eric, after war service in the army, worked for forty years for Worcester Gas Works at Lowesmoor.

DAPHNE MARCH AND HEATHER BELL

Just before and during the 1939-45 War, Daphne March, at first with her brother Christopher until he joined the Merchant Navy on the outbreak of the War, then with friends, used the family working boat *Heather Bell*, built in 1937 by Frank Nurser of Braunston, to carry various cargoes on the River Severn and along the W/B and other canals. Christopher March's keen interest in waterway carrying had been kindled by his experiences as a school boy of travelling in the holidays on the river tug *Alert* from Gloucester to Stourport and back, usually towing two or three barges and, behind them, several narrowboats in two columns, the narrowboats being mostly "Severners" loaded with sugar for Bournville. Downstream, occasionally, would be towed Tom Rice's boat *Poppy* carrying sand to Hardy & Padmore's foundry at the Blockhouse, Worcester. Christopher's interest was further fuelled by accompanying Tom Rice on a trip to Littleton Colliery and by exploring the canals around Gas Street Basin, busy with working boats, during his time at Birmingham University.

An article in the Worcester Evening News about Daphne March and her wartime work for Townshend's Mill on Heather Bell.

Heather Bell was used until 1939 for the occasional carrying of grain from Sharpness to Worcester for the family farm or for Townshend's Mill. Then, to quote Daphne's own account:

> The *Heather Bell* lay idle in Diglis Basin from September 1939 until August 1940 when I made my first trip to Cannock Chase with two friends and Tom Rice to show me the way. There were no sign posts in those days. Encouraged by my brother, home on leave, I decided to leave my job and see what I could achieve in the *Heather Bell*. The canal at Bournville, bombed early in December 1940, had been closed to traffic for 6 weeks when Denny Watton, lock-keeper at Diglis Basin, told me on 23 February that it would reopen the next day. The delay had given me time to find a crew, ask Mr Harry Townshend at Albion Mills if I could work for them, and collect my wits. There was much to learn about loading, unloading, and the Petter 10 hp engine. The next day we took on board 20 tons (320 sacks) of flour and I did the clothing up. We became so practised at this that at Sharpness, once loaded, we would let go and cloth up whilst under way. Until December 1945 we worked more or less non-stop. Weather sometimes delayed loading but made little difference to our schedule unless we were iced up.
>
> The round trip with flour from Worcester to Tipton, out light to the colliery at Cannock, back loaded with 'beans' to the mill, took four or five days. We did this three or four times a month, passing *Cressy* at the top of Tardebigge when Tom and Angela Rolt might give us tea or help us down the locks. We always took about three and a half hours to go up or down the 36 locks to or from Stoke Wharf where Winnie Wedgbrow ran a wonderful shop. From the Mill to Sharpness and back with grain took about two days, 9-10 hours down, 11-12 hours up, depending on how much 'fresh' there was if the river was in flood. These trips we did a couple of times a month interspersed with longer runs for Fellows, Morton & Clayton to Ellesmere Port, Oxford, Preston Brook or Wigan, occasionally for Cadbury's. A 12 hour day was not impossible in the winter if the moon was up; in the summer a 15-18 hour day was not unusual."

Daphne continued her carrying work with *Heather Bell* until after the end of the war. One of her early crew members, for several months in 1942, was Eily Gayford who went on to train other women to handle working boats on the Grand Union Canal during the war, as described in her book "The Amateur Boatwomen".

TOM MAYO

One of the very many boatmen who worked for the Severn and Canal Carrying Company on both horse and motor boats was Tom Mayo of Gloucester. His grandfather John Douglas Mayo had worked with his wife on boats for Danks and

Sanders and then, from 1873, for the S&CC Company under John Danks. When his wife died, their only son Jack worked with his father until his marriage. John then retired from the boats and worked on Gloucester Docks until the age of 83, whilst Jack and his wife Ada continued to work boats for the S&CC Company. They had altogether sixteen children, of whom nine were stillborn or died in infancy. Three of the four surviving sons, Tom, Charlie and Jim each worked with their father on his last S&CC boat *Fazeley*, Charlie and Jim only for a short period. Tom began working with his father at the age of 11 in 1927 and then only attended school a day or two at a time when they were back in Gloucester. On 11 December 1930 they took over the S&CC motor boat No.2 from Alf Parrot. When Jack took ill in 1932/3, Tom became skipper of No.2 at the age of 16. Jack died in 1936 and Tom, with various crew, continued to work the motor boat until 1939 when he ceased working for the S&CC Company and joined Jack Merrell on his salt boat *Joan* until it was destroyed in an air raid on Birmingham in 1941. He then served in the army 1942-7 and afterwards in industry.

A horse-drawn laden coal boat below the lock at Sidbury Bridge, Worcester, 1957. (Michael Dowty)

Tom took many varieties of cargo along the River Severn and into the Midlands via the W/B Canal. *Fazeley* was used to carry red sand from the Stour cut to Hardy and Padmore's foundry opposite the Blockhouse Lock in Worcester, using horses picked up from the S&CC Company's stables at Stourport and Worcester at each end of the intervening river section of the journey. Another frequent trip was the carrying of wheat from Sharpness up the Severn and along the W/B Canal to Brown's Mill and Watson Todd's Mill in central Birmingham. In 1929 Jack and Tom on *Fazeley* carried wheat on the last commercial trip down the Droitwich Junction Canal to Everton's Town Mill. Continuing with No.2, consignments of chocolate crumb and sugar were carried to Cadbury's Wharf at Bournville from Frampton on the Gloucester & Berkeley Canal and, on return journeys, empty sacks and mash butter. Other items carried along the W/B Canal to the S&CC Company's warehouse and other locations in Birmingham included tea, sugar, timber and copper.

On its trips up the W/B Canal motor boat No.2 was often accompanied by a butty consisting of a company's horse boat. Because of the narrow locks the butty would be horse drawn from Diglis to Tardebigge. The horse would then be stabled in the SND stables on the New Wharf and looked after by the lock-keeper, Joe Warner, until required on the return journey, whilst the butty was towed along the summit level between Tardebigge and Birmingham.

DANGEROUS CARGOES

The waterways were used, as are roads and railways today, to carry a few potentially dangerous cargoes. Gunpowder was carried on rare occasions for rock blasting or military use, oil and in more recent times petrol, and also chemicals, some of a hazardous nature. Oil and chemicals were carried on the W/B Canal for the most part safely, but there were accidents, the most spectacular of which occurred at Worcester in September 1905. The Bromsgrove Messenger carried the following report:

"ALARMING AFFAIR AT WORCESTER - NAPHTHA BOAT BLOWN UP
    "A canal boat belonging to Messrs Chadburn Son & Taylor of Gloucester arrived at Worcester with a cargo of 6,000 gallons of naphtha on its way to Messrs F.F.Fox & Co, Birmingham, and was placed in the lower canal basin at Diglis, close to the chemical manure works. Shortly before midnight, without any warning, there was a terrific explosion amongst the barrels of naphtha on board the boat, and flames broke out in all directions. The captain's mate Albert Harris who was the only person on the boat was blown through the hatchway badly burned on the face and hands, and his hair was singed, while a companion, William Maynall who was standing a few yards from the boat, was knocked down, and both men had to be removed to the Infirmary for treatment. With great

presence of mind, the toll collector, Mr Charles Wilmott, with assistance, towed the boat to the opposite side of the basin where there was a clear space, and the action undoubtedly saved the manure works from destruction. There was a great conflagration within minutes and the flames were visible from Malvern. The burning oil escaped from the barrels and covered a large portion of the canal basin, making it a sea of brilliant flame. The fire raged for nearly 9 hours. The boat eventually burnt out and sank, it being valued at £120 and the oil at £200."

RECENT CARRIERS ON THE CANAL

Since the end of regular carrying on the W/B Canal there have been several traders delivering coal from motor narrowboats to premises located by or near the canal. In the 1980s J & M Forth took orders in the spring for coal loaded at Atherstone Wharf for delivery later in the year from their 1981 built narrowboat *Newbury*. In the 1990s John Jackson and his mate Jenny have carried coal in their boat *Roach*, built in 1935 by Yarnolds of Northwich for Fellows Morton & Clayton, from their base at Wombourn for delivery along the Shropshire, the Staffs. & Worcs., the W/B and the Gloucester & Berkeley Canals.

In 1965 Charles (Sam) Waller and Graham Wigley founded The Birmingham and Midland Canal Carrying Company, with a fleet of boats based at Gas Street Basin, to carry freight on the canals. Most of their carrying was from Liverpool to the Midlands, but around 1967 they did carry timber up the Severn and along the W/B and Northern Stratford canals to Warwick.

Chapter 16

THE WELFARE AND SAFETY
OF CANAL EMPLOYEES, BOAT
PEOPLE AND BOAT ANIMALS

As with any responsible organisation with many employees and users of its services, the W/B Canal Company and its successors, the SND Company and British Waterways, have taken action at various times to promote the welfare and safety of its maintenance staff and the boat people using the canal. Other outside organisations and individuals have also shown concern for the physical, moral and spiritual care of boat people and the welfare of animals used to tow their craft.

SUNDAY WORKING

From time to time during the nineteenth century the W/B Canal Company, in common with other canal companies, received complaints about Sunday working by lock-keepers and boatmen. These complaints came mainly from the Worcester area. In June 1824 the Canal Committee heard that "Richard Woodyall, a Lock-keeper, and several Boatmen had been convicted before the Reverend Mr Clifton of following their worldly Calling on the Lord's Day", and four Committee members were deputed to communicate with the Worcester County magistrates on this subject. As a result, all lock-keepers were directed to padlock the lock gates on Sundays from 10.00 am to 1.30 pm and from 2.00 pm to 5.50 pm, and the magistrates were informed of this directive. However, by June 1831 these restrictions must have been somewhat relaxed, for we find Mr Tymbs, the Mayor of Worcester, in a letter to the Canal Committee, deploring the working of boats on Sundays. This complaint was referred to the General Assembly of Proprietors in July and the Committee subsequently agreed the following reply to the Mayor:

"This Company has given directions to prevent Boats passing on this Canal during divine Service on Sundays. But this Committee beg to observe that the attempts to stop the transit of Goods on this Canal on Sunday has from experience been found to produce more Immorality, by far, than the passing of Boats thereon, by Boatmen lounging and tippling in public Houses."

The Canal Company was evidently by now reluctant to take more than minimal steps to prevent Sunday working, and this attitude hardened in their reply, two years later in 1833, to a further official complaint from the "Mayor, Aldermen and Citizens of Worcester". This time the Committee ordered:

"That the Mayor be informed that this Committee are fully satisfied that any further interruption to Boats passing on this Canal on Sundays, than what at present takes place, would occasion by the Congregation of Drunken Boatmen a greater nuisance and have a much greater demoralising effect than their pursuing their worldly Calling; besides, this Committee can see no good reason why Traders should be prevented passing on this Canal on Sundays while Stage Coaches and Boats on other Canals are allowed to pass without interruption."

The latter argument was taken a stage further in 1836 in a tactful reply to an address from the Clergy of Worcester:

"This Company concur with the Clergy of Worcester in the propriety of preventing worldly Calling being carried out on Sundays, but they conceive the only way of effecting this is by procuring some legislative provision which shall operate on all persons alike and be compulsory."

In 1836 the Canal Company, through their lock-keeper John Waldron at the Blockhouse, Worcester, did take legal action against one of Crowley's steerers who broke a lock off the lock gate there on a Sunday during service time. But in general the Canal Company was much more tolerant and down-to-earth in its attitude to Sunday working than the well-intentioned sabbatarians, realising that most boatmen were unlikely to attend church services. Their working attire was anyhow hardly fitting and, for them, enforced idleness meant not only loss of earnings but also frustration and the temptation to be drunk and disorderly.

The Canal Committee received further appeals to them to ban the movement of working boats upon the canal on Sundays, but they refused to act unilaterally. In 1840 in response to organised petitions from citizens of Worcester and Stourport, the Committee instructed the Company's Clerk, Mr Hodgkinson, to send the following circular letter to the traders on the canal:

"Many applications having been made to the Committee of the Company of Proprietors of the Worcester & Birmingham Canal Navigation to put a stop to Trading upon their Canal on the Sabbath day, they respectfully request you will give directions to your Steerers to avoid such a practice as much as possible."

Thus the onus was passed on to the boat owners. To further similar pressure in 1852 and 1861, the reply was that the Committee "have no powers to prevent Trading on their Canal on Sundays."

In the latter part of the nineteenth century, there was a growing social concern for the general welfare of the working classes, and a new argument against Sunday working was that of reducing the number of working hours to provide time for rest and relaxation as well as the opportunity for Sunday worship. This was the motive behind the initiative of a consortium of boat owners following the SND takeover of the canal in 1874. In 1875 a "Memorial" was received by the Board of Directors from 55 signatories of carriers on the SND waterways, including Healing & Sons, John Corbett, Hardy & Padmore, and Lucy & Townshend, in favour of their crews enjoying Sunday as a day of rest and having the opportunity to attend Divine Worship with their families. In reply the Directors said they were not prepared to close the W/B Canal on Sundays and they suggested "to the Memorialists the propriety of giving instructions to any steerers in their employ to cease labour on the Sunday, and as almost all the traders have signed the Memorial they have the remedy in their own hands."

So the waterways, like the roads, continued to remain open on Sundays and it was left to the firms and individual traders on the W/B and other canals to make their own decision about Sunday working.

THE WATER-HIGHWAY CODE

For the protection of its structures, the efficient use of the waterway and the safety of those involved, the W/B Canal Company had to draw up and update from time to time a set of bye-laws to be observed by its employees and boatmen, together with penalties prescribed for their infringement. Many of these bye-laws were broadly in line with those of other waterways. The minute books of the Canal Company do not record any rules applicable during the first years of the use of the waterway. The first recorded set of "Rules, Bye Laws and Orders" were those agreed by the Assembly of Proprietors on 4 July 1809. They were ten in number and (abbreviated) laid down that (1) boatmen must not navigate without a helm, or helm first, (2) two boats must not be fastened together, (3) each boat must have a qualified helmsman and a person attending the horse, (4) empty boats must give way to loaded ones, (5) boats must be moored at both ends on the non-towpath side of the canal and at least 40 yards from any bridge, aqueduct or stop lock, (6) horses or other towing beasts must be muzzled, (7) boats must not strike bridges, aqueducts or stop gates, (8) goods must be unloaded on the Company's wharves only as directed by the Company's agent or wharfinger, (9) drawbridges must be put down after passing, (10) the metal of metal-ended shafts to be not less than 3 inches square at the end. These rules, together with the penalties for infringement, were to take effect from 1 August 1809 and were to be printed and displayed at the machine houses and elsewhere on the canal.

When the 1809 set of bye-laws came into operation the canal was open only as far as Tardebigge Old Wharf; there were no locks, and canal lifts instead of locks were a possibility. But when the canal was finally completed to Worcester in December 1815 there was the need for a new set of bye-laws to include the use of the locks. The January 1816 Assembly of Proprietors agreed sixteen new bye-laws drawn up by its Committee. They covered six main items:

First, the identification of boats and the means of determining their loads; they had to have their gauge number in figures at least 3 inches high and clearly visible above water level, and also four "indexes" (vertical measuring rods) fixed, one each end and one at the middle of each side of the boat, to enable the draught to be ascertained and the load determined from the boat's gauging records. (Gauging rods were apparently not yet in use.)

Second, concerning the use of locks; paddles to be checked before and after use, boats to enter locks as gently as possible, lower gates to be closed after use, no waste of water, ropes not to be wound or coiled around lock gear or parts of lock gates, side pounds at locks which have them to be properly used, boats using locks to have a stern strap or tail rope to restrain them, no boat to remain in a lock more than five minutes.

Third, the avoidance of damage to canal structures, banks, hedges and fences, masonry and timber; also to other boats through collisions or unmoored boats drifting.

Fourth, efficient use of the Company's wharves; boats to be unloaded within 12 hours and moved within 24 hours if not taking on more cargo.

Fifth, fishing gear not to be used without the consent of the owner of the fishery rights.

Sixth, in tunnels, boats to carry a lighted candle or lantern at the front, and when passing a boat travelling in the opposite direction to keep to the left.

These bye-laws came into effect on 25 March 1816, copies having been posted up at the machine houses and elsewhere, and distributed "among persons concerned in navigating Boats or other Vessels on the Canal". In their long-winded legalistic form with the penalty prescribed for each offence, they cover nine pages of Assembly minutes and would take some reading and digesting. But most boatmen would soon know what was expected of them and what the penalties for any breach of the bye-laws were liable to be.

From time to time, in the light of events and new situations, the bye-laws were added to or amended. For instance, following a complaint from Crowley. Hicklin & Co. about delays to their fly-boats, the Assembly in January 1825 agreed a new bye-law to give fly-boats priority over coal boats in their passage along the canal and through locks. After tunnel tugs were introduced by the SND Company in 1876, additional regulations included the prohibition of legging and the use of shafts in tunnels, the provision by each boat of a towrope, and the extinguishing of fires on board.

WATERWAY HAZARDS AND SAFETY MEASURES

All waterways are potentially dangerous, and over the years the W/B Canal has had its own mounting toll of accidents and drownings. Some of these have involved boat crews, lock-keepers and other canal employees; others have involved the general public, adults and children. At various times there have been calls for the Canal Company to take action to prevent such happenings. In 1822 the Worcester Humane Society (established in 1786 for the recovery of persons apparently dead from drowning or other causes and to reward those instrumental in their recovery) expressed concern about the danger of the locks on the canal. In response the Canal Committee advised that locks were not intended for public passage and people should keep away from the danger. Action taken by the Humane Society included the provision of "suitable apparatus" at various points on the River Severn and the W/B Canal for rescuing people from drowning. By 1825 the Humane Society had distributed to alternate lock houses along the canal, from Diglis to Tardebigge, rescue equipment including drags and hooks. In February 1828 Berrow's Worcester Journal reported that, using this equipment, the Blockhouse lock-keeper, William Bradley, had saved John Rigby of Tewkesbury, who had fallen into the lock, from drowning. The equipment certainly helped to save some lives, but many continued to be lost.

In 1834, following some child fatalities, the Mayor of Worcester, Mr Tymbs, sent a letter to the Canal Company expressing his concern. The Committee replied that it was up to parents to take proper care of their children. There was little that the Canal Company perceived it could do at that time to prevent accidents other than to urge care in the use of its canal by all concerned.

In recent years structural safety measures have been undertaken. These have included the fitting of lock ladders to facilitate escape from within partly-filled locks, and the making of steps up to the towpath from both portals of each of the tunnels with deep cuttings (i.e. all but Edgbaston Tunnel) to speed rescue efforts in the event of a tunnel accident.

PASTORAL MINISTRY TO BOAT PEOPLE AT THE BIRMINGHAM END

The nineteenth century saw a growing concern for the social and spiritual welfare of the labouring classes, including individuals and families living and working on boats and barges on the rivers and canals. In 1869 a canal mission was established in a rented building on the Worcester Wharf of the W/B Canal in Birmingham by the Incorporated Seaman's and Boatman's Friendly Society. The aim was to provide material, moral and spiritual help to boat people. Services were held on Sundays and teaching was provided for children on the boats tied up in Gas Street Basin. The enthusiastic superintendent of this "Boatmen's Bethel" was a Mr Cusworth.

Early in 1877 the premises used by the Bethel were no longer available, and in March the SND Committee received a letter from Mr Arthur Ryland requesting a possible site for another Bethel, school and hospital on the Worcester Wharf. Mr George was instructed "to obtain a return of the average number of children belonging to the boat population that attend the school at any time and of the average number attending Divine Service on Sundays." In May he reported that the average number of children at the Worcester Wharf did not exceed fifteen, including infants. The Canal Committee decided that a school was not necessary, but they informed the mission trustees, Messrs. Ryland, Martineau and Carslake, that they were prepared to lease a site for a reading room, offices and infirmary. In December the architect for the new Boatmen's Bethel applied on behalf of Miss Ryland for an

Outside the Boatmen's Hall adjacent to the Worcester Wharf, Birmingham, during a severe freeze-up in 1895. The collection for FROZEN-OUT BOATMEN was under the auspices of the Seamen and Boatmen's Friend Society. (NWMT)

extra piece of land. This was granted and the building went ahead. It is described in an article in the Birmingham Daily Mail of 5 March 1875: "The little 'Bethel' stands close to the entrance gate; it contains an infant schoolroom, and a gaily decorated large room for Sunday services and day scholars." It was quite well attended, the services being hearty and informal, and the men in charge were generally welcomed on their pastoral visits to families on their boats.

Miss Louisa Anne Ryland, who took a great interest in the Worcester Wharf mission, was a very wealthy lady and a great benefactor to the City of Birmingham. Her father Arthur Ryland was one of the above-mentioned mission trustees. Her wealth was inherited from the wire-drawing business of her grandfather John Ryland, and her benefactions included the gifts to the City of Cannon Hill Park and Victoria Park, Smallheath, as well as support for hospitals, churches and the welfare of boat families. When, to make way for the construction of the Midland Railway Goods Depot, the recently constructed Boatmen's Bethel, to which she had contributed some £2,000, had to be demolished, Miss Ryland was in charge of the Committee which superintended the construction of the new Boatmen's Hall at the junction of Bridge Street and Wharf Street which opened in 1885, the cost of which was met by the Midland Railway Company.

The new Hall had two floors. On the ground floor there was a refreshment room, a reading room and a games room with a billiard table. Upstairs there was a mission room where services were held and also a schoolroom for boatmen's children. The place provided a welcome social venue for boat people, advice and help, food and drink, simple religious services, and a Sunday School for their children. On Sundays the padre would visit the boats in the basin and invite the occupants to attend the service there. An article in the Birmingham Mail of 8 February 1886 gives an impression of the average boatman's use of the Boatmen's Hall:

> "He frequents the Boatmen's Mission Hall near the wharf quite as much as is to be expected of him, and when he is stopping in the town for a day or two he sends his children to the special canal children's school which is held there with commendable regularity. Comparatively speaking he is a sober man, and, perhaps to a certain extent because of the limited space at his disposal, he does not beat his wife as he sometimes does his horse. At present he gets his letters written for him at the Mission Hall, and gets his letters read there for him too."

The Boatmen's Hall was still open and busy during World War 2, but with the demise of working boats after the war it was closed and eventually demolished. In connection with the mission one of the memories of boat people is of Sister Cooper, a midwife, helping to deliver babies on boats in Gas Street Basin in the 1940s and early 1950s.

MISSIONS TO BOAT PEOPLE IN WORCESTER

At the Worcester end of the canal the first mission initiative was that of the Wesleyan Methodists who built a chapel in Lowesmoor opposite to the entrance to the basin. Berrow's Worcester Journal of 18 March 1824, in a news item, announced that Lowesmoor Chapel near the wharf would be opened on the following Tuesday, 23 March, "in order to give encouragement to the boatmen ... to attend Divine Worship." The minister and other church members were, no doubt, active in ministering to boatmen and their families and, whilst the locks were padlocked during the times of worship on Sundays, perhaps some of the boat people did attend the chapel services. However the chapel was taken over in 1838 by members of the Countess of Huntingdon's Connexion who were probably not greatly concerned about the canal community over the road. In more recent times the building has belonged to the Elim Pentecostal Church still functioning there.

Fifty-five years after the Methodists, the Rector of St. Martin's Parish, the Revd. Robert Blair, sought to establish a mission building on Lowesmoor Wharf. In 1879 he asked the Canal Company for the free use of an unoccupied tenement there and for permission to make the necessary alterations to fit it for a night school, reading and service room for boatmen. His request was granted for a nominal rental of five shillings per annum, all alterations and repairs to be executed by Mr Blair to the satisfaction of the canal engineer, Mr Hobrough, the Company reserving the right to repossession if at any time the building was unused or was required by the Company. Known as St. Mark's Mission Room, it is shown on the 1886 O.S. map as being a little way inside the wharf entrance on the left hand side, opposite to the weighbridge house. It was looked after by "Scripture Reader" T Turner and there were Sunday services at 11.00 am and 6.30 pm. It closed about 1894, having been in use for some fifteen years.

Unlike the situation at the Worcester Wharf, Birmingham, and at Lowesmoor, there was never any mission building at Diglis. The basins were in St. Peter's Parish, the church being close by at Sidbury, so maybe the parish clergy did take an interest in the boat people. One clergyman who certainly took an active part in caring for the crews of both river and canal boats was the Revd. John Davies. He was appointed Rector of the Parish of St. Clements, Worcester, in 1816, and was concerned at first for the welfare of prisoners in the City Jail and for patients in the Worcester Infirmary, both in his parish. In the 1840s he turned his attention to the needs of the watermen and their families. He travelled far and wide speaking of their plight and he raised money to build the Mariners' Chapel at Gloucester Docks and also to convert the old river barge *Albion* into a floating chapel at Worcester. The *Albion* was fitted up and furnished with seats, pulpit and communion table at a cost of £400 and was located on the river alongside Pitchcroft. Unfortunately it eventually sank and the resident caretakers had to be rescued through the roof. John

Davies died in 1858, and in his memory a new watermen's church made of corrugated iron was built near the quay at the bottom of Dolday in the old churchyard of St. Clement's, and the *Albion* was raised and put on brick foundations beside the church to serve as a schoolroom. Both structures outlived their necessity and were demolished in 1947. In the meanwhile they had been available to serve the needs of both river and canal boat people including those using the Diglis basins.

PASTORAL MINISTRY ALONG THE CANAL

Besides the missions to boat people at the Birmingham and Worcester ends of the canal, the spiritual needs of many boat families along the canal in the heyday of commercial carrying were often met by local parish clergy. George Bate remembered being told by his father and grandfather about the Revd. Harcourt Aldham and the Revd. Charles Stockdale, successive vicars of Stoke Prior, and Canon Allan Dickins, Vicar of Tardebigge, whose ministries covered the period from the mid-nineteenth century until World War 1, conducting the weddings and christening the babies of boat families. Some of these families were local, as at Stoke Works where many who crewed salt boats had homes at Causeway Meadows near to the canal and the Bowling Green Public House. Baptisms sometimes took place on the canalside using water from the canal.

There were funerals too, all too often of young children, victims of illness or accident, and also, in the early days, of leggers drowned in Tardebigge or Shortwood Tunnel, possibly the worse for drink when the Plymouth Arms at the New Wharf and the Navigation Inn at the Old Wharf were open. Tardebigge Church Registers contain the names of eight men, mostly young, who were drowned in one or other of the two tunnels between 1820 and 1846. Local clergy were usually ready to comfort and help passing boat families, as well as their own parishioners, in times of bereavement and distress.

Besides officiating at baptisms, weddings and funerals, local clergy also sometimes held canalside Sunday services. George Bate's grandfather John Bate, besides being licensee of the Queen's Head, was also the organist at Stoke Prior Church and he would accompany, on a harmonium, open air services on Stoke Wharf which were conducted by the Revd. H Aldham at times when enough boat people were assembled there on Summer Sunday afternoons. In his memoirs George tells how he himself, as a young lad with his father around 1909/10, saw at Tardebigge New Wharf "a clergyman along with a congregation of boatmen and a flock of women having an open air service. My father told me it was Canon Dickins. He used to come down from Tardebigge Church and conduct a service on some Sunday afternoons when sufficient numbers of boats had come up the locks during Saturday night and Sunday morning."

LOCAL HELP DURING CANAL STOPPAGES

In recent times winters have mostly been relatively mild and the canal has rarely been frozen over for long periods since the severe winters of 1947 and 1962/3. However, during the nineteenth century and on into the early years of the twentieth century, there were many years when in winter the canal was frozen over for weeks at a time and boats were at a standstill, trapped in thick ice. At such times the boat people suffered distress through lack of money, fuel and food. At many locations along the canal where boats were icebound, local people were pleased to help. On one such occasion in January 1861 the "Bromsgrove Messenger" reported:

Icicles inside Tardebigge Tunnel during the freeze-up of 1962/3. (Doris Colledge)

Tardebigge. "The boat people engaged on the canal, being in great destitution on account of the inclemency of the weather and the consequent stoppage of their ordinary employment, the Vicar, the Rev.C.A.Dickins, has exerted himself to obtain subscriptions for their relief. Soup and bread have been liberally supplied; on Wednesday ninety-six of these poor people received each three pints of soup. Mr. Samuel Taylor of the Plymouth Arms has also most kindly supplied the most pressing wants of many of the boatmen."

Stoke Prior. "The poor boatmen, whose barges have now been locked in the ice for five weeks, have received from various individuals, soup, also tickets to the value of 2s.6d. for bread and other necessities."

During another prolonged icy spell in January/February 1879 some forty boats were reported icebound in the vicinity of Stoke Prior Salt Works. Help given included distribution by Mr Hobrough, the canal engineer, of 73 quarts of soup and a quantity of bread on two occasions, a dinner for the boatmen at the Stoke Works Workmen's Club, and soup and bread provided by John Corbett the proprietor of the Salt Works.

These instances are typical of many such on the same and similar occasions.

THE COMPASSION OF THE CANAL COMPANY

As an employer responsible for its employees and its customers (the canal users), the W/B Canal Company has shown from time to time a practical concern for those in distress, whether through illness, accident or bereavement. Already mentioned in chapter 4 are steps which were taken to provide for the welfare of workmen injured during the creation of the canal, including a benefit club to provide help in time of need, the appointment of a surgeon and apothecary, and a subscription of 5 guineas a year to the Birmingham General Hospital where many injured workmen were treated. Other instances recorded in the Committee minutes include:

January 1795: "Payment of one guinea to Rhoades, a poor distressed Engineer to assist him on his Road."

February 1836: "Philip James of Tewkesbury be given £3.10s towards his loss by having a Horse drowned in the Canal."

January 1837: Recommendation of £40 compensation to the widow of Mr Lewis lately killed by the falling of a stale at Worcester Wharf "to place her in some way of business".

January 1861: "£10 to be paid to Mr B.F.Baldwin as compensation for the loss of a mare by falling into the Canal at Shortwood Tunnel."

This compassionate concern for canal employees and users continued under the SND regime. Special consideration was given to long-serving employees. For instance:

In August 1877 a donation was made to Mrs Colley, the widow of the lock-keeper at Astwood who had accidentally drowned.

In 1908 John Tallis, who had worked for the Canal Company for 65 years and was now unable to work, was awarded a pension of 5 shillings a week. Unfortunately he died the following year.

Reuben White, who after 27 years service at the Stoke Depot was unable to work in 1908 due to a cataract, was allowed to continue to live in the Company's house rent-free.

In 1920, the widow of George Colley who had served for nearly 40 years (his father and grandfather having also given long service) was allowed to remain in the Company's house.

THE CARE OF BOAT ANIMALS

The horses, donkeys and mules which were used to pull working boats on the canal were an important part of the workforce, yet their welfare was at times neglected by those who employed them. Boatmen who owned their own animals had every reason to care for them, to provide adequate drinking water, fodder and stabling. On the other hand animals which were hired from the Canal Company, as happened at Diglis for many narrowboats towed along the Severn by tugs, tended to be less well treated and sometimes cruelly beaten to increase their pace.

The W/B Canal Company was concerned from the outset to build stables, where necessary, at public wharves to supplement those provided by canalside hostelries. Stone troughs were also provided for animals to drink from. The only bye-law relating to boat animals was that passed by the Assembly of Proprietors in July 1809 "That no Boatman or other Person shall use any Horses or other Beasts for hauling of Boats or other Vessels upon this Navigation without being muzzled, under the Penalty of Ten Shillings for every such offence."

In the early years the Canal Company took little or no responsibility for the way boat crews treated their animals. But one simple device which did ease the strain on animals pulling boats out of the locks was the provision of metal hooks firmly embedded in the heavy stonework of the top of the forbays on the off-side. The towrope attached to the towing animal passed round a pulley block on the central mast of the boat and a loop on the end was placed over the hook. By this means the effort of the animal was effectively doubled, until a toggle in the rope a few feet from the loop hit the pulley, that part of the rope slackened and it slipped off the hook as the boat passed by. Most of these hooks, situated at both ends of a lock, are still there to be seen. The process for which they were intended was reenacted with two working boats on the Astwood Flight of the canal in 1997 and recorded for posterity on a videotape entitled "Towpath Encounter".

Soon after the SND Company took over the canal in 1874 it acquired many donkeys to hire out in pairs for canal boats arriving at Diglis from the river, and it took steps to deter those who hired these animals from ill-treating them. In July 1875 it was decided to issue notices offering a reward of £5 to persons giving information leading to the conviction of anyone found guilty of cruelty to any animal working on the canal. By October 1883, perhaps because of a costly spate of convictions, the reward had been reduced to 10 shillings, the Committee then remarking that no neighbouring canals offered such rewards.

Cases of cruelty, however, continued to be reported. The Bromsgrove Messenger of 31 October 1896 gave news of Boatman William Drinkwater who "was sent to Worcester Jail for two weeks hard labour by town magistrates who found him guilty of beating a horse with an iron handle. The incident happened between Halfway and Tardebigge as the poor animal struggled to pull a 30 ton cargo to Stoke. Drinkwater opted for jail as he claimed he could not afford the 5 shilling fine."

An earlier instance was reported in the Bromsgrove Messenger of 20 August 1892: "Rawson Merrill of 26 Causeway Meadows, Stoke Works, was fined 2/6d at Kings Heath court for cruelty to a mule. It appeared that the lazy Merrill, instead of leading the animal as it towed his barge along the canal towpath, sat on the bows and catapulted stones at the unfortunate animal to gee it up." Fortunately such cases of cruelty were the exception. Unreported were the many kind boatmen who valued and cared for their animals. One of these was Jack Merrell who, in the 1930s, used a mule called Smoker to pull a salt boat from Stoke Salt Works to Johnson's warehouse in Birmingham. The mule was well treated, having a home grazing ground at Stoke Pound and being, as Jack described him, "a real Christian", knowing from experience how to behave and what his duties were.

THE WELFARE OF BOAT PEOPLE

Just as the welfare of boat animals was not the responsibility of the Canal Company, so also were the conditions of people living and working on the boats. The state of the small cabins in which boat families lived varied from those which were kept clean, neat and tidy to those which were dirty and smelly, infested by bugs and vermin. Some boat cabins were very overcrowded with parents and children of both sexes sleeping in the same bed. As soon as they were able to do so, children helped to work the boats, and they received little or no schooling.

Following a campaign by George Smith and a book "Our Canal Population" researched by him and published in 1875 describing the hard life endured by many boat families, an Act of Parliament was passed in 1877, followed by an amending Act in 1884, requiring all boats used as dwellings to be registered with a local authority and to carry on board a certificate of registration. The size of the cabin had to be measured and the composition of the crew was limited by the stipulation that there should be not less than 60 cu.ft of air for each person over the age of 12 and not less than 40 cu.ft for each child under 12. Girls aged over 12 and boys aged over 14 were not allowed to live on a boat with their parents. Typically a boat crew would be limited to three adults or to two adults and two children under the prescribed ages. Each local Sanitary Authority had to appoint an inspector who could inspect a cabin boat at any time and report on its state and its occupants. The inspectors also had powers to see that the parents of children living on canal boats were arranging for their children to attend school, as much as possible, in the place where their boat was registered or elsewhere, in accordance with the Education Acts of 1870 and later.

Boats using the W/B Canal were liable to be inspected at Birmingham, at Droitwich if travelling along the Droitwich Junction Canal, and at Worcester. The reports of the inspectors at each of these locations are available, for Birmingham from 1912 to 1958 in Birmingham Reference Library, for Droitwich from 1891 to 1917 in the Worcester Record Office, and for Worcester from 1892 to 1960 in the City Council offices. The Birmingham and Worcester reports are brief and to the point, e.g. the cabin improperly occupied by a female above 12 years of age, or by a male above 14 years of age; no certificate of registration on board; the cabin

The registration, in accordance with the Canal Boats' Act of 1878, of one of T & M Dixon's horse boats in the charge of boat-master Thomas Colledge. (Archives Department, BRL)

overcrowded by parents with four or more children; boat without proper water vessel, dirty and dilapidated, needs repainting; roof of cabin leaking, unfit for habitation. Following an unsatisfactory report, faults were to be rectified and a further inspection would follow to check whether or not they had been.

The "Journal of the Inspector of Canal Boats" for the Droitwich Authority is more detailed and includes general remarks and a note of any action which was taken. The inspector's visits were often not welcome and at times he had a a very hostile reception, the police were called in and there were legal proceedings. For instance in 1892 *Fanny* owned by Mary Footman of Stoke Prior was visited. It had two men and one woman on board and the report stated: "Had a great deal of trouble to see certificate, boat in middle of canal, woman very abusive." In 1895 on the boat *Hellen* owned by W J Gorman, Ombersley, the report read: "All information refused. Man very abusive and offered to fight. Laid before Council and proceedings ordered. Fined 5/- and 12/6 costs." In 1906 the boat *Rover* owned by brickmakers W H Wynn of Alvechurch, master Robert Wood, was reported to be dirty and untidy. It had not been registered, although two men had slept in it overnight. In reply to a note of complaint sent to them, Wynns said the men had no right to sleep on board. But they soon registered the boat since the men did need to sleep overnight on some trips.

One interesting case reported on at length by the Worcester inspector related to the boat *Norah May*. In March 1923 the mate, Mr Thomas junior, was taken ill at Cannock and went home by train to Gloucester where he was diagnosed as having smallpox. There then followed a search for the boat as it proceeded down the W/B Canal. Telephone calls revealed that a woman on another boat *Bromsgrove*, accompanying *Norah May*, was ill as they passed through Offerton. She was the wife of Henry Thomas the skipper of *Bromsgrove* who was the brother of the smallpox patient, and she was feeling poorly because she had recently had a baby. Both boats were intercepted at Bilford Lane lock and the occupants were instructed to proceed to Diglis without mixing with anyone. At Diglis the boat cabins were well sprayed with Izal and strongly fumigated with formaldehyde and the personal clothing of the patient burned. All bedding was removed to hospital and put through the steam disinfector. Mr Thomas senior also went to hospital where he was disinfected and given a bath. Dr Andrews examined Mrs Thomas and the three children aged 5, 3 and 1 month on *Bromsgrove* and found them to be in good health. Finally the inspector telephoned the Gloucester authorities to inform them of the action taken.

There is no doubt that the Canal Boats Acts had a beneficial effect in raising the standards of cleanliness, hygiene and decency in the cabins of working canal boats and ensuring that children were not too greatly disadvantaged by their life afloat.

SCHOOLING FOR CANAL-BOAT CHILDREN

Before the passing of Mundella's 1880 Education Act, children did not have to attend a school and many of those living on canal boats with their parents received little or no schooling. Following the Act, the education of canal boat children became the responsibility of the School Board where the boat was registered or was usually based. Being for most of the time on the move, the children were expected to attend the nearest school wherever the boat happened to stop, so their education was disrupted, and, being behind their contemporaries, they were often put in classes with younger children. It was not easy for them, but it had to be endured unless, or until, the family could make other arrangements.

There are references in one of Tardebigge School's log books to canal-boat boys attending the school. In January 1891 James Thomas was admitted to the school for two weeks whilst his father's boat was immovable on the frozen canal. In 1901 Edward Bourne from a canal boat attended the school irregularly.

Because of the number of canal-boat children attending, albeit part-time, schools situated near various wharves along the canal, the SND Canal Company felt in duty bound to contribute towards the schools involved. In 1885 it was agreed to pay a subscription of 50 shillings per annum to the School Board in the Parish of Northfield. In 1891 a subscription of one guinea was agreed to Hanbury National School. £5 was granted to Alvechurch School Building Fund in 1895 and £5 to Hadzor Voluntary School in 1896. Until 1891 parents of children attending school had been charged 2 pence a week for their education, unless they were really poor. It is unlikely that the parents of children on icebound boats would have been able to pay any such fee, hence, perhaps, the obligation felt by the Canal Company to support schools attended by canal-boat children.

Chapter 17

CANALSIDE INDUSTRIES
ESTABLISHED BEFORE 1850

From the point of view of canal companies, anxious to increase their revenues, one of the welcome consequences of the creation of their waterways was the establishment of canalside industries. Even after the building of railways, the canals remained a convenient means of transport for heavy materials such as coal, bricks, metal ores, sand and timber. Over the years some twenty substantial industries were established beside the W/B Canal. Most of these are now bygones; in some cases they have disappeared virtually without trace; of others there are visible remains such as wharf walls, bridges over the canal or canal arms, and buildings, some derelict, others put to alternative use.

LIFFORD CHEMICAL WORKS

Soon after the W/B Canal had been authorised by Act of Parliament in 1791, and as it was being surveyed, Thomas Dobbs of Lifford was thinking of setting up a factory beside it. Born in 1745, he had been in business in Livery Street, Birmingham, as a roller of, and a dealer in, metals. Around 1780 he had bought all or part of the estate of James Hewitt, Viscount Lifford, at Kings Norton, including the Hall and the adjacent mill on the River Rea, which he used for rolling metals. As soon as he realised that the W/B Canal was planned to pass through Lifford, he bought more land along its line cheaply in order to sell at an inflated price to the Canal Company. This was, as we have seen, the beginning of a long series of disputes between himself and the Canal Company, during the period of the canal's construction, over such matters as his encroachment on the Canal Company's land, avoidance of tolls, and overcharging for his land required for Lifford Reservoir. At the outset, Dobbs decided to make use of the canal by setting up a chemical works on the land he owned on the west side of the waterway as it curves round from Breedon Cross towards Lifford Lane Bridge. In June 1792 he requested, and was allowed to buy, 50,000 bricks from the W/B Company's kilns for his factory, which was to produce nitric and sulphuric acids. Following the completion of the canal to Kings Norton in 1795-6, he added a wharf and other buildings including a canalside warehouse. Dobbs died in 1827, but the Lifford Chemical Works continued in existence, being shown on an 1840 map as Pratt's Works. By 1870 the chemical works had closed down and there was, for a time, a brickworks on the site.

WORCESTER ROYAL PORCELAIN WORKS

In 1791-2, at the southern end of the planned W/B Canal, another man, Robert Chamberlain, was setting up a porcelain factory on the site of the present Worcester Porcelain Works. He would have been aware of plans to cut the canal through Diglis Fields along the line of a small stream, the Frog Brook, and of the hope (alas not realised) that it would be completed through to Diglis in a few years time. As a lad of fourteen he had been one of the first, if not the very first, of the apprentices taken on by the porcelain works newly established in 1751 by the River Severn at Warmstrey House, now the site of the Worcester Technical College and the adjacent riverside car park.

Porcelain was first imported into this country from China and became popular in the early 18th century. So great was the demand that experiments were made to produce it in England and in the 1740s three factories were set up, located at Bow and Chelsea in London, and at Bristol. The Bristol enterprise, started in 1749, soon moved, in 1751, to Worcester. Leading light of the fifteen founder partners of the

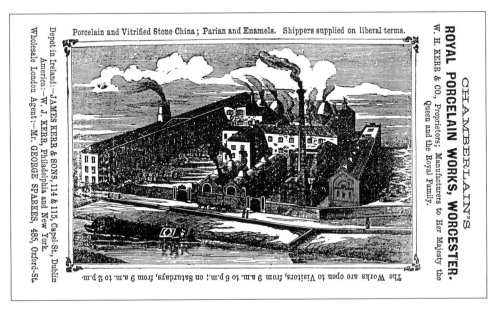

An engraving of the Royal Worcester Porcelain Works c.1860.

Worcester Porcelain Works wharf c.1900 featuring the bottle kilns, boats, and, on the wharf, china clay and other materials. (Royal Worcester Archives)

Worcester Company was Dr John Wall, local doctor, chemist and artist, whose name is associated with the earliest products. This early porcelain was made from "soaprock", or china clay, from near the Lizard in Cornwall, transported to Worcester by sea and river. Dr Wall died in 1776, and when the manager, William Davis, died in 1783 the business was purchased for £3,000 by Thomas Flight of Hackney, who had been the London agent, and the factory was managed by his sons Joseph and John Flight. In 1788, King George III and Queen Caroline visited Worcester and bought some of the firm's wares, following which, in 1789, the Company received the Royal Patent. In 1793, following the death of John Flight, Martin Barr, an able technician, was taken into partnership. Between 1793 and 1840 the Firm was known as Flight and Barr, then Barr, Flight and Barr, then Flight, Barr and Barr, as successive members of both families took control.

Soon after the business was sold to Thomas Flight in 1783, Robert Chamberlain, who was by now in charge of the enamelling department, decided to leave and, with his son Humphrey, to set up his own studio in King Street, Worcester. There he painted white porcelain bought from the Caughley Factory, Coalport, Shropshire, which had been started by another former employee of the Worcester Porcelain

Works, Thomas Turner. He would have needed little plant, beyond a kiln initially to fire his wares, but having successfully established his business, and with the W/B Canal in prospect, he decided to set up his own canalside porcelain factory. Robert Chamberlain died in 1798, long before the W/B Canal was completed to Worcester, and the factory was then managed by his two sons Humphrey and Robert as partners until 1827 when John Lilly joined the partnership and Humphrey retired. In 1802 the firm had an order from Lord Nelson, in 1806 one from the Duke of Cumberland, and in 1811, as manufacturers to the Prince of Wales, it introduced prestigious "Regent" porcelain. With the help of such patronage the business gradually expanded and prospered, so much so that their rivals, Flight, Barr and Barr, whose business in the 1830s had declined and whose principal partner, Joseph Flight, died in 1838, agreed to a merger with Messrs. Chamberlain and to move into their canalside works. Following this, and the death of Humphrey Chamberlain, a new company, Walter Chamberlain & Co. was set up in 1842, which paid £3930 to the executors of Humphrey Chamberlain for the factory, and in which a substantial shareholder was Henry Douglas Cardon, grandson of the Thomas Cardon who had played a large part in the creation of the W/B Canal. The old riverside Warmstrey Factory continued to be used for ten years or so to make encaustic tiles before it closed around 1850.

In 1850 W H Kerr, who was connected by marriage with the Chamberlain family, joined the partnership, and when Walter Chamberlain and John Lilly retired in 1851, he invited R W Binns to join him and undertake the artistic direction of the factory. In 1852 W Chamberlain & Co. was taken over by Kerr and Binns, being known thereafter as W H Kerr and Company. During the next ten years new buildings were erected and improvements made in standards of workmanship and artistry. Then in 1862 the Worcester Royal Porcelain Company was formed, and this, after so many changes of ownership, created a stability which enabled it to survive until 1967 when it amalgamated with Spode of Staffordshire to become Royal Worcester Spode Limited.

Until the 1960s the Worcester Porcelain Works continued to make use of the canal for transport and also for water for their engine boilers. China clay from Cornwall and Forest of Dean coal from the Lydney Coal Co. and Parkend Coal Co. came up river, carried in the early years by Soule's trows, later by Crowley & Co. and by Danks, Venn and Sanders. Coal, lime, salt for glazing and other materials came down the W/B Canal, conveyed by a number of carriers including Pickfords, Ryder Bird, Vaughan, Lloyd and Bromleys, in the early years. The works had its own small fleet of canal boats from at least 1827 when one was bought for £23.13s.5d. These were eventually phased out by 1907, some sold by instalments to individuals (e.g. Cabin Boat No.6 to Frederick Smith of Hylton Road, Coal dealer, for £18, at £1 per month, agreed in 1905), others to T S Townshend's Flour Mill. However, the use of canal transport by other carriers continued until around 1960.

A 1933 aerial view of Worcester with, centrally, the Cathedral and, in the foreground, the W/B Canal with Townshend's Mill and Silo and, beyond Mill Street Bridge, the Royal Worcester Porcelain Works with old bottle kilns. (Aerofilms)

Over the years there have been many alterations and additions to the factory buildings including the replacement of coal-fired kilns by electric ones. With the ending of the use of canal transport a tall canalside brick wall was built which now shuts off the factory and former wharf from view from the canal.

GRAINGER'S PORCELAIN WORKS, WORCESTER

Around 1806 Thomas Grainger and John Wood, both of whom had been apprentices and employees of Robert Chamberlain's porcelain works, started up their own porcelain factory in the Lowesmoor area of Worcester in partnership with Stephen Wilkins who owned the land there. This factory, which is believed to have been situated at the corner of Pheasant Street and George Street, was unfortunately burnt down on 25 April 1809. However, undeterred, Grainger, Wood & Co. soon built a replacement factory on a nearby site at the corner of St. Martin's Gate and Pheasant Street. It seems likely that the choice of location for these works was made in view of the proximity of the line of the yet-to-be-constructed section of the W/B Canal through Worcester. Once the canal was open Graingers rented a wharf at Lowesmoor Basin, used, no doubt, for unloading coal and raw materials, and probably for delivering some of their wares. In 1817 Thomas Grainger and other china manufacturers were negotiating with the Canal Committee over tonnages on coal.

Following the death of Thomas Grainger in 1839 the factory was run by his son George Grainger with several business partners at various times. Then after George Grainger's death in 1888, his son Frank sold the business in 1889 to the Worcester Royal Porcelain Company. The factory continued in production and traded as George Grainger & Co. until 1902 when it was sold. Over the years Graingers produced fine decorated porcelain, including table ware, vases, ornaments and figurines. They had a shop and showroom at 19 Foregate St. They continued to use their rented wharf at Lowesmoor, the lease of which was renewed in November 1865. In 1871 George Grainger applied to the W/B Canal Company for permission to erect an advertisement sign on a wall at Lowesmoor. The Canal Committee agreed to this but made a charge of five shillings per annum.

HARDY AND PADMORE

As the W/B Canal was nearing completion through Worcester in 1814, brothers Robert and John Hardy from Scotland began to set up an iron foundry in Blockhouse Fields beside it. In Berrow's Journal of 8 February 1816, just two months after the canal came into use, it was reported that Messrs. Hardy & Co. were producing "every sort of castings", and that this new industry was "one of the advantages the Canal has brought to this City." A map of 1824 shows the main foundry building fronting Foundry Road north of the Blockhouse Bridge and the foundry yard and wharf located just above the Blockhouse Lock. A corner of land between the foundry and the lock belonged to the Canal Company, which in 1821 agreed to sell it to Hardy & Co. but then reversed the decision as side ponds were planned for both the deep Sidbury and Blockhouse locks, but were never actually constructed. Because of these two narrow locks between Diglis Basin and the foundry, only narrowboats could be used for the transport to it of coal, sand, pig iron, timber and other items. During its existence the foundry did make extensive use of the waterways, not only for incoming supplies, but also for the delivery, where convenient, of heavy castings. The Company evidently owned its own boats and employed its own boatmen from time to time, but the only cabin boat registered by them in the Registers of the Birmingham Sanitary Authority from 1879 to 1960 was, in 1897, *Heart of Oak*, its master Charles Smith of Worcester, carrying pig iron, coal etc. and hauled by two donkeys. It is possible that other boats were registered with the Worcester Authority, but the early Worcester records are not available, presumed lost.

In 1818 Richard Padmore (1790-1881), son of Thomas Padmore of the Ketley Ironworks, Salop., joined the workforce. A capable and ambitions man, he was soon in a responsible position on the business side and a traveller for the firm. In 1823 he married Emma Jones of Worcester, and in 1829 he was taken into partnership and the business thereafter was known as Hardy and Padmore.

A receipt signed by Richard Padmore in 1825 on behalf of Robert Hardy & Co. describes the Worcester Foundry as "Manufacturers of every description of Stove Grates, Kitchen Ranges, Oven Grates, Shop and Ironing Stoves, Hot Air Stoves, ascending or descending; Boat and Barge Stoves, Furnaces and Pans, Furnace and Oven Doors, Grates, Bars, &c., Bookcases and Chests, Field and Garden Rollers, Cattle and Pig Troughs, Horse Racks and Mangers, Iron Pumps, Water Pipes, Spouting and Gutters, Plough Shelboards and Shares, Smiths' Troughs, Backs and Tue Irons; Columns and Pillars, Lamp and Street Posts, plain or ornamental; Pallisades, Railing, Gates and Hurdles; Window Frames, Wrought Iron Ploughs, &c.,&c.; PATENT Pipe Boxes and Bushes, Smoothing, Hatters', and Tailors' Irons; Engine and Mill Work Castings, Gas Apparatus fitted up to order, Iron Roofs, &c.,&c. with every other description of Casting, to pattern, drawing, or dimensions."

Over the years Hardy and Padmore's products were to be found countrywide in Great Britain, and also worldwide. They include the lovely dolphin lamp standards on the Westminster Embankment of the Thames in London, the cast iron railway bridge over Foregate Street in Worcester, also in Worcester the fountain in Cripplegate Park, the clock from the old Market Hall now on a building opposite the Guildhall, and the lamp posts on the River Severn bridge. Items not on the above list but later produced in large quantities were tram standards, machine tools, traffic

A working boat opposite Hardy and Padmore's Foundry buildings above the Blockhouse Lock, Worcester. (Max Sinclair)

bollards, park seats, manhole covers, drain grills and mangles. Also produced were spiral and straight iron staircases and waggon weighing machines.

In W D Curzon's book "The Manufacturing Industries of Worcester" (1881), there is a detailed description of the works. which included a pattern making shop, pattern store rooms, seven foundries, the largest being equipped with travelling cranes, dressing shops for grinding, polishing and finishing castings, a smith's shop, fitting shops for the assembly of cast parts into the finished products, and three warehouses. Each initial pattern was made in wood, but an iron casting was then used as the pattern.

Robert Hardy retired and left Worcester in July 1851 to return to his native Scotland, having distributed £100 amongst his workmen as a parting gift. His nephew Peter Hardy, son of John who had died, continued as a partner until 1874. Richard Padmore played a leading part in local affairs, being elected to the City Council in 1835, becoming Alderman in 1838, Sheriff in 1847 and Mayor in 1848 and 1852; and he was elected M.P. for the City of Worcester in 1860 and 1865. Also a magistrate and local benefactor, he retired from active interest in the foundry in 1872. In 1874, the business, though continuing to be known as Hardy and Padmore, was bought by Thomas Southall and his brother-in-law Joseph Hall. Then in 1895, on the death of Joseph Hall the business became a limited liability company and continued as such, mainly in the hands of three generations of the Southall family. Joseph Southall invented an early hot air engine and a tiny candle-power motor to power watchmakers' lathes. His "Ideal" patent oil and gas engines were used to power pumps, lighting sets and farm machinery. Another development was a range of rock-crushing machinery, sand and gravel washing and grading plant, and these were installed by Hardy and Padmore's employees in many parts of the world.

As late as 1964 the firm was flourishing when, due to a sales push abroad and increased production, a night shift was introduced. That same year Richard Southall died and three years later, in May 1967, regrettably, Hardy and Padmore went into voluntary liquidation and some 160 people lost their jobs when the works closed.

Throughout its existence the foundry had relied upon canal transport and, amongst the boatmen who brought red foundry sand from the Stour Pound off the Staffs. & Worcs, Canal and via the Severn and W/B Canal to the Factory, before and after World War 2, were Tom Mayo and Tom Price, both of whom had worked for the Severn and Canal Carrying Company, and Tom Rice of George Street, Worcester.

THE BIRMINGHAM GAS LIGHT AND COKE COMPANY

When in the early 1800s coal-gas was introduced for domestic and street lighting, it was desirable that, where possible, gas works should be located beside canals, water transport being used to supply coal, lime and other materials, and for the distribution of the by-products including coke, coal tar and ammoniacal liquor. In Birmingham, gas lighting had first been introduced at the Soho Works of Boulton and Watt in 1798. But in the use of piped gas for street lamps Birmingham was well behind London where it was introduced in 1807. By 1811 in Birmingham a few gas lamps had appeared outside the houses of private individuals producing their own gas supply. It was not until 1816 that the Street Commissioners advertised for tenders for the replacement of their whale-oil lamps by gas. The only response was from John Gostling of London who had installed gas-lighting in Parliament Street, Westminster.

Early in 1817 Gostling signed a contract to light ten main streets in Birmingham, to build the necessary gas works, lay pipes and provide lamps with three times the illumination of oil lamps. During 1817 he set about building his gas works on the west side of the W/B Canal and the new road soon to be known as Gas Street. Under this street an arm from the canal already ran into a basin which had been used by the Dudley Canal Company as a coal wharf. This basin was taken over and enlarged by the gas works and from it coal, off-loaded from canal boats, was moved to the retort house in waggons on an iron railroad.

Early in 1818 street lighting commenced, and from April onwards agreements were made with householders for house lighting. There were no gas meters nor gas mantles at that time and householders were charged according to the number of lamps and the days and hours of burning. At first payment was expected in advance, half-yearly, but this was soon changed to quarterly in arrears. In 1819 Gostling was asked to light sixteen more streets and, in order to raise the necessary capital, he formed a joint stock company, The Birmingham Gas Light and Coke Company, supported by a private Act of Parliament. This Company took over on 19 October 1819, having paid £25,000 for the plant, which included 28 cylindrical retorts each 7 feet long and 12 inches in diameter and three larger patent retorts, also four tar retorts, one cast iron cistern, two patent purifiers, one brick cess-pool for spent lime used in purifying the gas, two brick tanks for gasometers to float in, two gasometers together holding up to 55,000 cu ft of gas, pipes, retort house with chimney, lime and coke houses, and the iron railroad. Under its constitution the company was to be run by a committee of nine elected by the shareholders, and the committee included John Gostling until his departure for pastures new in 1821. The first company officials engaged in July 1819 were Alexander Smith as Engineer with a salary of £250 per annum plus house plus coal, Thomas Pemberton as Treasurer and Superintendent, salary £200 per annum, and Mr Evans as Clerk and Collector at £85 per annum plus house plus coal.

The relationship between the Gas Company and the W/B Canal Company was none too cordial at first, as the Canal Company saw the gas works as a hazard and feared that an explosion of gas might damage the canal. In June 1820 the W/B Canal Committee received a letter from Thomas Pemberton of the Gas Company seeking permission to pass a gas main of six inches diameter under the Holliday Street

Part of a panoramic view of Birmingham published in 1847 showing the canals and the Gas Works.

Aqueduct. This request was at first refused and further fears expressed: "The Company learn with alarm and anxiety that the Gas Company are putting down more Gasometers in their Works, which may in case of accident produce the most mischievous consequences to the Worcester and Birmingham Canal and also the lower parts of the town .... and in case of any accident taking place which may prove injurious to the Worcester and Birmingham Canal they shall hold the Gas Company liable to make good all such damages." The question of the safety of the proposed gas main under the aqueduct was referred to Messrs. Boulton and Watt for their opinion and, as a result, the Canal Company's fears were allayed. The Gas Company was on better terms with the Birmingham Canal Company which, in 1819, agreed to supply the Gas Works with piped water from their canal, and also asked the Gas Company to install gas lamps along the B.C.N. between Farmer's Bridge and Snow Hill. Eighteen lamps were soon installed by Gostling along this section of canal.

The Birmingham Gas Company, though keeping to the terms of its contract with the Street Commissioners, was not very accommodating, and so the Commissioners encouraged the formation of a rival company, The Birmingham and Staffordshire Gas Light Company, which was established in 1825 and soon supplied not only parts of Birmingham, but also West Bromwich, Tipton, Oldbury, Smethwick, Bloxwich, Wednesbury and Walsall. In Birmingham the two gas companies caused great inconvenience by their rivalry, claiming equal rights in the same streets and digging them up so frequently that the residents continually complained. In the confusion this caused it was not unusual for one company to supply a customer by mistake from the other's main.

Gas meters, invented by Clegg, were introduced in 1820, and the Birmingham Gas Company's charges to domestic consumers were 15 shillings per 1,000 cubic feet from 1820-25, reduced to 12 shillings in 1826, and down to 10 shillings in 1834. In 1830 jet burners were replaced free of charge by bat-wing burners. The charge for street lamps was £2.10s. per lamp in 1829, increased to £3.10s. by 1853. A new contract with the Street Commissioners was signed in 1840 for further street lighting, and the Gas Company had to set up additional works, first in Upper Windsor Street, Aston, and then, by 1860, in Fazeley Street beside the Warwick and Birmingham Canal at Bordesley. Responsibility for street maintenance and lighting passed from the Commissioners to the Borough Council in 1851, and the Commissioners in their final report to the Council complained of the poor quality of the gas and the street lighting compared with other towns. In 1865 the Corporation decided to employ and pay its own lamp-lighters and negotiated a reduction in the price of gas which saved it some £1,800 per year.

In July 1871 news broke that Joseph Harrison who had been the Secretary of the Birmingham Gas company for 25 years had swindled the company out of some £20,000 by including in the accounts, as debts owed by many large consumers, money which they had paid and which he had appropriated. As an investigation into the accounts began Harrison absconded and fled abroad. The shareholders set up a Committee of Enquiry to examine the affairs of the company and, after sitting for five months from October 1871 to March 1872, it reported widespread negligence and corruption amongst the company's employees, lax supervision of workmen, serious discrepancies in the company's accounts and superficial auditing. Of Harrison, it was said that he had, since 1857, defrauded the company of considerable amounts of money and that "His style of living and his expensive habits were of a character inconsistent with the salary paid to him by the Company." He had absconded with many missing papers, books and other documents belonging to the Company.

Following these revelations and the Committee of Enquiry's damning report of the inefficient way the Gas Company had been run, it was not long before the Birmingham Corporation moved to take it over. During his mayoralty Joseph Chamberlain obtained approval and the necessary funds to municipalise the gas supplies, and this was legalised by an Act of Parliament in July 1875. Almost immediately the Gas Street Works were closed and demolished, soon to be replaced by a metal works.

THE WORCESTER GAS LIGHT AND COKE COMPANY

At the other end of the canal the Worcester Gas Works had a rather less turbulent history. In April 1818 a number of leading citizens arranged a meeting in the Guildhall to promote "The Worcester Gas Light and Coke Company". It was soon fully subscribed and authorised by an Act of Parliament obtained in June 1818. The initial capital was raised by 750 shares of £20 each with a maximum individual holding of 20 shares. One of the original committee of five was H Chamberlain, Porcelain Works proprietor and Mayor-elect of Worcester. A contract for constructing the gas works at Lowesmoor beside the W/B Canal was signed in August. During the months of March, April and May 1819 the Engineer, Mr Bradley, gave a series of lectures to the general public in the Bell Inn and in the Guildhall on the theory, application, safety and economy of gas lighting. Thus reassured, the City was first lit with gas on 9 August 1819. By 1840, as reported in Bentley's History of Worcester, gas lighting was "used in most places of worship, all the streets, squares, &c., the principal shops, inns and public buildings, and in many private dwellings; and the city presents a very different appearance on a winter's evening now, to what it did 20 years ago."

However, in the early 1840s there was widespread dissatisfaction with the quality of the gas and its high price, 8s.4d. per 1,000 cu.ft The City Council and the Street Commissioners both considered but turned down the option to purchase the gas works, and instead a new company was initiated in 1846 and Parliamentary approval obtained for the compulsory takeover of the old works, for it to be improved and gas produced more economically. The Worcester New Gas Light Company was floated with a capital of £15,000 in £10 shares, and £14,408.13s.

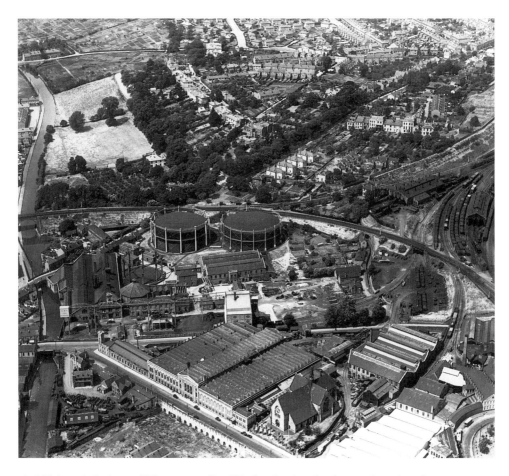

A 1934 aerial view of Worcester Gas Works, having both canal and railway access. (Aerofilms)

was paid for the old works in May 1846. Further capital was soon authorised by Acts of Parliament and after considerable improvements and additions to the works, the price of gas had fallen to 4s.0d. per 1,000 cu.ft by 1865 and was at its minimum of 2s.3d per 1,000 cu.ft in 1914 just before the outbreak of the 1914-18 War. In 1934, under a new General Manager and Engineer, George Porteous Mitchell, the Gas Works were modernised and extended; the old horizontal retort house by the canal was replaced by a large mechanised vertical retort house; a second large gasholder was constructed; a railway siding was laid into the retort house for coal supplies and an overhead telpher constructed between the retort house and the canalside for the conveyance of coke; also improvements were made to the processing plant.

From the beginning the canal, and later the railway, were used for bringing in coal and other materials such as lime used in purifying the gas, and in the distribution of coke. Gas tar was carried in a tanker narrowboat down to Diglis and there transferred to river boats for conveyance to Gloucester for distillation to produce various grades of oil, creosote and and pitch. In the 1930s, 40s and 50s, the horse-drawn tar boat *Maria*, owned by Butler's Oil and worked by Bert Thomas and his mate, each working day took two loads of tar, gravity fed into its tank at the Gas Works, along to the pound between the two broad locks at Diglis. There the tar was pumped into one of the River Severn tar boats, *Jolly*, *Derby* and *Isabel*. Mrs May Russell, wife of the Blockhouse lock-keeper, used to feed the horse drawing the tar boat from the Gas Works with cake, and it would wait, regularly, at the door of the lock house for this treat.

An old former employee of the Gas Works remembered that before 1934, when the Bridge Inn was located by the canal opposite the Gas Works between Rainbow Hill Road and Tolladine Road, there was a ropeway over the canal from the inn to the old retort house, and 4½ gallon casks of beer, suspended from a pulley block, were hauled along it to slake the thirst of the men who sweated in the heat of the retort house.

STOKE PRIOR SALT WORKS

In one of the minute books of the W/B Canal Committee there is a reference to salt springs being found in the bed of the canal as it was being cut through the Parish of Stoke Prior in 1812-13. Acting on this discovery, William Furnival, a Cheshire salt manufacturer who had set up in business in Droitwich in 1822, began in 1825 to dig for rock salt beside the W/B Canal on behalf of a new company, The British Rock and Patent Salt Company, in which he was involved. This pioneering mining venture met with only limited success. However, in 1828 the site was acquired by a Matthew Macalister who sunk pits and found brine at a depth of around 300ft. The brine rose to within 100ft from the surface and steam engines were installed to pump it up to a tank or reservoir, from which salt pans were fed. In 1831 Macalister's works were purchased by Alexander Reid, a Cheshire salt works proprietor, and run by Richard Parker. In 1836 The Imperial Salt and Alkali Company was established, with a capital of £75,000, to acquire the works, to pay off debts, and to expand the business with a chemical works to produce alkalis from salt, and also soap.

Meanwhile, another salt proprietor from Droitwich, Jonathan Fardon, having fallen out with other managers of his company, The Droitwich Patent Salt Company, came out to Stoke Prior at the end of 1827 and sank pits on the east side of the canal. He located rock salt some 300ft below the surface, and in 1829 bought the eight acres of land, already rented, on which he set up his salt works. Because mining rock salt at this depth was difficult, Fardon introduced water into the shaft to dissolve it so that the resulting brine could be pumped up. Very soon no more water was needed, as a connection was made with a natural brine spring.

In 1830 Fardon was joined by William Gossage, an industrial chemist who had been an apothecary in Leamington, to set up and manage a chemical works to manufacture various alkalis and soap from salt. The business was now known as Fardon, Gossage and Company. By 1835 the company was prospering but was in need of capital to expand, so Fardon and Gossage sold the business for £120,000 to a new company the "British Alkali Company". The original six directors of the British Alkali Company included Fardon and Gossage, who continued to run the works, and Francis Rufford, a Bromsgrove banker whose bank had invested heavily in the new company.

Thus by 1836 there were the two rival salt and chemical works on opposite sides of the canal. Both made extensive use of the canal, for the carriage of bricks and other building materials used in setting up and expanding their works, for bringing in supplies of coal and raw materials, and for the distribution of the salt and other products. The British Alkali Company, on the towpath side, had a canal arm which led into a long tunnel under the salt works where canal boats could be loaded directly from the panhouses by means of chutes. The Imperial Company had two canal arms into their works. Both companies, besides contracting with independent canal carriers, also had boats of their own, crewed by their own employees. The British Alkali Company sent salt by canal as far as London where it had its own warehouse and London agent, and it also leased a wharf and warehouse on the Gloucester and Berkeley Canal in Gloucester.

From the beginning the W/B Canal Company took a great interest in the development of the Salt Works. In the 1830s the Assemblies of Proprietors were kept informed of the benefits of the growing trade in salt along the canal. The Company cooperated in the construction of wharf walls and of sluices into the works. To encourage the use of the canal for the transport of coal and salt the Company allowed drawbacks on the tolls, especially to combat competition in due course from the railways.

In 1840 the Birmingham and Gloucester Railway was constructed alongside the Imperial Works and this enabled that Company to have sidings into their works and to begin to use railway transport. The W/B Canal Company was naturally concerned at this competition and in 1844 they opposed an application by the British Alkali Company for a railway bridge to be built over the canal to gain railway access to their works, but to no avail, for an Act of Parliament in 1845 empowered the Railway Company to construct the bridge and branch line into the British Alkali Works and these were completed in 1846.

Towards the end of the 1840s both salt companies found themselves in financial difficulties mainly due to fierce competition from the Cheshire and Droitwich salt

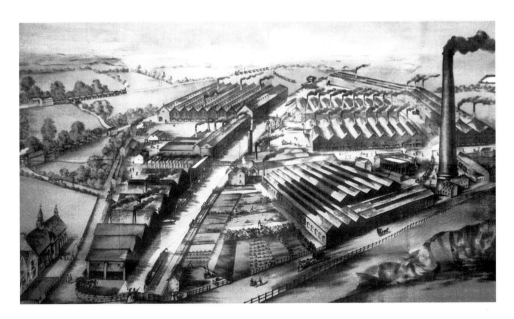

Stoke Prior Salt Works astride the canal c.1875.

producers, but partly, it is believed, because of the seepage of fresh water into the Stoke Works pits, causing a serious dilution in the strength of the brine. Also, perhaps due to the rural location of the works, the chemicals side of the business had proved unprofitable. One of the consequences of these problems was the departure of William Gossage in 1850 to Widnes with a number of key employees to found his own successful chemical and soap business there. Another was the failure in 1850 of the Bromsgrove Bank of Rufford, Biggs and Co., the British Alkali Company's bankers, together with the bankruptcy of Francis Rufford and his disappearance from public life (he had been M.P. for Worcester City and a Director of the Oxford, Worcester and Wolverhampton Railway). However, the British Alkali Company, heavily mortgaged, was able to continue in production on a reduced scale until January 1852 when John Corbett leased it from the Company. Due to similar problems the Imperial Company went into liquidation in 1850, owing its bankers over £90,000; it was put up for auction in London the following year, valued at £120,000, but there was no sufficient offer and it was eventually purchased at the knock-down price of £16,500 by John Scott. Under the ownership of Scott and later F C Hills the works continued to operate and trade as "The Imperial Salt Company" until 1858, when it was leased to John Corbett.

The connection of John Corbett with the Stoke Prior Salt Works had begun in 1845 when he became an agent of the British Alkali Company. Born in 1817, he was the eldest son of Joseph Corbett who had a canal carrying and boat building

267

business at the Delph, beside the Dudley Canal, near Brierley Hill. On leaving school he joined his father in the business and gained an extensive knowledge of the canal system. As an agent of the British Alkali Company, delivering and selling salt along the waterways, he must have followed with interest the firm's declining fortunes and, having undergone an apprenticeship at the Leys Iron Works, Stourbridge, he believed he knew how the Salt Works could be rescued and restored to prosperity. He had become a partner with his father in their carrying business; this was sold when Joseph retired, and John used his share of the proceeds to lease the British Alkali Company's works in 1852. He worked relentlessly, he made the brine pits watertight, he produced high quality salt and marketed it successfully, both locally and widely, mainly in London and the south-west, and also abroad. By 1867, he had become the owner and sole proprietor of Stoke Prior Salt Works, having in 1858 both bought the British Alkali Company and leased the Imperial Works, the latter being purchased nine years later.

In its heyday in the 1860s and 1870s, Stoke Prior Salt Works produced over 150,000 tons of fine salt and broad salt per annum, giving employment to over 500 people and at the same time making John Corbett a very rich man, enabling him to become a considerable landowner, a public figure, and philanthropist. He retained his interest in canal transport and built up his own fleet of some fifty canal boats for bringing in coal and delivering salt. Salt went by canal to his depots in London, Birmingham and Gloucester, and from Gloucester much was transhipped onto ocean-going vessels for export.

Corbett's takeover of the British Alkali Company included a boatyard run, since 1846, by Samuel Shellard on the west side of the canal beyond the railway bridge. When Shellard eventually retired in 1876, Corbett invited two brothers, George and Joseph Farrin from Flore in Northamptonshire, to take over the boatyard and he provided each of them and their families with one of his many workers' cottages in Stoke Works village. The Farrin brothers were to run the boat-building and repair business, assisted by Joseph's son Tom and other local craftsmen, for many years until the 1920s. From 1894 they managed it independently and kept a small fleet of boats which they hired out to canal carriers. After the closure of the boatyard around 1930, the site was tipped over and the ground level was raised.

During the 1880s the salt industry suffered generally from cut-throat competition between firms and price-cutting which greatly reduced profitability. The Salt Union came into being in 1888 following several years of negotiation to amalgamate the principal salt producers, and in March 1889 Corbett finally agreed to the sale of his works to the Salt Union for £600,000.

Under the Salt Union the Stoke Works continued to produce salt by the open-pan method of boiling brine in small pans to produce fine salt and by evaporating it at lower temperatures in large pans to produce broad (larger grained) salt. These

Stoke Prior Salt Works Vacuum Plant, in operation from 1950 to 1972. (B Poultney)

processes continued when Imperial Chemical Industries (I.C.I.) took over in 1937, and throughout the 1939-45 War. Following the War I.C.I. built a large Vacuum Plant on the west side of the canal for the more efficient production of salt by the evaporation under minimal pressure and at low temperature of purified brine heated by steam tubes in large vertical cylindrical vessels. The Vacuum Plant began to operate in 1950 and by 1956 open-pan production had ceased.

Because the extraction of brine at Stoke was blamed for continued subsidence in Droitwich, Stoke Prior Salt Works was eventually forced to close in 1972. The site is now mainly occupied by the Polymer-Latex Works and there is little remaining of the Salt Works to be seen apart from the railway bridge and a short length of the canal arm under the raised towpath.

In 1894 the Salt Union acquired about half of John Corbett's fleet of boats; by 1914 the number was reduced to eight boats, and by 1927 only two boats were in use, *Medway* manned by Jack and Denny Merrell and *Victory* by Jack Wright and Harry Bourne. Salt was carried by other canal carriers until around the 1930s. 1941 saw the last carriage of salt from the works by canal when a bomb was dropped on Henry Johnson's salt warehouse in Birmingham and the salt boat *Joan*, moored beside the warehouse, was destroyed. Fortunately the crew, Jack Merell and Tom Mayo, had slipped home for the night.

J & E STURGE LIMITED

John Sturge began the manufacture of chemicals in Bewdley in 1822 but, unable to find a suitable factory site there, he moved in 1823 to Wheeley's Lane in Birmingham where he was able to build his works with the advantage of its own canalside wharf. He was joined by his brother Edmund in 1830, hence the name of the firm. The following year they bought a large piece of land on the opposite side of Wheeley's Lane for further factory buildings, and later incurred the wrath of the Street Commissioners by constructing, without permission, a subway under the lane to connect the two factories. In 1833 another factory was built beside the canal at Selly Oak to make citric acid.

After John died in 1840, Edmund, from 1841 to 1855, had his brother-in-law, Arthur Albright, as partner. Under the care of Arthur Albright, phosphorus was produced at the Selly Oak factory from 1844 to 1854, after which it closed. In 1868 Edmund sold the business to C Dickinson Sturge and Francis Clayton. Following the retirement of C D Sturge in 1886, F Clayton sold out to brothers Henry and Alfred Wilson. However, the name of the firm remained J & E Sturge Ltd.

The Wheeley's Lane factories produced various chemicals including citric acid, bicarbonate of soda, cream of tartar and tartaric acid. In 1841 there began the large-

A water-colour impression of Sturge's Selly Oak Chemical Works in 1844. The site was later taken over by Elliott's Metal Works. (James Hyland)

scale manufacture of precipitated chalk (calcium carbonate), which had many uses in agriculture, food, metallurgy, pharmacy, dentifrice, fermentation, matches, paper and printing, paints, cosmetics, rubber and, later, plastics. In 1898 land was purchased and additional works erected at Lifford beside the Stratford Canal.

Besides using the canal for the transport of coal and chemicals, the original Wheeley's Lane Factory took water from it for the large condensing beam engine which was in use until 1920. It was not unusual for the valves of the engine to get choked by a shoal of sticklebacks which were probably attracted to the neighbourhood of the intake by the warm water from the return pipe.

The Wheeley's Lane factory closed in the 1960s, but the Lifford factory has survived to continue the large-scale production of precipitated calcium carbonate. Since the 1970s there have been several changes of ownership. In 1998 it became one of the many factories world-wide owned by Speciality Minerals of America.

BOROUGH FLOUR MILLS, BIRMINGHAM

In January 1831 the Committee of Works of the Canal Company considered a letter from William Lucy stating that he proposed to erect a steam mill in Birmingham on his property adjoining the canal close to Bridge No.3 and requesting the purchase of a small amount of the Company's land and permission to use water from the canal for the engine, the water to be returned to the canal. The requests were granted and the flour mill was built with a residence for the proprietor at the corner of Wheeley's Lane and New Bridge Street adjacent to Sturge's Chemical Works. The mill had a covered wharf and the canal was used for coal and grain deliveries. Around 1860 the business was taken over by relatives Charles Lucy & Nephew who were millers at Stratford-on-Avon and it became known as Borough Flour Mills. Closure took place about 1887.

WEBB'S CHEMICAL WORKS, DIGLIS

In December 1840 the Canal Company granted permission for James and Henry Webb to take over the warehouse at Diglis previously occupied by George Ryder Bird at a rent of £60 per annum. The Webbs were industrial chemists and they developed a business in chemical manures and fertilisers. In 1857 they leased from the Canal Company, for a new chemical works, the strip of land between the "New Basin" arm and the pound between the locks. The site included the engine house for pumping water from the river up to the basin, and Webbs undertook to maintain it. Leases of further land for extending the factory were obtained in 1863 and 1870. The second addition included the strip of land between the lane and the New Basin which was narrowed along most of its length to allow the construction of loading bays on the south side. By this time Henry Webb had died in 1861 and the business, known as Henry Webb & Company, was in the hands of his executors, Josiah and John Stallard.

The factory had the advantage of both river and canal basin frontage and made use of both river and canal carriers for their extensive import and export trade. Their products included chemical manures, phosphates, sulphuric acid and sulphate of ammonia, and they also sold the imported organic fertiliser Peruvian guano. Vast quantities of bones from home and overseas were treated with sulphuric acid to make bone manure. The factory closed around 1911. In 1916 the Canal Company sold the plant still there for £300. Subsequently the site was occupied by Evertons, boat builders. In recent years the arm has provided safe mooring for a number of pleasure boats.

The only remains of Webb's chemical manure factory now visible are the buildings still surrounding the canal arm, and the boundary wall at the river end. There used to be a large rambling house called "Severn Weir House" at the end of the

WORCESTER COMMERCIAL PROSPECTUSES.

ESTABLISHED TWENTY-EIGHT YEARS.

HENRY WEBB & COMPANY,

AGRICULTURAL CHEMISTS,

MANUFACTURERS OF

BONE SUPERPHOSPHATE OF LIME

ALSO,

SPECIAL CHEMICAL MANURES

FOR ALL CEREAL AND ROOT CROPS.

CHEMICAL MANURE, AMMONIA, BONE,

AND OIL OF VITRIOL WORKS,

WORCESTER.

SOLE CONSIGNEES FOR MESSRS. A. M. SMITH & CO'S. (LIVERPOOL), PALM-NUT MEAL.

LINSEED, COTTONSEED, AND RAPE CAKES.

WHOLESALE MANURE DEALERS SUPPLIED ON THE MOST ADVANTAGEOUS TERMS.

Works : Diglis, Worcester.
Warehouses : Diglis Basin, and Angel Place, Angel Street.
ATTENDANCE AT CORN EXCHANGE EVERY SATURDAY.
Pamphlets, Prices, Terms, and all information, may be had on application.

Webb's Chemical Manure Works shown in an advertisement in Littlebury's Guide to Worcester, 1869.

arm, with a large walled garden. Its last residents were the Smith family. Don Smith who grew up there eventually became keeper of the Bevere river lock north of Worcester. The house had been the home and office of the resident manager of the chemical works.

TOWNSHEND'S MILL, WORCESTER

About 1840 Thomas Lucy of Pershore Mill was residing in Worcester at the King's Head Hotel, Sidbury, to supervise the construction of a new steam-operated flour mill. The mill's location beside the canal between Diglis Basin and the first road bridge was strategic, for it could be served by Severn trows and barges bringing grain along the river and through the two barge locks, and also by narrowboats bringing coal via the W/B Canal from Birmingham and the Black Country and returning with flour for shops and bakeries in those populous areas.

The mill was in operation by 1843, and a few years later Thomas Lucy took into partnership Thomas Downing of Henwick watermill. This partnership lasted ten years; then Thomas Lucy made his son Edward a partner, and the firm was known as Thomas Lucy & Son until 1868. Thomas died in 1864, leaving the mill to his son who seems to have been less capable than his father and was probably glad when Thomas Suffield Townshend entered into partnership and took over the running of the mill in 1869. Edward Lucy died in 1874 aged only 36, leaving his estate to his wife and family. The business was known as Lucy & Townshend until 1881 when T S Townshend bought out the Lucy family.

Both Thomas Lucy and Thomas Townshend took an active part in civic affairs in Worcester, both becoming Mayor, Lucy in 1861 and Townshend in 1880. Unfortunately T S Townshend died in 1890 on an errand of mercy. On 19 December one of his carters was fatally injured when a fully-loaded waggon, taking sacks of flour from Tipton to Dudley, overturned in the snow and crushed him. Townshend went by train to Dudley Hospital to see the badly injured man and died there of a heart attack. It was fortunate for the mill that already Townshend's three sons, Frank, Percy and Conway, were involved in its running and, following his death, took over. From 1891 onwards the mill was known as T S Townshend & Sons.

In 1903 the Worcester Daily Times Trade and Industrial Edition described many of the mill's then recent innovations including measures to keep the machinery and environment dust-free, a novel but precarious passenger elevator between the cellar and the top floor of the mill, electric lighting and an electric oven for baking test loaves run from their own generator, and automatic chutes which loaded flour from any floor into boats or vans and which weighed and counted the sacks. The very latest addition was a silo storage building designed by Percy Townshend and just completed beside the canal, over 100 feet high, with six floors, and from which a mechanical elevator swung out over the canal to convey grain from river barges up into the storage rooms, whence it travelled by conveyor belt across to the mill to be washed, dried, milled and sacked. All the machinery of the mill was driven by belting from a a large steam engine with an 18 feet diameter flywheel.

From an early date Townshends relied largely on their own water and road transport. Until about 1930 their large river barge *Ceres* was towed up and down the Severn. It was converted for use as a family houseboat on the River Avon when replaced by two motor-driven barges, *Sunrisen* which carried 100 tons and *River King* which carried 90 tons. The latter in recent times has been based at Stourport and used for trips on the River. On the canal in the 1920s and 1930s Townshends had five horse-drawn narrowboats taking flour to their Tipton and Great Barr depots and elsewhere and bringing back slack for the boilers. The last of these in service,

T S Townshend and Sons' Flour Mill and Silo. (The Worcester Daily Times Trade and Industrial Edition, 1903)

Violet, was worked by Sidney and Jess Tombs with their two sons, followed by Tom and Eric Rice, until 1940. Stables in the basement of the mill off Mill Street held several horses used for drawing boats and waggons.

During World War 2 and until 1946 Daphne March used her family's motor boat *Heather Bell* to carry grain, flour and coal for Townshends (see Chapter 15). After the war Tom Rice and Jumbo Harris worked a boat together, and one of Charles Ballinger's boats crewed by Albert Tonks and his wife and children made three trips for Townshends every fortnight to the Black Country.

During the final decades of its operation, following the deaths of Percy, Conway and, finally, Frank Townshend, the mill was managed by further members of the family, Peter, Harry and John Townshend. At length in 1960 the business went into liquidation and closed due to competition from large combines such as Spillers and Rank, and the buildings were acquired by the nearby Worcester Porcelain Works. Soon after closure a disastrous fire in December 1960 gutted the top floors of the mill and it was reduced from eight to four storeys in height as it is now. The tall silo building with its rusting machinery was infested by pigeons until its demolition in 1982.

THE QUEEN'S HOSPITAL, BIRMINGHAM

The Queen's Hospital, with its entrance on Bath Row and with grounds at the rear bordering the canal, was planned in 1839 as Birmingham's second hospital, the General Hospital being already well established. It was intended as a clinical and teaching hospital in connection with the Royal School of Medicine and Surgery, soon to be known as the Queen's College. The foundation stone was laid on 18 June 1840, and Queen Victoria, who became one of its patrons, agreed to it being called "The Queen's Hospital". It opened on 18 June 1841 with two principal wings called "Victoria" and "Adelaide". The hospital was financed mainly by public subscription and fundraising events, one of which was a concert in Birmingham Town Hall by "The Swedish Nightingale" Jenny Lind in 1848. It had extensive grounds at first, but these were progressively built on as an outpatients' department was added, and a new mortuary and laundry built beside the canal in 1873, then additional wards and operating theatres in 1908 and 1927. The Queen's Hospital closed in 1940, but the buildings were reopened in 1941 as an accident and rehabilitation centre for wartime casualties. After serving as Birmingham Accident Hospital for over 50 years, it finally closed in August 1993.

For many years the hospital made use of the canal for supplies of coal, having been given permission by the Canal Company to construct its own wharf in 1845. In 1860, in common with other canalside premises, the hospital was no longer allowed drainage into the canal. For many years, commencing in 1847, the Canal Company subscribed 3 guineas a year to the hospital, where, no doubt from time to time, casualties amongst its employees and boat people received treatment.

Chapter 18

LATER CANALSIDE INDUSTRIES

BRICKWORKS

When the W/B Canal was created, the large quantities of bricks needed for its structures, including bridges, locks, tunnels, wharves and warehouses, were mostly made from the clay soil through which the waterway was cut from Selly Oak to Diglis. Small brickyards were located every few miles along the route. Manufacture was simple and labour-intensive. Clay was dug out of small pits, the remains of some still being visible in fields near the canal at places like Alvechurch and Tardebigge. The bricks were moulded by hand and burnt in simple kilns. Skill and experience were required on the part of the brickmakers to produce the good quality bricks required, and some of those engaged, whose bricks were inferior, had to be dismissed and replaced. With little shelter, brickmaking was a seasonal occupation which was suspended in the winter months, severe winters then being the norm.

Brickmaking as an all-the-year-round industry began to flourish in the middle of the nineteenth century following the invention and production of brick-making machinery and kilns designed for the mass-production of bricks. The machinery included pan mills in which two massive rollers crushed and pulverised solid marl, pug mills in which, in a vertical tub, rotating blades on a vertical spindle chopped and kneaded clay which was fed in at the top and extruded from the bottom, and devices to facilitate the forming of the clay into bricks. In the latter part of the nineteenth century massive brickmaking machinery, capable of carrying out a series of processes from the input of dry marl or soft clay to the output of bricks ready for drying and firing, was developed by Bradley & Craven of Wakefield. This and patent continuous kilns designed by Hoffman & Licht of Berlin and Danzig were used in many of the larger brickworks. These kilns were in the form of an annular archway, separated into a number of chambers, the temperature of each being controlled by dampers. In the centre of the circular building containing the annular kiln a tall chimney helped to create the draught needed in the kiln chambers. Bricks loaded into a chamber were dried at low heat, then fired at high temperature, then cooled before being taken out. The process was continuous as some chambers were loaded and others emptied day by day.

Because waterway transport afforded easy carriage for heavy goods like coal and bricks, and because abundant clay soil existed beside the W/B Canal, it is not surprising that a number of brickworks were located along its length. Of some, such as one at Breedon Cross shown on maps of the mid-nineteenth century, there is little record. Of others we have more details.

ODDINGLEY BRICKWORKS was situated beside the canal below where the lane down from Oddingley to the railway crossing runs parallel to the canal. It was a small works, set up around 1850 by William Aston who, besides being a brickmaker, was also a shopkeeper and beer retailer. He produced both bricks and tiles, and in the 1860s was also a lime burner, coal merchant and farmer, and lived at Netherwood Farm. In the 1870s the brickworks was taken over by Alfred Godard of the Lodge, Tibberton, and it continued in production until the 1890s, the chimney being demolished around 1900. The brickworks had its brick-walled wharf, the remains of which are still visible, and a boat *Alpha* which, owned by R.& A.Godard, registered in 1879 and worked by George Grundy of Tibberton, carried coal, timber,

limestone and night soil. The deep claypit below the lane was filled in with surplus soil from the building of the M5 Motorway in 1961. In the 1920s hay from local farms was loaded into boats on the wharf for use in Birmingham.

JOHN CORBETT'S BRICKWORKS were established in keeping with his policy of self-sufficiency. They were situated on the east side of the canal opposite the "Boat and Railway" Inn, where now is a social club and car park, and used between about 1860 and 1880 to make bricks for his salt works buildings and for his workers' cottages and school. When no longer needed the buildings were demolished and the claypit used for the disposal of night soil from the village privies and other waste before being eventually levelled.

BARKER'S PATENT BRICKWORKS were erected at Gregory's Bank, Worcester, on the east side of the canal just north of St. George's Lane bridge in 1869. The

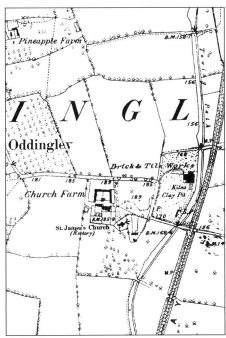

Oddingley Brick and Tile Works beside the canal shown on an O.S. map of 1886.

proprietor, D W Barker, came from Frome, Somerset. The Bradley and Craven brickworks machinery required forty railway waggons for its transport from Wakefield to Worcester. The Hoffman & Licht type kiln had twelve chambers and the tall central chimney was 160 feet high and had a base diameter of over 21 feet. Rocky marl was transported from the hillside behind the works by a tramway into the machine house to be pulverised, mixed, moulded and pressed automatically into bricks at a rate of about 1,500 an hour. Barker's bricks were used in the construction of many public buildings and factories in and around Worcester, including the imposing Powick Lunatic Asylum.

The brickworks made use of the canal for its supplies of coal and the delivery of bricks. It had its own wharf and stables and two boats, including, in the 1890s, *John* and *Maud* crewed by John Spragg, and, in the 1920s and 1930s, *Betty* crewed by Albert Hayes.

The production of bricks continued until the late 1950s, the manager in the 1920s and 1930s being Alan Wood. After the works closed to make way for industrial development, the great chimney was felled in 1961.

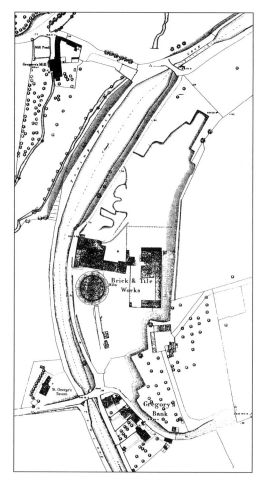

1886 O.S. map showing Barker's Brick & Tile Works, St George's Tavern, Gregory's Mill and nearby lock No.5 (WRO)

WYNN'S ALVECHURCH BRICKWORKS were constructed on the west side of the canal at Alvechurch between Scarfield Wharf and Wythybed Green in 1876. In July of that year, the Canal Committee received a letter from W H Wynn informing it of the work in hand and that he hoped to be making from 100 to 150 thousand bricks per week, initially with a 5 HP portable engine, but later with a 20 to 25 HP engine. He requested to know first "what rental you will charge for the water used. I shall most likely make dry pressed bricks, so shall only want water for the engine. Secondly, shall you be willing to put me down a wharf alongside the kiln, say two boats length. Thirdly, as Mr Reachill tells me he is leaving Alvechurch

Wharf, have you any objection in letting it to me." In reply Wynn was given permission to take water from the canal for his engines at a rate of five shillings per HP; a 140 feet long wharf wall would be built, Mr Wynn to supply the materials; and he could rent the Scarfields Wharf for £20 per annum.

The brickworks had a Bradley & Craven press with an output of 1,200 bricks per hour. From it the bricks were taken by wheelbarrow, forty at a time every two minutes, to the sixteen chamber continuous kiln, where "setters" filled the chambers in turn, for the bricks to be dried, then burnt, then when cool removed by the "drawers" to be stacked or loaded for delivery. Wynns had two canal boats registered in 1880, bringing coal from Hednesford and delivering bricks along the W/B and the Droitwich Canals, on the latter of which their boat *Rover* was inspected in 1906 and 1909.

In 1924 the brickworks was sold to Charles Boden, and he began to produce, besides bricks, tiles and other roof fittings with the help of experienced tilemakers brought in and housed in some of the company-owned Scarfield Cottages, Greenfield Cottages, and a row at Wythybed Green. From 1925 to 1929 two Foden steam lorries were used to deliver bricks before local haulage contractors took over. In 1939 the waterlogged claypit was exhausted and the works closed, just before the outbreak of World War 2. Since then the claypit has been filled in and levelled and the site put to industrial use.

HANBURY BRICKWORKS was situated in the area lying between the W/B Canal, the Hanbury Road and the railway, where now is a public refuse disposal depot. Its beginnings are uncertain. It could have been the site of one of the brickyards set up when the canal was cut, and also the source of bricks which came by canal from Hanbury for some early buildings of Stoke Prior Salt Works. In the 1890s bricks were being manufactured there by G H Grove. In the early 1900s the proprietor was Joseph Parkes, who in 1911 registered his canal boat *Harry*, and the manager was Fred Hingley who lived at the nearby Wharf House. By the end of the 1914-18 War the brickworks were almost derelict and in 1919 they were bought by T A Everton, who already with other relatives had extensive business interests in Droitwich. He soon invested in the latest machinery for hauling the clay in trucks from the pit and for making the bricks. In 1925 three oblong kilns, each with a 30ft chimney, were replaced by a large circular continuous kiln with eight chambers and a central 120ft chimney. In the 1930s a further continuous kiln with nine chambers and a 100ft high square chimney was built. When production was at its peak the works produced 30,000 bricks a day six days a week and employed twenty-five men. T A Everton built the two houses opposite The Eagle and Sun and the row of eight houses nearer the railway for his workers. During the 1939-45 War German and Italian prisoners were brought in. After the War T A Everton sold the works to Baldwins of Nottingham who used it to make electric cable covers. The last owner was K E Millward of Oldbury who made bricks. The brickworks closed in 1969 after a fire destroyed part of a kiln house.

In the early days coal came, and some bricks were transported, by canal. Bricks were loaded onto boats moored beside the towpath by barrows across planks, uphill to begin with, but as the boats filled they sank lower in the water and loading became easier. Occasionally a barrowload of bricks fell into the canal.

KINGS NORTON BRICKWORKS, situated on the east side of the canal south of Parsons Hill, were established around 1890, probably on the site of the brick kiln (No.4) set up near Kings Norton Wharf when the canal was cut. The entrance to the works was at the end of Cyril Road (now Ardath Road) in which many of the workers lived. There were three rectangular kilns, each with its chimney, on the bank above a 10ft wide canal wharf. Between the kilns and the large and deep claypit was the brick-making works with its engine and tall chimney and large drying shed. At first clay was dug out of the pit by hand and loaded into trucks which were hauled up to the works on rails manually, two men each side using grips to pull four trucks at a time. From 1934 JCBs were used. Springs of water flooded the claypit, which needed pumping, and children and cattle were at times drowned in it. In the early years John Hough was the proprietor, later his son Cyril, then Cyril Atkins, and finally Baylis until the works closed in 1969, the tall chimney being felled in August that year. 45 to 50 people were employed at the works, and up to the 1920s barrow-running (moving bricks to the kilns) was done by women. Slack for the brickworks was brought by canal until 1930, mainly by Fellows, Morton and Clayton and by Lloyds horse-drawn boats. The works did have a boat of their own, used for carrying bricks, until about 1923.

FRISBY'S TARDEBIGGE BRICKWORKS AND POTTERY, situated on the west side of the canal between London Lane Bridge and the accommodation bridge below the Top Lock, had a short life of only sixteen years. In 1896 the Earl of Plymouth, who had often visited Italy and had been impressed with Italian decorated terra-cotta pots, vases and garden ornaments, asked Samuel Frisby, a brickmaker of Perryfields, Bromsgrove, if he could reproduce some of these designs for the house and garden of his newly-built Hewell Grange. Samuel agreed and, as his Perryfields claypit was exhausted, he set up a new small brickworks and pottery on the Earl's land beside the canal. Access to the works was from London Lane, and at the far end facing the canal Samuel built a four-bedroomed house for himself, his wife Anne, and his son John and daughter Lena, both in their early twenties at the time. Besides the clay-processing and brick-making plant, the works included a potter's wheel; drying shed; two round kilns, each about 20ft in diameter with a chimney; and two steam engines, one for winching small waggons by wire hawser up from the claypit at the London Lane end of the site, the other for working the brick-making machinery. Water for the boilers and for brick-making was taken by

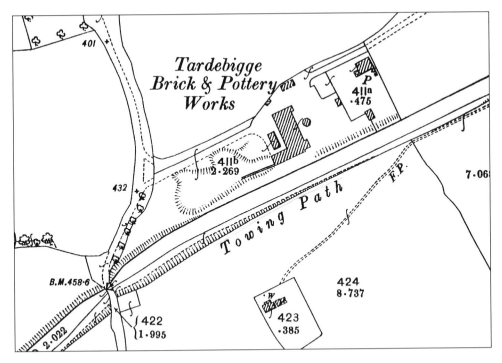

Map showing Frisby's Brick and Pottery Works beside the canal at Tardebigge.

agreement from the canal. A canal wharf was constructed, with its brick wall surmounted by sandstone blocks. The brickworks possessed, in succession, two horse-drawn boats with cabins, used occasionally for delivering bricks, but mainly for fetching coal from the Black Country. There was stabling for two horses.

When Samuel Frisby died in 1904, his wife Anne, who was a strong and assertive character, took over. Their son John, by this time married and living in Bromsgrove, continued to work for his mother, being treated and paid like other employees. Their daughter Lena worked in the office. Frisbys specialised in unglazed terra-cotta garden pots, vases and ornaments in all shapes and sizes, many attractively decorated. Their bricks were used by local house-builders, and they produced specialized bricks for the erection of Tardebigge Village Hall (now "The Tardebigge" public house) in 1911. By 1912 there was a building slump; Frisbys were owed a considerable amount by local builders and the claypit was exhausted, so the works had to close down. Anne and Lena moved from the Brickworks Cottage in 1930, since when it has had several occupants. The cottage remains, now a pleasant residence known as The Bridges House. The claypit, filled in mostly by canal dredgings, and the brickyard, cleared in due course of its derelict remains, were eventually tipped over to create a pleasant canalside garden.

CADBURY BROTHERS

In 1824 John Cadbury, aged 23, established a tea and coffee warehouse and shop at 93 Bull Street, Birmingham. He was soon producing "Cocoa Nibs", advertised as "an article affording a most nutricious beverage for breakfast". In 1831 he rented an old malthouse in Crooked Lane as a factory to manufacture his cocoa drink and by 1842 he was also making solid chocolate. When this factory building had to be demolished due to the making of the railway tunnel into Snow Hill Station in 1847, he moved to larger premises in Bridge Street beside the bridge over the arm of the B.C.N. leading into the Old Wharf. At that time he was joined by his brother Benjamin in a minor role and the name of the business was now Cadbury Brothers. It concentrated on manufacture and the Bull Street shop was handed over to John's nephew, Richard Barrow, and was long known as Barrow's Stores.

The Bridge Street factory was conveniently placed for supplies of coal from the Old Wharf and ingredients such as cocoa beans and sugar carried by river and canal from Sharpness or Gloucester Docks to the nearby Worcester Wharf of Gas Street Basin. The trade in cocoa and chocolate prospered in the 1850s and in 1854 Cadburys received the Royal Warrant, being noted for their good working conditions. By 1861, however, the business had declined, partly due to John's ill-health, and that year he retired and handed over responsibility to his two sons, Richard aged 25 and George aged 21. As a result of their efforts and enterprise the tide soon turned, mainly due to the vigorous marketing of an improved better-tasting cocoa drink. By the 1870s the number of employees had risen from a low of 20 in 1861 to 200, and a substantial export trade had been built up. At Bridge Street, Cadburys were the first firm to introduce a half-holiday on Saturdays and leisure activities for their workers. Daily morning Bible readings and prayers, voluntarily attended, were introduced in 1866 and continued until 1912.

By 1878, because the Bridge Street factory had become inadequate for their expanding business, Richard and George Cadbury decided to buy a fourteen-acre site for a new factory in open country about four miles from the centre of Birmingham. It was alongside the newly-constructed Birmingham West Suburban Railway and had road access to the W/B Canal on the other side of the railway. The factory was built during the early months of 1879 and was in production by the autumn of that year. Some of the equipment from Bridge Street was carried there by canal. The name Bournville was chosen for the location of the factory because the Bourn Brook (known as Gallows Brook when the canal was cut) ran through the factory site and it was French sounding because French chocolate was highly rated at the time. Twelve houses were initially built nearby for key workers. Other employees commuted from Birmingham by train to Stirchley Street Station (soon renamed Bournville Station) until rented accommodation was available in the 1890s in Cadbury's model village being built at Bournville.

The Bournville factory made much use of the railway for coal deliveries and the distribution of its products. Branch sidings were soon laid outside and into the works, and the firm obtained its own waggons and vans and one or two small steam locomotives to move them around. As the factory was being built in 1879, Sparrey's Wharf was leased from the Canal Company for 21 years. This wharf, which had been used by William Sparrey, a coal merchant, for many years, was a narrow strip of land on the east side of the canal just north of the aqueduct above Bournville Lane. It was reached from the lane by a steep slope up to the canal. Carriage between the wharf and the factory was by horse-drawn vans. Despite the awkwardness of the access, Cadburys used canal delivery for coal and many of their raw materials, and the lease of the wharf was renewed in 1900 for a further 21 years.

At Bournville, as the factory was extended and output grew, the workforce increased in number to some 2,700 by 1900, and by 1920 it exceeded 7,000. In the 1880s Richard Cadbury's sons Barrow and William joined the firm, as did George Cadbury's sons Edward and George in the 1890s. When Richard died in 1899 the family business was converted into a company, Cadbury Brothers Limited. The prosperity of the Company was greatly boosted by two new products. In 1906 "Bournville Cocoa", a slightly spiced blend, was introduced and became the popular standard brand. Earlier in 1897 Dairy Milk Chocolate began to be made, at first on a small scale, then by 1905 in large quantities as it caught on and widespread advertising helped it to become an enduring best-seller.

The advent of Cadbury's Dairy Milk Chocolate generated considerable waterway traffic in the early half of the twentieth century. At first large quantities of milk from dairy farms near canals came by boat in churns to Bournville. But because of the problem of milk turning sour in transit, especially during the summer months, and also the fact that about 7/8 of the content of milk is water, it was decided to set up condensing plants at strategic points, to which milk was delivered locally, some by day boats. Two of these plants, one at Knighton on the Shropshire Union Canal near Market Drayton which opened in 1911, the other, established in 1915 at Frampton on the Gloucester and Sharpness Canal, became subsidiary factories which produced "chocolate crumb" for many years. In the process, ground cocoa mass from Bournville went by boat to these factories where it was mixed with sugar and condensed milk, then dried in large ovens to produce the crumb which was then transported in 1 cwt bags on narrowboats to Bournville for the final stage of converting it into milk chocolate. A small amount of this sweet chocolate crumb tended to get "lost" en route to its destination as children at places along the canals enjoyed eating pieces given to them by passing boat crews.

Sparrey's Wharf had limited wharfage and facilities, so in 1908 Cadburys, with their waterway traffic increasing, secured a wharf and canalside premises just south of Mary Vale Road bridge over the canal. This additional wharf and the adjacent

Cadbury's canal boats at Mary Vale Road Factory wharf, 1911. (Stanley Holland Collection)

factory building were retained until 1929. In 1922/3 Cadburys, needing yet further transport facilities, bought a 27-acre strip of land with about half-a-mile of canal frontage between Sparrey's Wharf and Raddlebarn Lane and built on it a large warehouse with a partly canopied six-boats-length wharf which they called "Waterside". The southern end of the Waterside site was land previously built up to the level of the embankment by the tipping of waste on what was known as Stirchley Tip. In 1923 Cadburys obtained permission to build a skew railway bridge over the main railway line and the canal at the northern end of the factory site to connect the factory sidings with Waterside. The track was laid through the Waterside warehouse and alongside the wharf which was equipped with a number of moving hoists to facilitate the transfer of freight between canal boats, railway vans and the warehouse. The Waterside facilities continued in use until the last sporadic use of canal transport by Cadburys in the 1960s. The whole site was sold to developers in 1981, following which Waterside was demolished and the site cleared to make way for housing.

In 1916-17, in the midst of the First World War, a munitions factory was set up by the Government at Blackpole, Worcester, with a canalside wharf. After the War, in 1920, Cadburys decided to purchase the Blackpole factory from the Government for the purpose of making wooden boxes and packing cases in sections. These were made from timber brought in by river and canal and were taken by canal to Bournville. The W/B Canal Committee minutes of December 1920 record: "Messrs. Cadbury desired that the Canal should be enlarged so that 80 to 100 ton barges could be utilised to carry traffic from their Works at Bristol to Blackpole without transhipment." This proposal of George Cadbury, which would have meant widening the canal from Diglis, rebuilding bridges and replacing the intervening six narrow locks with barge locks, was too disruptive and expensive to be viable. From 1939-46 the factory was again taken over for the making of munitions. Then from 1946 Cadburys used it for making tins for cocoa and Bournvita, for preparing nuts and raisins for Fruit and Nut Chocolate and, in the 1960s until closure in 1971, for producing Cadbury cakes. The disused Blackpole wharf remains, now surrounded by factory development.

In the early years at Bridge Street Cadburys had had no wharf or boats of their own. But soon after the move to Bournville they did have a horse-drawn boat *Bournville*, registered in 1883, which was used to fetch coal from Hednesford and timber from Gloucester. Around 1910 the collection of milk locally around Knighton involved several day boats purchased from Fellows, Morton & Clayton. For the traffic in condensed milk between Knighton and Bournville two specially designed steel narrow boats, with steel decks and hatches to their holds and

Cadbury's Waterside canal and railway wharf in 1929, showing horse-drawn boats, a horse on the towpath, a steam locomotive and railway waggons. (BRL Cadbury Collection)

Timber being unloaded from canal boats c.1930 at Cadbury's Blackpole factory which, at that time, was producing wooden boxes and packing cases to be transported by canal to the Bournville factory. (Cadbury Trebor Bassett)

powered by 15 HP Bolinder engines, came into use in 1911. These boats, named *Bournville I* and *Bournville II*, had design faults and were soon replaced by a series of wooden motor boats and butties, named *Bournville 1* to *Bournville 17*, the last being registered in 1926. The butties were towed between Frampton and Diglis but hauled by horses along the W/B Canal to Bournville. In 1928 Cadburys disposed of their remaining fleet of four motor boats and five butties, but they still continued to use the waterways, relying mainly on the Severn and Canal Carrying Company for transport between Frampton, Blackpole and Bournville, and on Fellows, Morton & Clayton for transport between Bournville and Knighton and also for the collection of sugar and the delivery of Cadbury's products to various places via the W/B Canal northwards. Following World War 2 and the nationalisation of the canals, declining water transport continued using available carriers, including Ballinger's boats southwards from Bournville. The last crumb deliveries were in 1961 by Charles Ballinger from Frampton and by Charlie Atkins (known as "Chocolate Charlie") from Knighton.

The survival of the W/B Canal in the 1920s and 1930s, when it was losing money and faced possible abandonment, as happened to the Droitwich canals in 1939, owed much to its use by Cadburys, and especially to George Cadbury junior, who was Managing Director of the Company when canal transport was chosen to play a large part in the production of Dairy Milk Chocolate, and who became Chairman of the Directors from 1936 to 1943. He was a canal enthusiast, and in 1926 established a guarantee fund, supported by other businesses, to raise up to £2,000 a year for five years to subsidise the W/B Canal, on condition that it was kept open. He was co-author of a book advocating a revival of inland waterways transport, and he went on to serve as a Director of the SND Canal Company and as Chairman of the Severn & Canal Carrying Company. He died in 1954.

Besides their abandonment of canal transport in the 1960s, Cadburys also dispensed with their railway system, track and rolling stock, in 1976. Following the merger of Cadburys with Schweppes in 1969, Cadbury-Schweppes has remained one of the only two surviving W/B canalside industries, the other being Royal Worcester Spode.

DAVENPORT'S BREWERY, BATH ROW, BIRMINGHAM

The family brewery firm was started by Robert Davenport who in 1829 had premises in Hockley. The business expanded and in 1852 acquired the mansion "Bath House" in Bath Row, Birmingham, the extensive gardens of which stretched to the bank of the W/B Canal. By 1867 the business was concentrated there and registered as "John Davenport and Sons", John being the son of the founder, Robert. The gardens were completely built over as the brewery expanded. In 1904 Baron John Davenport started the "Beer-at-Home" service for which Davenports became widely known through its advertising and countrywide depots. Unfortunately the firm was taken over in 1986 by the Greenall Whitley Group, and the Bath Row Brewery which had employed over 200 people there was closed down around 1990.

In 1872 Davenports reached agreement with the Canal Committee for the purchase of a strip of land along the canal bank giving access to their malthouse from Granville Street Bridge. They had a wharf and probably received supplies of coal and made some deliveries by canal in the early years of the business before the advent of twentieth century motor transport. In December 1905 a dispute, which reached the County Court, between Davenports and the Canal Company over the pollution of the canal by an inflow of yeast from the brewery was settled amicably. The brewery paid the cost of disinfectants used in abating the nuisance.

KINGS NORTON PAPER MILL

In 1855 a piece of land known as New Meadow on the north side of the junction of the W/B and the Northern Stratford Canal at Kings Norton was for sale. The purchaser was James Baldwin. Since the early 1830s he had been in business in Newhall Street, Birmingham, as an engraver, printer and wholesale paper dealer. He had also been engaged in the manufacture of paper and gun wadding at his own paper mill situated at the corner of Sherborne Street and Morville Street with a canal arm from the Oozells Street loop of the B.C.N. In 1853, needing larger premises to expand his business, he made application to the W/B Canal Company for a piece of waste land adjoining the embankment of the canal at Kings Norton, but bought the New Meadow site instead when it came on the market and in 1856/7 built on it his new paper mill. The mill was known as Sherborne Mill for many years, also as Baldwins' Paper Mill, the Company name being James Baldwin and Sons.

Because the process of paper manufacture requires plentiful supplies of water, Baldwins' Paper Mill was ideally situated beside the W/B Canal and also the River Rea. As much as 30,000 gallons of water per hour was used for the steam engines and processing. Some was taken from, and discharged back into, the River Rea; some, by an 1860 agreement with the W/B Canal Company, from the canal, on condition that it was returned unpolluted to the satisfaction of the canal engineer. In 1870 the Canal Company had cause to complain to Mr Baldwin over the pollution of the canal and he promised to end the nuisance. By 1880 the used water was being filtered and deodorised before being returned to the river or canal. In 1904 a new

The boat Cossack and other coal boats tied up alongside Kings Norton Paper Mill with fuel for the engine house. (Colin Scrivener)

engine house was built and liquid effluent began to be discharged into local sewers under a Health Act banning discharge into the River Rea.

James Baldwin and Sons specialised in making various grades of brown wrapping paper, also paper bags of many types and sizes, including the blue sugar bags formerly used by Tate and Lyle. They also manufactured great quantities of gun wadding, much of which was exported. The raw materials from which these products were made included vast amounts of waste paper, rags, woollen fabrics, old rope and cord, carpet manufacturers' waste, sacking and wood fibre. Recycling has long been practised in the manufacture of paper.

In the Mill the raw materials were sorted by hand and suitably processed by machinery, cleansed, fragmented and pulverised to produce a semi-liquid pulp which was stored in chests to supply each of Baldwins' three paper-making machines. In these machines the pulp was fed over a moving sieve, and the deposited fibres forming a wet film were then spread evenly upon an endless moving woollen blanket which passed between huge rollers to squeeze out more liquid and produce a damp paper. This was dried by passing up and down round a succession of steam-heated rotating cylinders, and it was finally given a smooth finish by being fed through "calendering rolls". The paper thus produced in widths of 72, 66 and 50 inches on the three machines was wound onto wooden rollers each taking about 400 yards of paper. Each machine produced about 300 miles of paper a week. Elsewhere in the factory the paper was dyed if necessary, cut and packed in reams, and some used in bag-making machinery.

Baldwins made use of the canal for the transport of coal. In the late nineteenth century and early twentieth century they had their own fleet of six horse-drawn wooden cabin boats. These tied up beside the wharf wall where coal was unloaded and delivered through six portals. There could be up to four boats moored there at a time; two boatloads would arrive each day except Sunday. The boatmen used to lash two boats together and one man steered, so that two men and a horse could manage both. Some of the paper produced was transported by canal, much of this by Fellows, Morton and Clayton.

For many years James Baldwin and his family lived at Lifford Hall close to the mill. When he died in 1894 his three sons and one daughter took over the business, the eldest son Major James Baldwin being Managing Director. Eventually in 1926 the business was sold to a consortium and its name changed to Kings Norton Paper Mill Ltd. It continued to prosper until after World War 2, when plastics material began to replace paper for packaging. Production declined and the factory closed on 13 August 1965. The steam engines had been removed from the engine house in 1963. The tall chimney was demolished, brick by brick, in 1968. The engine house and some buildings, including the wharf wall, remain, the site having been used as a motor museum for some years.

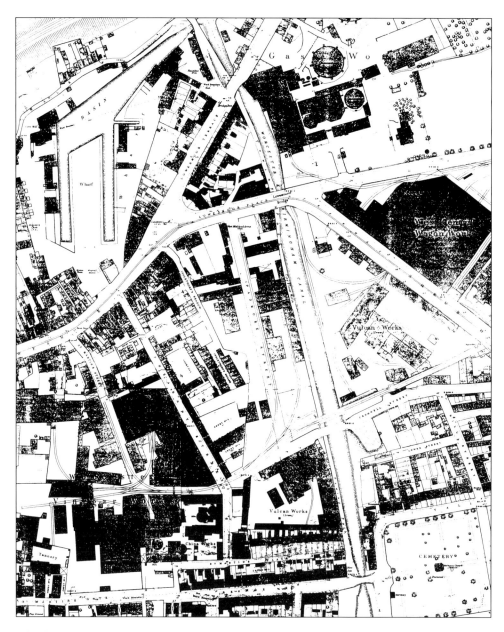

1886 O.S. map of the Lowesmoor area of Worcester, showing Lowesmoor Wharf with the Elephant and Castle PH, mission room, and weighing machine; the Gas Works; City Flour Mills; Vulcan Iron Works on both sides of the canal; Grainger's China Works; the Vinegar Works railway bridge over the canal; and the New Inn by George Street Bridge. (WRO)

CITY FLOUR MILLS, LOWESMOOR, WORCESTER

Established around 1860 and situated beside the canal below Lowesmoor Place bridge, the City Flour Mills changed hands several times. In 1867 it was Mainwarings, in 1869 Goodwin & Sons, then Weaver & Sons until 1898 when it became D.Redler & Co. Finally, from 1912 until its demolition in 1972, it was owned by John Barnett Ltd. who had a coal and corn business based at Lowesmoor Wharf. Over the years the mill underwent various changes, including installation of a 250 HP steam engine, early electrification, use of a special hoist to lift imported grain from canal boats up the top floor of the mill, and the latest machinery to produce high quality flour, bran and animal feeds. Water transport was used to convey consignments of flour to Birmingham, Wolverhampton and other destinations.

THE VULCAN IRON WORKS (MCKENZIE & HOLLAND), WORCESTER

After the opening of the Oxford, Worcester and Wolverhampton Railway and its station in Worcester in 1850, followed by the construction of engine and carriage sheds and goods yards at Shrub Hill, related industries were soon established nearby. One such was the Vulcan Iron Works, first located on the towpath (west) side of the canal between Cromwell Street and George Street. A second factory, with railway access into and around the works, was later set up between Shrub Hill and the east side of the canal on what had been Inglethorpe's Meadow. Situated as they were beside the canal, both factories evidently made some use of canal transport for supplies of coal and metal.

The business, started in 1857 and purchased in 1859 by Thomas Clunes, an engineer from Aberdeen, is listed in Kelly's Directory of 1860 as Thomas Clunes & Co., engineers, millwrights, iron and brass founders. In 1861 John McKenzie and Walter Holland became copartners and the firm, now McKenzie, Clunes and Holland, began to specialise in the manufacture of railway signalling equipment, interlocking and other safety devices, also the provision of signal boxes, water cranes, bridges and signal gantries. In 1870 they were commissioned to equip London's Liverpool Street Station.

Following John McKenzie's death in 1872 the business continued under copartners Thomas Clunes and Walter Holland, and when Clunes departed it was henceforth known as McKenzie and Holland. After Walter Holland's death in 1888 his namesake son Walter Holland became managing director. At the same time Samuel Dutton, who had joined the firm in 1861 as draughtsman and had by 1880 become manager and a partner in it, left to run his own rival company in the nearby Shrub Hill Engineering Works from 1888 to 1901.

By 1903 McKenzie and Holland had supplied signalling equipment to many railways at home and abroad. They had a workforce of around 700 in Worcester and others employed in subsidiary factories overseas, including two in Australia.

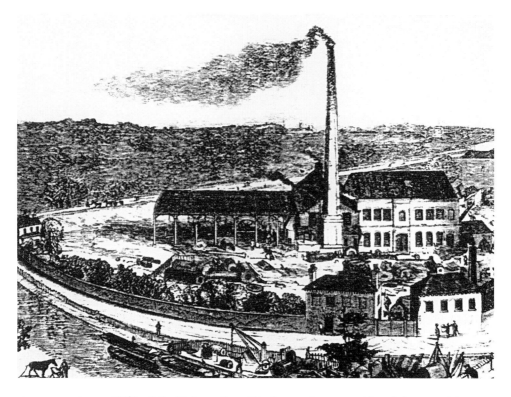

An engraving c.1860 of the Vulcan Iron Works on the west side of the canal in Worcester. Canal boats are being loaded or unloaded by crane.

Eventually they were taken over in 1921 by Westinghouse of Chippenham; the Worcester factories then closed and the premises were occupied by the engineering firm Heenan and Froude.

Early examples of Vulcan Iron Works structures are the iron-framed waiting rooms with decorative tiling on Worcester Shrub Hill Station, Platform 2, and the railway bridge alongside the main viaduct over Infirmary Walk in Worcester which carried the spur sloping downwards towards the long-removed riverside sidings of the North and South Quays. Some of McKenzie and Holland's sturdy mechanical signalling equipment is still in use on railways at home and abroad.

ELLIOTT'S METAL WORKS, SELLY OAK
In 1853 William Elliott of the Woodlands, Northfield, established his metal works on the site of the former Sturge's Chemical Works at Selly Oak, incorporating its buildings, canal arm, engine house and chimney. His factory was soon producing rolled brass and copper sheet, drawn brass and copper wire, and brass and copper

tubes. In 1866 Elliotts took over the business of Charles Green who had patented his invention of drawing seamless brass or copper tubes from a thick tubular ingot. A tube mill was then installed for producing boiler tubes and machinery was introduced for making locomotive boiler end plates. Another speciality of Elliotts was the production of metal sheets of an alloy, known as Muntz metal, a patent of George Frederick Muntz, used for sheathing the hulls of wooden ships. Over the years also amongst their products were vast quantities of telegraph wire for the Post Office and trolley wire for electric tramways. In due course the works extended from the Dingle over a large area alongside the canal towpath.

The works made considerable use of canal transport for incoming supplies of coal, copper, zinc and other materials, and for the dispatch of its products. In addition to the original canal arm leading into a basin equipped with a 30 cwt crane, a second one boat-length canal arm was cut across the towpath into the copper mill in 1875. In 1915 when the works was making munitions, the towpath was narrowed to create a canalside wharf with an overhead cantilever gantry crane projecting from the factory wall to facilitate loading and unloading. In 1877 the firm applied to the Canal Company for permission to erect a substantial bridge over the canal to carry a standard gauge railway siding from the Midland Railway into the works. This idea was shelved when the Canal Company, to offset the threat to its trade, stipulated as a condition a guaranteed minimum of canal business of £400 per year. In 1893, following the construction of a 3ft gauge tramway system to convey heavy items around the works on flat wagons pulled by horses and later by tractor, Elliotts made a similar request, this time for a bridge to extend the tramway over the canal into the Midland Railway goods yard. Again the plan was withdrawn when the Canal Company demanded a guaranteed minimum £125 tolls per annum as the condition.

For well over a century Elliotts was a thriving concern. The management included from 1897 to 1924 Neville Chamberlain who, after becoming Prime Minister, still kept in touch with former colleagues and employees. In 1928 Elliotts Metal Co. Ltd. became part of the I.C.I. Metals Group. By this time the use of canal transport was minimal, the arms and basin were soon disused and were filled in in 1938; the towpath overbridges were also soon demolished. During World War 2 the factory made, besides munitions, millions of rivets for army boots. Post-war, Elliotts continued to turn out non-ferrous metal products until the factory closed on 31 December 1964 when manufacture was transferred to the Kynoch Works, Witton. The site has since been untidily occupied as a small industrial estate using parts of the old buildings.

NETTLEFOLD & CHAMBERLAIN SCREW FACTORY, BREEDON CROSS
In 1842 J S Nettlefold, an ironmonger of Holborn, London, where he had had a small screw factory worked by water power, moved to 14 Broad Street, Birmingham. At the 1851 Exhibition in London he was impressed with an American screw-making

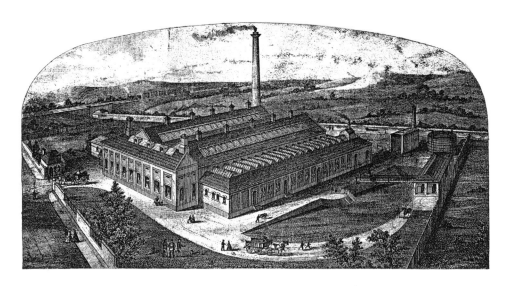

THE PATENT SCREW WORKS, KING'S NORTON.
(NETTLEFOLDS LIMITED.)

Nettleford's Screw Factory at Breedon Cross. This illustration from the firm's 1900 trade catalogue shows the W/B Canal on the far side of the factory and a train on the Birmingham and Gloucester Railway which crosses the canal. (Archives Dept., BRL)

machine and, with the help of his brother-in-law Joseph Chamberlain (father of the statesman) he secured, at a cost of £30,000, the English rights of using the machine. Three years later Joseph Chamberlain junior, then aged 18, came to Birmingham to share in the rapidly growing business. His cousin Joseph Nettlefold was in charge of management and production. He devoted himself to the commercial side of the business and established overseas sales in France and Ireland.

In 1866 the firm took over James, Son and Avery, manufacturers of wood screws, and moved into their new factory which had been built in 1862 beside the W/B Canal at Breedon Cross. In the early 1870s Nettlefold & Chamberlain obtained agreements with the W/B Canal Company for extra telegraph poles needed and wires along the canal from Breedon Cross to Birmingham, and also for canalside land for a wharf and for the construction of the wharf wall. The wharf was later extended and permission obtained for fences to be erected. Water was piped from the canal for the engines and water transport was used for incoming coal and the delivery of goods. During the 1870s Joseph Nettlefold required a night watchman to fire a musket promptly at ten o'clock every night, it is said, to make sure that he was on duty.

In 1880 the business was incorporated as Nettlefolds Limited. and later, in 1902, it became part of Guest, Keen and Nettlefold Limited (GKN). Over the years the factory was extended several times and in 1895 an adjacent recreation ground was provided for employees. By the 1950s there were around 500 people employed at the factory. It closed at the end of 1982, and the site, including the recreation ground, has since been occupied by a number of other businesses.

BIRMINGHAM BATTERY WORKS, SELLY OAK

The Birmingham Battery and Metal Company was established in 1836 and created its factory, with a rolling mill to make battery plates, tubes, copper and brass ware, at Digbeth. Of the thirteen original proprietors five were sons of Joseph Gibbins (1756-1811), a banker and button manufacturer from South Wales. One of the sons, Thomas Gibbins (1796-1863), played a large part in developing the business, and his two sons William and Thomas continued its expansion. In 1871 land was bought at Selly Oak at the junction of the W/B and Netherton (Dudley No.2) Canals and, not without opposition in the form of a round-robin from local people wanting to preserve the rural aspect of the location, the new factory was built, with access from the Bristol Road, and production began in 1873. The Digbeth branch was eventually closed in 1895 and administration and output concentrated at Selly Oak.

Developments at Selly Oak included: in 1880 and 1883 machinery for the manufacture of seamless copper tubes; in 1884 the erection of the very tall chimney which was a local landmark; in 1897 registration as a limited company with directors William, Thomas and John Gibbins; in 1900 installation of five new condensing steam engines to power the three rolling mills and two tube mills; and in 1902 the introduction of gas engines, in use from then until 1926, which entailed the building of a gas works to fuel them, as well as to enable gas lighting and the production of sulphate of ammonia and other useful by-products.

As at Digbeth, the firm made the most of its canalside situation. It used the large basin between the W/B Canal towpath overbridge and the stop lock on the Netherton Canal branch, also canal arms into the metal works and the gas works. Coal and metal ingots arrived by canal boats, some belonging to the Company. Water was extracted from the canal for the condensing engines. But the works also used water from their own wells, and during the severe droughts of 1914 and 1934 the Company supplied the W/B Canal with well-water, as much as 32,000 gallons per hour for several weeks. As at the same time the level of the nearby Harborne Reservoir fell, it was suggested that in fact the W/B Company was being indirectly supplied with, and charged for, some of its own water.

The Gibbins family were local benefactors. Some 30 acres of land for Selly Oak Park were donated by them in the early 1900s and the land for Selly Oak Library which opened in 1906 was given by Thomas Gibbins.

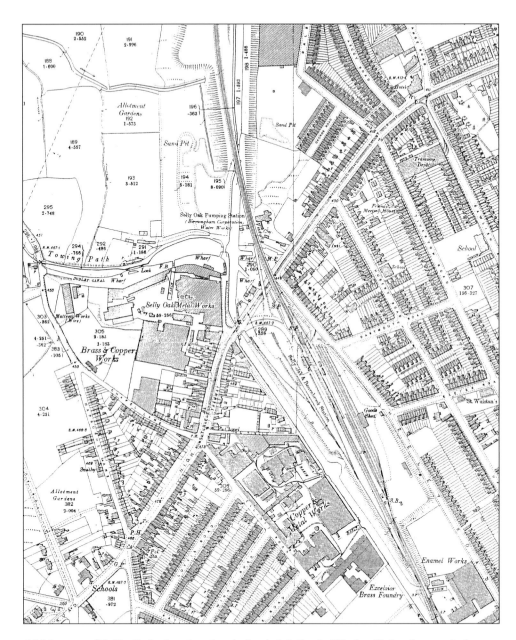

1904 map of Selly Oak showing (top) the Ariel Cycle Works, (left of centre) the Birmingham Battery Metal Works, (lower centre) Elliottt's Metal Works, and (bottom right) the Birmingham Enamel Works. Note the viaduct (part still in situ) and the bridge (later demolished) over the Bristol Road, of the original single-track Birmingham and West Suburban Railway.

The Battery and Metal Works continued to produce copper and brass products until its closure. Production declined in the final years. A large part of the factory area was turned into a business park around 1990 and the remaining part of the metal works closed in 2000. Only the original office building facing the Bristol Road now remains, it being a listed building. The use of canal transport ceased well before the closure of the Netherton Canal in 1953.

THE BIRMINGHAM PATENT ENAMEL COMPANY

It was in 1857 that Benjamin Baugh began to manufacture tough vitreous enamelled sheet wrought iron, by a process he invented and patented, at premises in Bradford Street in Birmingham. These enamelled plates came to be used widely for advertising various products on railway stations, shop fronts, and buildings, also for the inside decoration of walls and ceilings in places affected by dirt and damp as they could be easily kept bright and clean. By 1888 the firm had an expanding export business and its resources were so stretched that the then partners, Benjamin Baugh and William Walters decided to set up the Patent Enamel Company Limited with share capital of £150,000. The two partners became two of the three managing directors, the third being H W Elliott of the nearby Elliott's Metal Works.

In 1889 the Company moved into a new purpose-built factory at Selly Oak located between Heeley Road and the railway. The factory had twelve furnaces for fusing powdered glass and coloured oxides to produce the enamels, and two furnaces used in the process of scaling and flattening the sheet iron. There was a large printing room and an extensive area for steampipe drying. Agreement was reached with the Midland Railway for the construction of a canal arm through a tunnel in the railway embankment leading into a basin large enough to accommodate four or five boats, canal transport being used to bring in coal, sheet metal and other materials. There was also a railway siding into the factory and stabling for horses used for both water and road haulage.

In the manufacture of the enamel signs wrought iron sheet was cut to size, the protective grease was burnt off in muffle furnaces and the plates were then cleansed in acid and washed and dried. They were then dipped in a vat of paint to receive a special grey undercoat and moved by conveyor belt to be dried off. The coloured vitreous enamels were brushed or stencilled on, each colour being separately applied and fired, until the design was completed.

The 1920s saw the introduction of quality sheet steel suitable for vitreous enamelling and this gradually replaced wrought iron. But due to competition from other firms set up at home and abroad, business began to decline. There was a further fall-off in trade after World War 2 due to the increasing use of improved paper posters and plastics, and eventually the works closed suddenly in August 1965. The premises were then occupied by a number of small firms until a fire destroyed the factory

Aerial view, c.1950, of the Birmingham Battery Works (centre) and part of Elliott's Metal Works beside the W/B Canal (top). At the bottom is Harborne Lane Bridge over the Dudley No.2 Canal and, with its canal arm off the wide section of this canal, can be seen the Gas Works serving the Battery Works. (BRL)

complex in 1968, after which the site was soon cleared and occupied by a Comet Warehouse. By the 1950s the canal basin had fallen into disuse, except as a dump for rubbish and a watery grave for reject enamel plates. It was filled in when the factory closed, but the entrance to the arm on the canal side of the railway remains. Many of the Patent Enamel Company's advertisements are still around, some on heritage railway stations, and some, in good condition, have become collectors' items.

KINGS NORTON METAL COMPANY
Situated south west of Lifford Lane bridge and on the towpath side of the canal, the Kings Norton Metal Company's factory was built in 1889/90 by Thomas Baylis. He had previously been in business with his father-in-law John Abraham at Adderley Park Mills, Saltley, where rolled copper and brass, percussion caps and solid drawn

brass cartridge cases were produced, then guns and cycle components. Baylis continued there as managing director after the Adderley Park Mills were taken over by the Birmingham Small Arms Company (BSA) in 1873. When, fifteen years later, he decided to set up his own independent company to produce ammunition and rolled metals, the 27-acre site he chose for his new factory at Lifford had the advantage of a water supply from the canal and the use of water transport for the supply of heavy metal ingots as well as coal for his extensive steam-raising plant. In 1889 the Canal Company agreed to the construction of a canal arm into a basin in the works with an overbridge for the towpath, and for water to be taken for the engines and condenser at a cost of two shillings per HP per annum, water to be returned to the canal. The firm had to guarantee a minimum £75 worth of canal traffic per annum and to erect adequate fencing to replace the towpath hedge.

A 1936 aerial view showing (top) Kings Norton Paper Mill at the junction of the W/B and Northern Stratford Canals and the extensive Kings Norton Metal Works. (Aerofilms)

Over the years the busy factory complex was gradually extended over a further 30 acres. Additional rolling mills were built in 1900 and 1914 and they were kept working day and night to produce strip copper, brass and other alloys for cartridge cases and other components. During the 1914-18 War some 2,000 people were employed producing munitions. The factory employed highly qualified technical and scientific staff to design new machines and techniques.

In the early l900s the firm produced high quality blanks for coin making and in 1912 a complete minting plant was installed, licensed to produce coins with the KN mint mark. After the War the company came to the assistance of the Royal Mint, and under the 1918 and 1919 date-marks some 5 million (old) pennies with the KN mint mark were put into circulation.

Baylis died in 1914. In 1918 Kings Norton Metal Company was absorbed, along with other firms, into Nobel Industries Ltd., which in 1926 became part of the I.C.I. Metals Division. 1928 saw the decision to close the Kings Norton Factory and concentrate production at Witton. Some plant and machinery moved to Witton, as did many Kings Norton employees, but the Metals Group continued to rent some capacity at Kings Norton for rolling strip. From 1936 some of the Kings Norton plant, including the 1914 rolling mill still in situ, was used to produce aluminium sheet for aircraft. During the 1939-45 War the factory produced radiator tubes for aircraft. Research and production was also carried out there for the micropore filters needed to separate, from uranium metal, the active isotope 235 employed in the first atomic bomb and subsequently in nuclear power stations world-wide.

THE ARIEL CYCLE WORKS, SELLY OAK

The Ariel Cycle Works were in existence at Selly Oak in Dale Road below the canal embankment adjacent to the Bourn Brook aqueduct from 1893 to 1961. The first motor tricycle was made there in 1898 and the first motor cycle in 1905. The business, which in the 1930s employed 200 people, was taken over by the BSA Company in 1944 and production moved to Small Heath in 1961.

In 1895/6 the firm arranged with the W/B Canal Company for the installation of a chute from the canal bank down to the works for the delivery of sheet iron, coal and slack from canal boats. In 1897 a four-inch pipe was laid to supply water from the canal to the works. After 1961 the factory buildings were occupied by Boxfoldia Ltd., makers of packaging.

Chapter 19

ALONG THE SUMMIT LEVEL OF THE CANAL FROM GAS STREET BASIN TO TARDEBIGGE

In this and the two following chapters the aim has been to describe, in order along the canal from Gas Street Basin in Birmingham to Diglis Basins in Worcester, various features of the canal scene past and present, including wharves, stables, boatyards, shops and public houses, some of which are bygones, others still remaining. Mention will also be made of the locations of the canalside industries whose history and other details are recorded in chapters 17 and 18.

When the W/B Canal was constructed it was essential to create public wharves at strategic locations along its length where boats could load and unload their cargoes to serve the local communities within reach of the canal. Wharf walls of stone and brick, usually capped with blue bricks or large stone blocks, were constructed and the wharf area was firmed with stones and gravel. At the main wharves a weighbridge would be installed, together with an adjoining house for the attendant wharfinger. Stables would be provided and stacking areas allocated to local traders in coal, bricks and other commodities. For perishable goods one or more warehouses would be built. These amenities were provided initially, not only at the canal basins at Gas Street in Birmingham and at Diglis and Lowesmoor in Worcester, but also at Selly Oak, Kings Norton, Hopwood, Tardebigge each side of the Tunnel, Stoke Prior, and Hanbury. Also along the canal at convenient locations, usually where a road crossed the canal, simple public wharves were created where boats could tie up to load or unload coal, timber, road stone, farm produce and other items. In addition to the public wharves many private wharves were made at various times to serve factories and businesses located alongside the canal.

To supply the needs of boat people, enterprising people would build or rent a cottage near to or beside the canal and set up shop in a front room stocked with such things as oil, cigarettes, food and items of clothing. Some built stables where, for a

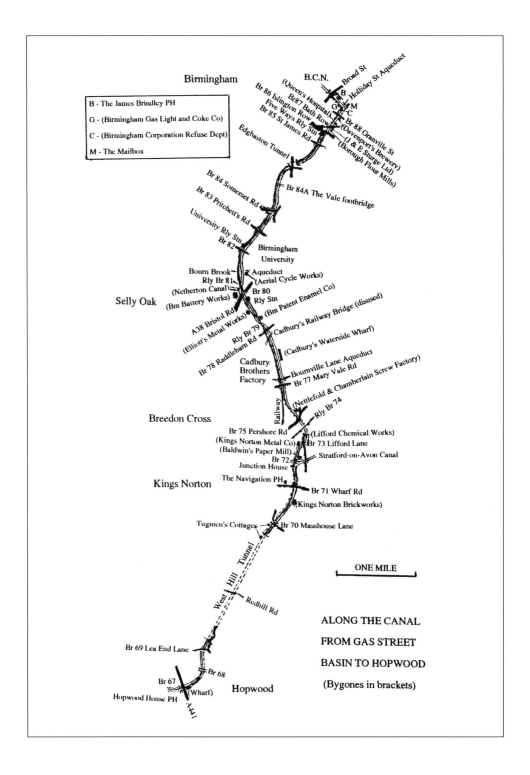

few pence, canal horses or donkeys could be accommodated when boats tied up for the night. In some cases the shops also obtained an off-licence to sell beer and cider, and some were developed into taverns or public houses where boat people and local people could congregate and spend a convivial evening. On the other hand, some canalside public houses were purpose-built.

Boat-building and repair yards were set up beside the W/B Canal at various places in the busy early years of canal carrying. A typical boatyard would have a timber-store, workshops, one or more slipways with winches and chains by which boats were launched or hauled out of the canal, a steam chest to enable planks to be bent to the required curvature for the sides of boats, and a tar pot for making watertight the joints packed with oakum. We know little about most of these early boatyards apart from their locations and the names of their proprietors.

GAS STREET BASIN

Until World War 2 Gas Street Basin remained busy with commercial boats, mostly bringing foodstuffs, materials and fuel for shops and businesses in central Birmingham. It was the rapid growth of motor transport from the 1920s onwards which caused the ultimate decline in water transport and the run-down state of most

Gas Street Basin c.1960, showing the Bar Look with plank and handrail crossing, the tunnel under Broad Street and the Church of the Ascension, the glassworks Chimney and the entrance to a canal arm and, in the foreground, loaded Corporation Salvage Department boats. (NWMT)

inland waterways, wharves and basins by the 1950s. From business records, contemporary photographs and the memories of old boatmen and canal maintenance staff we can gain a fair impression of life in Gas Street Basin in the 1920s and 1930s well before it became a scene of dereliction in the 1970s and 1980s, and latterly has been transformed with new waterside residential and commercial development on the Worcester Wharf and the offside of the canal as far as Five Ways.

The Worcester Bar remains an historic feature and, with the new traditional-style bridge over the stop lock, provides a pedestrian link between Gas Street and Bridge Street, as well as, with pontoons each side, moorings for an interesting collection of craft, including old working boats and residential boats. The stop lock has lost its four gates. When necessary, stop planks can be used there to create a barrier between the B.C.N. and W/B sections of canal.

The offices of the W/B section of the SND Company were at 46 (now renumbered 6) Gas Street until 1925 when the canal administration was transferred

Gas Street Basin in 1971 showing the Worcester Bar, the gateless stop lock and, soon to be demolished, the Severn & Canal Carrying Company's warehouses.

to Gloucester. Unfortunately, as George Bate witnessed at the time, many of the old documents and records stored there were then burnt and destroyed. But the building, which has a quite imposing frontage on Gas Street, remains and has non-waterways business use. On the towpath side the entrance to the canal arm which ran under the offices has been bricked up to form part of the wall of the building. The towpath bridge over the arm was at the same time removed.

There used to be two toll offices, one at each end of the Bar Lock. The last remembered W/B toll clerks were Arthur Dance and Thomas Bird who lived in cottages on the Worcester Wharf. The B.C.N. toll office clerk was Caesar Jones. To ascertain the tolls due, boats were gauged by the Birmingham clerk if travelling onto the B.C.N. and by the W/B clerk if passing onto the W/B Canal. The W/B toll office building has been used latterly as a café, an amenity available to the increasing number of people attracted to the waterway scene in this area.

The two canal arms under Gas Street, created at the outset, continued in use until the 1930s. The one on the B.C.N. side of the Bar Lock was used in the later 19th century by a firm of lead manufacturers and finally, until the 1920s, by Fraley

Granville Street wharves c.1910. On the right-hand side are rubbish boats tied up alongside the Birmingham Corporation Salvage Department wharf. (Birmingham Museum and Art Gallery)

& Sons, stone masons. It is now filled in but the entrance portal remains. The other arm, which in the early years led under the W/B offices into the Gas Works basin, later served the Anchor Tube Works built on the Gas Works site. The hump over it in Gas Street remains together with a small watered section of the arm beyond. In the nineteenth century both arms were extended under Berkley Street to serve other metal businesses.

Still on the Gas Street side of the Basin and beside the towpath beyond the old offices is first a substantial warehouse building and then stables later converted into the "Opposite Lock" restaurant and night club. The stables were in three sections, one reserved for seven horses of the S&CC Co., one for seven horses of other boats, and one for up to ten donkeys. There used to be two stablemen, one on duty days and one on nights. Towards the end the sole stableman was a former boatman, Billy Perkins, who slept in a hut at the stables and cleaned them out, but boatmen had to feed their own animals.

Beyond the stables and the Holliday Street aqueduct was the Birmingham Corporation Refuse Department's extensive depot dating from 1859 when land was first leased for it from the Canal Company. Its entrance was in Holliday Street and its wharves extended alongside the Basin and round the corner towards Granville Street. The Department had many of its own boats and, for its cart horses and boat horses, there were by the 1890s two substantial three-storey buildings, each with stables on the two lower levels, and a granary above. Animals reached the first floor level up an external ramp. Rubbish, including night soil, went, some through the Bar Lock and down "The Thirteen" (locks) or towards the Black Country, and some along the W/B Canal to Bournville and Lifford tips and beyond. The regular use of the canal for carrying away rubbish had ceased by 1965 when the last remaining twelve corporation boats were displayed in Gas Street Basin and sold. After years of disuse the stables beside the canal were last used briefly in 1987 to house two horses, one of which pulled a working boat used to clean up rubbish around the canals, whilst the other towed a dray to collect rubbish from city centre streets. Since this nostalgic exercise the canalside stables have been used as an arts and craft centre. Now the whole site is due to be developed to include a new Register Office and residential accommodation but retaining the canalside stables building.

On the east side of Gas Street Basin the Worcester Wharf extended from the Bar to the Severn Street Arm. Its entrance was from Bridge Street and along its length there were at one time five cranes. Nearest the Bar was a cement and lime wharf with warehouses, known as Graham's Wharf, which was occupied by Thomas Graham and also Greaves, Bull & Lakin. Next, with a four-boat arm and canopy covered wharves alongside the Basin, were the timber-built warehouses of the S&CC Co. Next on the Worcester Wharf were two saw mills and premises occupied by timber merchants Williams & Farmer for many years. Between these and the Severn Street arm was a large open wharf where agricultural produce, hay, straw, etc. from along the W/B Canal and beyond were unloaded. There was a weighbridge in the centre of the wharf, kept for many years by Walter Harris, and at the back of the wharf there were cottages for wharfingers and toll clerks. On both sides of the entrance to the Severn Street Arm were the wharves and storage tanks of oil merchants, on the Worcester Wharf side William Butler & Co., and on the other side William Fox & Sons of Bristol. Both firms had fly-boats carrying oil and tar between Birmingham and Gloucester. William Butler & Co. and Williams & Farmer were the last firms in business on the Worcester Wharf, remaining there until the early 1970s.

The short Commercial Street Arm had wharves and warehouses for two businesses, Moreland's matches which came by boat from Gloucester, and Noakes salt and coal, the salt arriving by canal from Droitwich. Between the Commercial Street arm and Granville Street Bridge there were other wharves with boats, including holiday craft, moored alongside until the 1990s.

Just as the Severn Street Arm narrowed to go under Holliday Street Passage, there was a draw bridge, known as the "heave-up bridge" because its platform was raised for boats to pass by being lifted vertically by gears up four pillars. This bridge, together with a nearby crane, was demolished in 1927 by George Bate and other workmen and the metal parts were sent by canal to Jackson's metal scrapyard at Lowesmoor Basin, Worcester. Another bridge, also demolished around that time, was a footbridge across Gas Street Basin from the hay wharf to the stables. It was known as the "Tay Bridge", perhaps because it was not very safe.

The development of Gas Street Basin in the latter part of the twentieth century has involved in 1975 the demolition of the S&CC Co's warehouses, in 1988 the completion of the James Brindley public house and the erection of the cast iron bridge over the stop lock, replacing the previous small swing bridge, to provide access from Gas Street to the pub. Subsequently in the 1990s Worcester Wharf was covered with modern business and residential buildings. Opened in 2001, the Mail Box complex replaces the former Post Office transport depot and later sorting office built on part of the marshalling yard of the old Midland Goods Station and occupying land which included the filled-in Severn Street Basin. A small section of the Severn Street arm has been reexcavated and watered and a new modern-style footbridge over the Basin has been installed to connect the towpath at the Worcester turn with Commercial Street.

The remaining old canalside buildings in Gas Street are now grade 2 listed and will hopefully be preserved. In recent years the resident boating community, some with traditional boats, have given life and character to the Basin.

FROM GAS STREET BASIN TO SELLY OAK

Between Gas Street Basin and Selly Oak wharfage facilities were restricted partly because they were banned by the 1791 Act through the Calthorpe estates in Edgbaston and partly because a large section of the canal consists of cuttings and embankments. But at the Birmingham end there were a number of industrial and public wharves on the off-side of the canal. Davenport's Brewery and the Queen's Hospital between Granville Street and Bath Row had their own wharves, as did the Malthouse, Sturge's Chemical Works and the Borough Flour Mills between Bath Row and Islington Row. Between Islington Row and St James Road there were two public wharves. By the bridge was the Islington Wharf with its smithy, where Herbert King's coal business was located. He had his own boats, one worked by his son. Further down the canal was Wheeley's Road Wharf with a weighbridge in the entrance way between houses which backed onto the wharf. On Wheeley's Road between the two wharves was the Navigation Inn. All these are now bygones.

The only other wharf along the canal beyond Edgbaston Tunnel in the Selly Oak direction was a small one at Pritchett's Road Bridge where roadstone was unloaded. But a little further along the embankment there was a large frame with a lid in the centre of the towpath, giving access to an underground tunnel. This enabled waste material to be unloaded from boats and taken under the railway to Metchley Park Tip near to the site of the Queen Elizabeth Hospital. This hospital, built on land donated by Cadbury Brothers, was opened in 1938.

On this section of the canal between Five Ways and Selly Oak the canal, accompanied by the railway, passes through the Edgbaston Tunnel and over the two lofty embankments across the Chad Valley and the Bourn Brook Valley. On the off-side are Birmingham University Halls of residence, now accessible from the towpath by the new footbridge, and, bordering the canal towards Selly Oak, the extensive University Campus.

SELLY OAK

It was the establishment of industries beside the canal at Selly Oak in the middle of the nineteenth century which led to the rapid urbanisation of what had been a rural area, the population rising from about 250 in 1841 to nearly 3,000 by 1871. When, or soon after, the canal was opened to Selly Port in 1795, the wharf with its entrance on the Bristol turnpike road was provided with a weighbridge, an office and two canal arms. In Jacob's 1828 plan of the wharf one arm is labelled a boat dock, the other a basin, and beside the dock are shown five lime kilns. In 1822 the Canal Company approved the takeover by William Povey of the coal and lime business already established on the wharf by a Mr James. In 1836 the Canal Committee agreed to transfer the tenancy of the wharf to James Whitehouse of Frankley. He lived on the wharf, carrying on a business in coal and lime and also keeping a shop, until the 1870s.

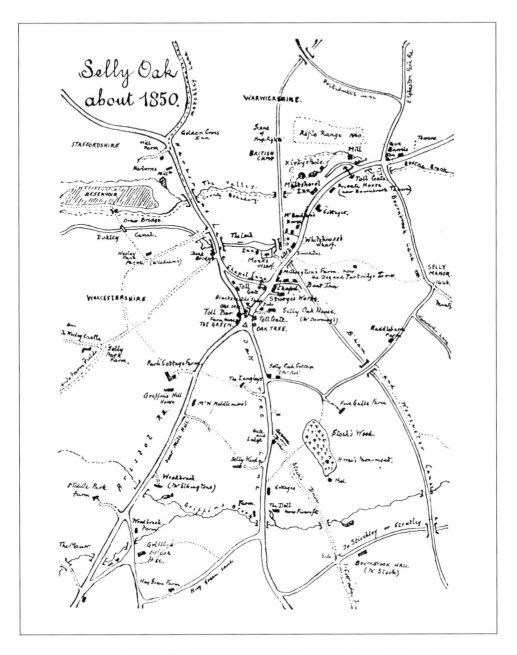

A map of Selly Oak c.1850 showing many canal features including Harborne Reservoir, Whitehouse's Wharf and limekilns, the Boat Inn, Sturge's Works, and aqueducts over Bourn Brook, Griffin's Brook and Stirchley Street. (F W Leonard, The Story of Selly Oak)

Goodman's wharf and canal arm at Selly Oak, where building materials were delivered and stored, viewed from the towpath bridge over the junction with the Dudley No.2 Canal. (Jeremy Goodman)

Several boat-building firms existed at various times at Selly Oak. Alongside the Dudley No.2 Canal near its junction with the W/B Canal John Smith was boatbuilding in the 1820s, then James Price, followed in the 1850s to 1870s by William Monk. On the W/B Canal, using the Company's boat dock, William Hetherington was in business as a boatbuilder from the 1870s until 1894 when the Canal Committee agreed to Edward Tailby occupying the boatyard which he had purchased from Hetherington. The manager of Tailby's initially was Matthew Hughes until he left to set up his own boatyard by Harborne Lane bridge; Matthew Hughes and Sons were in business there until the 1930s. Edward Tailby closed down his Selly Oak business around 1923 but continued boat-building at Perry Barr.

Following Tailby's departure his canal arm and boatyard site was taken over by Goodmans, builders' merchants, who had opened a branch in 1905 on the corner of the wharf nearest the railway bridge and had already used the wharf basin for their boats bringing in bricks, slates, sand, cement and other building materials. Their use of canal transport finished in the 1930s and the canal arms were filled in around 1947. Goodmans continued in business on the Bristol Road, using the former wharf area as a builders yard, until the year 2000. The firm, in its heyday, had had several branches and had supplied materials for major buildings including Birmingham Town Hall.

In the early years at Selly Oak there was a small public house, "The Boat", kept by Mr Kinchin, beside the canal at the bottom of the Dingle, as shown on a map of 1850 in "The Story of Selly Oak" by F W Leonard. An 1873 plan of the Birmingham West Suburban Railway shows a large building, The Junction Inn, situated on the canal wharf at the junction of the W/B and Dudley No.2 Canals before the Birmingham Battery Works took over the site. There is mention of another canalside hostelry in the minutes of the W/B Committee of the SND Company of August 1875. The landlord of the "Malt Shovel" at Selly Oak was "to be asked to pay an annual rental for the use of the banks of the canal adjoining his pleasure grounds. If he refuses the ground will be fenced off and the trees cut down and sold." There is unfortunately no mention of the outcome, nor of the exact location of the pub., but it was probably in the Dingle area and possibly "The Boat" renamed.

FROM SELLY OAK TO KINGS NORTON JUNCTION
Between the Bristol Road and Raddlebarn Road (formerly Fieldings Lane), Elliott's Metal Works on the towpath side and the Enamel Works under the railway on the off-side had their own basins and wharves. On the towpath side, just before the canal narrows under the railway bridge, there were the two canalside cottages, long ago demolished, built in the late 1870s for toll clerk W J Parish and his assistant J Miles. The last occupant of the toll house there from 1937 to 1953 was Herbert Hancox who was lengthsman from the West Hill Tunnel to Gas Street Basin. He followed Albert Coleman, son of boatman Tom Coleman of Stoke Pound. Albert had previously been the Stoke Flight lock-keeper.

High above the canal beside the cutting at Raddlebarn Road Bridge is the Country Girl public house. This had been built on the W/B Canal Company's land and was owned by the Company in the latter part of the nineteenth century. In 1876 the landlord, Mr Round, was permitted by the Canal Company to continue to occupy the premises at a rent of £15 per annum, rising to £20 after one year. In 1881 a Bristol brewer, E W Cotterill, was allowed to take over the Country Girl and its grounds at £20 per annum, provided he paid the rent arrears owed by Mr Round. A fourteen year lease was agreed. In 1882 the Canal Company agreed to pay £100 towards the cost of repairs and extensions to the pub. and to its being sublet to Alfred Allen for 21 years. The alterations and repairs were completed by November of that year and the Company deducted £40 from their share of the cost, £30 for Round's rent arrears and £10 for the half-yearly rent. In due course the pub. was sold. It has been much altered and rebuilt over the years. Unfortunately it is not easily accessible from the canal.

Along the canal past the now disused Cadbury's railway bridge was their Waterside wharf and warehouse with railway access via the skew bridge to their factory. On the wharf site there is now a small housing estate. At the far end of the

The guillotine stop-lock between the W/B and Stratford-upon-Avon Canals at Kings Norton with, on the left, the old toll house, long demolished (NWMT)

embankment, with access from Bournville Lane, was Sparrey's Wharf used by Cadbury's when their Bournville factory was first built. Then as the canal enters a shallow cutting there were wharves by Mary Vale Road bridge and beside a number of canalside businesses including Ashby's cycle accessories and roller skates factory, Showell's Metal Works, and, approaching Breedon Cross, Nettlefold's screw factory.

At Breedon Cross in the latter part of the nineteenth century there was a brickworks beside the canal between the screw factory and the bridge and, near to the bridge, the Cross Inn. Around 1900 the then landlord sold the old Cross Inn and moved to larger premises, named The Breedon Cross Inn, on the other side of the canal on the corner of Pershore Road and Lifford Lane. This pub., which for many years in both locations was patronised by boatmen and wharfingers, closed down around 1993 and was soon devastated by a disastrous fire.

In July 1867 it was reported in the Canal Committee minutes that their engineer, Mr Boddington, "had arranged with the engineer of the Midland Railway Company for the construction of the Dock or Basin near Breedon Cross Bridge in connection with the proposed siding to that place." The siding was constructed from the old Birmingham and Gloucester Railway near Kings Norton Station and curved round under the main line beside the canal to Breedon Cross Wharf which was busy as merchandise was transferred between canal boats and railway waggons and vans. Today the only remaining visible reminders of the siding's existence are the second arches of the railway bridge and of the road bridge over the canal through which the railway passed, much of the trackbed and the wharf now being occupied by industrial development.

On the curve of the canal between Breedon Cross and Lifford Lane Bridge, just beyond the railway bridge and on the towpath side, were the Lifford Refuse Disposal Works. Here refuse from Birmingham Corporation's Holliday Street depot was off-loaded from their canal boats. The three straight boat-length bluebrick-edged sections of wharf wall built in the 1890s remain, but the refuse tip has long lost its canal access.

Between Lifford Lane and the junction of the Stratford and W/B Canals, there were, on the towpath side, the Kings Norton Metal Works with its canal arm and, further along on the off-side, Baldwins Paper Mill with wharfage for three boats. The 1796-built Junction House remains. It was used as a canal toll office for many years. Along the Stratford Canal branch, on the towpath side just before the guillotine stop lock and Lifford Road bridge, there used to be another toll house beside the lock where boats could be conveniently gauged.

KINGS NORTON

In May 1816 Thomas Monk & Son, members of a family with many relatives involved in commercial carrying and boat-building in the nineteenth century, were given permission by the Canal Committee to construct a dock and a house on the off-side of the canal by Wharf Lane bridge. There is no evidence that the dock was ever made, but a wharf there was let in August 1817 to William Monk and Thomas Holyoak for £10 per annum. In later years this small wharf was used for the delivery of road stone and also by local farmers for loading their produce onto boats for transit to Birmingham. This wharf has long disappeared, the canal bank there having been raised.

Whilst the canal was busy with commercial traffic, the Canal Company's wharf on the towpath side at Kings Norton, with its entrance from Wharf Road, was well used. Beside the wharf house there was a coalyard with a weighbridge and in 1865, when George Reachill rented the wharf following William Brant's tenure, stables were added.

Beside the towpath north of Wharf Road there are three dwellings. The first of these, now much altered, used to be a public house, the "Boat". It was built in the

The Navigation Inn along Wharf Road, Kings Norton, c.1880. The lady to the left of the entrance is probably the licensee, Mary Rogers. (Kings Norton Library)

early days of the canal and continued in business until around 1925. In the 1850s it was kept by Abraham Evans, listed as a beer retailer and butcher.

The other canalside cottages at various times housed canal workers and one in the 1870s was a shop. Along Wharf Road toward the centre of Kings Norton there is "The Navigation" Inn, which has been in existence at least since the mid-nineteenth century and is now much modernised. In the 1850s and 1860s the licensee was John Rogers, and in the 1870s Mary Rogers.

Between Wharf Road and the high bridge over the canal (latterly rebuilt) where Masshouse Lane becomes Primrose Hill was situated the wharf of Kings Norton Brickworks. On the top of the embankment on the towpath side adjacent to the high bridge are two cottages, originally built for tugmen and their families. Below, in the cutting towards the West Hill Tunnel entrance was a winding hole for the tunnel tugs to turn in, and on the off-side of the canal a crane and a coal shed. At the approach to the tunnel mouth the towpath rises steeply up to the two tunnel cottages above the tunnel in which lived another pair of tugmen and their families and to the beginning of the route for boat animals over the tunnel. This route now passes through a housing estate before following a country lane towards the Hopwood end of the tunnel.

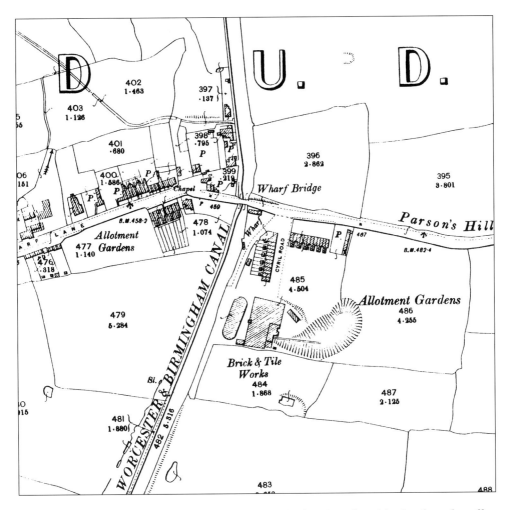

Map of the W/B Canal at Kings Norton c.1900, showing the old wharf on the off-side of the canal, the Kings Norton Brickworks and nearby workers' cottages and, top left, the canal feeder from Wychall Reservoir.

HOPWOOD

On the south side of the West Hill Tunnel the canal has a rural setting as far as Hopwood Wharf, the only intermediate road crossing being provided by the high bridge over the tunnel cutting for the lane between Hopwood and Lea End. From 1797 to 1807 Hopwood was the southern terminus of the canal, and during those ten years the wharf was much busier than when the canal was further extended. Initial facilities there included a coal wharf, weighbridge, wharfinger's cottage and stables. Soon to follow were limekilns and an inn beside the wharf. Richard Parkes was the inn-keeper and coal dealer at the time of the 1840 tithe map, followed in the 1850s by Thomas Merry. The 1840 tithe map also shows that a few hundred yards along the canal towards Bittell cutting there was, at that time, a beerhouse and garden, the occupier being John Eades.

In 1867 a new Hopwood Wharf Inn, now the Hopwood House Hotel, was built on the west side of the old humpback road bridge. Over the years its licensees also carried on various trades. One, James Terry, in the 1870s was a lime burner and manufacturer of bricks. His successor, Robert Southan, in the 1880s was a shopkeeper. On the off-side of the canal opposite the inn, there was a smithy and adjacent blacksmith's house with a corner shop and post office, all demolished after World War 2.

When the narrow brick bridge, which had long been a bottleneck for traffic, was replaced to take a wide main road in 1913, part of the canal wharf was taken for the widening of the bridge. On the remaining wharf and adjacent land a boatbuilding business was carried on by John Pinder in the 1970s. The two canal cottages near the wharf have housed canal maintenance workers including the man who attended to the gas engine which was used to extract smoke and fumes from the central shaft of the West Hill Tunnel.

FROM HOPWOOD TO TARDEBIGGE OLD WHARF

Between Hopwood and Tardebigge Old Wharf there were several small wharves. One of these, known as Bittell Arm Wharf, was on Jacob's Cut by the road across Lower Bittell Reservoir. Another, known as Bittell Wharf, was by the bridge where the road from Barnt Green to Alvechurch crosses the canal at the other end of the embankment; it served the nearby Barnt Green area. By the Lane House aqueduct was a wharf where night soil from the Birmingham conurbation used to be delivered for nearby farms, including Lane House Farm. John Burman at the adjacent house "Kingfishers", in whose garden was the wharf, attributed the excellence of his roses to this night soil.

Near the south end of the new cutting under the M42 Motorway was Coopers Hill Wharf, known in the old days as the New Wharf to distinguish it from the old Alvechurch wharf at Scarfields which was created when the canal was made. Also, since the wharf was close to Callow Hill Farm, now a housing estate bordering the canal towpath, it was also known as Callow Hill Wharf. The Wharf was used by the nearby New Wharf Farm for its own coal and farming business located there. It is said that the three stone buttresses of the stables beside the road came from the old Saxon chancel of the parish church of Alvechurch when the chancel was demolished in 1860. From around 1840 to 1880 George Greaves followed by Mrs Catherine Greaves ran the farming and coal business and the wharf then came to be known as Greaves Wharf. They had their own boat, the boatman being Thomas

Withers. The wharf was also used by another local farmer and coal dealer, John Beck of Coopers Hill, in the 1850s, 1860s and 1870s. From around 1890 to 1920 the wharf was used by Austin Withers, farmer and coal dealer, of Coopers Hill. There is now a 2ft depth of soil covering the old coal yard, forming the gardens of the two cottages into which the old stables were converted.

On the west side of the canal between Coopers Hill Wharf and Scarfields Wharf is Withybed Green with its public house, the Crown Inn. Because the

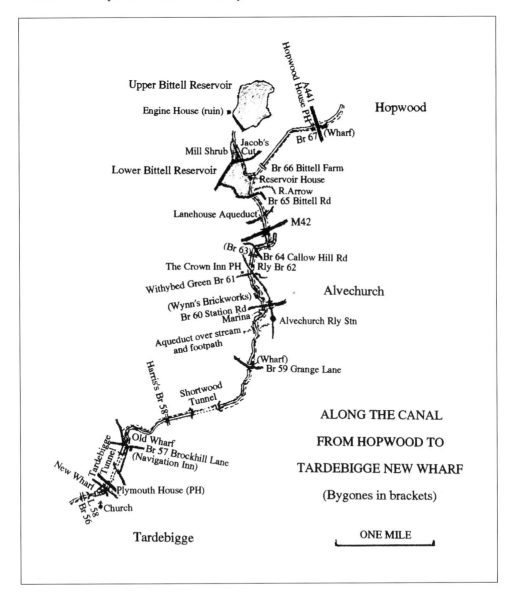

Upper Bittell Reservoir

Engine House (ruin)

Hopwood

Br 67 (Wharf)

Jacob's Cut

Mill Shrub

Br 66 Bittell Farm

Lower Bittell Reservoir

Reservoir House

R. Arrow

Br 65 Bittell Rd

Lanehouse Aqueduct

M42

(Br 63)

Br 64 Callow Hill Rd

The Crown Inn PH

Rly Br 62

Withybed Green Br 61

Alvechurch

(Wynn's Brickworks)

Br 60 Station Rd

Marina

Aqueduct over stream and footpath

Alvechurch Rly Stn

(Wharf)

Br 59 Grange Lane

Harris's Br 58

Shortwood Tunnel

ALONG THE CANAL

FROM HOPWOOD TO

Old Wharf

Br 57 Brockhill Lane

(Navigation Inn)

TARDEBIGGE NEW WHARF

New Wharf

Tardebigge Tunnel

Plymouth House (PH)

(Bygones in brackets)

L 58

Br 56

Church

Tardebigge

ONE MILE

The bridge together with The Crown Inn at Withybed Green, 1985.

The old stables at Scarfield Wharf, Alvechurch, 1985.

bridge near the inn was originally a vertical lift bridge, the inn itself used to be referred to by boatmen as "The Drawbridge" or "The Heave-up". In the 1840s it was in the hands of William Penzer, maltster and victualler, then run briefly by Job Penzer who was the local excise officer. After several other publicans, the pub was run by Augustus Whitby and then by his daughter from 1901 to 1981. The Crown Inn was much patronised by boat people, as it is today. The part of the building nearest to the canal, now converted, was a stable block for 5 or 6 horses with a hayloft above.

On the off-side of the canal towards Scarfields wharf is the site of the former Wynn's brickworks which, with its own wharf and boats, was in operation from 1860 to 1939. In the 1930s the canal wharf was still used, not for unloading coal or loading bricks, but for taking clay from the claypit in the Canal Company's work boats for puddling the bed of the canal.

Scarfield Wharf, today the location of Alvechurch Boat Centre, was established initially by the Canal Company as a public wharf a few months after the canal was opened to Tardebigge Old Wharf in 1807. In the summer of 1808 the wharf became the southern terminus of a horse-drawn packet boat service conveying goods and passengers between Alvechurch and Birmingham. Run at first by Thomas Cartwright, and following his death by Thomas Jenkins, the packet boat continued to operate for at least five years, the date of its demise being uncertain. In 1847 the wharf house at Scarfield, then occupied by J Greaves, was enlarged. In 1861 a stable and warehouse were erected on the wharf. From 1854 to 1865 Joseph Beck was in business as a boat owner, coal dealer and carrier at the wharf, followed from 1865 to 1896 by George Reachill, shop keeper and coal dealer. Later, from 1914 to 1919, George Colledge, a son of T & M Dixon's boatmaster Thomas Colledge, had a coal business on the wharf, together with his brother-in-law Jack Lewin. The coal came from Cannock in their boat *Snowdrop*. Unfortunately both men died in the severe influenza epidemic following World War 1 and the boat was then acquired by Dixons.

Between Alvechurch Boat Centre and Grange Lane there is an aqueduct over a small stream which comes down from Cobley Hill and beside the stream a public footpath also passes under the canal.

Alongside the Grange Lane humpback bridge over the canal, on the towpath side, is a house which was occupied for many years by a family who ran both a shop and coal business. Noah and Charlotte Knight were the proprietors from 1850 until Noah died in 1889 followed by Charlotte in 1891. Then their son Thomas who had lived with them continued to run both businesses until World War 1. Noah Knight had his own boat *Samuel No.3*, whose master was George Withers, for fetching coal from the collieries to his private wharf known as Grange Wharf.

Through Shortwood Tunnel the first bridge is an accommodation bridge for Stoney Lane Farm. Over the years it has been known as Harris's Bridge since the farm was in the hands of Samuel Harris when the canal was cut and, after Samuel and his wife Mary both died in 1829, their son Thomas Harris continued to manage the farm until his death in 1892. T & M Dixon took over Stoney Lane Farm from its next occupant around 1902 and their motor boat *Enterprise* which took produce from Tardebigge Old Wharf into Birmingham each day from 1806 until the 1930s would stop at Harris's Bridge to pick up churns of milk destined for the General Hospital and other Birmingham customers. The bridge used to be a favourite spot for workers from the Enfield Motorcycle Works in Redditch and other local people to come to, in order to swim or bathe in the canal.

TARDEBIGGE OLD WHARF

In the early years after its opening, Tardebigge Old Wharf was a hive of industry with six firms having been allotted their own single boat-length moorings and stacking grounds for coal, and with several local merchants allowed warehouse facilities. Also there was a convenient hostelry, "The Navigation", built on land at the corner of Brockbill Lane opposite the wharf entrance with stables and grazing for boat horses. Farmers and tradespeople would have come with their horse-drawn

Tardebigge Old Wharf c.1900. The crane was there from 1885 to 1914, brought from Tardebigge New Wharf for unloading stone and other materials for the building of the new Hewell Grange. (Phillip Coventry)

waggons and carts to collect coal and merchandise and to send their produce by canal to Birmingham. Following the completion of Tardebigge Tunnel in 1811 some of this trade, especially for the Bromsgrove area, would have transferred to the New Wharf. But the Old Wharf continued to be convenient for Hewell Grange and for Redditch, via Brockhill Lane, and so it remained busy.

The "Navigation Inn" continued in business for about thirty years. It closed around 1840, being shown on the tithe map of 1839 but not being listed in the 1841 census returns. The innkeepers, John and Catherine Hunt, remained at the Old Wharf as farmers and coal dealers for many more years, the business being later carried on by their son Richard and his wife Emma until the early 1900s. The closure of the inn may have been due to a falling off of custom when the canal was finally open throughout in 1815; some of the original businesses occupying boat lengths began to withdraw, and there was competition from "The Plymouth Arms" and local alehouses "The Elbows" and "The Squirrels" in Hewell Lane. By the latter part of the nineteenth century only Dixons remained permanent occupiers of the Old Wharf. As their business expanded they practically monopolised it and it became known as Dixons Wharf. On it they established a retail market where customers could buy their farm produce, meat and poultry, vegetables, milk, butter and eggs, as well as coal.

Until the use of the wharf by Dixons ended after World War 2 the weighbridge remained, but it was then removed. The weighbridge house, extended, is now a private house. The two disused lime kilns beside the winding hole at the north end of the wharf were used by Dixons in connection with the slaughter of pigs from their intensive piggery close by. Their long piggery was served by a 2ft gauge overhead tramway on which waste food and manure, brought from Birmingham markets and Davenport's Brewery by canal boat, was transported and tipped into the sties. In the fields adjoining the Old Wharf great numbers of free-range poultry were at large during the daytime. Eggs and mushrooms found in the fields beside the canal furnished many a boat crew with a tasty meal.

Over the years a number of humble dwellings were built on the wharf, some long demolished or replaced. Their occupants were at first wharfingers and canal workers, later mainly Dixons' employees. Of the two semi-detached cottages opposite the wharf on the west side of the canal, now used by a boat-hire firm, the one nearest the bridge was for many years a shop. It was kept from the 1870s onwards until the 1910s by Edward Tustin and his wife, then in the 1920s and until 1937 by Fred Davies and his wife Annie. It also became a post office in 1922 after the closure of the one on the New Wharf. Following Mr and Mrs Davies, the shop and post office were run by S Johnson.

The wharf was unusually busy during the seven years that it took for the building of the grand new mansion of Hewell Grange from 1884 to 1891. The edifice was built of dark red sandstone which came from quarries at Runcorn in Cheshire by canal boat to the Old Wharf. From there it was transported by a specially constructed horse-drawn tramroad up to Hewell. The canal Committee minutes of 26 February 1885 record that Mr Hobrough was to repair and remove the Tardebigge New Wharf crane to the Old Wharf "for unloading the heavy materials coming by Canal required for building Lord Windsor's mansion at Hewell Grange." The cost of repairing and moving the crane was to be paid by the builders. The crane, which was sited on the wharf beside the canal opposite the weighbridge, remained in situ until December 1914 when it was reported to be unsafe and was ordered to be pulled down. The circular stone base which surrounded the crane post remains a feature of the wharf.

TARDEBIGGE NEW WHARF

The New Wharf, which was opened to traffic in January 1811, has remained over the years, in spite of changes, the hub of a small community of canal workers and their families, living in cottages at the wharf. By the entrance to the wharf is the weighbridge house built when the wharf opened. The weighbridge, mainly used for weighing cartloads of coal, was in front of the house, and it is still possible to see the metal surround of the platform. The mechanism was in a cellar below the front of the house. It was no longer in use by 1920 when it was removed to Stoke Prior to replace the one there which had been condemned. On the other side of the entrance to the wharf the present house was built in 1912/13 for Frank Rowles the superintendent of the new depot. The previous house on the site had been the turnpike toll house which was there when the canal first arrived. Including the weighbridge house there are five old cottages facing the wharf. Of these cottage No.3 used to be a post office and shop. The location of the post box beside the front window can still be seen. The postmaster from 1869 to 1880 was James Timms. Then from 1881 to 1918 it was nominally Tom Colledge who could neither read nor write. He was chief boatman for the local coal and farming business of T & M Dixon. It was his wife Mary who ran the post office and shop, open from 7.00 am to 8.00 pm on weekdays. It closed in 1922 when Tom Colledge's married daughter, who then ran it, emigrated to New Zealand. The post office then moved to the Old Wharf. Successive members of the Colledge family lived at the No.3 New Wharf cottage for over 130 years.

The large stone warehouse beside the canal, which was built originally for the storage of perishable goods, was eventually taken over by T & M Dixon for use as a mill for producing animal and poultry feeds. The machinery was driven by a portable steam engine. In recent years, after a period of industrial use and subsequent neglect, the listed building has been restored and will feature as part of the canal heritage centre planned for the wharf.

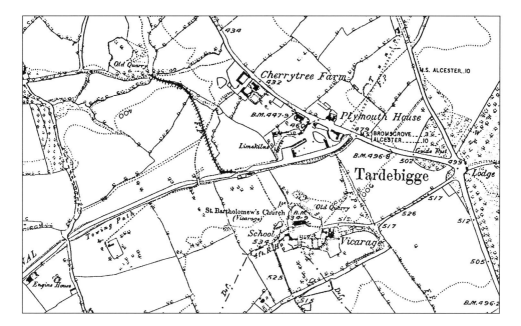

Map c.1890 showing the Tardebigge New Wharf area before the maintenance depot moved there, including the Church and the two quarries. The track of the tramway from Dusthouse Quarry to the stone wharf below the top lock has been added along the footpath, formerly the trackbed.

The 90ft square basin which was ready for use initially is some indication of the Canal Company's expectation that the wharf would be extensively used and would need adequate moorings and stacking space. The basin also served as a winding hole. By 1831 the demand for boatlengths was such that it was necessary to construct the canal arm from the corner of the basin towards the centre of the wharf area to accommodate an extra four boats with stacking ground for coal beside it. In addition to the boats carrying coal and other commodities, there were those which brought limestone from Dunhampstead to the five lime-burning kilns at the south-west corner of the basin. The disused kilns, long covered with an earth bank, have recently been excavated and exposed and it is hoped that one or more of them can be restored.

Soon after the SND takeover of the W/B Canal in 1874, the wharf became the station for the steam tug which towed boats through Tardebigge and Shortwood Tunnels, and the Tug Row of four houses was built in the lane outside the wharf for the tugmen and their families. These people came from the Gloucester area, but they were soon integrated into the local community.

Major changes at the wharf occurred from 1909 to 1911 when maintenance facilities were transferred to it from Stoke Prior following the retirement of the

Canal Engineer, F W Hobrough, in 1908. The move was made in order that the servicing of the tugs could be combined with general maintenance work. Some of the buildings have their date on and some incorporate a metal brick inscribed "SND" (Sharpness New Docks, the abbreviated title of the Canal Company). At the corner of the basin and the canal is the carpenters shop where, for many years, George Bate the foreman carpenter worked, making and mending lock gates and other items. The date 1909 can be seen roughly inscribed on a concrete slab at a corner of the building. In the middle section of the building were the Canal Company's own stables, and at the far end beside the canal arm was the fitting shop. The small detached building set back from the canal, and dated 1911, was the smithy where Tom Insull the blacksmith worked for many years. By the entrance to the compound is the office building, dated 1910, less used in recent times since the canal administration moved to Lapworth. In 1924 a dry dock was constructed in the canal arm and this remains in use: its date can be seen in the dock wall below the pump used to empty the dock. On the far side of the dry dock are a large wooden building and a brick building, both latterly used for industrial purposes, which housed the sawmill, timber store and workshop. The crane which remains in the yard adjacent to the canal came from Halesowen Wharf in 1953. It replaced a previous crane which had been in use at Sharpness Docks and was installed at Tardebigge in 1911. This earlier crane which was of iron apart from its timber jib had an SWL (Safe Working Load) of 12 tons in 1911, but by 1951 the SWL had been reduced to 7 tons and it was declared unsafe and was dismantled. Both cranes were used to lift lock gates and other heavy items onto and from canal boats. There used to be another crane by the sawmill which was used to load and unload logs and timber. For the animals of working boatmen there was a stable block with a saddlery above it set back behind the basin. This was demolished in 1957, being by then no longer needed.

A little way along the off-side of the canal between the basin and the top lock is a stone plinth with, on top, a memorial plaque with the inscription: "AT THIS SPOT IN 1946, ON BOARD 'CRESSY' TOM AND ANGELA ROLT FIRST MET ROBERT AICKMAN AND DECIDED TO FOUND THE INLAND WATERWAYS ASSOC. ERECTED BY THE WORC-BHAM CANAL SOCIETY". The meeting actually occurred in 1945. Tom Rolt was a civil-servant/engineer who lived with his wife Angela on his converted fly-boat *Cressy* moored at this location during and immediately after the War, from 1941 to 1946. He had come to realise the necessity of some organisation to campaign for the preservation and conservation of the canals as commercial carrying dwindled. Rolt's book "Narrow Boat" published in 1944, but written before his sojourn at Tardebigge, and his subsequent books on canals, helped to bring to the public's notice the plight of many canals in danger of abandonment, and the opportunities for their future leisure use. Over the

years the Inland Waterways Association which he and Robert Aickman founded
has done much to help save and preserve many semi-derelict and abandoned canals
in cooperation with local initiatives.

THE PLYMOUTH ARMS, TARDEBIGGE

The Plymouth Arms, now Plymouth House, situated across the road from the New
Wharf, was built as an Inn and Public House when Tardebigge Tunnel was
completed and the New Wharf opened in 1811. Through his agent, Mr Attwood, the
Sixth Earl of Plymouth, who owned the land thereabouts, was able to purchase
200,000 bricks from the Canal Company at a cost of 30 shillings per thousand to
build the Georgian-style hostelry, which, together with the coach house and stables
opposite, was completed in 1812. Soon after its opening it hosted a combined
housewarming and celebration of the birthday of the Earl of Plymouth. Some verses
penned by a local poet present at the proceedings include:

*Tardebigge New Wharf with, beyond the basin on the left, Tug Row; centrally
above the depot buildings, Plymouth House, formerly the Plymouth Arms Inn;
and, beside the canal on the right, the old warehouse.*

It was the second day of July
The people all met, I'll tell you why;
To celebrate my Lord's birthday
When mirth and joy each did display.

And that noble Inn the Plymouth Arms
Their jovial hearts gave loud alarms.
In joy and mirth they spent that day,
And satisfied they went away.

Mr Woodhouse builder of the lift
To drink his glass he will make shift.
He's an ingenious man with talents good
To work in iron, stone or wood.

The first innkeeper and his wife were John and Elizabeth Barron; their daughter Ann was baptised in Tardebigge Church in 1816. In the 1820s the tenancy passed to John Durham who held it until about 1852 when his son-in-law Samuel Taylor and his wife Eliza took over. In 1853 their son John Durham Taylor was baptised in Tardebigge Church.

Samuel Taylor was a colourful and enterprising character. In his time the Plymouth Arms was well-known locally for its social events, which included an Annual Ball held early in January. For the 1862 Ball "an efficient Quadrille Band" was engaged and tickets cost six shillings for gentlemen and five shillings for ladies. The Bromsgrove Messenger reported: "This gay affair was a decided success. The friends and patrons of Mr Taylor, the worthy host, assembled in full force, and, having footed it right merrily all night, sat down, thanks to Mrs Taylor, to a sumptuous breakfast in the morning." Besides running the Plymouth Arms, Samuel Taylor farmed the surrounding 20 acres of land and he rented the fishing rights on Tardebigge Reservoir from the Canal Company and advertised the availability of boating and fishing facilities upon it.

The last publican was Ambrose Moythan from 1869 to 1878/9, when the inn closed. Its closure is said to have been brought about by the drownings of drunken leggers in Tardebigge Tunnel. The Tardebigge Parish registers from 1818 to 1846 do contain the names of eight men and an eleven-year-old lad who met their deaths in this way. But the leggers had been replaced by tugs in 1876. In 1878 the young Lord Robert Windsor-Clive came of age and took up residence at Hewell. He was a promoter of "The True Temperance Society" and was concerned about the dangers of alcohol. The Plymouth Arms was one of a number of public houses on his estates which were closed down and put to other uses.

An engraving of the Plymouth Arms Inn, Tardebigge, c.1840 with, across the road, the coach house and stables. (Stephen Price)

Since ceasing to be a public house the premises, rechristened Plymouth House, have been occupied as a guest house, and latterly as a nursing home. Today the three-storey building remains largely unchanged. The cellars with brick-arched ceilings remain intact. The one-storey brick lean-to to the left of the front of the building was added at an early stage to provide a special bar for the use of boatmen and labourers, segregated from the more respectable guests and customers. The stable-block has been used for business purposes, including a funeral and removal business, and to provide residential accommodation.

Chapter 20

ALONG THE CANAL BETWEEN TARDEBIGGE NEW WHARF AND HANBURY WHARF

THE LOCK COTTAGES AND LOCK-KEEPERS

The lock-keepers and their wives and families along the canal from Tardebigge down to Worcester were, in the days of working boats, a help in many ways to passing boat people. They could supply water, vegetables, and small items needed, and also local news and news of other boats which had passed recently.

The original lock cottages were built to a general pattern, with kitchen, scullery, living room, upstairs bedrooms, lean-to washhouse and an outside privy. As roofing tiles and welsh slate were not generally available at the time, they initially had thatched roofs. Most had a small garden and a pigsty and also a built-in store room, with a wide door, for the storage of tools, timber and logs, coal and other items. They had a low wall, usually capped with blue bricks, and a gate, a few feet from the front of the building. Over the years, and especially in recent times, most of the lock houses have been modernised and some greatly altered. However many still retain original features, including windows topped with a shallow brick arch.

THE TARDEBIGGE FLIGHT

The flight of thirty locks from Tardebigge to the Queen's Head at Stoke Pound is famous as being numerically the greatest consecutively locked stretch of narrow canal in the UK. Apart from the pound between the two top locks 57 and 58, the pounds between the locks are quite short, mostly about seventy yards in length. For many years the myth was perpetuated that the top lock was the deepest narrow lock in the country with a 14ft change of level. This was believed in and repeated even by Tom Rolt and George Bate. It goes back at least to statistics for the W/B Canal listed in a document "Returns made to the Board of Trade ... in respect of Canals and

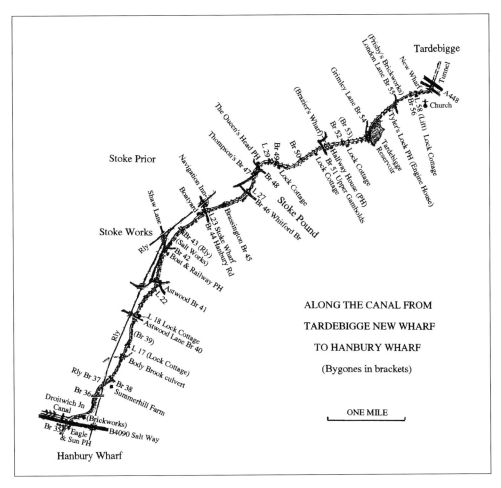

Tardebigge

(Prisby's Brickworks)
London Lane Br 55

New Wharf

L 58 (Lift) Lock Cottage
Br 56
Tyler's Lock PH (Engine House)

Grimley Lane Br 54

Tunnel
A 448
Church

(Br 53)
Br 52

(Brazier's Wharf)

Lock Cottage
Br 51 Upper Gambolds
Lock Cottage
Halfway House (PH)
Lock Cottage

Tardebigge Reservoir

The Queen's Head PH

Thompson's Br 47

Stoke Prior

L 29
Br 49
Br 50
Lock Cottage
Br 48

Navigation Inn

L 27
Br 46 Whitford Br
Stoke Pound

Boatyard

L 23 Stoke Wharf
Br 44 Hanbury Rd
Brassington Br 45

Shaw Lane

Stoke Works

Br 43 (Rly)
(Salt Works)
Br 42
Boat & Railway PH

Rly

Astwood Br 41

L 22

L 18 Lock Cottage
Astwood Lane Br 40
(Br 39)

Rly

L 17 (Lock Cottage)
Body Brook culvert

ALONG THE CANAL FROM

TARDEBIGGE NEW WHARF

TO HANBURY WHARF

(Bygones in brackets)

Rly Br 37

Br 38
Summerhill Farm

Br 36

Droitwich Jn
Canal

(Brickworks)

Br 35
Eagle
& Sun PH

B4090 Salt Way

ONE MILE

Hanbury Wharf

Navigations in the United Kingdom" for the year 1898, where the dimensions of Tardebigge Top Lock are given as length 75ft 2in, width 7ft 3in, depth on cill 5ft 4in, and rise 14ft. But the lock was made to replace Woodhouse's lift which was constructed to give a change of level of 12ft, and in fact, as measurements confirm, the lock does give a rise or fall of about this amount.

The duties of the lock-keeper resident at the top lock house in the days of commercial carrying included that of clerk and toll collector. He was expected to check and record the passage of boats, the cargos carried, both their content and weight, and to send in weekly returns. He would also supervise the working of the deep top lock which involved the use of the side pond beside his house which was in use until around 1950. The side pond paddles were dismantled by George Bate in May 1957, but the paddle frame remains. The side pond has recently been cleared to show its features.

Former lock-keepers at the top lock-house include Thomas Lander from around 1839 to 1870, Henry Willmott in the 1870s, William Hill in the 1880s, J H (Henry) Harrison in the 1900s, and William (Joe) Warner from around 1920 to 1955.

FROM TARDEBIGGE TOP LOCK TO UPPER GAMBOLDS

On the off-side of the canal between the top lock and the accommodation bridge is the site of the stone wharf where stone from Dusthouse Quarry, conveyed by horse tramway, was loaded onto canal boats. The accommodation bridge which served the nearby Cherry Trees Farm still retains the telephone line insulator brackets under the arch at each side. It also has its bridge number, 55, with the digits inset in concrete blocks over the archway at each side. It is believed that about 1900 a supply of these blocks of moulded concrete was made to insert into the brickwork of bridges and locks being repaired or rebuilt, and they can be seen below the mitre gates of a number of the locks and on the arches or abutments of some of the bridges.

Also on the off-side, between the accommodation bridge and London Lane, Frisby's brickworks and pottery existed from 1896 to 1912, with a wharf for its boat used for fetching coal and delivering bricks. On the towpath side between London Lane and lock 57 there is the old engine house which was converted into a restaurant and night club, and then, after complaints from local people about the noise and rowdy late-night leavers, was taken over to become a popular restaurant self-styled "Tyler's Lock", a name with no historic or local links. On down the canal the cottage below the towpath, for some years the home of George Bate, was the brickworks cottage. It was there when the canal was constructed and bricks were made from clay dug from the site which was later further excavated to create the reservoir. The lock cottage beside lock 53 was the home of Pat Warner, authoress of the book "Lock-keeper's Daughter". Her father Jack Warner, in addition to being lock-keeper, issued fishing permits for the reservoir which is overlooked by the lock cottage. The appearance of the lock cottage has been transformed by successive non-waterway occupants in recent years. Below lock 54 there is the overflow weir which allows surplus water in the canal to cascade down into the reservoir.

The pound just above lock 50 by Grimley Lane bridge used to be known as the Round Pond and there was a small farm wharf there. The wharf was used in the 1890s and early 1900s by Thomas Frazier and Son of nearby Patchett's Farm. They had a horse boat *John Bull* whose master was the son, Alfred George Frazier, and it was used to take farm produce to Droitwich and Birmingham and bring back manure. Between Grimley Lane and Upper Gambolds is situated the Upper Halfway lock cottage which, because of the lie of the land, was built below the level of the canal. A long-demolished accommodation bridge nearby just below lock 47 gave access to the farmhouse of Hill Farm, also long demolished, on the off-side of the canal. As the remaining bridge abutment is vertical like those of Upper

Gambolds bridge, it must have been a girder bridge. Here was one of the "bathers" where people, mostly children, used to bathe and swim in the canal, using the abutment as a diving platform.

THE HALFWAY HOUSE

Situated beside the canal, and just below lock 43 halfway down the Tardebigge Flight of 30 locks, the Halfway House was for over 130 years a popular venue for boatmen as well as for fishermen and local people. It was also the farm house of a small farm of 26 acres bordering the towpath between Tardebigge Reservoir and the Upper Gambolds road bridge by lock 41. An original house on the site was replaced in 1830 by the present house. Sandstone blocks for the cellar and house foundations came down by canal from Dusthouse Quarry at Tardebigge. Behind the house with its lounge, bar and smokeroom at the front, and living room, kitchen and dairy at the back, was a yard with stables on the canal side and a cowshed and barn on the other side. Beyond the stables a narrow gate in the hedge beside lock 43 provided access from the towpath to the yard and the rear entrance to the pub.

The first farmer-publican was Mark Gibbs. He was a tenant as the land and property were part of the Windsor Estates. He used to breed horses, and many were shipped to America for use during the Civil War of 1861-5. In 1864 Gibbs departed when convicted and sent to prison, it is said, for smuggling merchandise off canal boats. The spirit licence was then removed and thereafter the Halfway House remained an ale and cider house.

The next tenant from 1864 to 1890 was Thomas Sanders whose daughter married William Thompson of Cobley Hill. William was a carpenter and cabinet maker to the Earl of Plymouth and was rewarded for his services by being granted the tenancy of the Halfway House following his father-in-law. William and his wife had three sons of whom the eldest, Thomas, succeeded his father when he died in 1919.

Thomas, known to all as Tommy Thompson, was a blunt man, shortish and with a moustache. He usually wore breeches with polished leather leggings and a jacket. He was married to Beatrice Wormington of Ham Green Farm, Feckenham, in 1919 and they had three sons, Ron, Ken and Douglas. Beatrice's brother James Wormington later moved to Patchett's Farm adjoining the Halfway House land. In 1946 when the Plymouth Estate was sold, the Thompsons bought the Halfway House, and they continued to run the farm and pub until Tommy died in 1963 at the age of 76, when the farm was sold and the licence lapsed. It has since been occupied as a private residence.

Many people have pleasant memories of the Halfway House in the time of Tommy Thompson. In its rural setting beside the canal it attracted many local people including employees of the waggon works and the railway at Aston Fields. Many fishermen came by train from Birmingham to Bromsgrove and walked the one and a half miles up to the Halfway to fish the canal and enjoy the Thompsons' hospitality. Some brought their wives who would call at the house for a quart of tea which cost 6d. whilst their husbands settled down to fish. At 12.00 noon, opening time, they swarmed into the pub yard behind the house, and at 2.00 pm, closing time, it was difficult to get them out.

In the evenings boat people would leave their boats in the nearby pounds or walk down from Tardebigge New Wharf. Donkeys and horses were accommodated in the Halfway stables for 6d. per night. The end stable was known as "the mortuary" because it was used for laying out people drowned in the canal until the undertakers arrived. In 1919 it housed a boat-horse which, after a heart attack, fell into the canal and was drowned, until the knackers arrived.

In the evenings at the Halfway House boat people and local regulars enjoyed convivial get-togethers. To the accompaniment of a mouth organ there was the singing of many favourite songs such as "Irish Eyes" and "Just a Song at Twilight". The nightly contribution of Jack Warner, the reservoir lock-keeper, was "Nellie Dean". In the 1920s and 1930s Jim Bishop from the nearby Halfway lock cottage usually called at the pub when passing by, whether it was open or closed, for a drink round the back of the pub. He was always accompanied by his dog, a bull terrier, which used to fight the Thompsons' terrier "Snooker". When the two dogs got their teeth into each other all hell was let loose, and the only way to part them was to pitch fork them both into the canal.

Altogether the Halfway House was, in its heyday, a busy bustling establishment which, like many other canalside pubs, provided welcome evening cheer for boat people after a hard day's work.

BRAZIER'S WHARF, UPPER GAMBOLDS

The Building firm of J & A Brazier of Bromsgrove, with offices in Worcester Road, was founded around 1860 by Jonathan Brazier, then landlord of the nearby Britannia Inn. Following Jonathan's death in 1895, his two sons John and Albert continued to run the thriving business which built, over a wide area, many public buildings and churches as well as private houses. In 1898 the firm entered into an agreement with the SND Company to rent the land on the off-side of the canal between locks 41 and 42 at Upper Gambolds for a private wharf. There had been a small reservoir at the site, by this time mostly filled in. This Halfway Wharf, as it was called, was used by Braziers until the 1920s for the unloading of bricks, sand, gravel, lime, pipes and other building materials from canal boats, and for their storage until required. Some of these materials were moved by canal boat to canalside wharves which happened to be conveniently near to buildings being erected or extended.

Before they rented the Halfway Wharf, Braziers had obtained most of their red bricks locally, but because the two Bromsgrove brickworks, Frisbys of Sidemoor and Tetleys of Buntsford Hill, had closed down in 1896 and 1898 respectively, they

*A 1908 post-card picture of Brazier's Wharf and the Halfway House. Note the
telegraph poles carrying many Post Office telephone wires, soon to be removed.*

had to get supplies from further afield. The renting of the canal wharf enabled them
to have deliveries by boat from a number of canalside brickworks, including
Wynns of Alvechurch, Frisbys of Tardebigge and Barkers of Worcester. Each of
these firms had their own boats for fetching coal and delivering bricks, as also did
some makers of blue bricks, including Hambletts Ltd. of West Bromwich and the
Ketley Brick Co. of Stourbridge, who supplied Braziers at their wharf.

From 1898 until 1918 the annual rent of the wharf remained at £1 per year and
it then rose to only 25 shillings per year from 1919 to 1924. By renting their own
private wharf Braziers were able to save the wharfage charges levied by the Canal
Company for goods remaining on their public wharves over 24 hours, as well as
saving on transport costs. Security on the wharf seems to have been a very minor
problem. A three-rail oak fence was adequate, and from 1898 to 1916 the local lock-
keeper, Jim Bishop, who lived at the Halfway lock cottage just down the canal,
received an annual Christmas Box of five shillings for keeping an eye on things.

For the early years from 1898 to 1907 there are many entries in Braziers' ledgers
of allowances paid to boatmen of from 1/- to 2/6 for unloading bricks from the
boats. This was strenuous manual labour, thirsty work, and the allowance would, no
doubt, have been mostly spent on beer or cider in the nearby Halfway House.

The Halfway Wharf was used intensively at first, but 1907 saw the first steam
traction engine introduced in the Bromsgrove area by C H Lambe, who, besides being

the licensee of the Mitre Inn, also had an extensive haulage business. Steam traction meant that bricks, hitherto hauled by road in maximum cartloads of 350 by horse, could now be drawn in loads of 2,000 or more over longer distances. Petrol lorries were also appearing by the time of World War 1, and so, as road transport improved, the conveyance of bricks and other building materials by canal steadily declined. This led to the abandonment of the Halfway Wharf by Braziers at the end of 1924.

One of the most unusual jobs undertaken by Braziers was in 1904 when eleven of their craftsmen were engaged in fitting out a special horse-drawn houseboat, the hull of which had been built by George Farrin at his Stoke Prior boatyard. The work involved adding the superstructure, furniture and fittings, including a winebin and a teak running rail round the boat. A forerunner of modern luxury holiday narrowboats, this pioneer craft was 71ft 6in long, 7ft wide, and had a large dining saloon, kitchen, three cabins, boatman's cabin, lavatory etc. All the fittings were of varnished pitch pine. The boat, named the *Riplet*, was intended by its owner, Mr E P Bilbrough of London, to be used on the Thames and possibly on waterways in Ireland and Holland. A report on its launch in the Bromsgrove Messenger stated that "through the courtesy of Mr and Mrs Bilbrough the families of Messrs Hobrough, Shirley, Farrin and J & A Brazier, and a number of friends partook of refreshments, after which the owner complimented the builders on the admirable way in which the whole of the work had been carried out."

BETWEEN UPPER GAMBOLDS AND STOKE POUND

The bridge over the canal at Upper Gambolds is an interesting structure. The roadway is supported by six curved arches of brickwork between seven girders across the canal. Between the brick abutments the road has wooden fencing inside metal railings.

The Halfway lock house facing the pound between locks 40 and 39 has had few structural alterations apart from the early addition of the right hand end containing the store room, the evidence for which can be seen in the brickwork. The lean-to washhouse-cum-brewhouse which used to have a chimney to the boiler is at the left hand end and the outside privy was in the building at the right hand end. The occupier of the cottage since 1984 erected a tall radio mast, being, like his neighbour in the next cottage below the canal between locks 34 and 33 which also has a similar mast, a keen radio ham.

At the mitre-gates end of lock 33 a wooden cantilever bridge gives safe access from the towpath to a footpath across the fields towards the railway. The gap allowed the towrope of animal-drawn boats to pass through. The so-called Stoke Flight Lock Cottage between locks 32 and 31 was in a dilapidated state when purchased by the Landmark Trust in 1991 to let as a holiday cottage. It was carefully restored and vehicle access arranged across farmland to a parking space on the off-side of the canal. It had its first holiday bookings in 1994.

The cantilever footbridge beside the mitre gates (with hydraulic paddle gear) of lock 33, designed to allow the towrope of animal-drawn boats to slip through.

There are two accommodation bridges in this section of canal. Bridge 50, which was in a sad state with a covering of vegetation and its southern parapet broken down, was restored in 2000 by British Waterways with the help of the W/B Canal Society and a donation from the Inland Waterways Association. On its north side an unsightly black 2ft diameter pipe across the canal encloses a water main. Bridge 49 which has a smaller pipe on its south side serves Stoke Court Farm through whose land the canal was cut.

STOKE POUND AND THE QUEEN'S HEAD
The area known as Stoke Pound in which a short stretch of the canal is crossed by country roads at bridges 46, 47 and 48, derives its name, not from a pound of the canal, but, it is believed, from there being there at some time a pound or enclosure where lost and strayed farm animals were impounded.

Now a large restaurant with bar facilities and a spacious car park, the Queen's Head at Stoke Pound started as a small unpretentious shop and pub around 1850. The original brick building beside the canal bridge was actually two semidetached houses, the one next to the canal being the shop and pub and having basement stables for 3 or 4 horses, the other, known as Forge Cottage, being, for many years, the home of blacksmiths who worked in a smithy on the canal wharf. The road

The Queen's Head shop and off-licence and the smithy on Bate's Wharf, 1971, before the smithy was demolished to make way for the extension of the Queen's Head into a licensed restaurant.

frontage, with the two doorways remains basically unaltered, though the old "Queen's Head" inn sign has been replaced.

The first licensee of the "Queen's Head Inn", as it was known at first, was William Yeates who ran it with his wife Elizabeth until 1869. Then John Bate, who had been a blacksmith and licensee of the "Red Lion", Bradley Green, moved with his wife and family to the Queen's Head and he continued to work as a blacksmith, setting up his workshop and forge on the wharf behind the Inn which was long known as Bate's Wharf. During his time there John Bate decided to surrender the public house licence and it became an off-licence. This decision was made in order to protect his children from the bad language used by drinkers in the bar which was situated in the room to the right of the shop entrance.

From 1901 to 1940 the Queen's Head was at first in the hands of Mr and Mrs Ted Harris, then, when Ted died, his son Bob took over assisted by his mother until she died, and then by his wife. From 1941 to 1958, the licensees were Mr and Mrs Knight who continued to run the shop and off-licence. In the meanwhile from 1901 to 1915 the blacksmith living in Forge Cottage was Ernest Clewer. In February 1915 George Bennett and his wife Amelia moved into Forge Cottage from California, Birmingham, where George had been blacksmith at the brickworks beside the Netherton Canal near the entrance to the Lapal Tunnel. George, soon assisted by his son Jack who was aged 13 when they moved, ran the smithy until 1929 when Jack took over and George then assisted for some time. In 1958 the brewery which then owned the Queen's Head, Forge Cottage and the two nearby cottages, put them up for sale and Jack Bennett and his wife Hetty bought the whole property and moved into the Queen's Head. In 1970 the Bennetts sold all four properties to local entrepreneur Malcolm Giles. He was able to recover the wine and spirit licence and to modify and extend the Queen's Head into the canalside restaurant as it is today. In the process of development the old stables were converted into two pleasant bars, but the old smithy was demolished.

Over the years the smithy was used by the various blacksmiths from John Bate to Jack Bennett to shoe the horses of canal boats moored at the wharf. But the bulk of their trade was in the repair of agricultural equipment for local farmers, and in the earlier years this included the skilled work of a wheelwright.

Bridge 47 just below lock 28 is still known as Thompson's Bridge, so named because for over 40 years, from 1859 to 1900, Henry Thompson with his wife and daughter Kitty lived in the house beside the bridge and lock where they kept a general

Whitford bridge with its concrete number blocks embedded in the brick abutment and with its diamond-shaped notice, long removed, prohibiting the passage of heavy vehicles over it. (John Brown)

store. He also ran a coal business, renting part of the Stoke Wharf coalyard. In the 1900s Banner & Tolley ran a bakery at the house. It changed hands in 1910 and the baker then until the 1920s was Roland White. Alf Clisset was shopkeeper there in the 1930s.

At bridge 46, known as Whitford Bridge, the first of the row of cottages beside lock 27 was occupied for many years by boat families, until 1920 by Thomas and Eliza Coleman, and then by their daughter Alice and her husband Dennis Merrell. They were canal carriers for the nearby salt works. The bridge is similar in appearance to no.51 at Upper Gambolds, but the roadway here is entirely supported on a metal girder base. Both the bridge and the adjacent lock are numbered using concrete blocks embedded in the masonry. The lock-keeper for the six locks 23-28 usually lived in one of the three canalside terraced cottages alongside the towpath below Whitford Bridge, the other two being occupied by other canal employees. On a triangular plot of ground by the bridge, now part of a large garden, there used to be a small cottage owned by the Canal Company. It is said that when the canal engineer, W F Hobrough, got to know that there were several women living there made pregnant by the tenant, he ordered it to be filled with straw and burnt down.

STOKE WHARF, STOKE DEPOT AND THE NAVIGATION INN

When the canal was completed it was decided to locate the maintenance depot at Stoke Wharf about halfway between Tardebigge and Diglis, conveniently situated to deal with any problems on this section with its many locks. The necessary land was purchased in 1816 and a blacksmiths' shop, a store for materials and a carpenters' shop were built in that order alongside the canal, followed later by a fitting shop and the dry dock. Access was along the narrow lane parallel to the canal, which led on, past a sawpit on the right-hand side, to the Canal Company's donkey stables and donkey fields. The dry dock, whose entrance is still visible, was filled from the canal and emptied into the small stream which runs at a lower level nearby. The imposing Bridge House was built for W F Hobrough by the SND Company when he was appointed as Engineer of the W/B and Droitwich Canals, as befitted his status and importance and the standard of living he had become used to. It had a coach house and stables, servants' quarters and a smallholding. It replaced the humbler abode of the two previous engineers, George Rew and Richard Boddington. Following the building of the new maintenance depot at Tardebigge in 1909-11, part of the Stoke depot, including the dry dock, continued to be used until the 1920s. After a period of industrial use the dry dock (filled in) and some of the old canal depot buildings have been occupied by the boat building firm of J L Pinder & Son, noted for building the sailing boat *Spirit of Birmingham* in which yachtswoman Lisa Clayton sailed round the world in 1993.

At the old octagonal turnpike toll house (136 Hanbury Road) lived from around 1890 until his death in 1928 John Lewis who was gardener for W F Hobrough and keeper of the Canal Company's donkey fields and stables beyond the depot.

On the wharf, opposite to lock 23, the first house now known as Wharf Cottage was the weighbridge house and toll office. One of the first toll and weighbridge clerks was William Edkins who served from around 1840 until well over the age of 80 in the 1860s. Edward Shirley, who served from 1880 combined his duties as canal agent with running a hay, straw, corn and coal business on the wharf and he continued to deal in these commodities on the wharf after his move to Meadow Bank opposite the Navigation Inn around 1910.

Just before and during World War 1 the toll clerk was William Timbell. His son David who was born there in 1913 remembered his mother attending to the office work, including the issue of donkey tickets, whilst his father was away on war service. He recalled the alarming occasion when, due to some incident higher up the canal, the canal overflowed onto the wharf and the weighbridge house was flooded. He also remembered the Company launch *Little Sabrina* for which his mother made curtains and which was kept cosily in the boathouse beyond the wharf. On one side of the wharf were sheds containing hay etc., and along the wharf was a coal yard. On the canalside a corn warehouse, still there, was in use; it contained an engine which was blamed for causing a blaze which was extinguished by his father and others carrying buckets of water from the canal up the stone steps. William Timbell was the last toll clerk at Stoke Wharf. On returning from war service he was told that due to diminishing trade his job was gone. In 1919 he and his family and their furniture moved by narrowboat to Gloucester where he obtained employment as a docks policeman.

Following the Timbells the next occupants of the Wharf Cottage until 1964 were Mr and Mrs Charles Wedgbrow and their daughter Winnie. Charles Wedgbrow was employed by the Canal Company as a carpenter and chauffeur to the Section Inspector, Frank Rowles. Winnie Wedgbrow kept a well-stocked general store there at the wharf, patronised by boat crews and local people, from about 1927 until 1947.

Back in January 1816, a few weeks after the canal was completed, an application was received from James Hammond to occupy Stoke Prior Wharf. He was allowed to do so on condition that he paid a yearly rent of £25 and agreed to spend at least £100 on buildings to be approved by the Company. Hammond continued to rent the Wharf until 1842/3, the rent being raised to £32 in 1825. He probably built and lived in the house next to the weighbridge house, now known as Wharf House. The canal between lock 23 and lock 24 was, and still is, known as Hammond's Pound.

In the 1840s the Wharf House was rented by John Potter who set up as grocer, beer retailer and coal merchant. His wife Jane assisted, and also their daughter Selina who continued as shopkeeper and beer retailer for many years following the death of her parents until her own death in 1911 at the age of 78. In her later years she was known affectionately as Granny Potter. She wore a hair net, took snuff, and always used a red handkerchief. The next resident of the Wharf House was the canal engineer W T Griffiths who added the glass verandah facing the wharf.

Whilst the maintenance depot was at Stoke Prior, the Company's committee boat was kept in a covered mooring in Hammond's Pound, with, nearby, a convenient winding hole. The boat was named *Harriet*, after W F Hobrough's first wife. It had an iron hull and was steam powered. It was eventually converted into the steam tug *Droitwich*. The last committee boat *Little Sabrina*, with a timber hull built at Farrin's boatyard in 1913, was steam powered at first, then converted to petrol engine; the steam engine is now preserved in Stoke Bruerne Canal Museum.

Along the Hanbury Road, the five houses of Navigation Row were built in 1849 for canal employees, usually a lock-keeper and maintenance men and their families. This terrace probably replaced previous humbler dwellings in the same location, since the Navigation Inn, which was in existence in the 1830s, is sited beyond Navigation Row. Of the many innkeepers over the years, one, Edmund Knight, in the 1870s and 1880s was also a farmer and hay, corn and coal merchant on the wharf and he owned two working boats *Edmund* and *Live and let live*.

THE BOAT AND RAILWAY, STOKE WORKS

Stoke Works is the name of the village which grew with the creation and development of the salt works on both sides of the canal north of Shaw Lane bridge. Soon after the canal was completed a shop and ale house was built on the corner of Shaw Lane by the bridge ready to supply the needs of both boatmen and the workers who arrived in the 1820s to set up and run the new salt works nearby. The premises were soon extended alongside the lane and canal to create a public house, "The Boat Inn", which became a separate establishment. In 1847 the shop, which had living accommodation, a bakehouse and stable, was sold by auction, together with the Boat Inn and other houses and land on both sides of the canal south of Shaw Lane bridge, following the death of the property owner Charles Guise. The sales' particulars described the Boat Inn as "All that substantially built MESSUAGE, now used as A LICENSED PUBLIC HOUSE, comprising good Kitchen, Brewhouse, and Back Kitchen, Bar, and Parlours, five Bed Rooms, and three Attics, with Closets; TWO LARGE CELLARS and VAULT, BOWLING ALLEY, and GARDEN, with all necessary Conveniences, in the occupation of Mr. James Hickman." The shop and public house shared a pump and common access at the rear.

By this time the Birmingham and Gloucester Railway had arrived in 1840, with the Stoke Prior Station situated near the railway bridge over Shaw Lane. When the branch line to Droitwich was opened in 1852, the station was moved to a new location on the branch close to the new bridge over the lane. The novelty of the railway prompted George Francis, the landlord of the Boat Inn in the 1850s, to change its name to "The Boat Inn and Railway Tavern", as it is listed in Billing's

Dixons' new motor-boat Enterprise *at Farrins' Dock, Stoke Works, in 1906.*

Worcester Directory of 1855. But in later directories it reverts to simply "The Boat", perhaps because its customers were chiefly boat people and local salt workers rather than railway users. It was not until the 1900s that it became "The Boat and Railway".

The jovial licensee of the public house in the early 1900s was William Crumpton who, on a postcard picture of himself, wrote: "I live near the water. Pleased to see my friends drop in at any time." He was succeeded by his son Jonah Crumpton who was the licensee during World War 2. Jonah is remembered as being, like his father, short and portly. He was the life and soul of the village, its unofficial mayor, and he had a heart of gold. His wife Jesse, who was tall and slim, kept the pub and its patrons in order and, to the consternation of the local inhabitants, drove a vintage Austin Seven car round the village "in the manner of a Grand Prix driver".

Over the years The Boat has had many licensees and some modifications, but it remains structurally the same, and the bowling alley is still there. The corner shop which continued to serve the village until recent times is now the Bridge Cottage. For many years the shop was kept by a dear old lady, Mrs Moore, who always wore a lace cap, assisted by her daughter-in-law, and they sold home made food, including cooked meat and bread pudding. There was another shop in the village, Hope's, serving as a general store and post-office, which was taken over by J B Wilson and Sons of Bromsgrove and also catered for boat people as well as local customers.

Since the salt works closed in 1972 Stoke Works Village has been transformed. Sagebury Terrace of 56 solidly-built houses, provided by John Corbett for his salt workers and their families, has been replaced by modern residences. Shrubbery Terrace beside the canal, next to The Boat and Railway and opposite to the old school built by Corbett, was also demolished and its site is now a pleasant grassy verge between the lane and the canal.

Further along, Jubilee Terrace of four dwellings, built by John Corbett for his salt workers, has survived, having been recently modernised with added kitchens and bathrooms. The adjacent Butchers Arms public house began as a butcher's shop and off-licence managed by William Reeve in the mid-nineteenth century. It backs onto the canal and, like The Boat and Railway, was patronised by boatmen as well as by villagers. It has recently been converted into four dwellings.

BETWEEN STOKE WORKS AND HANBURY WHARF

The Astwood Flight of six locks extends from lock 22 south of Astwood Lane at the southern end of Stoke Works to lock 17 at the northern end of the Five-mile Pound. A feature of these locks is that the side overflow weir entrances are all under stone edging and a grass verge, and then there is an open-air section where the overflow, before disappearing into a round brick culvert, flows over a little waterfall.

Opposite lock 18 by the bridge on the road between Wychbold and Hanbury is the Astwood Flight lock-keeper's cottage with its well-kept garden on the opposite side of the lock. Between locks 18 and 17 there is a slight narrowing of the canal where there used to be an accommodation bridge. The lower brickwork of the off-side abutment of the bridge remains, as also does the raised farm road to the bridge on the towpath side where the fields are well below the level of the canal. Across the lower entrance to lock 17 there is a wooden plank footbridge with handrails for a footpath which crosses the canal. Beside this lock there used to be on the towpath side a large toll-house which was built at the time of the construction of the Droitwich Junction Canal for the collection of tolls from boats coming down the W/B Canal and onto the Junction Canal and vice-versa. This toll house, which was very isolated and had no nearby road access, was unoccupied, vandalised and demolished in the 1960s.

Along the Five-mile Pound, about 250 yards south of lock no.17, there is an aqueduct over Body Brook which drains the surrounding countryside and has an appreciable flow after heavy rain. The brook passes through a brick culvert well below the level of the canal. On the off-side of the canal there is an overflow which allows surplus flood water in the Five-mile Pound to drain into the brook. Body Brook was chosen as the southern boundary of the section of canal from Tardebigge, with 42 locks, which was the responsibility of John Woodhouse, the contractor, when the waterway was being constructed between Tardebigge and Diglis.

Lock 18 of the Astwood Flight and the lock cottage with its garden across the lock and its notice advertising cups and mugs of tea obtainable there in 1971.

Between lock 17 and Hanbury Wharf the Five-mile Pound is crossed by the former Birmingham and Gloucester Railway near to Summerhill Farm and by the farm's two accommodation bridges. Further along on the towpath side is the site of the former Hanbury Brick Works, now occupied by a refuse disposal depot. Here, where the canal broadens out to form a winding hole, was the wharf where boats which brought coal or transported bricks tied up. Just north of the Hanbury Road bridge the Droitwich Junction Canal joins the W/B Canal.

Chapter 21

ALONG THE CANAL FROM HANBURY WHARF TO THE SEVERN AT DIGLIS

HANBURY WHARF

The wharf is actually situated in the Parish of Hadzor on the south side of the Hanbury Road, the north side being in the Parish of Hanbury. The Canal Company initially built the two semi-detached cottages, nos.1 and 2, facing the canal, also the cottage no.3 and the weighbridge house no.4 along the Hanbury Road. There were stables under nos.1 and 2 and a separate stable block with a hay loft above it was built alongside the bridge approach; the hay loft was demolished many years ago, the remainder more recently. The first occupant of the weighbridge house was the machine clerk John Bolding; he soon moved to Tardebigge. Other cottages were occupied by canal workers, including a wharfinger and a stableman.

First to set up in business on the wharf was William Tredwell who had been one of the contractors for cutting the canal between Offerton and Diglis and who carried out further earth-moving contracts for the Canal Company until the 1830s. In March 1816 he was permitted to build a house on the wharf, not less than 20 yards from the machine house and the warehouse. The substantial house he built just beyond the weighbridge house is known as The Wharf House. Tredwell dealt in coal and had his own boat, being allotted one of the three available boat lengths, the others being for the salt trade. In April 1816 the Canal Company applied on Tredwell's behalf to the Revd. Richard Amphlett, Rector of Hadzor, for permission to open a public house adjoining the wharf. This was refused. But a further recommendation by the Canal Committee in 1822 for Tredwell to open his house "as a common Alehouse - a much needed requirement for the accommodation of Traders on this Canal" was, it seems, successful, for the Wharf House continued to be licensed for many years. By 1850 Tredwell had moved from Hanbury Wharf to Witton and was busy as a railway contractor.

ALONG THE CANAL FROM
HANBURY WHARF TO THE
RIVER SEVERN AT WORCESTER

(Bygones in brackets)

ONE MILE

Up to the time the Droitwich Junction Canal opened in 1854 the wharf was busy with salt arriving by road from Droitwich for dispatch by canal to the Birmingham area, and with coal brought down by canal for carting to Droitwich salt works. Sheds were erected on the wharf for the accommodation of the salt trade. Extra boat lengths were soon needed, and in 1834 the canal arm was made. In 1825 a crane was bought for £65 from Stourport and installed on the wharf mainly for loading logs onto boats for transport to timber yards in the Birmingham area. The conveyance of timber from the Hanbury area by canal continued for many years until around 1940. The crane was dismantled by George Bate in 1950 but the crane tree (now disguised as a lighthouse) remains on the wharf.

When the Birmingham and Gloucester Railway opened in 1840 a station was built, known as Droitwich Road, a few hundred yards along the Hanbury Road from

A working boat is moored near the old stables with hayloft above at Hanbury Wharf c.1960. The remaining post of the old crane was later transformed into a lighthouse. (Colin Scrivener)

the canal wharf. This station continued in use, in the later years only for goods, until the early 1900s, long after the Droitwich Town station opened on the Oxford, Worcester and Wolverhampton Railway in 1851. The Railway Tavern, now The Eagle and Sun, was built in the 1840s to serve both railway and canal users. It was kept in the 1850s by Mary Bourne, then in the 1860s by David Simpson, listed in directories as "innkeeper and barge owner". The name was changed to The Eagle and Sun around 1900. An old stable building remains behind the present modernised public house.

In the 1850s John Bickley and his wife Emma arrived on the wharf. They lived in the Wharf House and he carried on a varied and thriving business as beer retailer and dealer in coal, timber, hay and straw. He also farmed, and he had his own boat in the 1870s and 1880s, the boatman being Benjamin Footman from Tibberton who came to live on the wharf with his wife Emily and their children. By the 1870s the Wharf House was known as The New Inn. The Bickleys continued to live there but the inn was kept from 1870 to 1875 by John Cope, from 1876 to 1891 by Maria Cope, then from 1891 to 1898 by Harold Wyer and his wife Maud, finally in the 1900s by Miss Jane Cope. Until it closed around 1914 The New Inn was, reputedly, more popular amongst boat people than the Railway Tavern.

In 1996 the occupant of the Wharf House, Ian Parsons, in a letter to the W/B Canal Society Magazine "Fifty-Eight", wrote "In the garden there is a large stable with hay loft above and adjoining tack room and there have been other outbuildings in the past. On the wall of the house facing towards the canal is the remains of a sign painted on the brickwork which has been painted over. It measures about 10ft by 5ft and one can just make out the following;

THE NEW INN
FINE SPARKLING
BEERS & ALES
GOOD STABLING
ALES

Remains of previous wordings are also visible."

In the early 1900s the Misses Footman, whose father had been John Bickley's boatman, lived in cottage no.1 on the wharf; they kept shop and looked after the Canal Company's stables by the bridge. Around the 1900s T A Everton of Droitwich, who later took over the Hanbury Brickworks along the canal, sold coal and building materials on the wharf. Until recent years the weighbridge house was known as the Round House because it was semi-circular at the back to make it easier for carts to get round onto the weighbridge at the side of the building. In recent times the rear of the house has been altered to rectangular shape.

Hanbury Wharf today is busy with many pleasure boats moored there and a number of firms providing boat-building and repairs, chandlery and other amenities. Moorings are also available along the short section of the Droitwich Junction Canal above the restored top locks.

FROM HANBURY WHARF TO DUNHAMPSTEAD

Proceeding southwards along this section the first bridge is unique on the W/B Canal being a brick-built footpath bridge only 3 feet wide between the parapets and with steps up each side. It has always been known as the Coffin Bridge, perhaps because coffins were carried over it from Huntingdrop Farm to nearby Hadzor Church. Today it is no longer a footpath crossing; it simply provides access from the towpath to private off-side linear moorings which extend from Hanbury Wharf to well beyond the bridge. Most of these moorings have canalside gardens with huts, garden furniture and washing lines.

Two accommodation bridges, Hadzor Bridge and Hammond's Bridge, both in use, occur before Shernal Green road bridge is reached. Hadzor bridge has its number 33 in concrete blocks above the arches. Along this section the canal is thickly tree-lined on the off-side and tall reeds reduce the navigable width in places.

On Shernal Green road bridge there are rusted remains of weight restriction notice brackets and in some blue corner bricks beside the towpath there are deep grooves caused by the tow ropes of horse-drawn boats over many years. On the off-side of the canal south of the bridge, where now is a garden, there used to be a wharf where roadstone was unloaded and farm produce was picked up for delivery by canal.

On the towpath side as the canal bends round to the right towards Dunhampstead Tunnel there is an extensive wild area, much of it low-lying. This is the site of the basin where from about 1820 to 1850 limestone conveyed by a horse tramway from quarries in the Saleway Farm and Himbleton areas was stacked and loaded onto boats destined for lime-burning kilns beside the canal at Tardebigge and elsewhere. Until the 1980s, when the nearby railway track was realigned, there was a tunnel under the railway embankment through which the horse tramway went.

Dunhampstead Tunnel provides less headroom than the others of the W/B Canal. Its height above water level is only 9ft, compared with Tardebigge 11ft, Shortwood 11½ft, West Hill 12½ft and Edgbaston 13¾ft. This made it possible for animal-drawn boats to be legged through by a legger lying on the roof of a boat cabin. The tunnel was provided with hand rails to enable boats also to be pulled through by hand.

The boatyard arm by the road bridge at Dunhampstead is a fairly recent development. For many years wharves both sides of the bridge on the towpath side were used mainly for the delivery of coal and for loading limestone from quarries and timber from woodlands in the direction of Himbleton.

The Fir Tree Inn between the canal bridge and the railway level crossing has a long history. It is marked on Ebenezer Robins local canal map of 1816 which also shows John Wythes coal wharf by the bridge nearest the inn. In 1968 Alan and June Picken bought the Fir Tree Inn which was then in a run-down state and rebuilt and reestablished it. They also ran a trip boat *Cypress* and a hire boat business from the wharf, together with a little museum/shop in the old forge building opposite, under the business title "Water Folk". The Pickens left Dunhampstead in 1978 to try, against the odds, to resurrect the Coombe Hill Canal before moving on to establish their successful museum and boat business on the Brecon and Abergavenny Canal.

ODDINGLEY

South of Dunhampstead there are two accommodation bridges over the canal marked Lake Bridge and Oddingley No.3 on the 1904 O.S. map. Just before Lake Bridge there is a winding hole. On the west side of the canal between Oddingley no.3 and the road bridge (no.2) there existed from around 1850 until the 1890s the Oddingley brick and tile works with a brick-walled canal wharf and, on the far side away from the canal, a deep claypit. Undulations in the field indicate the position of parts of the works which were demolished around 1900.

The field beside the canal below Oddingley Church and the adjacent house was the location of the first of the two notorious Oddingley murders. On 24 June 1806, before the canal was cut here, the Rector, the Revd. George Parker, who was threatening to raise the tithes, was shot dead in this his field by Richard Hemming who had been hired as assassin by farmer Capt. Samuel Evans of the Church Farm. Hemming was then himself murdered by Evans and an accomplice, but his remains were not discovered until 24 years later when a barn at Netherwood Farm nearby on the east side of the canal was dismantled and the mystery of his disappearance resolved. By this time both his murderers had died and so escaped the gallows.

Along the stretch of canal between accommodation bridge 29 and the road bridge at Tibberton, the waterway runs alongside the railway for a short distance, and a little further on there is an isolated winding hole.

TIBBERTON

The Bridge Inn at Tibberton is an example of an establishment which began as a house adjacent to the canal bridge and canalside wharf whose occupant, described in early county directories as "beer retailer and shopkeeper", supplied boatmen and their families, as well as villagers. The Plough Inn, further up the village street, was already well-established. Then in 1855, for the first time, the canalside shop and off-licence was designated "The Bridge Inn". The licensees in the 1850s to 1870s were James Chambers and his wife, followed later by James Seeney and, in the early 1900s, William Oakley. From 1923 to 1970 the licensees were Mr and Mrs Tandy and from 1970 to 1992, their married daughter Mrs Meigh. Various previous members of the Tandy family had been shopkeepers in Tibberton in the nineteenth century. In the early years of the Tandy's stewardship the Bridge Inn was a typical tavern with its bar, coach house, stables and pigsties. They made their own cider from apples in their orchard, using the cider press at the village blacksmiths. Boatmen stabled their animals free in the stables in return for their custom. Amongst Mrs Meigh's memories is that of boat people collecting snails at the back of the pub and boiling them to eat. In recent times the inn has been much altered; it now has a restaurant and a car park and previous outbuildings have gone. With adjacent canalside moorings, it remains a popular venue for today's boat people.

A short distance along the road from Tibberton Bridge back towards Oddingley, the first house by the canal had a private wharf, known to boatmen as "Footies Wharf". Here for some years before and after 1900 William Footman, his wife and her father Henry Elt ran a coal business using the boat *Fanny* owned by Mary Footman of Stoke Prior. As early as 1816 the Canal Committee minutes refer to a coal wharf at Tibberton, occupied by Mr Featherstone, which could well be the same one.

BETWEEN TIBBERTON AND LOWESMOOR

From Tibberton the canal takes a westward course alongside Foredraught Lane, where at one time there were two alehouses, then on through a delightful wooded cutting and under the M5 Motorway before descending by the six locks of the Offerton Flight towards the outskirts of the City of Worcester. Beside lock no.15 is the Offerton Flight lock cottage, still the home of a lock-keeper whose duties now extend far beyond the Offerton Flight. Between locks 11 and 12 of the flight a concrete bridge for the B4084 road between the M5 roundabout and Martin Hussingtree has long replaced the original brick-built one. Just below the mitre gates of Offerton Bottom Lock No.11 the new tall metal-framed utility footbridge links the rugby football grounds on opposite sides of the canal.

At the A449 trunk road bridge we come to the Worcester City boundary. From here the towpath is well kept with a firm crushed brick surface and is used by many local pedestrians and cyclists. Industrial buildings proliferate on the towpath side as far as Blackpole. Beside lock no.10, Tolladine Lock, there existed a lock house until 1977 when it was quickly demolished after being empty and vandalised. Between Tolladine and Blackpole locks there used to be two accommodation bridges but the one nearest Blackpole road was demolished as recently as 1989, being in a poor state and targeted by vandals.

Between Blackpole Road and the railway bridge Cadbury's Wharf and small warehouse with its canopy, long disused, survive on the off-side of the canal, surrounded by industrial development. Beyond the railway bridge two accommodation bridges give access from the housing estate, mostly screened from the canal by the towpath hedge, to Monarch's Way and the open countryside on the off-side. The lock house beside Bilford lock no.8 has been rebuilt and its occupation is a deterrent to vandals who in recent times have caused damage to the nearby locks. At Bilford there used to be a maintenance depot for the Worcester gang who maintained the canal from Diglis to Hanbury Wharf. The depot was by the winding hole between Bilford Road bridge and lock no.7. Another lock-keeper's cottage which was situated beside Gregory's Mill lock no.6 was demolished in about 1960.

At the bridge just below Gregory's Mill lock no.5 the towpath changes from the eastern to the western side of the canal. The present bridge, constructed like others at around the same time by the SND Company, is supported by steel girders between brick abutments with shallow arches of brickwork between the girders. It replaced a former brick turnover bridge. Looking down from the towpath south of the bridge the Barbourne Brook can be seen. This stream, which used to run from Perdiswell under a bridge on Bilford Road, had a mill leat which supplied water to power Gregory's Mill. The mill was in use until after World War 1 but was eventually demolished.

St. George's Tavern and St. George's Road North Bridge over the canal, Worcester, before road widening involved the building of a replacement public house, The Cavalier, and a new bridge. (WCCHC, G N Hopcroft)

Along the canal north of St. George's Lane bridge and on the opposite side to Worcester City Football Club's ground, was the location of Barker's Patent Brick Works. Beside the canal at St. George's Lane the present public house "The Cavalier" replaced the old St. George's Tavern which was demolished when the new road bridge over the canal was constructed in 1968. The old Tavern had stables where boat animals could be accommodated.

On the towpath side of the canal both sides of bridge 11 (Lansdowne Road) are the sports grounds of Worcester Royal Grammar School. On the off-side, between this bridge and the Rainbow Hill railway bridge over the canal, the rough open land which rises up to Lansdowne Crescent contains some allotments, whilst on the towpath side there are interesting terraces of

Postage stamp, issued in January 1994, showing a Hall Class G.W.R. locomotive pulling a passenger train on Rainbow Hill Bridge over the canal.

late Victorian houses built in the 1890s. The distinctive lofty Rainbow Hill railway bridge over the canal with its two large circular holes in the structure was featured on a postage stamp issued in January 1994.

LOWESMOOR BASIN

It was the hope of the proprietors of the W/B Canal Company, once a decision had been made to construct narrow locks from Tardebigge down to Worcester, that the canal should have four barge locks from the River Severn to allow river traffic, barges and trows, access to a large basin located where the canal is near to the centre of the City on its east side. However, financial constraints together with land acquisition difficulties led to the decision to create instead two Worcester ports, one at Diglis, the other at Lowesmoor, the latter limited to narrowboats. Lowesmoor Basin is so named because its entrance is in the street named Lowesmoor leading from the city centre. Its design, with the two arms and stacking areas off the main basin, was similar to the layout of the Old Wharf of the B.C.N., but less prestigious, being smaller and having a far less imposing entrance and office buildings. Facing the entrance gates from Lowesmoor was the port house, a substantial dwelling (which still survives) together with a machine house and weighing machine (long gone). Until the 1890s the resident manager of the basin was known as the Portmaster, the last such being Samuel Westwood. Opposite the canal entrance to the basin through the towpath bridge there is a large winding hole made to enable boats to turn to enter or to leave the basin.

For the security of boats and merchandise, the basin soon had boundary walls and gates, and also a night watchman with his customary hut and brazier. Initially the Company built two main warehouses of which one was purchased by Pickfords who made Lowesmoor their Worcester base, and the other was available for letting to various traders.

The main commodities arriving at Lowesmoor by canal were coal, corn, hay and straw, timber, and building materials. Over the years a large number of coal merchants had stacking grounds and offices in the port area. Their number rose from around five in 1820 to over twenty by the 1850s. Corn, hay and straw, delivered mainly from canal and riverside farms, were needed for the many horses pulling carts as well as boats before the age of motorised transport, and there were several long-established dealers in these with storehouses at Lowesmoor. Timber and building materials were required in great quantities as industries were established around the Lowesmoor area and intensive housing was built for the workers and their families.

In the early years the main carriers by water based at Lowesmoor and listed in Lewis's Directory of 1820 were Pickfords and James Bromley with their own rented warehouses, Joseph Smith & Sons and Worthington & Co. operating from Bromley's warehouse, Whitehouse and Sons, and Crowley, Lealand and Hicklin. James Bromley was the only locally-based firm; the others were established ones with their main depots elsewhere. Most of them operated regular fly-boat services to places on the canal network countrywide.

The two brothers, James and John Bromley, dominated the Lowesmoor scene for some thirty years until the 1840s. Besides having a warehouse available for the use of several canal-carrying firms and having their own fleet of working boats with a daily schedule of departures for Birmingham, they were also brickmakers and coal merchants. By 1851 they had moved off the wharf and were located nearby, James being in business as beer retailer, hay, straw and coal dealer in Pheasant Street, and John having a coal business in Lowesmoor Terrace.

By 1835 there were two boat-builders with boatyards at Lowesmoor, John Hepwood and George Hill. John Hepwood's business was probably taken over by the latter around 1840, since only George Hill is listed as boat-builder and blacksmith in the 1840s and 1850s. After 1860 the business was in the hands of William Hill, one of the sons of George Hill. The Hill family had other business interests at Lowesmoor, for they were also involved in managing the Navigation Inn and the music hall which replaced it.

There were three public houses serving the boat crews, other workers and traders at Lowesmoor initially. The Boat Inn, located outside the port area along the street towards the City, was established by 1820. It survived over the years at No.17 Lowesmoor until demolished with other properties to make way for the City's inner ring road. There was also the Union Tavern in Lowesmoor amongst the shops and small businesses which sprang up there. The Navigation Inn, first listed in 1822, was built to the right of the port entrance. Its proprietor from the mid 1840s until 1869 was George Hill, already in business in the wharf area as a boat-builder and blacksmith. In 1869 the Navigation Inn was pulled down to make way for the New Worcester Concert Hall. Its proprietor was John Hill, and for twelve years it provided entertainment every evening, one of its most celebrated female artistes being Vesta Tilley who performed as a male impersonator. In 1881 the concert hall closed and it was taken over by the Salvation Army as its Worcester headquarters. From the early 1900s until the 1960s there was the Elephant and Castle public house within the wharf area amongst dwellings on the left hand side through the entrance gates. The Bridge Inn, now situated in Lowesmoor Terrace, used to be on the other side of the road beside the canal facing the gas works.

Following the arrival of the railway at Worcester in 1850, canal transport to and from the City began to decline, and Lowesmoor in particular suffered from the nearby presence of Shrub Hill Station and railway goods yards. By the mid 1850s none of the above-mentioned early canal carriers remained in business at Lowesmoor. To offset this loss the W/B Canal Company had taken advantage of legislation permitting canal companies to run their own carrying businesses and the W/B Canal Carrying Company was formed and based at Lowesmoor. A number of coal dealers continued to use their own boats to bring coal from the collieries to

Lowesmoor, and remaining canal carriers such as Danks, Venn & Sanders, did deliver to the basin. Individual boat owners, Frederick Wagstaff in the 1850s, and Henry Webb in the 1860s, also ran canal carrying businesses based at Lowesmoor.

The steady decline in the use of the dock area for businesses dependent on canal transport meant that space became available there for the establishment of other minor industries. In the 1860s corn merchant George Smith set up a steam mill at the corner of the basin where now are the offices of a boat hire firm. The mill was working until the 1890s.

For many years two main firms of corn merchants had premises and warehouses at Lowesmoor. Needham & Co. occupied the east side of the basin with a grist mill, grain and manure warehouses, stables and offices. The firm was started at Lowesmoor in 1818 by William Bass. It was expanded in the mid-nineteenth century to include a coal and canal-carrying business by his nephew Francis Haywood Needham who was appointed the manager of the W/B Canal Carrying Company whilst it was in existence. As many as a hundred operatives were employed by Needhams around 1900, some making and repairing sacks, tarpaulins, oil cloth and canvas covers for the conveyance of their products to customers over a wide area. The firm specialised in supplying farmers with animal and poultry feeds and with manures for various crops and soils. By the time Needhams closed down around 1930 the canal-carrying side of the business had long ceased.

The other large firm of corn and coal merchants at Lowesmoor was established in 1873 by John Barnett and it became a Limited Company in 1900. The main shop and office, in an imposing building (No.71 Lowesmoor) to the left of the entrance to the canal basin, closed early in 2002. Behind, on the wharf, Barnetts had brick warehouses for their wares, corn, seed, hay and farm feeds. They also had a considerable trade in quality coal brought by canal from various collieries. In their earlier years they made use of canal transport for the import of grain and the delivery of their products. In recent times the firm, which has long had branches elsewhere in Worcester and places around, has given up its coal business. It still deals in corn and animal feeds and now supplies the needs of pet owners and horticulturalists.

Of the many Lowesmoor coal merchants, John Tustin was an interesting character. His father, James Tustin, farmed at Ronkswood, east of Worcester, and in 1822 he was allowed to build a stable on the wharf at Lowesmoor. The Tustins evidently used the wharf for obtaining coal supplies by canal, and by the 1850s and 1860s John Tustin, still living at Ronkswood, had a flourishing business as haulier and coal merchant. He fell in love with the daughter of a wealthy baronet, Sir Henry Wakeman, but hopes of their marriage were soon dashed on the grounds of the incompatibility of class, he being much below her station. Later, to John Tustin was entrusted the task of hauling from Worcester, by means of a team of shire horses, the great statues which had been carved for the fountains of Witley Court for Lord Ward who became the Earl of Dudley.

The demise of Lowesmoor as a port on the canal system continued in the early 1900s, as canal transport dwindled. Some of the businesses in coal and corn remained, but the site suffered increasing dereliction. It did not help when a new business, Butchers' Hide, Skin and Wool Co. Ltd. was set up on the wharf before World War 1 and continued to operate until after World War 2. Skins from animals slaughtered at butchers' shops on Mondays and Tuesdays were brought by lorry to the wharf building to be salted and processed, and the hides, skins and wool were dispatched by road and rail later in the week. The smell in the locality was terrible and there was a profusion of blow flies and maggots, the latter collected by local fishermen for bait. The salt used got impregnated into the stone paving and brickwork, making them damp and unpleasant. With the accumulation of rubbish, rats infested the wharf area. The last major occupier of the derelict basin was Ernest Jackson, coal dealer, carrier and scrap-iron merchant. He had two working boats. Gradually the basin and canal arms were filled with rubbish of all sorts and old cars for scrap were piled high on the wharf between the canal arms.

Around 1970 British Waterways sold the lease of Lowesmoor to a developer, Stennard Harrison. The basin was sealed off by a dam behind the towpath bridge and the arms were filled in to be built over. At this time there was a Worcester City plan to build a river bridge by Pitchcroft with a link road over Lowesmoor basin. In

Lowesmoor Basin in 1967, a scene of dereliction. (Bill Meadows Picture Library)

1972 the W/B Canal Society held a widely publicised and well-supported protest rally of boats on the canal at Lowesmoor to support the Civic Society and other interested parties in their campaign to save and conserve Lowesmoor Basin. Fortunately the new bridge and associated road plans were soon ditched. In the following years the basin was cleared of many tons of rubbish and in 1982 a boat-hire firm, "Viking Afloat", took it over and established offices and a shop in the old mill building. The Elephant and Castle pub and six old cottages at the back of the basin were converted into residential accommodation. The rest of the wharf area was developed to provide premises for workshops and small businesses. There were plans for the former music hall/Salvation Army Citadel with its imposing facade to be transformed into the Vesta Tilley Centre with two floors of shops and other amenities, but the location was unsuitable and the building, now known as Vesta Tilley House, is occupied by a business firm. The old port house at the entrance to the wharf, with its ivy-covered walls and front garden, is now used as the Lowesmoor estate offices.

BETWEEN LOWESMOOR AND DIGLIS BASINS

The canal through Worcester City between Lowesmoor and Diglis has only ever been partially industrialised. Most of the industry was concentrated in the section north of George Street bridge and it included the Gas Works, the Vulcan Iron Works (both sides of the canal) and the City Flour Mills. The former Cromwell Street road bridge has been replaced by an arched concrete footbridge. The brick abutments of the road bridge remain in place, as also do those of the long demolished railway bridge alongside which carried a single rail track over the canal to serve Hill Evans Vinegar Works and the Vulcan Iron Works on the west side of the waterway.

At George Street bridge the towpath crosses from one side of the canal to the other. On the south side of the bridge on the off-side Tom Rice & Sons had a small holding, a house and wharf, being canal carriers and dealers in coal and other items, and on the opposite side of the road there used to be a public house, the New Inn. When the inn and adjacent properties were demolished in 1974, its sign as an alehouse, dating back to 1835, was discovered. The hostelry had stables, and must have supplied the needs of boatmen and their animals for well over a hundred years.

From George Street bridge the canal curves round to the Blockhouse Lock. Behind the lock house across Lock Street is an old building in which boat animals were stabled. This five-horse stable belonged to a former pub "The Lame Dog". Not far from the canal bridge, a little way along Park Street, a building, now "Chapel Court", was built as a Methodist Chapel in the mid-nineteenth century then converted into the Apollo Cinema in 1910 with its projection box overhanging the street outside the window above the entrance. The cinema, if not the chapel, was, no doubt, an attraction to boat families tied up nearby.

Opposite the Blockhouse Lock was Hardy and Padmore's Foundry, and below the lock beside the bridge on the off-side of the canal there used to be a coal wharf. This wharf was used in the late nineteenth century by Richard Dayus and in the early 1900s for many years by John Greenway who had his own boat.

Beside Sidbury lock can be seen the entrance to what was a short canal arm parallel to the lock which was part of the Kings Head Wharf. Here, for some fifty years, licensees of the adjacent King's Head Inn had coal delivered for sale to the public. In the 1840s and 1850s boatbuilders George Glover and Samuel Lee also had a boatyard at Sidbury Wharf.

The King's Head Inn existed long before the canal. After innkeeper William Hodges became insolvent in March 1813, the Kings Head was taken over by Thomas Vaughan from the Coachmaker's Arms who advertised in Berrow's Worcester Journal of 15 April 1813 offering "desirable accommodation for Travellers, Butchers, Gardeners etc., there being a large Yard behind the Inn to receive up to 300 Coaches, Gigs, Waggons or Carts, and having a small Farm adjoining the Inn can accommodate his Friends with Grass for Horses or Cows. N.B. Good Stabling." Thomas Vaughan was an enterprising man who realised the business potential of the canal being constructed alongside his inn, and who, having obtained his own boat, had it ready with a cargo of coal at Tardebigge to be the first to reach Worcester on 4 December 1815 when the waterway officially opened. He it was who created his own wharf and the one boat-length canal arm beside the lock which was mostly filled in 1860 to strengthen the adjacent lock wall which had collapsed. Thomas Vaughan and succeeding innkeepers of the Kings Head were retailers of coal, hay and straw, until around 1870.

On the towpath side of the canal above the lock is the Commandery, founded around the year 1100 as a hospice outside Sidbury Gate catering for wayfarers. It has been involved in various historic events including the Battle of Worcester in 1651. It now houses an interesting museum of local history.

On the off-side of the canal between Sidbury Bridge and the Diglis Basins are the buildings of the Worcester Porcelain Works and, west of Mill Street Bridge, the remains of Townshend's Flour Mill. On the same side, towards the dry dock and occupying a large area were Whilesmith's saw-mills and timberyard, long gone.

DIGLIS BASINS

Of the two basins the one immediately above the two barge locks and facing the lockhouse has long been known as the "outer basin"; the other through the swing bridge beside the old warehouse building being the "inner basin".

Despite the various changes which have taken place over the years to the buildings surrounding the two basins and the transition from a busy commercial port to a quiet haven for river and canal pleasure craft, Diglis has retained many of its historic features. Unlike Gas Street Basin and Lowesmoor Basin where canal arms have been filled in and built over, Diglis has lost little of its navigable water area. Of the two original side ponds to the barge locks between the River and the inner basin, the lower one has long been filled in and concreted over; the other, overgrown and hardly noticeable behind the dry dock, can still be used but there is only occasionally any need to do so. The lockhouse, built in 1816, has been little altered, save for the bow window added by 1869. The adjacent building alongside

A 1961 aerial view of Diglis Basins, showing the old warehouses on the east side of the inner basin (demolished in 1973), the Webb's chemical manure factory's buildings surrounding the canal arm, bottom left, and, along the canal on the left and just before Mill Lane bridge, Townshend's silo and flour mill. (Aerofilms)

the towpath between the locks was the W/B Canal Company's stables, with a hayloft above. It was erected in the 1830s and could accommodate some 14 horses. Two swing bridges, one over the canal at its junction with the River, the other over the connection between the two basins, were necessary from the start. A third was soon needed when the "New Basin" arm was created around 1820. All three have been repaired and renewed at various times. The weighing machine and machine house and office near the road entrance to the basins were erected in 1820. The living quarters provided for the machine clerk seem to have been later incorporated into the adjacent Anchor Inn. The machine house is now used as a chemical closet disposal point.

At the outset the Canal Company gave carriers and traders at Diglis the option of either renting all or part of a company built warehouse or of building their own warehouse. In 1816 Messrs. Tyler and Danks opted to build their own warehouse between the basins close to the swing bridge between them. This robust brick warehouse is still standing. It was occupied for many years by Samuel Danks & Co of Stourport in partnership with other carriers, and it is still known as Danks' warehouse. In 1859 the W/B Canal Company took over the warehouse for use by its own carrying company formed at that time.

Just north of the original Danks Warehouse is another old brick building with a substantial canopy overhanging the basin and a rounded southern corner. This building, latterly in need of extensive repairs and restoration, was built as an extra warehouse by Danks around 1825 and was subsequently let to other firms. It was last used by Mick Wade, marine engineer. Added onto it is a later addition with corrugated iron superstructure. This, on the site of what had been a coal wharf, was constructed by Ratcliffe Tysoe, corn and seed merchants, who acquired the entire building and used the extension as a grist mill. The "Grist Mill Boatyard" has latterly occupied the grist mill premises.

Other early buildings which have survived include the Severn and Canal Carrying Company's large stable block and the attached stableman's house built in 1871. They initially belonged to J.Fellows & Co. who amalgamated with Danks & Co. in 1874 to form the S&CC Company. On the basin side of the stable block is a small brick building, known as the horse hospital, in which sick animals were treated and cared for. The Canal Company's donkeys were kept, when not working, in the so-called donkey meadows alongside the river towpath south of the Diglis basins.

The last ostler to live in the stableman's house at Diglis was Percy Preen from 1937 to 53. He looked after as many as 28 horses belonging to the S&CC Company. A burly man of some 17 stone weight, he was used to dealing with belligerent boatmen when they demanded the use of a particular horse which was already out. He used to cut the horses' hair with a hand-operated Lister horse-trimmer. One interesting feature of the stableman's house is the cast metal brick at one corner with the letters SND on it, indicating ownership by the Sharpness New Docks Company. The building has recently been occupied by MW Marine and by the Grist Mill Boatyard as offices.

Early buildings which have been demolished include four Canal Company warehouses on the east side of the inner basin. First built and ready as the canal opened in December 1815 were two semi-detached warehouses, numbered 1 and 2, at the northern end. These were soon followed by a third one at the southern end, then in 1826 by the fourth between the others. The annual rents per warehouse were fixed at 7½% of the cost of building them. The first applications for warehouse space in the Company's warehouses were from G R Bird, from Gibbins, Small & Co. and from Coleman & Co. G R Bird was granted the whole of No.1 on condition that it was kept as a public warehouse with space available to other carriers. Danks & Co. who wanted the exclusive use of No.2 warehouse were turned down and so applied to build their own. Space in No.2 was let to the other two applicants, with room for other traders. The warehouse at the southern end was rented by the canal carrier William Partridge before being let to Pickfords. The fourth Company warehouse built in 1826 was rented by Hood and Wall, carriers and wharfingers. Of these warehouses No.1 was taken over in 1840 by lead and paint merchants J & H Webb, and No.2 by Evans and Lewis. Both premises were eventually adapted for use as the pickle and sauce factory of Lewis & Co., later Becks. The southern warehouse was vacated by Pickfords in 1847 and taken over a few years later by J.Fellows & Co. followed by their successor the S&CC Company who were still using it in the 1930s. All four old warehouse buildings on the east side of the inner basin were finally occupied by Windshields who made windscreens for road vehicles. They were all demolished in 1973, leaving the site clear for access to pleasure boat moorings.

One facility soon available at Diglis was the dry dock and adjacent boatyard. The dry dock was built in 1817 by Charles Bird & Son who remained in business there for some thirty years. After the death of the father in 1847 the dock was taken over by the Hill brothers who already had a family boat-building business at Lowesmoor. They obtained permission for a house to be built near to the dock for the resident boat-builder Edward Hill and his family. It was known as the Dock Cottage. When the Hills left around 1878, the house and boatyard were taken over by Samuel Lee from Sidbury who lived there with his family and several workmen. He was followed by John and Silas Cotterill in the 1890s and 1900s. The Dock Cottage has long been demolished but the large dry dock, some 30 yards long and 10 yards wide, continues to be used for work on pleasure craft. The modern roof is a replacement for previous ones. The gate to the dock is hinged horizontally at the bottom; it used to be raised manually but is now lifted by a winch. The dock is emptied through a small trapdoor in the corner of the floor nearest the pound between the locks. The trapdoor is hinged horizontally, and when it is raised by a chain, the water flows out through a culvert into the pound.

The long arm, which in the early years was known as the New Basin, provided extra moorings and wharfage for working boats, In 1870 it was leased to Webb's chemical manure factory and partly filled in on the south side to make room for loading bays. Substantial low-built premises, including loading bays, were built each side of the arm and these have not been demolished as was the rest of the factory a few years after it closed in 1912. Soon after Webbs closed down the arm was taken over by boat-builder J H Everton who had been in business on the riverside below Worcester Bridge since 1870. The boatyard eventually closed down in 1979, after it had been carried on by other operators. The arm has in recent years provided secure moorings for several pleasure craft.

Whilst the carrying trade continued at Diglis there were five cranes in use on the wharves, two for the inner basin and three for the outer basin. The only one remaining, but unusable, is of all-metal construction. It is anchored to the wall of what used to be the millwright's warehouse near the Anchor Inn and is in a dilapidated condition.

At first the nearest public house within easy reach of Diglis was the King's Head at Sidbury. In July 1822 the Canal Committee supported Thomas Chandler's application to the magistrates for his new large house to be licensed as a common inn and alehouse. The application was successful and the Albion Inn at the junction of Diglis Road and Bath Road opened to serve the needs of boat crews and trades people at the nearby basins. In the following years a number of auctions of trows, barges and canal boats were held there. The Albion Inn remains in situ.

In 1834 the Canal Committee received a letter from the County coroner about drunken boatmen from a beerhouse on the Company's land at Diglis who had fallen into the water and drowned. The beerhouse had been erected without the knowledge or consent of the Committee, and they decided it should be closed. However, perhaps because it was actually on land belonging not to the Company but to the local landowner, the Revd. Shapland, it survived and by 1838 it had become the Anchor Inn situated beside the entrance to the basins in Diglis Road. Over the years there have been a number of alterations to the building, but the Inn has changed little in character.

For over 25 years following World War 2 the Severn Trow *Spry* lay sunk and resting on the bottom on the south side of the outer basin. With a corrugated-iron canopy, it was used as a workshop and store, until in 1977 the Severn Trow Preservation Society had it pumped and floated and conveyed to Stourport to be restored. It is the last remaining of many sailing barges which used to work on the River and carry cargoes to and from Diglis basins.

Diglis was the venue for a non-event reported in Berrow's Worcester Journal of 23 April 1829. Handbills had been distributed in Worcester "announcing that an agile gentleman would, on Easter Sunday, dance upon a rope extended across the basin of the Canal at Diglis." A great crowd congregated in expectation, but there was no exhibition and the crowd dispersed to the jeers of those who were not "taken in".

When it was originally decided to create basins at Diglis, it was only after it was ascertained that the wharves and warehouses would be above the highest known flood level. However there have been rare occasions when the River Severn has risen to submerge the barge locks and reach the water level of the basins. One instance is recorded by an inscription on the side of the stone coping beside the off-side bottom gate of lock no.2 which against the flood level mark reads FLOOD MAY 1886. Another happened in 1947, when the river boat *Sunrisen* with grain for Townshend's Mill sailed directly from the swollen river into the outer basin.

Today Diglis basins are busy with pleasure boats, mostly occupying long-term moorings. Some 200 boats are laid up there over the winter, including sea-going cruisers, river launches and narrowboats. Visitor short-stay moorings are confined to the towpath side of the canal between the outer basin and Sidbury.

To facilitate the safe and orderly entry of pleasure boats from the river into the first lock, a floating landing stage has been installed downstream of the canal entrance in recent years. Previously great care was needed, especially when the river was fast flowing and unpowered boats were travelling downstream, to hold them and manoeuvre them into the lock. In these circumstances, Eric Rice recalled: "One little acrobatic act I used to have to do was when we got to the entrance to the bottom lock of the W/B Canal from the River at Worcester. As we got there my brother used to steer as close to the bank as he could get; I had the long river shaft and I used to have to carry out a pole jump from the boat to the bank; this was for me to catch the rope ashore and to put the rope eye on the mooring post by the entrance to the lock to stop the boat; then a light line would be thrown to me to haul the boat into the lock. This was a tricky manoeuvre, requiring some skill, and, of course, if you missed, the next stop was Diglis River Lock and weir. However we always did get into the lock okay."

It is to be hoped that recent proposals for residential development of the area around Diglis basins will be restrained so as not to spoil the open vista around the basins and their continued use by both river and canal boats. The remaining older buildings should be preserved and used, some as features of a Worcester heritage waterway visitor attraction.

Chapter 22

THE RECREATIONAL USE OF
THE CANAL AND RESERVOIRS

A lthough created for commercial use, canals have from the beginning provided opportunities for recreational activities, whether boating, fishing, walking or cycling along the towpaths, observation of the wildlife for which they provide an attractive environment, or an appreciation of canal architecture and canal structures.

PLEASURE BOATS ON THE CANAL

We tend to think of pleasure boating on canals as a relatively recent pursuit, but it has taken place from the beginning, and various canal Acts have included regulations on the use of pleasure boats. A common restriction was that such boats should not use the locks in order to conserve water and to avoid interrupting the passage of working boats. This limitation was prescribed in the abortive 1786 Bill for the Worcester Canal from Stourbridge; but there was no reference to pleasure boating in the 1791 Act for the W/B Canal.

On the W/B Canal the long summit level from Gas Street Basin to Tardebigge, with its rural aspect even near the city centre, has long been an attractive stretch of water for pleasure boats, and this was especially so in the 19th century before extensive suburban development took place. Many wealthy business men made their homes in Edgbaston in splendid villas with large gardens, some of them bordering the canal, and some obtained permission from the Canal Company to build boat houses and to use the canal for boating. Some of these boat houses are marked on large scale maps produced in the 1880s and later, and there are interesting references in the Canal Committee minutes to the use of boats for pleasure.

It seems that until 1867 there had been no charge for the use by individuals of their own private pleasure boats on the canal, for in August 1867 the Committee of Works decided "That Notice be given to all parties who have pleasure Boats on this Canal that they will in future be required to take out a Licence for which they will be required to pay £1 per Annum per Boat." It was soon duly recorded that "Notice has been given to the following parties - Messrs J. & T. Davenport, Bath Row - Gibbins Junr., Carpenter Road - Thos. Gilbert, Wheeley's Road - Osborne Junr., Carpenter Road - Messrs. Carter, Lady Wood - James Whitehouse Junr., Selly Oak."

In July 1869 George Cadbury was given permission to erect a boat house on the canal bank for a rent of £1 per annum, an agreement to be drawn up at Mr Cadbury's expense. The following month a Mr Hunt applied for similar permission. Around that time there was some concern on the part of the Committee about the effect of pleasure boats, especially steam-powered boats, upon the banks of the canal, and the Company's engineer, Richard Boddington, was instructed to investigate. He went for a nine-mile trip on Mr Davenport's boat, and was satisfied that no damage would be done. But he had observed a Grand Junction Canal steam trading boat on the canal three years earlier, the wave from which would damage the banks. The Committee resolved "That Messrs. Davenport be informed that they will be permitted to use their Steam Boat upon the Canal on payment of £5.5.0d. per annum until further notice."

Steam pleasure boats were evidently the new "in thing". For, a few months later, in November 1869, Mr Perks applied for permission to place a small steamer on the canal. He was permitted to do so between Birmingham and Tardebigge on payment of 2 guineas per annum and allowed to make a small dock at Selly Oak for his boat. In July 1870 the Company's engineer reported that he had no objection to Mr Perks's steamer working on the canal.

Following the takeover of the W/B Canal by the Gloucester and Sharpness Company in 1774, pleasure boating continued. In 1877 Mr Davenport was allowed reduced charges for the use and moorage of his steamer and permitted to use the locks at and below Tardebigge on payment of the usual lockage fees. New licence fees for pleasure boats were introduced in January 1882, as follows:- "For plying between Birmingham and Tardebigge Upper lock, for Rowing Boats 21/-, for Steam Yachts 42/-", and "an extra charge of 15/- be made on each occasion for passing Tardebigg Upper Lock, such charge to clear the Boat to the Severn either via this or the Droitwich Section. Steam Yachts to be approved by the Company's Engineer before Licences are granted."

The popularity of pleasure boating on the canal is highlighted by a report in the Sunday Mercury of 29 October 1892 describing a carnival organised by the Islington Canoe Club from Birmingham:

"There were pleasure boats going to and fro, all preparing for an afternoon's trip together as far as Kings Norton, and the canal looked, for the time being, like a river at holiday time. The illusion was heightened by a steamer, the Merlin, in the middle distance, getting up steam. Presently a great commotion was seen to take place among the large number of boats collected, and the cause was not long in making itself known, for a second steamer, the Phoenix, was steaming through the bridge under Islington Row. The start was finally made at about three o'clock, when the small boats were taken in tow by the steamers for the purpose of keeping in close proximity during the afternoon."

The flotilla of boats arrived at Kings Norton at about 5.30 pm and the party enjoyed a substantial tea at the Navigation Inn before re-embarking for an illuminated procession of boats back to Birmingham through the cold night air which unfortunately marred the enjoyment of the return journey. Mention of the canoe club is a reminder that canoeing on the canal has been at times a permitted leisure activity.

In 1908 the SND Company decided that no new pleasure boat licences would be issued and that the cost of existing licences would be increased to 31/6 per annum for rowing boats and 3 guineas for motor or steam boats, the latter to be raised after three years to 5 guineas. This decision to limit pleasure boating was evidently made because of the introduction of towing by tug along the summit level at that time. In 1915, summit level towing having ceased, the question of the issue of new licences was reconsidered and it was decided to allow them for pleasure boats to run only on the summit level.

At various times over the years working boats have been used by their owners to convey parties of adults and children on pleasure cruises along the canal. For instance, the Canal Committee in July 1875 granted Palmer & Sons free passage to take the children of St. Asaph's School on a trip on the canal from Birmingham to Kings Norton, and a similar privilege to the children of the Boatmen's Bethel on Worcester Wharf, Birmingham. In 1897 the Committee authorised Mr George to let the Canal Company's committee boat be hired by select parties for pleasure, to be in charge of the Company's men, the inclusive hire charge to be 4 guineas per day; a Board of Trade licence was needed if more than 12 passengers were to be carried. In 1919 an application was received by the Committee for the licensing of a motor boat to carry passengers between Birmingham and Tardebigge; it was decided to issue a licence at the usual fee for pleasure boats but with an additional payment per passenger in addition.

In 1917 Cadburys organised the first of a series of annual educational canal boat trips from Bournville for youths under the age of 18 who were employed there and who were obliged to attend a day continuation school one day a week. Each trip lasted a week and took twenty or more lads who camped at night beside the canal on the outward and return journeys and at their canalside destination. They had lessons about the canals and the surrounding countryside and visited places of interest. At first Cadburys used one of their own boats, Bournville No.6, pulled by two donkeys.

By 1919 the boat was equipped with a temporary wooden superstructure with windows and a canvas roof. Later other boats were used, horse-drawn and then motor-powered. From 1947 to 1959 Charles Ballinger and his wife used their boat *Olive* for these Cadbury school trips which continued for over 40 years.

So pleasure boating, though obviously limited, was a feature on the W/B Canal long before it became popular after World War 2, and pleasure steamers were seen on it long before Norman Terry's *Phoenix* and Pat Ireland's *Lady Disdain* appeared in recent years.

SWIMMING IN THE CANAL

In recent times bathing and swimming in the canal have been officially prohibited by a bye-law of British Waterways. But many older people today have memories of themselves and others as children learning to swim in the canal, and of dangerous feats performed such as swimming through the shorter canal tunnels. We are now much more aware of the danger to health and safety due to the pollution of canal water by motor boats, drainage and rubbish tipped into the canal, as well as the danger of accidental drowning. There used to be, along the length of the canal, popular places for bathing and swimming, such as, in the Tardebigge and Stoke Prior areas, Harris's Bridge upstream from Tardebigge Old Wharf, Brassington Bridge upstream from Stoke Wharf, and the no-longer-existing accommodation bridge upstream from the Halfway House. Many of these locations were known locally as "The Bather".

The accommodation bridge below the top lock at Tardebigge was a very popular location for swimming. Up to around 1950 there was a notice on the bridge "BATHING BRIDGE". In the 1920s and 30s Mr L F Lambert, the agent of the Earl of Plymouth at Hewell Grange, had a wooden hut erected close to this bridge on the off-side of the canal. He taught many young people to swim, using a pole with a belt attached to it, and the hut was used as a changing room. Many people were attracted to the "BATHING BRIDGE" for bathing and swimming, especially at weekends.

Evidently bathing and swimming in the canal were tolerated and not prohibited by the Canal Company in days gone by, but conditions were laid down. For instance, in July 1877 the local inhabitants were given permission to bathe in the canal "between the 1st. and 2nd. locks at Hanbury" provided bathing took place between 9.00 am and 6.00 pm, and a charge of one shilling per annum was made for the use of a "bathing shed" on the Company's land. In June 1895 it was resolved "that bathing will be permitted in future in the canal at all hours, but that no bathing be allowed without bathing drawers being used." The Bromsgrove Messenger of 23 July 1898 carried a report of a 200 yards swimming match in the canal, which was the highlight of a sports day programme organised by the Sick and Dividend Club of the Boat Inn, Stoke Works.

FISHING IN THE CANAL

In the 1791 Act for the making of the W/B Canal, it was stated that Lords of the Manor and other landowners should have fishery rights in those parts of the canal and its associated reservoirs, trenches and sluices to be made over their property, provided there was no obstruction to the passage of boats along the canal and no letting of water out of the canal; also that the landowners should continue their rights to game over their land taken over by the Canal Company. Boatmen and others on boats were prohibited from carrying "any Fishing Net, or other Engine, for taking or destroying Fish or Game", the penalty for infringement being five pounds. The owners of lands upon which canal reservoirs were to be made were entitled to let out the water from such reservoir once every seven years "for the purpose of taking the fish therein, the Water to be taken out in the Month of November, and at no other Time".

It is unlikely that the large landowners would have allowed would-be fishermen, apart from their friends, to fish in their stretch of the canal in the early years, because of the fear of damage and trespass on their estates.

By the early l900s fishing rights on the canal had been leased by landowners, including the Hewell and Corbett estates, to the Severn Fishery Board. On its behalf fishing permits were issued to fishermen by the Canal Company through local lock-keepers.

In recent years the fishing rights over most of the canal have been owned by the Birmingham Angling Association. Its area extends from Blackpole in Worcester to the south end of the West Hill Tunnel, with the exception of a short stretch between bridges 48 and 51 which is leased by BW to Harris Brush Works Angling Club. Worcester and District United Angling Federation have the fishing rights in the City of Worcester from Mill Street Bridge, Diglis, to Blackpole. Several small angling clubs operate in the Birmingham area north of the West Hill Tunnel. All angling clubs pay rent to BW for access to the towpath.

The species of fish in the W/B Canal are those found in most other waterways. They include carp up to 10 lb in weight, bream up to 4 lb, chubb, roach, perch, gudgeon, also goldfish and terrapin as a result of unwanted pet fish being dumped into the canal.

The angling clubs have large memberships and many people turn out to line the canal towpaths for fishing competitions, as well as at other times for individual pleasure.

FISHING AND BOATING AT TARDEBIGGE RESERVOIR

The reservoirs must have been stocked with fish soon after their construction, and fishing in them enjoyed by those permitted to do so by the contiguous landowners in accordance with terms agreed when land for the reservoirs was originally purchased by the Canal Company.

From the Canal Committee minutes we learn that by 1827 Lord Windsor of Hewell Grange owned the land surrounding Tardebigge Reservoir together with the fishing rights. In 1879 the Committee received a complaint from Lord Windsor's agent, Mr Tomson, that the estate had sustained a loss of £20 due to the destruction of fish when the reservoir had been emptied in order to repair the valve at the base of the dam which controlled the release of water into the culvert taking it back down into the canal near to the Halfway House. Perhaps because of this, when the outlet valve needed attention again in the summer of 1933, the reservoir was not emptied; instead a platform was constructed on the bank above and from it a diver was lowered down to repair it. More recently, British Waterways who now own the reservoir have drained it to enable repairs to be carried out to the culvert and the control gear accessed by manholes halfway down and at the base of the massive earth dam. When, on occasions such as this, the reservoir needs to be drained completely, the fish are removed temporarily.

Back in the 1860s the landlord of the Plymouth Arms, Samuel Taylor, rented the fishing rights on Tardebigge Reservoir from the Hewell Estates. In May 1861 a news item in the Bromsgrove Messenger announced: "On Saturday last, Mr.S.Taylor, the energetic Landlord of the Plymouth Arms Hotel, invited a party of friends to inaugurate the launch of a new paddle boat, named the 'Nancy Dawson' which he has built expressly for fishing purposes. She can, however, be used as a pleasure boat. She is beautifully painted and lettered in vermillion, the national colours red, white and blue, encircling her in broad bands." The paddle boat was 15ft long, 9ft wide across the paddle boxes, with three and a half feet clear width across the boat, and took 12 persons, two abreast. There was also a rowing boat. In the summers of 1861 and 1862 Samuel Taylor was advertising excellent fishing and pleasure boats on the 50-acre reservoir, including "Boats upon the most approved principle for the use of anglers and pleasure parties."

For many years Cadburys of Bournville owned the fishing rights on Tardebigge Reservoir, having leased them on 16 June 1914 for the benefit of the Bournville Athletic Club Angling Section. From 1916 until he retired in 1950 the local lock-keeper, Jack Warner, was maintained by Cadburys to look after the reservoir and to act as water bailiff, being paid £3 a year at first, rising in stages to £20 a year. His duties included selling fishing permits to members of the Bournville Angling Club which included others besides Cadburys' employees. He had a punt with oars available for the use of fishermen. Pots of tea and bottles of soft drink could be bought at the lock house. The reservoir was replenished with fresh stocks of fish brought in by road from time to time. At weekends, especially in the summer, the reservoir was a popular resort for fishermen and their families, some of whom camped out beside it.

In the mid 1990s British Waterways, into whose ownership the reservoir had passed, took over the fishing rights of Tardebigge Reservoir following the termination of Cadbury's lease. Since then permits to fish there have been obtainable at a local agency in Aston Fields, Bromsgrove.

THE BITTELL RESERVOIRS; FISHING AND SAILING

Soon after the completion of Upper Bittell Reservoir in 1832 it was reported in the Canal Committee minutes that many applications had been received to fish in it. By this time, July 1840, a Keeper of the Reservoir had already been appointed, living in a cottage built on the south-west side of the reservoir. The Committee decided that fishing there should be restricted to themselves and others in their company, and the Keeper of the Reservoir was informed of this order and expected to enforce it. But the restriction must have soon been relaxed, for in 1844 John Maugham of Barnt Green applied for, and was given, permission to use "Bow nets" there several times a year on the grounds that fish taken by angling were too small to be of any use.

In 1847, the land around Upper Bittell having been acquired by the Hewell Estates, the Hon. Robert Clive, who had married Lady Harriet Windsor, applied for permission to make a drive round the reservoir, to erect a cottage and boat house on the southern bank, and to lease the fishing rights which, in the case of this new reservoir, belonged to the Canal Company and not to the original owners of the land purchased. The lease was agreed at £20 per annum. In 1876 Lord Windsor, through his agent, Mr Tomson, obtained agreement to build a new boat house and to plant trees by the reservoir.

Both Bittell Reservoirs are now owned by British Waterways. Lower Bittell is securely fenced and is leased to Barnt Green Fishing Club for trout fishing. Upper Bittell is leased to Barnt Green Sailing Club and also to Barnt Green Fishing Club for coarse fishing.

THE USE OF COFTON AND LIFFORD RESERVOIRS

As with the Bittell reservoirs, the land around Cofton Reservoir was owned for many years by the Hewell Estates, until it was sold by auction in September 1919. The reservoir was used for fishing and in 1879 the Canal Committee approved an application from Lord Windsor for a boat house there. The fishing rights were, until recently, leased by British Waterways to the West Midlands Transport Fishing Club.

Lifford Reservoir, when no longer needed for supplying water to working mills on the River Rea, was acquired by Birmingham Corporation as a public amenity. For some time, until his death in the 1950s, Samuel Harris hired out pleasure boats on the reservoir and issued fishing permits. Fishing permits have since been available from a local agent.

HARBORNE RESERVOIR

Until its closure and dewatering around 1957, Harborne Reservoir had long been used for pleasure boating and fishing. In the nineteenth century ownership of the Northfield Estate, on part of which the reservoir had been made, passed to Joseph Ledsom and then to his son Goddington Ledsom who, around 1913, leased the remainder of the reservoir land in Harborne Parish. In 1923, or thereabouts, John Philip Monk, whose mother Rebekah had been the reservoir keeper for the Ledsoms, acquired the lease of the reservoir and the fishing rights, and he and his son John Philip Monk junior ran a boat business, hiring out rowing boats, canoes and skiffs and issuing fishing permits, until the reservoir was done away with and the two boat houses, one brick-built and the other wooden, on the south side of the reservoir were demolished.

EELS IN THE CANAL

Soon after the the W/B Canal was completed in 1815, there was inevitably a growing eel population in it, as eels were plentiful in the River Severn. It was accepted that eels were not to be counted as fish and therefore they were exempted from the restrictions which applied to the catching of fish. Eels were caught by boat crews and others, including lock keepers, and were cooked and eaten as a great delicacy.

In the August and September 1972 issues of the W/B Canal Magazine "Fifty-Eight" there appeared an article in two parts by George Bate on fish and eels in the W/B Canal. His memories going back as far as 1908 include the following:

> "When a pound was drained for maintenance work the eels were always caught and sold to the workmen or local inhabitants by auction at the lockside at the end of the day's work. Fish were never sold, always transferred to water in other pounds. On some occasions when a long pound or several pounds were to be de-watered, the Severn Fishery Board would be notified so that they could come and collect and sort the fish.
>
> "When commercial traffic was numerous from Gloucester coming off the River Severn, during the spring tides when elvers (young eels) were coming up river in shoals with the tides, the elvers would adhere closely to the sides of the boats and barges working up into the basins and boats working up the locks. The elvers would drop off at the different locks along the length of the canal, the flushing of water when the paddles were drawn would cause lots to drop off. This process happened many times during the spring of the year, therefore we had a population of eels in the canal in the rural areas. Elvers were not very big, about the size of a small worm, and some so fine as to be no bigger than a piece of cotton thread. It usually takes them 8 to 12 years to grow to maturity and suitable for jellied eels or stewing with parsley and mushrooms (highly delicious.)

"The auction sales of eels caught at repair stoppages got less and less as the eel population diminished with declining commercial traffic, until today there are not many eels to be found in the canal above Stoke Works, and they are few and far between below. Some contamination could account for the scarcity of fish and eels up this way in the Tardebigge flight of locks.

"It always appeared to me that only timber sided boats brought the elvers off river, the oakum seams, hollow tar blisters, and crevices on the sides of timber planking were ideal for clinging to.

"Sometimes when steam tugs were approaching Shortwood Tunnel from Tardebigge, the skipper would stand on the stern-end deck with a long-handled landing net and, as the water receded from the bank side an eel or eels would slide out of holes and the skipper would be ready with the net for the eels to drop into. Also in those days a lot of the boatmen would carry a long-handled gaff or eel-spear trident for the purpose of catching an eel now and then when they fancied one. They could also use a catapult very skillfully in getting a rabbit; in my younger days a lot of the boatmen lived off the waterways and the land each side in the rural areas.

"Lock-keepers in the locks of years ago would catch eels when running off storm water through the paddles from lock to lock right on down to the River Severn, the notable places being Tardebigge top lock, locks nos. 17, 16 (the bottom of the Five-mile Pound and the best place), 10 (Tolladine), 8 (Bilford), 6 (Gregory's Mill), 4 (Blockhouse), and 2 (Diglis). A net on an iron frame with a timber handle long enough to reach up to be tied to the paddle stand post was used. The iron frame, usually made in half-inch round, would lie across the face of the paddle frame; the paddle would then be drawn up fully and any eels going along with the flow of the water would be trapped in the net. When the net was full of eels, the lock-keeper would know because the flow of water would be slowed down owing to the eels and other debris such as water-logged leaves. It would be heavy to pull up with the net extended out; however a lot of eels could be caught by this method, and some of the lock-keepers' cottages had an eel pit at the back to keep the eels in until such time as they could get together with a fishmonger to come and collect them. This was a source of income. Nowadays the canal has had several large weirs constructed and this does away with the water running in heavy rain storms that the lock-keepers and lengthsmen had to contend with, usually at night time."

WILDLIFE ALONG THE CANAL

Besides the fish and eel population of the waterway the W/B Canal and its environs provide habitats for many other creatures including insects such as dragonflies, mammals especially water voles, waterfowl including mostly mallards and swans, but also moorhens and coots, and many birds including kingfishers, herons, and reed-warblers. These creatures are mostly to be seen along the quiet unspoilt stretches of countryside through which the canal passes, away from the urban sprawl of the cities of Birmingham and Worcester. But there is plant life and there are swans and ducks to be seen along the canal in both cities. Unseen on the bottom of the canal are freshwater mussels, and these can often be seen amongst the spoil when the canal is dredged. Along the canal the undersides of bridges and the interiors of tunnels provide habitats for bats, and when bridges are repaired crevices are often left for their occupation.

Due to the presence of mink at various places along the canal, water voles are, as elsewhere in the country, an endangered species, but they are still around in favoured locations where rocky edges to the waterway with nooks and crannies provide protected habitats.

In the spring the hedgerows on both sides of the canal, especially along the Tardebigge lock flight, are a lovely sight with blossom; and later in the summer and autumn there are crab apples, wild damsons, blackberries and elderberries to be found.

Unfortunately the prolific growth of reeds, especially in parts of the Five-mile Pound, has tended to narrow the navigable channel to such an extent that boats are impeded. The reeds are a habitat for birds such as the reed warbler, so dredging and cutting them back are preferable to chemical spraying to destroy them.

The Worcestershire Wildlife Trust, with its headquarters at Smite Farm close to the Oddingley Flight of locks, and British Waterways are both concerned about wildlife conservation along the W/B Canal. There is much to see and, by those with a keen interest and watchful eyes, much enjoyment to be had in observing the wildlife along the waterway.

BOAT BUSINESSES ALONG THE CANAL

With the growth of pleasure boating following World War 2, a number of boat businesses have been established along the canal at various times. These include boat-hire firms, boat builders and repairers, marine engineers and boat chandlers. Over the years some have gone out of business. Others have been taken over or superseded. In the 1970s Hopwood Marina Ltd., located at Hopwood Wharf, offered boat hire, sales and service and the fitting out of boats, until the widening of the main road bridge reduced the size of the wharf and the business closed. The Tolladine Boat Company which also existed in the 1970s, was located at Blackpole Wharf, Worcester, before transferring, for a brief period, to Stoke Wharf. There are now no boat businesses at Hopwood or Blackpole.

Five boat-hire firms remain on the W/B Canal. At Scarfields Wharf, Alvechurch, the Alvechurch Boat Centre established in 1975 replaced an earlier boat-hire firm, Warwickshire Cruisers. The Alvechurch Boat Centre is now an extensive concern. It operates a large fleet of holiday craft for hire, it builds and sells boats and provides full marina services. It created its own canal basin to provide mooring facilities for many craft throughout the year and it now owns other boat businesses elsewhere on the canal system.

Next down the canal is Anglo-Welsh Holidays at Tardebigge Old Wharf. Its premises include the two semi-detached cottages which in earlier days housed a shop and post office. Here, besides holiday boat hire, boats may be hired for a day's cruising on the canal. Anglo-Welsh is the successor to two previous boat businesses there, Tardebigge Boat Company in the 1970s and Dartline in the 1980s and early 1990s. Dartline used to run a 42-seater trip boat for day cruises on the canal.

At Stoke Wharf, just beyond the old warehouse building beside the canal, is one of five Black Prince Holidays hire-boat centres. Their office is located in the warehouse building. Here previously in the 1960s and early 1970s a boat-building and repair business was run by J G A Thornett.

At Dunhampstead, operating from a short private arm on the off-side of the canal beside the road bridge, is Brook Line Holidays with holiday boats for hire. Founded in 1981, the firm took over the canal arm made and used by Alan and June Picken who, under the name "Water Folk", ran day cruises on the Five-mile Pound. The Pickens also developed a little museum and shop in the former smithy on the other side of the canal, as well as owning and running the nearby Fir Tree Inn.

The saving of Lowesmoor Basin from complete abandonment and infilling made possible the establishment there of one of the four hire-boat operating centres of Viking Afloat, the Worcester offices being located in the old mill building in a corner of the basin.

To serve the needs of pleasure boaters there are, in addition to these hire-boat firms, several boat-building and repair businesses and chandleries.

Now occupying buildings which belonged to the old canal maintenance depot south of the road bridge at Stoke Wharf is the boat-building and repair firm of J L Pinder & Son, Marine Engineers, which moved here from premises in Bromsgrove in 1987. They build both sea-going vessels and canal boats and manage the dry docks at Tardebigge New Wharf and Diglis Basins. The entrance to the old dry dock of the Stoke maintenance depot, (the two-boat width dock being filled in and concreted over as part of the workshop floor) is now used as a slipway.

Hanbury Wharf Chandlery and the New Boat Company now dominate what has recently been christened Hanbury Wharf Canal Village, which includes the Eagle and Sun public house and the old wharf cottages. Before the present boat businesses took over there were two previous ones, Ladyline in the 1970s followed by Saraband in th 1980s. The New Boat Company is a boat-building and repair firm.

Whilst there is no hire-boat facility located at Diglis, there has been, for many years, a boat building and repair business located at the Grist Mill Boatyard between the basins, and also a yacht chandlery using, until recently, one of the old Danks' warehouse buildings.

THE STRUCTURES AND HISTORY OF THE CANAL

With ever increasing interest in local history and industrial archaeology, it is to be hoped that the surviving listed structures alongside the W/B Canal will be preserved and that at places such as Tardebigge New Wharf and Diglis there may be established visitor centres where students and the public may be able to learn about the history of the W/B Canal and associated waterways. Interest in our canal heritage is a growing recreational activity for which increased provision needs to be made.

WALKING AND CYCLING ALONG THE TOWPATHS

Following the neglect of W/B Canal towpath maintenance in the 1970s and 1980s, especially along some sections in the countryside such as the Bittell Cutting and the Five-mile Pound south of Hanbury Wharf, the 1990s saw great improvements, especially within the Birmingham and Worcester City boundaries. The towpath is now well maintained by the lock-keepers and other canal employees, and much of it is surfaced with crushed brick. Within the suburbs of Birmingham there used to be, until quite recently, very few access points to the canal towpath; now it is possible to join or leave the towpath at most of the bridges over the canal, as has long been the case elsewhere along the waterway.

Cycling along the towpath, long discouraged, and for which a small annual charge used to be levied for a permit, is now encouraged, a code of conduct being available from BW to promote consideration for walkers, fishermen, and others. Walking the towpath, whether as a means of travel or as a form of recreation, is a peaceful and potentially interesting occupation. A number of brochures are available from BW with details of local walks featuring the towpath and interesting locations along the waterway.

APPENDICES

I. ICE-BREAKING ON THE CANAL

During the 1800s and the 1900s, up to the end of commercial canal carrying following World War 2, there were many winters when the canal was frozen over for long periods. To enable boats to move when the ice was forming or melting and was not too thick, a boat with a strong iron or iron-clad hull was used to break the ice. Following World War 1 the motor tug *Sharpness* was often used for this purpose. Previously, specially-built ice-boats were used. They were open boats pulled by a team of up to ten or twelve horses lent by local farmers. Each had a longitudinal hand-rail to which several warmly-clad canal workers clung as they rocked the boat from side to side as it crushed the ice. It was a spectacular operation, usually attracting a multitude of onlookers.

The horse-drawn ice-boat at Stoke Works c.1950. (B Poultney)

The tunnel tug Sharpness *in use as an ice-breaker. (Birmingham Post and Mail)*

The need for an ice-boat for the W/B Canal is first mentioned in the Committee minutes of July 1807 soon after the waterway opened to Tardebigge Old Wharf a few months earlier. But, because of the expense, no action was taken until October 1810, when it was ordered that the boat which John Woodhouse had obtained for the early trials of his lift should "be prepared as an ice-boat without loss of time." This could not have been very satisfactory, for a year later, after a fruitless advertisement for an ice-boat in Berrow's Worcester Journal, an estimate for a new one was obtained from the Birmingham boat-builder James Taylor. His estimate of £140 for the boat, exclusive of iron sheathing, a costly outlay at a time of financial stringency, caused the acquisition to be postponed until the canal was nearly completed. It was in September 1815 that two ice-boats were ordered from Mr Taylor. These, and others which replaced them over the years, were in use most winters as spells of icy weather often occurred.

II. THE WORCESTER AND BIRMINGHAM CANAL SOCIETY

In 1967 Norman Cox and his wife Doris were bringing their boat *Lulu IV* from Kingswinford to new moorings at Hanbury Wharf when, due to engine trouble, it broke down at Stoke Wharf. Luckily they were able to obtain the assistance of Alan and June Picken whose boat business "Water Folk" was at that time located there. The Coxes enquired of the Pickens whether there was a canal society for the W/B Canal and, on learning that there was none, the four agreed such a society was desirable. Support for the idea was obtained from other local canal enthusiasts and in the Autumn of 1968 fourteen people met at the Crown Inn, Withybed Green. An ad hoc committee was formed and a public inaugural meeting was advertised and held at Parkside School in Bromsgrove on 20 February 1969, attended by 150 people. The guest speaker was one of the founders of the Inland Waterways Association, Robert Aickman, and it was decided to launch the W/B Canal Society. The first general meeting was held at the Boat and Railway Inn, Stoke Works, on 15 April 1969, when officers and a committee were elected and the constitution and rules of the society were agreed. Norman Cox was elected chairman and Marion Thornett secretary and 63 members joined.

The Society has as its aim "To promote the use, care and restoration, as appropriate and necessary, of the Worcester and Birmingham Canal, together with its adjacent waterways including those abandoned or derelict." In the pursuit of its aims the Society has endeavoured to cooperate with the planning departments of the cities of Worcester and Birmingham and the Wychavon and Bromsgrove District Councils, and also with the British Waterways Board and its officials. It has played an important role in improving the state of the W/B Canal, as a pressure group and through working parties. It has also supported the restoration of the Stratford-on-Avon Canal and the Droitwich Canals, and more recently the Lapal Canal restoration project.

Meetings of the Society have been held almost continuously over the years at the Boat and Railway Inn on the first Tuesday of each month, except July and August, usually with a speaker. Boat rallies at locations on the W/B Canal have been organised most years, mainly as social events, but sometimes to promote a cause, as in 1972 at Lowesmoor to campaign for the preservation of the basin, and in 1986 at Selly Oak to encourage the transformation of the Dingle which had long been in a dilapidated state. The society has a library available at meetings and a mobile shop, selling canal items and books both at meetings and various waterway events. The shop, besides raising money, helps to publicise the society. Also organised are an annual dinner, social and fund-raising events, and outings to other waterways and places of interest.

The magazine of the Society, entitled "Fifty-Eight", is published monthly with a combined edition for July/August. It was started in April 1969. Its contents include canal news, reports of meetings and events, correspondence, and articles on canal cruising and canal history.

In 2002 the Society acquired the 70ft narrowboat *Cecilia*, equipped with eight berths and all the usual amenities. It is available to groups of people of all ages with special needs, handicaps or learning difficulties, to enable them to experience the enjoyment and interest of a canal holiday.

Further information about the Society and membership can be obtained from the secretary, c/o the Boat and Railway Inn, Shaw Lane, Stoke Prior, Bromsgrove, Worcs., or via the Society's website: www.wbcs.org.uk

DOCUMENTARY SOURCES

ABBREVIATIONS USED

BRL	Birmingham Central Reference Library
BCCA	Birmingham City Council Archives in BRL
NRO	National Archives (Record Office), Kew
NWM	National Waterways Museum, Gloucester
WBCS	The Worcester and Birmingham Canal Society
WBCS 58	The Worcester and Birmingham Canal Society monthly magazine "Fifty Eight"
WCCHC	Worcestershire County Council History Centre, Trinity Street, Worcester
WRO	Worcestershire Record Office, County Hall, Worcester

The primary sources of historical information throughout the book have been the recorded minutes of the W/B Canal Company and the Sharpness New Docks Company, both kept in the National Record Office at Kew, references RAIL 886 and RAIL 864 respectively; quotations from them are mostly referred to in the text by their date. The dates of quotations from newspapers are also given. The records of Berrow's Worcester Journal and other Worcester newspapers are available in the Worcester Local History Centre, those of the Bromsgrove Messenger in Bromsgrove Public Library, and of Aris's Birmingham Gazette and other Birmingham papers in the Birmingham Central Reference Library.

CHAPTER 1

Relevant minutes in NRO of the Dudley Canal Company, RAIL 824; the Stourbridge Canal Company, RAIL 874; the Birmingham Canal Company, RAIL 810; the Staffs, & Worcs. Canal Company, RAIL 871; and the Droitwich Canal Company, RAIL 822.

House of Commons Journal, Vol.42 (1786), BRL.

House of Lords Journal, 1786, BRL.

"John Snape, Land Surveyor, 1737-1816" (typescript) by A F Fentiman. Copy in Sutton Coldfield Public Library.

CHAPTER 2

Various W/B Canal documents amongst the papers of William Brooke, in WRO, Ref. 705:288.

Snape's plan for the W/B Canal, BRL 910239.

House of Commons Journal, Vol.45 (1790) and Vol.46 (1791), BRL

CHAPTER 3

Many copies exist of the 1791 Act for making and maintaining the W/B Canal; one in WRO 7799/1 Ref.899:1

Josiah Clowes, 1735-1794. Biographical articles by Christopher Lewis in Waterways News, April and May 1978.

CHAPTER 4

The Robins Collection in BCCA MS275 contains many maps relating to the construction of the W/B Canal. Ebenezer Robins was a surveyor employed by the W/B Company at the time.

"Waterways to Stratford" by Charles Hadfield and John Norris, 1962, David & Charles.

CHAPTER 5

Plymouth Estates documents 1803-11 re concern over suspected loss of water to the canal and the consideration of possible legal action, WRO 1188/8(i).

Gloucester and Berkeley Canal Act 1874 (NWM Archives). The second schedule consists of the agreement made in 1873 between the donees of leasing powers under the will of Other Archer, Earl of Plymouth, deceased, and the W/B Canal Company concerning fishing rights and the use of canal water for the Hewell Lakes.

Outrams's Report on the Worcester and Birmingham Canal and Railways, 8 January 1799, together with Observations by the Committee. An original in private hands; a copy in the possession of the author.

Tardebigge Parish Registers re the Hunt Family at the Old Wharf.

CHAPTER 6

"Lives of the Engineers" Vol.2 by S Smiles re John Rennie.

CHAPTER 7

"Canal Inclines and Lifts" by David Tew (Alan Sutton, 1984), for details of other canal lifts.

"A Description of the Patent Perpendicular Lift, erected on the Worcester and Birmingham Canal at Tardebig, near Bromsgrove." by Edward Smith. (W.H.Smith, 1810)

Letter to the Proprietors of the Worcester and Birmingham Canal, with comparative estimates of the expence of lifts and locks and results of the trials of the Lift at Tardebigge, from W.W.Eagle and Geo. Hallen, March 22, 1811 (W/B Canal Society archives).

Patent No.2912 (1806) John Woodhouse. Describes four improvements relative to canals including a double vertical boat lift (no diagrams).

Patent No.3324 (1810) John Woodhouse. Describes two improvements relative to canals including a single vertical boat lift (no diagrams). Details of the lift are based upon that at Tardebigge, but with additional ideas such as a heating system within the building to prevent the water and machinery from freezing up in very cold weather, padded buffer beams on the inside of the paddles of the trough to protect them from damage when struck by boats, and a modified version of the lift for where a canal joins a river, involving a trough with a fixed end next the river and a valve to allow it to fill with water and sink well below river level so that a boat could float into and out of it over the fixed end.

CHAPTER 8

William Crosley. Information in various regional histories of canals published by David and Charles.

CHAPTER 9

A copy of the 1804 Writ of Mandamus, BRL 375174

The Boulton and Watt Collection, BCCA Box 1/11/1-16; correspondence re the proposed pumping engines to raise water from the Severn to the summit level, 1809-10, and correspondence re the pumping engine to raise water from Lower Bittell to Upper Bittell Reservoir, 1836-39.

"The Bittell Waterways System", booklet by Ian Hayes, Lickey Hills Local History Society.

CHAPTER 10

Droitwich Junction Canal Minutes, NRO RAIL 823.

"Proposed Birmingham Ship Canal". 1886 report by Robert Capper for the Committee formed to promote the undertaking. BRL 209885.

"The Birmingham and Bristol Channel Improved Navigation", 1887 pamphlet, BRL.

Collections of newspaper cuttings re canals, 1886-1907, BRL 243972; 1923-33, BRL 1017623; re ship canal schemes.

CHAPTER 11

Coombe Hill Canal Company minutes, Gloucestershire Record Office.

Gloucester and Berkeley Canal Company minutes, NRO RAIL 829

CHAPTER 12

The Gloucester and Berkeley Canal Act 1874. Copy in NWM Archives.

"The Tunnel Tugs *Worcester* and *Birmingham* of the W/B Canal" - an article by Cath
    Turpin in Waterways Journal Vol.7, 2005, The Boat Museum Society, Ellesmere Port.

British Waterways journals for information about administrative organisation
    changes in recent years.

CHAPTER 13

"Stone Blocks and Iron Rails" by Bertram Baxter, 1966, David & Charles.

Birmingham and Gloucester Railway plans in WRO, BA1254.

Birmingham West Suburban Railway, plans etc., 1876, BRL 436226.

CHAPTER 14

Microfilm of parish registers and census records in Worcester Local History
    Centre for information about individuals.

Obituary of W F Hobrough in the Bromsgrove Messenger, 19 Oct 1912. A
    personal housekeeping accounts book in the possession of the author.

Worcester Evening News 1956 re Golden Wedding of Albert Bishop.

CHAPTER 15

Early Birmingham and Worcester Directories in BRL and WCCHC for lists of
    canal carriers and their itineraries.

"Traffic and Transport (Pickford's)" by G L Turnbull, 1979.

George Ryder Bird, Diary of a Wharfinger, BRL 662750.

"A Worcestershire Dynasty (Dixons of Tardebigge)" by Alan White, 1987, Brewin
    Books.

"Working Life on Severn & Canal" compiled by Hugh Conway-Jones, 1990, Alan
    Sutton. Includes reminiscences of working boatmen on the W/B Canal.

CHAPTER 16

Louisa Anne Ryland is featured in "Edgbastonia" February 1889 (monthly
    magazine), BRL 34824; also in an article in the Birmingham Post, 27 Dec. 1988.

"Old Worcester: People and Places" by Bill Gwilliam, 1993, Halfshire Books, re
    the Revd. John Davies.

"Our Canal Population" by George Smith, 1875, Houghton & Co. London.

Canal Boats Registrations:

    Birmingham Sanitary Authority, 1879-1960, BCCA MS316.

    Droitwich Sanitary Authority, 1879-1912, WRO 7526/1 Ref:497

    Worcester, 1917-1956, due to be deposited in the Worcestershire Record Office.

    Gloucester, 1879-1952, Gloucestershire Record Office.

Canal Boats Inspectors' Reports:
  Birmingham, on canal boats, 2 vols., 1912-1943 BCCA MS316.
  Birmingham, Journal of Inspectors, 5 vols., 1934-1957, BRL MS316.
  Droitwich, Journal of Inspector, 1891-1917, WRO 7526/2,
  Worcester, Complaints Book 1892- 1960, WRO.
"The Horse on the Cut" by Donald J Smith, 1982, Patrick Stephens,
  Cambridge.
Report on the Health of the City of Birmingham 1905-6, BRL 194999, contains
  the section on canal boat children.

CHAPTER 17

"The Origin and Early History of the Manufacture of Porcelain at Worcester" by
  R W Binns, 1862 booklet, Deighton and Son.
"History, Topography and Directory of Worcestershire", 1860, Bromsgrove Public
  Library, re Worcester Porcelain Works.
"Chamberlain - Worcester Porcelain, 1788-1852" by G A Godden, 1982, Barrie &
  Jenkins.
Documents, Account books, etc. in the archives of the Dyson Perrins Museum,
  Worcester Porcelain Works.
"Grainger's Worcester Porcelain" by Henry & John Sandon, 1989, Barrie &
  Jenkins.
"The Manufacturing Industries of Worcestershire by W D Curzon, 1881, re Hardy
  & Padmore.
Memory Lane, article by Michael Grundy on Hardy & Padmore, Worcester
  Evening News 4 Feb. 1986.
Birmingham Gas Light and Coke Company. Minute Books in BCCA: Agreements
  with householders and businesses 1818-21, BRL 89163; Enquiry 1871-2, BRL
  390475; Report in Birmingham Daily Post 11 July 1871; Birmingham Gas
  Dept. History, 1923, BRL 663386.
The Worcester Gas Company. Illustrated booklets (1) Inauguration of Extensions,
  1934; (2) to mark the centenary of the Worcester New Gas Light Company
  1846-1946. Both contain historical and descriptive details. Copies supplied by
  British Gas West Midlands, Solihull.
"Worcestershire Salt: A History of Stoke Prior Salt Works" by Alan White, 1996,
  Halfshire Books.
John & E Sturge Ltd., a review of the past hundred years, 1923, BRL 626008
Borough Flour Mills, Birmingham. Birmingham Directories.
Webb's Chemical Works. "The Basins and Canal at Diglis, Worcester", by Pat
  Hughes, typescript report, 1991, for BW and Worcester City Council. Article in
  Littlebury's Directory for 1873, page 810.

Townshend's Mill. Article in WBCS 58, March 1988, by Alan White.

The Queen's Hospital, Birmingham. "The Making of Birmingham" by Robert K Dent, 1894, Allday. Also hospital newspaper cuttings files in BRL Local History Dept.

CHAPTER 18

"Bricks and Brickmaking" by Martin Hammond, Shire Publications Ltd. A description of Barker's Brick Works in Littlebury's Directory of Worcester, 1873. "The Alvechurch Brick Company" by Harold Fenn, 1984, typescript, Alvechurch Historical Society. Frisby's Brickworks, article in WBCS 58, December 1985, by Alan White.

Cadbury Brothers. Articles by Stanley Holland in Waterways News: Centenary at Bournville, August and September 1979; Waterside - the end of an era, February 1981; Farewell to Frampton, May 1982.

"George Cadbury 1839-1922" by Walter Stranz, 1973 (Shire Publications Ltd.)

"The Firm of Cadbury, 1831-1931" by I A Williams, 1931 (Constable & Co. Ltd.)

Davenport's Brewery. "Fifty Years of Progress" (Souvenir Book), 1935. 1984 short typescript history received from firm.

Kings Norton Paper Mill. Article in WBCS 58 September 1990 by Alan White.

City Flour Mills, Worcester. Article in Worcester Evening News when the mill closed for demolition, 22 February 1972.

Vulcan Iron Works (McKenzie & Holland). Section in the Worcester Daily Times Trade and Industrial Edition, "Worcester at Work", 1903, WCCHC L609.42448. Two-part article by Ralph Dunham in Newsletters Nos. 18 and 19 of the Worcester Industrial Archaeology and Local History Society based on a talk given by Edward Dorricot on Samuel Telford Dutton.

Elliott's Metal Works. Article in WBCS 58, June 1988, by Alan White.

Nettlefold & Chamberlain's Screw Factory, Breedon Cross. Brief history in "Images of Stirchley" by Linda Chew. Copy in Stirchley Public Library.

"Birmingham Battery & Metal Works 1836-1936", BRL 453183.

Patent Enamel Works, Selly Oak. Article in WBCS 58, January 1990, by Alan White.

"The Kings Norton Metal Company Limited" by Richard Chadwick, 1985, typescript notes supplied by him.

CHAPTER 19

"A Gas Street Trail" by Ray Shill, 1994, Heartland Press.

The Plymouth Arms, Tardebigge, Article in WBCS 58, May 1989, by Alan White.

CHAPTER 20

Parish records and census returns in WCCHC for information about lock-keepers and other individuals.

"Lock-keeper's Daughter" by Pat Warner, 1986, Shepperton Swan.

The Halfway House. Articles in WBCS 58, February and March 1986, by Alan White.

Braziers Wharf. Articles in WBCS 58, February and March 1987, by Alan White.

Copy of 1847 Sales particulars of Boat Inn etc., in W/B Canal Society archives.

CHAPTER 21

Worcestershire directories for information about individuals at Hanbury Wharf, Tibberton, Lowesmoor.

"Old Worcester People and Places" by Bill Gwilliam, 1993, Halfshire Books, re Lowesmoor's portmaster, James Tustin and Vesta Tilley.

"The Basins and Canal at Diglis" by Pat Hughes, 1991, Report for BW and Worcester City Council.

CHAPTER 22

Nicholson's Guide to the Waterways No.2, Severn, Avon and Birmingham, contains a guide to the W/B Canal, pubs, restaurants, boatyards and places of interest along the waterway from Worcester to Birmingham.

"Walking the Waterways". A series of folders of circular walks from various locations on the canals, including Kings Norton and Tardebigge. Available from BW.

Walking over the tunnels. Leaflets showing the walking routes over the West Hill, Shortwood and Tardebigge Tunnels. Available from BW.

INDEX

Malt Shovel, Selly Oak, 311
King's Head, Worcester, 272, 357, 361
Navigation, Kings Norton, 314, 365
Navigation, Lowesmoor, 353
Navigation, Stoke Prior, 340
Navigation, Tardebigge, 63, 81, 244, 320, 321
New Inn, Hanbury Wharf, 346, 347
New Inn, Worcester, 290, 356
Plymouth Arms, Tardebigge, 71, 102, 121, 244, 245, 321, 325-327, 368
Queen's Head, Stoke Pound, 200, 335-337
St. George's Tavern, Worcester, 278, 351
Union Tavern, Lowesmoor, 353

Q
Quarries:
Dusthouse, 70, 72, 73, 175, 176, 182, 323, 330, 331
Limestone, 176-178, 197, 348
Tardebigge Church, 72, 133, 175, 323
Queen's Hospital, 275, 308

R
Railways:
Birmingham & Gloucester, 138, 151-153, 177-181, 188, 190, 192, 217, 266, 313, 340, 343, 345
Birmingham & Worcester Direct, 153, 176, 181-183, 197
Birmingham and West Suburban, 155, 185-189, 282, 296, 311, 312
London & North Western, 154
Midland Railway, 152.155, 157, 181, 184, 186, 188-191, 242, 293, 297, 307, 312
Oxford, Worcester & Wolverhampton, 138, 140, 153, 154, 180, 181, 183, 184, 267, 291, 346

Redditch, 184
West Birmingham, 154, 184, 185
Worcester & Hereford, 184
Rammill, Thomas, 209
Reachill, George, 183, 313
Rennie, John, 66, 67, 75, 77, 82-87, 89, 93, 103, 115-117
Reservoirs:
Cofton, 13, 65, 68, 109, 114, 118, 122, 125-127, 205, 369
Harborne, 13, 65, 109, 111, 126, 309, 370
Lifford, 13, 65, 68, 109, 113, 126, 369
Lower Bittell, 13, 57, 59, 65, 68, 96, 109, 111, 112, 122, 124-127, 175, 205, 316, 369
Tardebigge, 119-122, 125-127, 200, 330, 367-369
Upper Bittell, 122-127, 205, 369
Wychall, 13, 65, 100, 108-111, 117, 118, 125-127, 315
Rew, George, 97, 99, 101, 120-122, 126, 129, 137, 174, 177, 196, 197, 338
Rice, Jacob & Son, 226
Rice, Thomas & Sons, 229, 231, 232, 259, 274, 356, 362
Roberts, W A, 6, 7, 10, 13, 14, 24, 53, 107, 138
Robins, Ebenezer, 130, 131
Robinson, Corbet & Co., 216
Rolt, L T C, 211, 232, 324, 325, 328
Rowlands, Richard, 105, 200
Rowles, Frank, 161, 162, 199, 322, 339
Russell, May, 263
Ryland, Louisa Anne, 241, 242

S
Salt Works, 151, 165, 175, 184, 190, 226, 245, 248, 263-269, 338, 340, 342, 345

Worcester and Birminghar

MILEAGES from place to place, and Tolls and Charges leviable, as enacted by No. 3 (C

Junction with the Birmingham Canal ...	0 Junction with the Birmingham Canal.										
Granville St. Bridge and intermediate places	½ Granville St. Bridge and intermediate places.										
Davenport's Brewery	½ 0 Davenport's Brewery.										
Sturge's and Bloxham's Wharves	¾ ¼ ¼	Sturge's and Bloxham's Wharves.									
Edgbaston Brewery	1¼ ¾ ¾	½ Edgbaston Brewery.									
Islington and Wheeley's Road Wharves ...	1¼ ¾ ¾	½ 0 Islington and Wheeley's Road Wharves.									
Stop Gates, Worcester end of Edgbaston Valley	2¾ 2¼ 2¼	2 1½ 1½	Stop Gates, Worcester end of Edgbaston Valley.								
Pritchett's Wharf	3½ 3 3	2¾ 2¼ 2¼	¾ Pritchett's Wharf.								
Metchley Park Tip	3¾ 3¼ 3¼	3 2½ 2½	1 ¼ Metchley Park Tip.								
Kirby's Pool Tip	4¼ 3¾ 3¾	3½ 3 3	1½ ¾ ½	Kirby's Pool Tip.							
Selly Oak Wharves	4½ 4 4	3¾ 3¼ 3¼	1¾ 1 ¾	¼ Selly Oak Wharves.							
Netherton Canal	4½ 4 4	3¾ 3¼ 3¼	1¾ 1 ¾	¼ 0 Netherton Canal.							
Elliott's, Hudson's, and Enamel Works ...	5 4½ 4½	4¼ 3¾ 3¾	2¼ 1½ 1¼	¾ ½ ½	Elliott's, Hudson's, and Enamel Works.						
Stirchley Street Tip	6 5½ 5½	5¼ 4¾ 4¾	3¼ 2½ 2¼	1¾ 1½ 1½	1 Stirchley Street Tip.						
Cadbury's, Sparrey's, and Prescott's Wharves	6½ 6 6	5¾ 5¼ 5¼	3¾ 3 2¾	2¼ 2 2	1½ ½ Cadbury's, Sparrey's, and Prescott's Wharves.						
Endurance Tube &c. Company's Works ...	6½ 6 6	5¾ 5¼ 5¼	3¾ 3 2¾	2¼ 2 2	1½ ½ 0	Endurance Tube &c. Company's Works.					
Nettlefold's and Breedon Cross Wharf ...	7¼ 6¾ 6¾	6½ 6 6	4½ 3¾ 3½	3 2¾ 2¾	2¼ 1¼ ¾	¾ Nettlefold's and Breedon Cross Wharf.					
Vale's Timber Yard & Lifford Goods Station	7¼ 6¾ 6¾	6½ 6 6	4½ 3¾ 3½	3 2¾ 2¾	2¼ 1¼ ¾	¾ 0 Vale's Timber Yard and Lifford Goods					
Kings Norton Sanitary Authority's Wharf ...	7½ 7 7	6¾ 6¼ 6¼	4¾ 4 3¾	3¼ 3 3	2½ 1½ 1	1 ¼ ¼	Kings Norton Sanitary Authority				
Kings Norton Metal Company's Works ...	8 7½ 7½	7¼ 6¾ 6¾	5¼ 4½ 4¼	3¾ 3½ 3½	3 2 1½	1½ ¾ ¾	½ Kings Norton Metal Company				
Baldwin's Works	8 7½ 7½	7¼ 6¾ 6¾	5¼ 4½ 4¼	3¾ 3½ 3½	3 2 1½	1½ ¾ ¾	½ 0 Baldwin's Works.				
Stratford-on-Avon Canal	8¼ 7¾ 7¾	7½ 7 7	5¼ 4¾ 4½	4 3¾ 3¾	3¼ 2¼ 1¾	1¾ 1 1	¾ ¼ ¼	Stratford-on-Avon Ca			
Kings Norton Wharves	8¾ 8¼ 8¼	8 7½ 7½	6 5¼ 5	4¼ 4¼ 4¼	3¾ 2¾ 2¼	2¼ 1½ 1½	1¼ ¾ ¾	½ Kings Norton Wha			
Kings Norton Tunnel Tug Coal Shed ...	9¼ 8¾ 8¾	8½ 8 8	6½ 5¾ 5½	5 4¾ 4¾	4¼ 3¼ 2¾	2¾ 2 2	1¾ 1¼ 1¼	1 ½ Kings Norton T			
Hopwood Wharf	11¾ 11¼ 11¼	11 10½ 10½	9 8¼ 8	7½ 7¼ 7¼	6¾ 5¾ 5¼	5¼ 4½ 4½	4¼ 3¾ 3¾	3½ 3 2½	Hopwood W		
Bittall Arm	12½ 12 12	11¾ 11¼ 11¼	9¾ 9 8¾	8¼ 8 8	7½ 6½ 6	6 5¼ 5¼	5 4½ 4½	4¼ 3¾ 3¼	¾ Bittall		
Bittall Arm Wharf	13 12½ 12½	12¼ 11¾ 11¾	10¼ 9½ 9¼	8¾ 8½ 8½	8 7 6½	6½ 5¾ 5¾	5½ 5 5	4¾ 4¼ 3¾	1¼ ½ Bitta		
Bittall Arm	12½ 12 12	11¾ 11¼ 11¼	9¾ 9 8¾	8¼ 8 8	7½ 6½ 6	6 5¼ 5¼	5 4½ 4½	4¼ 3¾ 3¼	¾ 0 ½	I	
Bittall Wharf	12¾ 12¼ 12¼	12 11½ 11½	10 9¼ 9	8½ 8¼ 8¼	7¾ 6¾ 6¼	6¼ 5½ 5½	5¼ 4¾ 4¾	4½ 4 3½	1 ¼ ¾		
Lane House Wharf	13 12½ 12½	12¼ 11¾ 11¾	10¼ 9½ 9¼	8¾ 8½ 8½	8 7 6½	6½ 5¾ 5¾	5½ 5 5	4¾ 4¼ 3¾	1¼ ½ 1		
Cooper's Hill Wharf	13½ 13 13	12¾ 12¼ 12¼	10¾ 10 9¾	9¼ 9 9	8½ 7½ 7	7 6¼ 6¼	6 5½ 5½	5¼ 4¾ 4¼	1¾ 1 1½		1
Withybed Green	13¾ 13¼ 13¼	13 12½ 12½	11 10¼ 10	9½ 9¼ 9¼	8¾ 7¾ 7¼	7¼ 6½ 6½	6¼ 5¾ 5¾	5½ 5 4½	2 1¼ 1¾		1
Wynn's Brick Works	14 13½ 13½	13¼ 12¾ 12¾	11¼ 10½ 10¼	9¾ 9½ 9½	9 8 7½	7½ 6¾ 6¾	6½ 6 6	5¾ 5¼ 4¾	2¼ 1½ 2		[illegible]
Scarfield's Wharf	14 13½ 13½	13¼ 12¾ 12¾	11¼ 10½ 10¼	9¾ 9½ 9½	9 8 7½	7½ 6¾ 6¾	6½ 6 6	5¾ 5¼ 4¾	2¼ 1½ 2		1
Grange Wharf	14¾ 14¼ 14¼	14 13½ 13½	12 11¼ 11	10½ 10¼ 10¼	9¾ 8¾ 8¼	8¼ 7½ 7½	7¼ 6¾ 6¾	6½ 6 5½	3 2¼ 2¾		2
Shortwood Tunnel Wharf	15¼ 14¾ 14¾	14½ 14 14	12½ 11¾ 11½	11 10¾ 10¾	10¼ 9¼ 8¾	8¾ 8 8	7¾ 7¼ 7¼	7 6½ 6	3½ 2¾ 3¼		2
Harris' Bridge	15¾ 15¼ 15¼	15 14½ 14½	13 12¼ 12	11½ 11¼ 11¼	10¾ 9¾ 9¼	9¼ 8½ 8½	8¼ 7¾ 7¾	7½ 7 6½	4 3¼ 3¾		3
Tardebigge Old Wharf	16¼ 15¾ 15¾	15½ 15 15	13½ 12¾ 12½	12 11¾ 11¾	11¼ 10¼ 9¾	9¾ 9 9	8¾ 8¼ 8¼	8 7½ 7	4½ 3¾ 4¼		3
Tardebigge Crane	16½ 16 16	15¾ 15¼ 15¼	13¾ 13 12¾	12¼ 12 12	12½ 10½ 10	10 9¼ 9¼	9 8½ 8½	8¼ 7¾ 7¼	4¾ 4 4½		4
Tardebigge New Wharf	17 16½ 16½	16¼ 15¾ 15¾	14¼ 13½ 13¼	12¾ 12½ 12½	12 11 10½	10½ 9¾ 9¾	9½ 9 9	8¾ 8¼ 7¾	5¼ 4½ 5		4
London Lane and Engine House ...	17½ 17 17	16¾ 16¼ 16¼	14¾ 14 13¾	13¼ 13 13	12½ 11½ 11	11 10¼ 10¼	10 9½ 9½	9¼ 8¾ 8¼	5¾ 5 5½		5
Round Pond	18 17½ 17½	17¼ 16¾ 16¾	15¼ 14½ 14¼	13¾ 13½ 13½	13 12 11½	11½ 10¾ 10¾	10½ 10 10	9¾ 9¼ 8¾	6¼ 5½ 6		5
Half-way House Bridge	18¼ 17¾ 17¾	17½ 17 17	15½ 14¾ 14½	14 13¾ 13¾	13¼ 12¼ 11¾	11¾ 11 11	10¾ 10¼ 10¼	10 9½ 9	6½ 5¾ 6¼		5
Bates' Wharf	19¼ 18¾ 18¾	18½ 18 18	16½ 15¾ 15½	15 14¾ 14¼	14¼ 13¼ 12¾	12¾ 12 12	11¾ 11¼ 11¼	11 10½ 10	7½ 6¾ 7¼		6
Thompson's House	19½ 19 19	18¾ 18¼ 18¼	16¾ 16 15¾	15¼ 15 15	14½ 13½ 13	13 12¼ 12¼	12 11½ 11½	11¼ 10¾ 10¼	7¾ 7 7½		7
Stoke Wharf	20¼ 19¾ 19¾	19½ 19 19	17½ 16¾ 16½	16 15¾ 15¾	15¼ 14¼ 13¾	13¾ 13 13	12¾ 12¼ 12¼	12 11½ 11	8½ 7¾ 8¼		7
Stoke Works Central	21 20½ 20½	20¼ 19¾ 19¾	18¼ 17½ 17¼	16¾ 16½ 16½	16 15 14½	14½ 13¾ 13¾	13½ 13 13	12¾ 12¼ 11¾	9¼ 8½ 9		8
Gittus Mill	21¼ 20¾ 20¾	20½ 20 20	18½ 17¾ 17½	17 16¾ 16¾	16¼ 15¼ 14¾	14¾ 14 14	13¾ 13¼ 13¼	13 12½ 12	9½ 8¾ 9¼		8
Pastoral to	22¾ 22¼ 22¼	22 21½ 21½	20 19¼ 19	18½ 18¼ 18¼	17¾ 16¾ 16¼	16¼ 15½ 15½	15¼ 14¾ 14¾	14½ 14 13½	11 10¼ 10¾		10
Groves' Brick Works	23½ 23 23	22¾ 22¼ 22¼	20¾ 20 19¾	19¼ 19 19	18½ 17½ 17	17 16¼ 16¼	16 15½ 15½	15¼ 14¾ 14¼	11¾ 11 11½		11
Droitwich Junction Canal	23¾ 23¼ 23¼	23 22½ 22½	21 20¼ 20	19½ 19¼ 19¼	18¾ 17¾ 17¼	17¼ 16½ 16½	16¼ 15¾ 15¾	15½ 15 14½	12 11¼ 11¾		11
Hanbury Wharf	23¾ 23¼ 23¼	23 22½ 22½	21 20¼ 20	19½ 19¼ 19¼	18¾ 17¾ 17¼	17¼ 16½ 16½	16¼ 15¾ 15¾	15½ 15 14½	12 11¼ 11¾		11
Hadzor Wharf	24¼ 23¾ 23¾	23½ 23 23	21½ 20¾ 20½	20 19¾ 19¾	19¼ 18¼ 17¾	17¾ 17 17	16¾ 16¼ 16¼	16 15½ 15	12½ 11¾ 12¼		11
Dunhampstead (Old Tramway Wharf) ...	25¼ 24¾ 24¾	24½ 24 24	22½ 21¾ 21½	21 20¾ 20¾	20¼ 19¼ 18¾	18¾ 18 18	17¾ 17¼ 17¼	17 16½ 16	13½ 12¾ 13¼		12
Dunhampstead Wharf	25½ 25 25	24¾ 24¼ 24¼	22¾ 22 21¾	21¼ 21 21	20½ 19½ 19	19 18¼ 18¼	18 17½ 17½	17¼ 16¾ 16¼	13¾ 13 13½		13
Oddingley Brick Works	26¼ 25¾ 25¾	25½ 25 25	23½ 22¾ 22½	22 21¾ 21¾	21¼ 20¼ 19¾	19¾ 19 19	18¾ 18¼ 18¼	18 17½ 17	14½ 13¾ 14¼		13
Tibberton Wharf	27¼ 26¾ 26¾	26½ 26 26	24½ 23¾ 23½	23 22¾ 22¾	22¼ 21¼ 20¾	20¾ 20 20	19¾ 19¼ 19¼	19 18½ 18	15½ 14¾ 15¼		14
Hindlip Wharf	28¼ 27¾ 27¾	27½ 27 27	25½ 24¾ 24½	24 23¾ 23¾	23¼ 22¼ 21¾	21¾ 21 21	20¾ 20¼ 20¼	20 19½ 19	16½ 15¾ 16¼		15
Tolladine Private Wharf	29 28½ 28½	28¼ 27¾ 27¾	26¼ 25½ 25¼	24¾ 24½ 24½	24 23 22½	22½ 21¾ 21¾	21½ 21 21	20¾ 20¼ 19¾	17¼ 16½ 17		16
Blackpole Wharf	29¾ 29¼ 29¼	29 28½ 28½	27 26¼ 26	25½ 25¼ 25¼	24¾ 23¾ 23¼	23¼ 22½ 22½	22¼ 21¾ 21¾	21½ 21 20½	18 17¼ 17¾		17
Bilford Bridge	30¾ 30¼ 30¼	30 29½ 29½	28 27¼ 27	26½ 26¼ 26¼	25¾ 24¾ 24¼	24¼ 23½ 23½	23¼ 22¾ 22¾	22½ 22 21½	19 18¼ 18¾		18
Gregory's Mill	31 30½ 30½	30¼ 29¾ 29¾	28¼ 27½ 27¼	26¾ 26½ 26½	26 25 24½	24½ 23¾ 23¾	23½ 23 23	22¾ 22¼ 21¾	19¼ 18½ 19		18
Barker's Brick Works and Wharves ...	31¼ 30¾ 30¾	30½ 30 30	28½ 27¾ 27½	27 26¾ 26¾	26¼ 25¼ 24¾	24¾ 24 24	23¾ 23¼ 23¼	23 22½ 22	19½ 18¾ 19¼		18
Lansdown and Horn Lane Bridge ...	31½ 31 31	30¾ 30¼ 30¼	28¾ 28 27¾	27¼ 27 27	26½ 25½ 25	25 24¼ 24¼	24 23½ 23½	23¼ 22¾ 22¼	19¾ 19 19½		19
Lowesmoor Wharves to Tallow Hill	32 31½ 31½	31¼ 30¾ 30¾	29¼ 28½ 28¼	27¾ 27½ 27½	27 26 25½	25½ 24¾ 24¾	24½ 24 24	23¾ 23¼ 22¾	20¼ 19½ 20		19
Tallow Hill, Blockhouse, and Sidbury	32¼ 31¾ 31¾	31½ 31 31	29½ 28¾ 28½	28 27¾ 27¾	27¼ 26¼ 25¾	25¾ 25 25	24¾ 24¼ 24¼	24 23½ 23	20½ 19¾ 20¼		19
Porcelain Works and Townsend's Mill	32¾ 32¼ 32¼	32 31½ 31½	30 29¼ 29	28½ 28¼ 28¼	27¾ 26¾ 26¼	26¼ 25½ 25½	25¼ 24¾ 24¾	24½ 24 23½	21 20¼ 20¾		20
Diglis Basin	33 32½ 32½	32¼ 31¾ 31¾	30¼ 29½ 29¼	28¾ 28½ 28½	28 27 26½	26½ 25¾ 25¾	25½ 25 25	24¾ 24¼ 23¾	21¼ 20½ 21		20
Diglis—Junction with the River Severn	33 32½ 32½	32¼ 31¾ 31¾	30¼ 29½ 29¼	28¾ 28½ 28½	28 27 26½	26½ 25¾ 25¾	25½ 25 25	24¾ 24¼ 23¾	21¼ 20½ 21		20